MEASURING BUSINESS INTERRUPTION LOSSES AND OTHER COMMERCIAL DAMAGES

PATRICK A. GAUGHAN

JOHN WILEY & SONS, INC.

Copyright © 2004 by John Wiley & Sons, Inc. All rights reserved.

Published by John Wiley & Sons, Inc., Hoboken, New Jersey
Published simultaneously in Canada

Library of Congress Cataloging-in-Publication Data

Gaughan, Patrick A.
  Measuring business interruption losses / Patrick A. Gaughan.
    p. cm.
Includes bibliographical references and index.
  ISBN 0-471-26656-6 (CLOTH)
  1. Lost profits damages—United States.   2. Business losses—United States.
  3. Forensic economics—United States.   I. Title.
  KF1250.G38 2004
  657'.48—dc22

                                                            2003015147

10 9 8 7 6 5 4 3 2 1

To Kerry with Love

In Memory of John Gaughan, Jr.

CONTENTS

PREFACE

Over the past few decades the field of litigation economics, sometimes referred to as forensic economics, has grown dramatically. This work often involves measuring various types of economic damages. One of the most prominent areas of economic damages is commercial damages. This involves estimating the economic losses of corporations who are alleging that other entities have caused them to incur losses. A common cause of such damages is the interruption of a business's operations. The first half of this book is devoted to this very common type of commercial damages. In doing so, the book provides a methodological framework for the measurement of such losses. The second half of the book then focuses on other related types of commercial damages.

The anticipated audience is a combination of accountants, attorneys, and economists. For economists and accountants, the book is designed to give them assistance in their role as experts in litigation. For attorneys, it should aid them in working with and challenging such experts. Given the breadth of the audience, a detailed analysis of particular specialties is not attempted. Rather, an overview of these special topics is provided. The reason for this is that the goal of each subsection is to provide the reader with an introduction to topics in certain subfields. It is assumed that the reader does not have an in-depth familiarity with many of the issues in these areas.

The knowledge and skills required to work as an expert measuring commercial damages are extensive. Few experts possess strengths in all related areas. For this reason, experts who are strong in one area—say, accounting—may find the introduction to the relevant economic topics useful whether attempting to do some of this analysis on their own or working on a team with economists. Conversely, readers who are economists will repeatedly find that the strengths of accountants are touted throughout the book. Readers who are attorneys working with experts will gain a better understanding of how these different experts interact and what each can and cannot do. Attorneys will also learn how damages should be measured so as to arrive at a nonspeculative opinion. Armed with such knowledge, they will be better able to challenge the work of experts who have not measured losses properly or who have done so in a speculative manner.

This book is organized so that readers who seek to learn about a particular topic do not have to read the entire book or preceding chapters to gain an understanding from the selected reading. This is particularly true for topics in the second half of the book. However, the cost of presenting more "self-contained" chapters is some repetition. Readers of the entire book will note that some topics that have already been covered are briefly discussed a second time. While this is done to a limited extent, it is done by design, allowing readers of selected chapters to gain the maximum from the time they invest in the book. This format may be helpful for the professional who has very high time costs.

It is hoped that *Measuring Business Interruption Losses and Other Commercial Damages* will add to the limited literature that exists in the field of commercial damages, spurring further developments as others build on what is provided in this book.

1

INTRODUCTION

This book is designed to provide a methodological framework for how lost profits should be measured in business interruption litigation. Such a framework is provided so that a standard approach can be followed in the measurement of such damages.

In following the discussion, readers will notice the interdisciplinary nature of commercial damages analysis. Depending on the type of case, the expert who seeks to measure a plaintiff's lost profits needs to possess a well-rounded knowledge of the research and practices in certain major subfields of economics (macroeconomics, microeconomics, econometrics, and forensic economics), several subfields of finance (investment analysis, capital market theory, and corporate finance), and accounting. Given the broad range of expertise that may ultimately be needed and that few individuals would be experts in all of these fields, a team of experts, such as economists working with accountants, is often the optimal solution.

This book is not meant to present an exhaustive review of all the issues relevant to commercial damages analysis. Rather, it is meant to discuss those issues which are the most important and fundamental. It is necessary to bear in mind, however, that each case brings with it a unique set of factors which need to be considered on an individual basis. No broad-based book, such as this one, can anticipate all of the unique circumstances that may be encountered. For this reason, this book focuses on those circumstances that are most commonly encountered and attempts to present a general damages evaluation framework capable of handling most of them.

DEVELOPMENT OF THE FIELD OF LITIGATION ECONOMICS

The field of litigation economics, which is sometimes referred to as forensic economics, has developed significantly over the past two decades. During this time period, the National Association of Forensic Economics (NAFE) was formed. It is a national body of economists who work in the field of litigation economics and who may provide expert testimony in court proceedings. The organization is composed primarily of Ph.D. economists, many of whom have academic affiliations. In addition to the advent of NAFE, three well-received, refereed, academic journals devoted to the field of litigation economics have been created. They are the *Journal of Forensic Economics, Journal of Legal Economics,* and *Litigation Economics Review.* These journals have given litigation economics an academic stature similar to other subdisciplines in the field of economics. In addition to this forum for respected scholarly work in the area, most of the major meetings and the leading professional conferences of economists in the United States, including the annual meetings of the American Economics Association and the Western Economics Association, now have several sessions, sponsored by NAFE, devoted exclusively to litigation economics. Such conferences have allowed an exchange of ideas that has further developed the methodologies in the field.

At present, the leading use of damages experts, often economists, is in personal injury and wrongful death litigation. This is not surprising, since this type of litigation is the most common.[1] While there are some similarities between lost profits analysis and the estimation of damages in personal injury and wrongful death litigation, there are major differences which cause them to be two separate fields, often including different groups of practitioners. Most economists who do personal injury damages analysis have a background in labor economics but may not have a background in finance. Many of these experts are sole practitioners who often have a full-time academic position. Experts in business interruption matters, however, tend to be a more diverse group. Some of them work for large firms, including some public companies. They come from a variety of backgrounds, the most common of which are accounting, economics, and finance.

LOST PROFITS BUSINESS INTERRUPTION ANALYSIS COMPARED TO PERSONAL INJURY AND EMPLOYMENT LITIGATION

As noted above, economists are often called upon to provide testimony on damages in personal injury and wrongful death litigation. These cases utilize a methodology which does not vary significantly among cases. This methodology has been well developed in the forensic economics literature. In addition, a con-

---

[1]Lanie Bachmier, Patrick Gaughan, and Norman Swanson, "The Volume of Litigation and the Macroeconomy," *International Review of Law and Economics,* forthcoming.

cise statement of many of the generally accepted steps in the damages measurement process for personal injury cases has been set forth in *Economic Expert Testimony: A Guide for Judges and Attorneys.*[2] The methodology usually involves projecting lost earnings and fringe benefits (net of mitigation in personal injury cases) over the work-life expectancy of the plaintiff, as well as valuating lost services over a time period that may approach the life expectancy of the plaintiff/decedent. The work-life is the generally accepted standard for the terminal date of lost earnings estimates, while the life expectancy is often used as a guide to establish the length of the loss period for the valuation of lost services (the life expectancy may be reduced to reflect the diminished ability to provide services due to the aging process).[3] Both the life expectancy and the work-life expectancy are based upon statistical data that establish averages from demographic and labor market characteristics. This contrasts with lost profits analysis in which the loss period is usually determined by a different set of circumstances, such as a time period set forth in a contract. Naturally, there may be differing interpretations of this contract and what it means about the length of the loss period.

In personal injury litigation, the monetary amount that is presented is usually derived from the historical earnings of the plaintiff or decedent. For those who have not yet had much of an earnings history, lost earnings may be derived from government statistics which list earnings as a function of age, sex, and education. Where appropriate, historical compensation data may allow the expert to measure the value of fringe benefits. Once the total compensation base has been established, the expert constructs a projection by selecting a proper growth rate. The projected values are then brought to present-day value terms through the application of an appropriate discount rate.

In employment litigation, the expert may project damages using similar methods as those employed in personal injury cases. However, the role of the economist can be expanded when there are claims of bias or other discriminatory practices. Here, in addition to possibly measuring the damages of the plaintiff, the economist may be called upon to utilize his or her econometrics background to render an opinion on the liability part of the case.[4]

---

[2]Thomas Ireland, Stephen M. Horner, and James Rodgers, "Reference Guide for Valuing Economic Loss in Personal Injury, Wrongful Death and Survival Actions," in *Economic Expert Testimony: A Guide for Judges and Attorneys* (Tucson, AZ: 1998), 1–108.

[3]Michael Brookshire and Frank Slesnick, "A 1990 Survey Study of Forensic Economists," *Journal of Forensic Economists* IV (2) (spring/summer 1991): 125–149.

[4]Michael Piette, "Economic Methodology and the Analysis of Employment Discrimination," *Journal of Forensic Economics* IV (3) (fall 1991): 307–316.

Business interruption lawsuits, on the other hand, tend to vary considerably. Although some of the evaluation techniques used may be similar, the circumstances often vary more widely from case to case. In addition, the industries involved can be very different and may each present unique issues. Given this wide variability, business interruption cases present a greater degree of complexity than the two types of litigation mentoned previously. They typically involve significant time demands for the expert who must conduct a thorough analysis. These time demands often are greater than those associated with a typical personal injury or wrongful death loss analysis, thereby making an expert business interruption analysis a more expensive proposition.

Another important difference between business interruption analysis and personal injury or wrongful death loss analysis is the role of cost analysis. The losses of a worker are typically wages and benefits; job-related expenses usually are not a significant factor. In business interruption analysis, however, costs related to lost revenues are generally quite important. It is here that the skills of an accountant may be most useful in measuring the appropriate costs that would have been incurred in order to realize certain lost revenues. This is why we have devoted an entire chapter to cost analysis.

QUALIFICATIONS OF AN ECONOMIC EXPERT

It is important that the business interruption expert possess a well-rounded background in order to measure the damages reliably and withstand the criticisms that will come during cross-examination. While courts are generally somewhat lenient in whom they accept as an expert, the "expert must possess requisite skill, training, education, knowledge, or experience from which it can be assumed that the opinion is reliable."[5] Given that these are generic attributes, it is important to evaluate the expert's specific credentials relevant to measuring economic damages.

The desirable qualifications of an economic expert witness are given in various publications in the field of litigation economics. Examples can be found in Stuart Speiser's *Recovery for Wrongful Death and Injury*, Michael Brookshire and Stan Smith's *Economic/Hedonic Damages*, Gerald Martin's *Determining Economic Damages*, and Baker and Seck's *Determining Economic Loss in Injury and Death Cases*.[6] The qualifications listed in these publications focus on appli-

---

[5]*Mattott v. Ward*, 48 N.Y. 2d 455, 423 N.Y.S. 2d 645 (1979).

[6]Stuart Speiser, *Recovery for Wrongful Death and Injury*, 2nd ed. (The Lawyer's Cooperative Publishing, 1988); Michael L. Brookshire, and Stan V. Smith, *Economics/ Hedonic Damages, The Practice Book for Plaintiff and Defense Attorneys* (Anderson

cations in personal injury and wrongful death litigation. The requisite qualifications for competently estimating business interruption lost profits and rendering an *expert* opinion are similar. However, the expert qualifications in business interruption matters are normally broader. These have also been set forth in the forensic economics literature.[7]

A list of the desirable qualifications of an economist who could provide expert witness testimony on business interruption losses includes:

- Ph.D. in economics, finance, or accounting
- Background in finance or financial economics
- University teaching position, preferably at the graduate level
- Scholarly publications in economics, finance, or accounting
- Professional presentations in economics, finance, or accounting
- Experience in industry analysis and forecasting
- Experience in commercial damages analysis

The qualified witness may not possess all of the above, but may have strengths in one area that outweigh deficiencies in other areas. Courts and juries should consider such factors when weighing the testimony of individuals who have been presented as experts but who may lack many of these attributes or who only possess minimal levels of the listed qualifications. Other individuals who are strong in most or even all of the areas may "bring a greater level of expertise to the table."

Example of How Courts Weigh and Compare Credentials of Experts

When hearing the opinions of two opposing damages experts, courts will naturally consider the credentials of the experts when deciding how much weight to give their opinions. This was very clear in *United Phosphorous, Ltd. v. Midland Fumigant, Inc.* In discussing the respective credentials of two economists put forward as damages experts the courts summarized their backgrounds as follows:

Publishing, 1990); Gerald Martin, *Determining Economic Damages* (James Publishing, October 1995); W. Gary Baker and Michael K. Seck, *Determining Economic Loss in Personal Injury and Death Cases* (Shephard's/McGraw-Hill, 1987).

[7]Patrick A. Gaughan, "Economics and Financial Issues in Lost Profits Litigation," in *Litigation Economics*, Patrick A. Gaughan and Robert Thornton, eds. (Greenwich, CT: JAI Press, 1993).

Hoyt received a B.S. degree in Milling Technology from Kansas State University in 1962, and a Ph.D. in Agriculture and Applied Economics from the University of Minnesota in 1972. Hoyt previously held a teaching position at the William Mitchell College of Law in St. Paul, Minnesota and served as a guest lecturer at the University of Minnesota and at St. Olaf College. Hoyt has published a total of seven articles in his entire career, two of which appear in agricultural economics journals, and two of which were published in law reviews, and were therefore not subject to peer review by economists.

In contrast, Dr. John Siegfried is a professor of economics at Vanderbilt University and has served as a professor there for 24 years. Siegfried earned a bachelors degree in economics from Rensselear Polytechnic Institute in 1967, a masters of arts degree in economics from Penn State University in 1968, and a Ph.D. in economics in 1972. At Vanderbilt, Dr. Siegfried served as chair of the department of economics from 1980 to 1986. He taught numerous courses at Vanderbilt, including undergraduate and graduate courses on industrial organization and antitrust economics.

The court continued with a discussion of Dr. Siegfried's credentials and then addressed his publication record:

Siegfried has authored over 100 articles, which have been published in economics journals or as chapters in various books on economics. Siegfried currently serves on the editorial board of three economics journals, and frequently "referees" articles submitted for publication as a contribution to scientific knowledge in the field of economics.[8]

It is interesting to note that the court put particular emphasis on the relative publication and scholarship records of the two experts. One had a more limited publication record, a record which was not focused on the areas upon which he was testifying. The other had an extensive publication record and was also a referee for such publications. The court seemed impressed with these credentials and it is not surprising that it put more weight on that expert's opinions.

QUALIFICATIONS OF AN ACCOUNTING EXPERT ON DAMAGES

In lost profits litigation, the courts have consistently ruled that economists and accountants are appropriate expert witnesses to testify on damages. While attor-

---

[8]*United Phosphorus, Ltd. v. Midland Fumigant, Inc.* 173 F.R.D. 675; 1997.

neys sometimes hire accountants to do lost profits analysis, CPAs generally have a limited background in economics and finance and therefore lack the expertise to conduct a thorough economic analysis. However, accountants may provide valuable expertise on certain issues such as cost analysis and preparation of *pro forma* financial statements. This is why for some business interruption cases an interdisciplinary approach combining the fields of economics, finance, and accounting, perhaps through the use of more than one expert, is useful. This may mean that only one expert testifies, and that the testifying expert relies upon the work of other experts.

The typical accountant possesses a bachelor's degree in accounting and is a certified public accountant (CPA). Some accountants may not have passed the CPA exam and lack this certification but it is unusual to see such individuals presented as experts—especially when there is such an abundance of accountants who are CPAs. Many CPAs also possess a higher degree—usually a Master's in Business Administration. This degree may feature a specialization in certain relevant areas such as accounting or finance. The characteristics of an MBA degree and what it implies about an expert's credentials will be discussed later in this chapter.

As the practice of accounting has gotten increasingly competitive, accountants have attempted to branch out into more lucrative areas of consulting. Litigation expert consulting is an area which has recently seen an influx of accountants. In order to enhance accountants'expertise, and in recognition that the typical training of an accountant does not address many of the issues that arise in expert work, the accounting profession has developed certifications that address specific aspects of a forensic accountant's work. Perhaps the most common is the certified fraud examiner (CFE).

INTERDISCIPLINARY NATURE OF COMMERCIAL DAMAGES ANALYSIS

Most commercial damages analysis is performed by an expert from one discipline—economics, finance, or accounting—who does not draw on the acumen of those outside his or her field. This is unfortunate because in many business interruption cases, the necessary skills and expertise transcend traditional discipline boundaries. The skills of an economist may be invaluable in analyzing the relevant economic environment, doing an industry analysis, and constructing reliable projections. A finance expert may be necessary for analyzing relevant variables from financial markets, such as rates of return. An accountant may be useful for conducting a costs analysis or performing other work, such as the reconstruction of financial statements (including cash flow statements). The needs just described are not generally part of the training that one acquires in these disciplines. However, it is common to see an expert from one field try to conduct the entire damages analysis for a given case. In such instances, the expert may do a competent job on the part of the analysis that is within the individual's expertise yet be inadequate elsewhere. A preferable approach is to use a team of experts, with one leading expert providing the methodological structure for the analysis and performing the part that is within his expertise. Other experts will then provide their own input upon which the leading expert will rely to put forward the loss measure.

While it is acceptable for one expert to rely on the opinions of other team members when putting forward an opinion, it may be useful to have more than one expert on the team testify. In this manner, each expert stays within his own knowledge base and is capable of handling the cross-examination on the relevant issues that arise.

Relative Strengths of Economists versus Accountants

Economists have training in various forms of macroeconomic and microeconomic analysis. Often economists have extensive training and expertise in statistical analysis and econometrics, skill areas which may be invaluable in forecasting. However, unless they have separately acquired a background in finance, many economists have limited familiarity with financial statements and are not involved in the preparation of such statements. Rather, this is the domain of accountants who have specialized training in areas such as cost accounting, which is most useful when determining profit ratios to apply to forecasted revenue levels. As noted earlier, some accountants have a Master's degree in Business Administration; others have an undergraduate degree in accounting with a CPA. It is important to note that even though an MBA is a graduate degree, most MBA programs provide only general business training. The economics and forecasting courses in MBA programs are often elementary and provide the student with only limited training in these areas, training that would not be considered expertise by economists. These courses are not comparable to the training that a Ph.D. economist normally receives. In addition, some accountants have Ph.D. degrees and also possess such training. However, one of the strengths of accountants is their field experience: it is particularly useful if it is in the industry that is being considered in the lawsuit. Accountants with Ph.D. degrees may be academics and *may* not have the experience of a practicing accountant.

An example of the court's reaction to opposing experts who possessed some of the strengths and shortcomings discussed above can be found in *Digital &*

Analog Design Corporation v. North Supply Company. The plaintiff introduced an expert who had a Ph.D. and who presented himself as an expert in economics and business finance. While the court appeared confused by the forecasting methods the economist employed, it was notably impressed.

> In this regard DAD's economic expert in the field of economic analysis, with a large number of publications and professional activities to his credit. The evidence would reasonably support his technique of cost-profit analysis, the so-called "time series analysis and projection."

> NSC, by comparison did not produce a comparable expert. Instead, NSC relied upon the testimony of a certified public accountant, an employee controller of NSC, a Mr. Simon, neither of whom it appears had as extensive training or expertise in the time series analysis method as had Dr. Zinser, and neither of whom utilized a competing method of analysis to calculate a lesser amount of profits.[9]

Although impressed by the economist's forecasting abilities, the court found his cost analysis lacking. The economist applied the gross margin to projected lost sales without more carefully measuring incremental costs along the lines of what is discussed in Chapter Six. A solution that neither side attempted would have been to have an economist do the lost revenue projection and an accountant conduct the analysis of the costs associated with the forecasted lost revenues. Such an approach is advocated throughout this book.

DIFFERENCE BETWEEN DISCIPLINES OF ECONOMICS AND FINANCE

Attorneys are more aware of the relative skills of economists versus accountants than they are when comparing specialists in economics versus finance. This is partly due to the fact that the fields are interrelated. Many economists consider finance to be a subfield of economics. Indeed, there is a field called financial economics which applies economic analysis to financial markets. However, there are several differences between a Ph.D. in finance and a Ph.D. in economics. For one, finance degrees are often conferred by a college of business within a university; economics degrees, however, may be offered by the university outside of

---

[9]*Digital & Analog Design Corporation v. North Supply Company*, 44 Ohio St. 3d 36; 540 N.E. 2d 1358, 1989.

the college of business. This difference is not important. What is more relevant is the different training of the individuals.

A finance Ph.D. and an economics Ph.D. provide different training. A Ph.D. in finance may have some training in accounting and may have taken certain courses taught in business school which economists are not required to take. Many economists lack any knowledge of finance and financial statements. It is possible, for example, to get a Ph.D. in economics without ever having even seen a financial statement (as shocking as this sounds). Indeed, many economists do their work in complicated and esoteric areas and consider topics such as the analysis of financial statements simplistic. Nonetheless, it is important that the economists in commercial damages analysis have a broad knowledge base that goes beyond the training received in graduate school. Those, for example, who write their dissertation on a financially-related topic may get this background as part of their thesis research. Each expert has a unique combination of credentials, training and experience. The court and jury will have to consider this set of credentials and then determine the weight to apply to the testimony.

FINDING A DAMAGES EXPERT

There are many ways for an attorney to find a damages expert. One of the most often used is "word-of-mouth" referrals, whereby an attorney consults with colleagues he or she respects and gets the names of experts who have successfully performed for them. If this process is not productive, other methods must be employed.

There are certain media that advertise the services of experts. They include regional legal publications as well as legal reference diaries. It is important that references be gathered and checked, particularly in cases where the attorney does not have any information on the expert other than what the advertisement lists. This review process can be enhanced by a verdict search which may reveal the names of cases in which the expert has testified.[10] The attorneys that retained the expert in the past and the attorneys that cross-examined the expert in prior matters can be consulted for feedback. However, an adversarial attorney may fail to give an objective review, particularly an attorney who did not do as well as he would have liked in the case in question.

Other sources where one can obtain information on experts are the expert referral companies. These are firms that maintain names and *curriculum vitae*

---

[10]*Verdict Search*, Moran Publishing Company, East Islip, NY.

(CVs) of experts with many different specialties whom they refer to attorneys for a fee.[11] A CV is a document that lists an expert's credentials. The fee that these companies charge may include an initial charge as well as a built-in hourly charge incorporated into the expert's fee. This causes the expert's fee to be different than what it otherwise would be were he contacted directly without a referral intermediary. However, referral agencies can greatly speed up the process of finding an expert—particularly if one is looking for unique expertise from a specialist in a narrowly defined industry.

Another source of experts is local universities. A professor at a nearby university may have a certain appeal to a jury from the same community. In addition, professors may possess the ability to explain complicated concepts clearly. However, attorneys have to be very careful if they hire an academic who lacks litigation and testimony expertise. It takes a certain personality to withstand the rigors of the adversarial litigation process in the United States. Furthermore, the way one voices arguments and positions in an academic environment is very different than how one expresses those same arguments and positions in an adversarial litigation environment. As obvious as this sounds, many would-be litigation experts who are pure academics may find this difficult to comprehend. Therefore, attorneys need to exercise caution in using untested experts—their testimony may be somewhat unpredictable. The role of experience will be discussed later in this chapter.

There are several economic consulting firms which offer litigation-related services. Some specialize in commercial matters while others offer a variety of damages-related services. These economic consulting firms range from small "boutiques" to large national firms. Many possess well-qualified individuals but attorneys still need to carefully evaluate the experts working on their case.

Still another source of experts is the major consulting arms of accounting firms and other larger litigation companies. In recent years, accounting firms have aggressively expanded their consulting operations after they discovered that the profit margins on traditional accounting work, such as auditing, were shrinking from competitive pressure and corporate cost-cutting. These firms can bring larger quantities of manpower to a project. However, though it may seem comforting that such firms can apply many professionals to a given project, usually only one expert ends up taking the stand and testifying. An army of accountants may be of limited benefit when that expert testifies on his personal credentials, the analysis that was performed, and the opinions that were developed. The specific credentials and track record of the expert are more important than the quantity of staff that a firm employs. It should not be inferred, however, that larger firms are infe-

---

[11]Technical Advisory Service for Attorneys, Blue Bell, PA.

rior to small ones. Rather, the expert selection process is individualistic and should focus on the expert or team of experts who will ultimately testify.

In the wake of the accounting scandals of the past few years, the issue of accountants' independence has been called into question. Accountants who are not independent may be more of a liability than an asset. This should give attorneys pause when they consider retaining the consulting division of an accounting firm that does other work for their client.

CRITICALLY REVIEWING A POTENTIAL EXPERT'S CURRICULUM VITAE

Many attorneys take at face value the content of a potential or opposing expert's curriculum vitae (CV). They merely give the CV a cursory scan and conclude from the length of the CV that the expert possesses impressive credentials. A closer review of the listings included on the CV, however, may possibly expose the misleading nature of the items. For example, in lieu of quality publications, an expert may list presentations made before attorneys, which are nothing more than marketing appeals and sales pitches. A CV may list very general articles published in legal newspapers and magazines. These articles, though, do not enjoy the scrutiny that a peer-reviewed or refereed journal article or book would. Sometimes what is listed as a publication is a paper or article that has not even been published.

Degrees

Some basic comments on degrees are mandatory. The most fundamental characteristic of a degree as it relates to litigation is the relevance of the degree. It is very common for experts to want to testify in an area that is outside their expertise. Courts, though, have been supportive of objections to experts who testify outside their expertise.[12] In the area of commercial damages, one sees a variety of individuals present themselves as experts. Courts are often liberal in accepting such individuals and rely on the *voir dire* process and cross-examination to expose any deficiencies. However, attorneys should be aware that Ph.D.s in some fields provide little or no training in the areas that are relevant to most types of commercial damages analysis. For example, fields like engineering or operations research may provide little training relevant to measuring damages in litigation.

---

[12]*Wright v. Williams*, 47 Cal. App. 3d 802, 121 Cal Rptr. 194 (1975).

Attorneys should be very wary of the "mail-away Ph.D." These are Ph.D. degrees which one can earn at home. Several institutions offering such Ph.D.'s have sprung up and some even advertise their degrees in major publications. If the degree-granting institution is unknown, the attorney should read its catalog course descriptions and degree standards to review the criteria employed for issuing degrees. When encountering experts with such degrees, this can be a very fertile area of inquiry. With the development of the Internet and the opportunities that are now available for online courses, it is important to ensure that the courses taken and the degrees conferred are from legitimate institutions of higher learning—not the product of bogus academic offerings.

Published Books

Published books are impressive credentials for an expert to have. These books are even more noteworthy if they are published by major publishers who can afford to be more selective. Books that have received acclaim or won awards for their quality are even better. In addition, books that have been used as textbooks may also provide the author with credentials that other experts who have not published any books may lack. Books in the area in which the expert is testifying can be invaluable. It is ideal to use as an expert the person "who wrote the book" in the area.

Beware of books published by vanity publishers. These publishers "publish" a book for an author—for a fee. They are not unlike photocopy houses as opposed to the more traditional publisher. Having a book published in such a way implies that none of the reputable publishing houses considered the work worthy of publication. It also implies that the book in question has a very limited readership and may not be regarded as authoritative by anyone in the field.

Refereed or Peer-Reviewed Journal Articles

In addition to published books, another important standard used for evaluating scholarship in academia is *refereed,* or peer-reviewed, journal articles. A refereed journal is one that utilizes a group of experts to blindly review articles submitted to the journal in their speciality. A journal's editors will allocate the articles to the referees and ensure that the process is completed without revealing the names of the authors or the referees. These referees judge the quality of the article and decide if it is worthy of publication. Peer-reviewed articles are very different than articles that undergo editorial review; in the latter case, an editor simply decides whether a piece is of interest to the readers.

As noted earlier, there are three refereed journals in the field of litigation economics. They are the *Journal of Forensic Economics, Journal of Legal Economics,* and *Litigation Economics Review.* While many of their articles focus on areas other than commercial damages, a certain quantity of articles on business interruption losses have been published in each of these refereed journals. Other refereed journals which feature articles in the area of commercial damages can be found in the closely related field of law and economics. This is a subfield of economics in which someone getting a Ph.D. in economics can specialize. The four leading journals in the field are the *Journal of Law and Economics, Journal of Legal Studies, International Review of Law and Economics,* and the *Journal of Law, Economics and Organization.* A new journal called *The Journal of Empirical Legal Studies* has just been established. In finance, there are many refereed journals. These include the *Journal of Finance, Journal of Financial Economics, Journal of Applied Corporate Finance, Financial Management, Financial Analysts Journal,* and *Journal of Accounting and Economics.* In econometrics, there are several quality journals such as *Econometrica, Journal of Econometrics,* and the *Journal of the American Statistical Association.*

In the field of accounting, *Accounting Review* and *Accounting Horizons* are two leading refereed journals. *Accounting Horizons* is published by the American Accounting Association. While not a refereed journal, the *Journal of Accountancy* is published by the American Institute of CPAs and is widely distributed to all members of the Institute. In addition, the *Journal of Corporate Accounting and Finance* is known as a source of quality articles in accounting and finance.

Presentations

An expert's CV often contains lists of presentations. In the academic world, the publication process often begins with a refereed presentation to one's peers in the specific area of the article. Refereed presentations are those that are accepted after a "call for papers" has been announced and submitted articles are reviewed by the organizers of paper sessions at academic conferences. The standards for acceptance vary widely but are usually higher than those for nonrefereed presentations. Attorneys should be wary of listings that are merely promotion sales—presentations made before potential clients.

Concluding Comments on CVs Content

The expert witness arena has become quite crowded—professionals from many fields have discovered that they can charge substantial fees by serving as experts in litigated matters. They have learned that they may be better able to get the assignment if they have a long CV filled with impressive-sounding contents. Therefore, it is incumbent on the attorneys to carefully review the listed items and ascertain their quality. When reviewing the contents of an opposing expert's CV, one's own expert can be invaluable. For example, it has been observed on many occasions that experts who lack publications may try to compile a list of alternative credentials that may take up several pages. As noted above, one tactic employed by such witnesses is to list testimonies. It is not unusual to have an expert with marginal credentials present a CV that is six or even ten pages in length. This may include several pages of testimony lists and marketing presentations but little scholarly, peer-reviewed work. The retaining attorney must then decide if a list of court appearances as an expert witness is truly a credential, particularly if there is little else on the CV. Another example of misrepresentation is what may be listed under the heading of publications. Experts who lack legitimate publication credits often list items that range from papers which were not even published to speaking appearances. A cross-examining attorney may expose such misrepresentations. Therefore, it is the retaining attorney's responsibility to review the contents of an expert's CV carefully.

One additional comment on expert credentials is necessary. As noted earlier, it is common that attorneys merely give a CV a cursory scan prior to retaining or cross-examining an expert. They often conclude that if the CV is several pages in length then the individual must possess sufficient expertise. Often, attorneys who know that the expert has testified several times assume that there is no point in challenging the individual's expertise. This is sometimes an error. It could be that many of these other testimonies were simply the product of negligence on the part of the opposing attorneys. Moreover, prior courts could have concluded that the expert was allowed to testify but that the jury could hear the challenges and accord the testimony whatever weight it wanted to. The fact that an expert has testified does not indicate anything about what weight the jury ultimately gave the testimony. If there is a legitimate concern about the strength of an individuals expertise, the opposing attorney should not hesitate to pursue this.

Credentials versus Experience in Litigation Analysis

Attorneys needs to be aware that litigation-related analysis is a specialized field and not all highly credentialed experts can perform well in it. One classic example of an expert who possessed extremely impressive credentials but who lacked a familiarity with litigation analysis occurred in a recent antitrust case where the class action plaintiffs hired the Nobel-Prize winning economist

Dr. Robert Lucas.[13] With respect to his credentials, the court had the following comments:

> We next come to Dr. Robert Lucas and the opinions he expressed, particularly as regards to the alleged collusion engaged in by all of the Defendants. First, it is proper to recognize Dr. Lucas' eminent and distinguished credentials. He is affiliated with the University of Chicago, indisputably one of the finest educational institutions in the world. He is also a past recipient of the Nobel Prize in Economics, an award without equal in recognition of scholarship and contributions in his chosen discipline. It was with high expectation that the Court anticipated his testimony and denied requests from the defendants to preclude his testimony or to conduct a separate Daubert hearing out of the presence of the jury.

However, with respect to his analysis the court was not as complementary.

> Sad to say, Dr. Lucas' testimony did not measure up to his unique qualifications. Among other things, his testimony showed the following:
> - He abdicated entirely the concept of the independence of the expert witnesses and simply became the sponsor for the Class Plaintiff's theory of the case
> - He was ignorant of material testimony and other evidence
> - His essential opinions were not only not based on the evidence, they were inconsistent with it
> - His opinions were offered without any scientific basis or having been subject of economic methodological testing
>
> Dr. Lucas reached his conclusions within 40 hours of his engagement and before he undertook any substantial or detailed study of the prescription drug industry. Most of the facts upon which he based his opinions and conclusions were supplied by Class Plaintiffs' counsel, although he admitted he did not expect Class Plaintiff's counsel to have a balanced presentation. His expert's report was redrafted by Class Plaintiff's counsel in its entirety and only included what counsel wanted. In Dr. Lucas' own words: "I don't think there is a single sentence in this affidavit that's intact from the first draft that I proposed."

It seems that in the above case, the attorneys who retained Dr. Lucas probably thought that presented with such a notable expert, the court would simply adopt his opinions. The expert's credentials can certainly add weight to the presentation, but the expert's work has to be able to hold up under scrutiny. Notable academic articles that one has written along with awards for prior work can be very helpful,

---

[13]*In Re Brand Name Prescription Drugs Antitrust Litigation*, 1999 U.S. Dist. Lexis 550, January 19, 1999 (*decided and docketed*).

but the work done in formulating and supporting the opinions expressed in the current case has to maintain a high standard.

GETTING THE DAMAGES EXPERT ON BOARD EARLY ENOUGH

One of the errors that attorneys sometimes make in commercial, as well as other types of litigation, such as personal injury and employment litigation, is not retaining the damages expert early in the process. Attorneys often devote much of their time to the liability side of their case while paying less attention to the damages aspect. Sometimes when they focus on damages, such as when gathering necessary damages-related documents, attorneys attempt to do so without the aid of a damages expert. This may result in a failure to collect important documents or to ask essential questions in depositions.

This error occurs for a variety of reasons. One is that the attorney may think he knows enough to gather the necessary damages-related materials and to conduct a complete deposition on his own. Another reason is that there may be cost constraints driving the litigation; the client is trying to control litigation expenses and the attorney does not want to add to the client's costs by hiring an expert—until the last minute when it can't be put off any longer. This often happens when deadlines for naming experts are near and the client has to either incur this cost or proceed without an expert. While the attorney may believe that he has gone to great lengths to keep his client's costs down, failing to retain the damages expert may cause the damages side of the case to suffer. If this happens, the apparent cost consciousness may in the long run be a disservice to the client.

In commenting on the failure to retain an economic damages expert early in the process, one expert noted:

> A typical disaster scenario. The damage expert gets hired two days before the deadline for expert disclosure. A pile of documents and depositions arrive at the expert's office a week later. When the expert calls the attorney to ask for key data that was not in the pile, the litigator says, "It looks like we never asked for that in the document request or at depositions. Oh by the way, they want to take your deposition next week." The expert must do a damages analysis that makes assumptions about key facts and then alter those assumptions depending on trial testimony. This often results in a poorer analysis and increases experts costs by a factor of 2 or 3.[14]

---

[14]James Plummer and Gerald McGowan, "Ten Most Frequent Errors in Litigating Business Damages," *Association of Business Trial Lawyers (ABTL) Northern California Report*, November 1995.

COURT'S POSITION ON EXPERTS
ON ECONOMIC DAMAGES

Courts have underscored the importance of expert testimony on economic damages. In fact, in *Larsen v. Walton Plywood Company*, the court stated:

> Respondents point out that a reasonable method of estimation of damages is often made with the aid of opinion evidence. Experts in the area are competent to pass judgement. So long as their opinions afford a reasonable basis for inference, there is a departure from the realm of uncertainty and speculation. *Expert testimony alone is a sufficient basis for an award for loss of profits.*[15]

The *Federal Rules of Evidence* are quite broad regarding what is considered acceptable expertise in an expert witness. Rule 702 states that "A witness may be qualified as an expert by *knowledge, skill, experience, training or education.*" With such broad criteria, a wide variety of individuals may serve as experts. However, an individual who possesses some of the necessary criteria set forth in Rule 702 may still be unqualified to testify if opposing counsel can demonstrate to the court that the expertise is not specific enough to the areas in which the expert is testifying.

Not all states, however, have adopted standards similar to the Federal Rules. Some states, such as California, employ broad standards and will allow a wide array of individuals to testify if their testimony will be of assistance to the jury in reaching its decision. Even in the face of such broad rules, opposing counsel may be able to exploit the weakness in an expert's credentials on *voir dire* which may reduce the weight that a jury gives the expert's testimony.

Using Management as Experts

In some cases, attorneys have tried to utilize management and the company's officers as experts at trial. Courts have accepted such testimony. In *Aluminum Products Enterprises v. Fuhrmann Tooling*, the court allowed the plaintiff's president to testify based upon his knowledge of the business and the industry.[16] The

---

[15]*Harold Larsen et al., Respondents, v. Walton Plywood Company et al., Appellants*, Washington Plywood Company, Inc. No. 36863, Supreme Court of Washington, Department One, 65 Wash. 2d 1; 390 P. 2d 677; Wash.

[16]*Aluminum Products Enterprises v. Fuhrmann Tooling*, 758 S.W. 2d 119, 112 (Mo. Ct. App. 1988).

disadvantage of such testimony is that the witness is an interested party in the litigation. On the other hand, the witness brings firsthand knowledge from working in the industry every day. Depending on the facts of the case, a combination of internal fact/expert witnesses and outside experts may be very effective. This is the case when internal financial witnesses, such as company controllers, are used to authenticate and describe the collection of data (such as cost data) upon which the outside damages expert is relying. It also is helpful when the expert lacks a significant background in the industry. The internal expert can be used to testify on trends and practices in the industry. Such an expert can also confirm numerical trends that the external expert may testify that he has found when analyzing industry data. The internal expert may be able to verify that these quantitative trends, such as reduced sales of distributors caused by manufacturers' selling directly to retailers, were experienced by those who worked in the industry.

Using an Expert as a Consultant

A damages expert can be invaluable to an attorney even if the individual never testifies; an expert can assist the attorney in understanding an opposing expert's report and opinions. Often an attorney may not have specialized training in the field in which the opposing expert is testifying. The fields of economics, finance, and accounting are very specialized, and it is difficult for an attorney to be knowledgeable in the law and also have expertise in these other related areas. In addition, like many other scientific fields, disciplines such as economics, finance and accounting have their own jargon, notation, etc. that may require interpretation. Having a knowledgeable expert to rely on can be of great benefit. Such an expert can be used to interpret the opposing expert's report or to prepare detailed lines of cross-examination for deposition and trial. The expert-consultant can also check for the presence of errors in the opposing expert's report. Without the necessary background, the opposing attorney may not be able to do a careful quantitative review of the opposing expert's analysis. Attorneys should be aware that such work can be surprisingly time-consuming. This is because an opposing expert's report may be intentionally cryptic and may not fully reveal the derivations of the various numerical values. The consulting expert may have to invest substantial amounts of time discerning exactly how the numbers were computed. In addition, once the method used by the opposing expert is known, counsel may want to stage different scenarios using more favorable factual and economic assumptions to see their impact on the loss estimates. This is a very thorough way of pursuing the damages part of the case. However, attorneys should know that such work may be time-intensive and may require the consulting experts to invest more time than even the opposing expert.

STANDARDS FOR ADMISSIBILITY OF EXPERT TESTIMONY

For approximately 70 years between 1923 to 1993, the standard applied in Federal Court for admissibility of expert testimony was the *Frye* test. This was based upon the 1923 criminal case *Frye v. United States* in which expert testimony on the results of a lie detector test was ruled inadmissible.[17] The *Frye* test focused on whether the analysis and testimony was based upon methods and standards that were generally accepted within the given field. That the Federal Rules of Evidence superceded the *Frye* test was decided by the United States Supreme Court in 1993 in the *Daubert v. Merrill Dow* case.[18] This case dealt with damages claims resulting from a mother ingesting Bendectin; the Supreme Court ruled that Rule 702 of the Federal Rules of Evidence is inconsistent with and supercedes the *Frye* test. The court stated that it did not find anything in the Federal Rules that requires general acceptance. The Supreme Court indicated that one should look to what is contained in the Federal Rules to determine whether testimony is admissible.

The court stopped short of putting forward a checklist of characteristics to which expert testimony must adhere.[19] Nonetheless, the court did set forth a list of four factors which expert testimony should possess:

1. **Testing.** This factor is most applicable to the physical sciences.[20] However, insofar as statistical analysis involves various forms of statistical testimony, such as hypothesis testimony, this factor could become relevant in business interruption cases.

2. **Peer Review and Publication.** Another factor that the United States Supreme Court highlighted was peer review and publications. This is particularly relevant for unique methodologies. If they have been subject to peer review, such as through the publication process in refereed journals, there may be a greater degree of reliability.

---

[17]*Frye v. United States*, 293 F1013 (D.C. Cir. 1923).

[18]*Daubert v. Merrill Dow*, 509 U.S. 579 (1993).

[19]Robert Dunn, *Expert Testimony: Law and Practice* (Westport, CT: Lawpress, vol. I, 1997), 195–201.

[20]Lawrence Spizman and John Kane, "Defending against a *Daubert* Challenge: An Application in Projecting the Lost Earnings of a Minor Child," *Litigation Economics Digest* III (1) (spring 1998): 43–49.

3. **Known Rate of Error.** If the analysis has a known rate of error, then this may be an indicator of its reliability. This can be applied to the case of statistical analysis which, for example, provides confidence levels for the value of a coefficient generated by a regression analysis which is used to project lost revenues.

4. **General Acceptance.** While the Supreme Court did not explicitly rule that general acceptance is required, it did point to such acceptance within the relevant community as one factor that a trial judge could use when evaluating such proposed testimony. The components of the loss measurement process that are described in this book are standard components of related disciples and general acceptance is normally not an issue. However, to reinforce this point, commonly used texts are cited throughout this book to emphasize this issue.

The *Daubert* standard is relatively new and its applicability to damages testimony will be developed over time. There have been some examples of *Daubert* being used to deny economic expert testimony in the areas of hedonic damages (the use of certain research studies in labor economics to value a human life or show the loss of the enjoyment of life).[21] However, in the commercial damages arena, many of the techniques that are used, such as forecasting methods and cost accounting methods, are quite standard and not controversial. Therefore, the fact that *Daubert* has replaced the *Frye* test may be less relevant to economic damages testimony than it is for other areas of expert testimony.

Applicability of *Daubert* to Economic Damages Testimony

Courts have held that while *Daubert* originally focused on scientific rather than economic and financial issues, it is also relevant to such matters.[22] One court specifically focused on economists when it concluded that *Daubert* should be applied when assessing the admissibility of their testimony.[23] In *Frymire-Brinati v. KPMG Peat Marwick,* the appellate court ordered a new trial partially because

---

[21]*Hein v. Merck & Co.*, 868 F. Supp 203 (M.D. Tenn. 1994) and *Ayers v. Robinson*, 887 F. Supp. 1049 (N.D. Ill. 1995).

[22]*Liu v. Korean Airlines Co.*, 1993 Westlaw 478343 (S.D.N.Y.).

[23]*Garcia v. Columbia Medical Center*, 996 F. Supp. 617, 621 (E.D. Tex. 1998).

the plaintiff's economic damages expert did not satisfy its interpretation of the relevance and reliability standards raised in *Daubert*.[24] In applying *Daubert* standards, the court in *Newport Ltd. v. Sears Roebuck & Co.* allowed the expert to utilize econometric techniques such as multiple regression analysis, a method which has long been accepted by many courts, particularly in the area of employment litigation. However, the court recognized that such analysis is dependent on specific assumptions which must be considered consistent with the relevant facts of the case in order for them to be probative.[25] This court required that in order for the plaintiff's economic expert to testify using this type of analysis, the relevance and accuracy of the assumptions must first be established.

    Daubert has also been found to be relevant to the closely related field of business valuations.[26] In *Ullman-Briggs, Inc. v. Salton-Maxim Housewares, Inc.* the U.S. District Court for the Ninth District of Illinois agreed with the defendant's argument that the proposed expert witness put forward by the plaintiff was not really an expert and did not utilize a reliable methodology. In its ruling the court stated:

> *Ullman-Briggs* contends that the *Daubert* test does not even apply to Goldfarb's testimony, beause *Daubert*, and nearly all the cases that follow it, deal with the admissibility of scientific expert testimony, and not the many areas in which expert opinion testimony may be proffered, but for which the methods and procedures of science are simply not available. It argues that the valuation of a business is not a matter of scientific knowledge, is not the subject of scientific testing or experimentation, and is not an area in which peer-reviewed journals evaluate the research methodology of prospective experts.

Later in its opinion the court clarified its reasoning:

> *Ullman-Briggs* reads *Daubert* much too narrowly. While business valuation may not be one of the "traditional sciences," it is nevertheless a subject area that employs specific methodologies and publishes peer-reviewed journals.

The court then went on to point out that the plaintiff's expert was not truly an expert but was really a dealmaker. It found that he did not employ a realiable methodology but really only supplied a bottom line value that was arrived at by

---

[24]*Frymire-Brinati v. KPMG Peat Marwick*, 2 F3d 183 (7th Cir. 1993).
[25]*Newport Ltd. v. Sears Roebuck & Co.*, 1995 Westlaw 328158 (E.D. La.).
[26]*Ullman-Briggs, Inc. v. Salton/Maxim Housewares, Inc.*, 1996 Westlaw 535083 (N.D. Ill.).

others. It stated that "an expert who supplies nothing but a bottom line supplies nothing of value to the judicial process."

EXPERT REPORTS

In the Federal Rules of Civil Procedure, Rule 26 (a) (2) requires that the expert provide a signed expert report. According to Rule 26, this report should include the following items:

- A complete statement of expert's opinions
- The basis for these opinions
- Data and other relevant information considered
- Exhibits to be used in the support of these opinions
- Qualifications of the witness
- List of all publications authored by the expert in the last ten years
- Compensation paid for report
- List of cases in which the expert has testified as an expert, at trial or in deposition, over the prior four years

The above disclosure is required in all federal cases. States, however, vary in their report disclosure requirements. Some follow the Federal Rules and some do not.

Although the Federal Rules require more disclosure in reports, leeway can still be applied in determining how detailed reports are. One school of thought advanced by attorneys is to provide a very detailed report showing the other side that the analysis is very thorough and that the damage estimates are firm. Armed with such a report, attorneys may believe that the case is more likely to settle. Further justification of abundant disclosure is that providing extra report details prevents the opposing counsel from objecting on the grounds that the proper pre-trial disclosure was not made. Conversely, the other school of thought is to provide only the minimum required under the Rules so as to avoid providing fodder for cross-examination. Both approaches have pros and cons.

Testifying Outside the Bounds of the Expert Report

While there may be variances in the degree of disclosure, courts have excluded testimony which is clearly outside the bounds of the expert's report. In *Liccardi* the court stated that expert testimony should have been excluded where such testimony went "far beyond the scope of [the expert's] report."[27] Other courts have reached similar conclusions.[28]

Supplementary Reports

Rule 26 (e)(1) stipulates that a supplement to pre-trial disclosures be provided when there are meaningful changes in the opinions and their bases given in the original report. The Rules are not clear as to exactly when such information is to be provided. They merely indicate that such information should be supplied at "appropriate intervals." If the expert's report is not appropriately supplemented on a timely basis, then the expert may be limited to his original report. This was the case in *NutraSweet Company v. X-L Engineering Company*.[29]

Net Opinions

Opinions that are vague and provide a conclusion without any supporting basis for the opinion may be considered "net opinions" and may not be admissible. Rule 26 requires that the expert provide the basis for his opinions. Although this still leaves room for interpretation, simply stating the opinion without any support for it may be insufficient.[30] Given the complexity of many business interruption cases, it is unlikely the expert would try to submit a very terse statement of opinion. However, opposing counsel should review the opposing report carefully to make sure that it fulfills the requirements of Rule 26 and is not a net opinion in disguise.

Expert's Knowledge of Relevant Facts

It is important that the damages expert be familiar with the relevant facts of the case. One way for a defendant to challenge a plaintiff's expert is to point out that he was not aware of important facts, facts that could change his opinion. Some-

---

[27]*Liccardi*, 140 F3d at 364.

[28]*Eastern Auto Distributors, Inc. v. Peugeot Motors of America, Inc.*, 795 F2d 329, 338 (4th Cir. 1986); *American Key Corp. v. Cole National Corp.*, 762 F2d 1569, 1581 (11th Cir. 1985); and *Merit Motors, Inc. v. Chrysler Corp.*, 187 U.S. App. D.C. 11, 569 F2d 666, 673 (D.C. Cir. 1977).

[29]*Nutrasweet Company v. X-L Engineering Company*, 227 F3rd 776 (7th Cir. 2000).

[30]*Bank Brussels Lambert v. Credit Lyonnais*, 2000 WL 1762533 (S.D.N.Y.).

times an expert is not fully informed of the relevant facts because he was not given a budget necessary to conduct a proper review. Some attorneys think that this is an appropriate cost-saving measure. If, however, an expert is not given all relevant facts that would affect his ultimate opinion, this "cost-saving" can be disastrous. This was the case in *United Phosphorous v. Midland Fumigant, Inc.* In this case the court found that an expert's (Dr. Richard Hoyt) lack of knowledge of relevant facts, including deposition testimony, violated *Daubert* standards.

> The court determines, based upon the foregoing, that Hoyt violated a fundamental principle of economics when he failed to consider in his report the actions of Midland in estimating a value for the Quick-Phos trade name. Hoyt did not read any of the depositions (notably Fox, Lynn, or Estes) before he rendered his report. Consequently, he was required to evaluate the Quick-Phos trade name with little knowledge about the facts of the case, and no knowledge about the underlying admissions from Midland's president and sales managers. The court finds that such ignorance of undisputed facts violates *Daubert's* requirement that an expert report and opinions must be based upon "scientific knowledge."[31]

Retaining attorneys need to be very careful when they try to control costs by limiting what their experts can review. One practice that is fraught with potential problems is providing the expert with only excerpts from depositions rather than the whole deposition. It is often the case that depositions may focus on issues that are unrelated to damages. Sometimes attorneys try to choose the parts that they think are relevant for the expert's needs. This practice puts the expert in a position of being asked if he only read what the retaining attorney wanted him to read. In the long run, it is usually better to simply give the whole deposition to the expert and let the expert decide what is relevant to damages.

DEFENSE EXPERT AS A TESTIFYING EXPERT, NOT JUST A CONSULTANT

There is one view within the defense bar which contends that a defendant should not put his own expert on the stand for damages. The idea is that if the defendant gives alternative damages testimony (even though that testimony may put forward a lower damages value), such testimony might lend credence to the claim that there really are damages. There is also the concern that if a jury hears two damages amounts—a higher one from the plaintiff and a lower one from the

---

[31]*United Phosphorous Ltd v. Midland Fumigant, Inc.*, 173 F.R.D. 675 (D. Kan. 1997).

defendant's expert—then they may simply average the two, particularly if they cannot decide which is more appropriate. On the other hand, the strategy of failing to call a defendant's damages expert can prove disastrous. One of the classic examples of this was the *Texaco v. Pennzoil* case in which the defense decided not to put on its own damages expert and relied on attacking the plaintiff's damages analysis.[32] When the jury found the defendant Texaco liable, there was no damages testimony for the jury to consider other than the plaintiff's presentation. The huge award that resulted underscored the drawbacks of this strategy.

> Our problem in reviewing the validity of these Texaco claims is that Pennzoil necessarily used expert testimony to prove its losses by using three damages models. In the highly specialized field of oil and gas, expert testimony that is free of conjecture and speculation is proper and necessary to determine damages. (cite omitted) Texaco presented no expert testimony to refute the claims but relied on its cross examination of Pennzoil's experts to attempt to show that the damages model used by the jury was flawed. Dr. Barrows testified that each of his three models would constitute an accepted method of proving Pennzoil's damages.

The fact that the ultimate award, which included punitive damages, resulted in the bankruptcy of Texaco underscores the risk of not calling a damages expert.

Another case in which the court highlighted the failure of the defendant to present alternative damages testimony is *Empire Gas Company v. American Bakeries Co.*

> A great weakness of American Bakeries' case was its failure to present its own estimate of damages, in the absence of which the jury could have no idea of what adjustments to make in order to take into account American Bakeries' arguments. American Bakeries may have feared that if it put in its own estimate of damages the jury would be irresistibly attracted to that figure as a compromise. But if so, American Bakeries gambled double or nothing, as it were; and we will not relieve it of the consequences of its risky strategy.[33]

The success of the defense's use of an expert was seen in *Associated Indemnity Co. v. CAT Contracting Inc.*, a case in which the court followed the analysis of the defense's expert in molding its damages award.[34] The Court of Appeals of Texas

---

[32]*Texaco Inc. v. Pennzoil Co.*, 729 S.W. 2nd 768 (Tex. App. 1987), *cert. dismissed*, 485 U.S. 994 (1988).

[33]*Empire Gas Company v. American Bakeries Co.*, 840 F2d 1333, 1342 (7th Cir. 1988).

[34]*Associated Indemnity Co. v. CAT Contracting, Inc.*, 918 S.W. 2d 580 (Tex. App. 1996).

reversed a prior seven figure award and instead awarded an amount that was a fraction of the original award. In this case, a construction joint venture sued a surety. The court was impressed by the argument of the defense's expert: the plaintiff's own financial history should be used to measure losses rather than just the industry averages used by the plaintiff's damages expert. The defense's expert testified as to what the lost incremental revenues were and what the profit margins associated with these revenues would be. The court then used these amounts, rather than the computations of the plaintiff's expert, to arrive at a damages award.

In cases where the defendant believes that the plaintiff has mitigated his damages and, therefore, has not really incurred any net damages, it is best for the defense to put on its own damages expert to demonstrate the point. In these cases, if the analysis is sufficiently thorough and convincing, the court may ignore the plaintiff's damages presentation and deny an award based upon the testimony of the defense's expert. The defense may be able to reduce the effectiveness of the plaintiff's damages presentation by showing that while its actions may have resulted in some lost profits, the plaintiff was able to substitute other business which resulted in profits being essentially unchanged from prior years. Such a result occurred in *Alcan Aluminum v. Carlton Aluminum of New England, Inc.*[35]

Discovery of Nontestifying Experts

An opposing counsel may not be able to gain access to the file, such as through a deposition, of a nontestifying expert; access to the individual may be impossible as well. The work of nontestifying experts is usually considered privileged and not subject to discovery. An exception occurs when opposing counsel can demonstrate a need for discovery to gain access to information or materials that are not available from other sources.[36] This was the case in *Delcastor, Inc. v. Vail Assoc., Inc.* where the court concluded that important data involving a construction site that was destroyed would not be available other than through access to a nontestifying expert's report.[37] However, in *Hartford Fire Ins. Co. v.*

---

[35]*Alcan Aluminum v. Carlton Aluminum of New England, Inc.,* 35 Mass. App. 161, 617 N.E. 2d 1005 (1993) *review denied,* 416 Mass. 1105, 621, N.E. 2d 685 (1993).

[36]Steven Babitsky and James J. Mangraviti, Jr., *Writing and Defending Your Expert Report* (Falmouth, MA: Seak, 2002).

[37]*Delcastor, Inc. v. Vail Assoc., Inc.,* 108 F.R.D. 405 (D. Colo. 1985).

Pure Air on the Lake Ltd. the court concluded that the defendant did not prove to the court's satisfaction that it could not gain access to relevant information through other sources beyond what was available through the plaintiff's non-testifying witness.[38]

QUANTITATIVE RESEARCH EVIDENCE ON THE BENEFITS OF CALLING A DEFENSE EXPERT

Dr. Robert Trout, of Economatrix Research Associates, Inc. and Lit-Econ, conducted a study which attempted to measure the impact of economic testimony on damages awards. His 1991 study found that when only the plaintiff called a damages expert, the average award was $418,355.[39] However, when the defendant also presented his own damages expert to counter the plaintiff's damages expert, the average award was less than a quarter of the plaintiff's only expert alternative—$98,567. Dr. Trout summarized the results of his analysis as it relates to the benefits of the defendant calling his own damages expert as follows:

> The findings concerning the use of economists suggest that a reasonable strategy for the defense counsel should be to use an economic expert whenever the plaintiff uses an economic expert, except in cases where the defense's economic expert testimony might increase the chance that liability would be found against the defendant or support the testimony of the plaintiff's economist.[40]

TREATMENT OF THE RELEVANT CASE LAW

This book focuses on the methods of conducting a damages analysis. It does not focus on the relevant case law. It should not be inferred that this is an unimportant issue. The case law provides a framework within which losses can be presented in court. Readers, however, are directed to other fine works in this area for a discussion of the issue. One of the leading books in this field is Robert Dunn's *Recovery of Damages for Lost Profits*.[41] Another is William Cerillo's *Proving Business*

---

[38]*Hartford Fire Ins. Co. v. Pure Air on the Lake Ltd.*, 154 F.R.D. 202 (N.D. Ind. 1993)

[39]Robert R. Trout, "Does Economic Testimony Affect Damage Awards?" *Journal of Legal Economics* 41 (March 1991): 43–49.

[40]Ibid., 47.

[41]Robert L. Dunn, *Recovery of Damages for Lost Profits*, 5th ed. (Kentfield, CA: Lawpress, 1998).

Damages.[42] These works are used in this book to provide guidance on the court's position concerning the methods of measuring damages. They are regularly updated in supplements that include recent cases on damages-related issues.

LEGAL DAMAGE PRINCIPLES

In measuring damages, experts should be familiar with the basics of legal damage principles. This section touches on some of the major relevant principles. For a more in-depth discussion, readers are encouraged to pursue the abundant sources available.

Proximate Causation and Reasonable Certainty

In order for damages to be recoverable, they must be *proximately caused* by the wrongful acts of the defendant. In addition, damages must be proven within a *reasonable degree of certainty.* A key word in the latter phrase is reasonable. By applying the modifier reasonable, the courts have acknowledged that it may not be possible to compute damages with 100 percent certainty. Therefore, a degree of certainty less than 100 percent is acceptable. It is here that the opinion testimony of an expert can be used to establish the reasonable limits of acceptability. In allowing a level of certainty less than 100 percent, courts recognize that, even for historical damages, the actions of the defendant may have permanently changed events such that one may never know exactly what would have transpired in the absence of such actions. For future damages, the course of events can never be known with certainty. If a 100 percent standard were adopted, damages might never be established. In addition, the defense would be able to take advantage of the fact that, through wrongful acts, it moved the plaintiff to a situation where it may never know the exact magnitude of its damages.

Occurrence of versus the Amount of Damages

It is important to make the distinction between establishing the fact of damages within a reasonable certainty and the actual measurement of those damages.[43]

---

[42]William A. Cerillo, *Proving Business Damages*, 2nd ed. (New York: Wiley, 1991).
[43]Dunn, 1.3.

The reasonable certainty is applied to the fact that the damages actually occurred. However, a lesser standard is applied to measuring the magnitude of the damages themselves. Here the courts have recognized the particularly difficult problem that arises in the measurement of damages that may have or will occur after the actions of the defendant may have permanently changed the course of events. The courts do not allow the defendant to benefit from the fact that its causation of the plaintiff's damages may render such damages unable to be proved within a 100 percent degree of certainty. On the other hand, if the occurrence of the damages is uncertain, then the plaintiff may not be able to recover such damages.

This reasoning is articulated in *Story Parchment Co. v. Paterson Parchment Paper Co.*[44] In this case, in which the plaintiff sought damages for antitrust violations of the defendant, the Supreme Court stated the following:

> Where the tort itself is of such a nature as to preclude the ascertainment of the amount of damages with certainty, it would be a perversion of fundamental principles of justice to deny any relief to the injured person, and thereby relieve the wrongdoer from making any amend for his acts. In such case, while the damages may not be determined by mere speculation or guess, it will be enough if the evidence shows the extent of the damages as a matter of just and reasonable inference, although the result is only approximate. The wrongdoer is not entitled to complain that they cannot be measured with exactness and precision that would be possible if the case, which he alone is responsible for making, were otherwise.

Reasonable Basis for the Damages Calculation

There must be a *reasonable basis* for the damages put forward. This basis is sometimes referred to as a *rational standard.*[45] The courts may try to serve as a filter through which speculative presentations are prevented from being used by the jury to arrive at a damages award. The range of acceptability is still quite broad and the expert is allowed to adopt the damages methodology to fit the unique requirements of each case. As the Supreme Court of Kansas stated in *Vickers v. Wichita State University:*

> As to evidentiary matters a court should approach each case in an individual and pragmatic manner, and require the claimant furnish the best available proof as to the amount of loss that the particular situation admits.[46]

---

[44]*Story Parchment Co. v. Paterson Parchment Co.*, 282 U.S. 555, 563 (1931).
[45]*Vickers v. Wichita State University*, 213 Kan. 614, 620, 518 P.2d 512, 517 (1974).
[46]Dunn, 391–392.

Forseeability

Another important legal principle in the field of commercial damages is the *forseeability rule.* In order to be recoverable, the damages must be foreseeable by the defendant at the time the defendant acted in a way which resulted in the damages. For example, in a breach of contract, the defendant must be able to foresee that when it breached the contract with the plaintiff, the defendant was going to cause the plaintiff to incur damages. This legal principle arises out of the very famous English case, *Hadley v. Baxendale.*[47] This case is similar to many business interruption claims which occur today. It involves a mill owner who sued a shipper for lost profits due to the late shipment of an iron shaft necessary to run the mill. The court concluded that the lost profits were not recoverable, as they were not within the contemplation of the parties.

Foreseeability can become clear when the plaintiff explicitly communicates its anticipation of damages to the defendant at the time of the defendant's actions. In the absence of such direct communications, the courts are put in the position of determining what was *within the contemplation of the parties.* This means that if the defendant is capable of understanding how its actions might have an adverse effect on the plaintiff, then those actions are within the contemplation of the defendant. For example, if the defendant has contracted with the plaintiff to provide certain services or products, the defendant likely knows of the use to which the plaintiff may be putting such services or goods. The defendant may be further able to anticipate the impact on the plaintiff if the latter were to do without such services or goods. In such cases, the actual contract between the parties may provide some useful information for determining what is within the contemplation of the parties. Other evidence of this can come from testimony or knowledge of communications between the parties, where the use to which the plaintiff was putting the goods and services was communicated to the defendant. The plaintiff would ease its burdens of proof if, at the time he entered into the contract, he explicitly advised the defendant of the anticipated damages should the defendant fail to complete his contractual obligations.

A clue to the reasonable foreseeability is the fact that a given transaction was commercial. Continuing with the contract example, the court may conclude that the defendant knew in advance that the plaintiff was using the goods or services for some commercial purpose in hopes of generating profits. Accepting this, a court may conclude that there would be a loss of profits if the contract were breached. It is even clearer if both parties were unambiguously aware of how the plaintiff used the goods or services provided by the defendant.

---

[47]*Hadley v. Baxendale*, 156 Eng. Rep. 145 (1854).

Collateral Transactions

A party may claim damages from a *collateral transaction*—a transaction contingent upon another. A party may claim that the failure of the defendant to perform the first transaction resulted in losses in another transaction that hinged upon the performance of the first transaction. Damages resulting from such transactions may not be recoverable unless it can be demonstrated that the damages were foreseen and within the contemplation of the parties at the time of the agreement. The plaintiff may have a clearer case if he can demonstrate that the second transaction flows directly from the first; this is different from an indirect route in which the plaintiff argues that had he been able to enjoy the proceeds from the first contract, he would have pursued another venture (in turn, generating additional lost profits which he claims as damages). The plaintiff's argument is stronger if he can show that he gave the defendant notice of the dependence of the second transaction on the first. Such notice, however, is not necessary in the case of a reseller where the seller knows the nature of the buyer's (reseller) business. Here, foreseeability is presumed given the nature of the buyer's business.

Contract-Related Damages

Parties to a contract can incur damages in a number of ways. A buyer may lose profits due to the failure of a seller to deliver. Such a failure may cause the buyer to incur *incidental* and/or *consequential* damages. Incidental damages are those expenses that the buyer may incur from having to secure replacement goods. Consequential damages are those which the plaintiff may have incurred as a consequence of the defendant's failure to perform. Once again, the defendant must have been able to foresee these damages and the plaintiff must not have been able to avoid such damages by securing performance from other parties. This alternative performance is sometimes referred to as *cover.* The plaintiff, however, may be able to cover the transaction by securing the goods or services elsewhere but still incur damages. This would be the case if the cover price were higher than the contract price. The damages would be the price difference plus any incidental damages.

The law carries with it a requirement that the plaintiff make efforts to mitigate its damages from securing alternative sources or cover. The situation becomes more problematic when the goods or services in questions are unique and not readily available in the marketplace. Mitigation of damages is discussed in Chapter Six.

Contractually-Related Liability Limitations

The seller may include provisions in the contract to limit its liability to the buyer. In a sale of goods, such as machinery, these provisions may limit the seller's obligations to repair the goods without any allowance for the recovery of consequential damages, including any lost profits. Courts have concluded that if the limitations are very extreme, they may be found *unconscionable*.

Breach of Covenant of Good Faith and Fair Dealing and Breach of Termination Clauses

Although the parties to a contract may have a contract period that is explicitly defined, the agreement may also provide for its termination under certain circumstances. If one of the parties exercises the termination provision, they may still be liable for damages if they violate the *covenant of good faith and fair dealing*. This was the court's conclusion in *Sons of Thunder, Inc. v. Borden, Inc.*[48] The New Jersey Supreme Court agreed with the trial court's differentiation between obligations which are controlled by a termination provision and obligations that are governed by the covenant of good faith and fair dealing.

> It seems to me that as a general rule where you have a contract that is terminable by its express terms, a party terminate, regardless of motive; however, that is separate from determining whether there has been good faith exercised in the performance of the contract; that you can look at good faith separate and apart from just looking at motive alone and pigeonholing it.

The importance and extent of the obligations under the covenant of good faith and fair dealings varies with the laws of different states. The State of New Jersey places relatively greater emphasis on such obligations.

> In our state, it is the law that where a party to a contract follows an agreement or provision in a contract regarding the termination of that contract, its motives or reasons for terminating are irrelevant . . .
>   Now it is also the law in New Jersey that each party to a contract must deal fairly and in good faith with the other in their performance under the contract.

Damages arising from a breach of the covenant of good faith and fair dealing can give rise to damages over a period that is not very clear. In *Sons of Thunder,*

---

[48]*Sons of Thunder, Inc. v. Borden, Inc.,* 148 N.J. 396; 690 A.2d 575, 1975.

Inc. v. Borden, Inc. the trial court awarded an additional year of lost profits. Once a jury determines the relevant time period the standard methodology for measuring lost profits that is set forth in this book applies. When the time period that a jury would find appropriate is unclear, one solution is for the expert to compute damages for various alternative time periods so that a jury can select the relevant damage period and associated amount.

Warranty-Related Damages

A breach of warranty is a contract-related claim. Under the Uniform Commercial Code, there are two types of warranties—express and implied. In an express warranty, the seller clearly delineates which characteristics of the goods that he sells are guaranteed. In an implied warranty, the promise is less clearly stated and a more general guarantee is given, such as general merchantability. The normal standard of warranty-related damages is the difference between the value of the goods as warranted and the value of the goods that were accepted. While this is an important area of commercial damages, it is not the focus of this volume.

OTHER TYPES OF DAMAGES CASES

A complete listing of all the different types of cases in which there is a claim for commercial damages is well beyond the scope of this section. However, it may be useful to highlight a few of the more common types which may give rise to a lost profits claim.

Distributor, Manufacturer's Representative, and Franchisee Relationships

Several contract cases arise involving the representations by a manufacturer or another goods or service provider. A *distributor* is similar to a *manufacturer's representative*. Both represent the manufacturer, but a distributor often takes possession of the goods and maintains an inventory of the products, while a manufacturer's representative augments the seller's sales force without physically storing an inventory. Each may or may not have exclusive territories. A *franchisee* may be given the right to market a company's products within an exclusive territory. Disputes often stem from the termination of these agreements with the terminated party claiming damages for lost profits under the agreement. These disputes may be caused by the franchisee or distributor failing to perform or the franchiser failing to live up to its obligations—neglecting to provide agreed-upon marketing support for the product, for example. The franchiser may contend that it terminated the franchisee because the latter did not properly market the product.

Despite the wide variety of these lawsuits, the methodology used to measure damages can be found within the framework described later in this book. The method usually involves constructing revenue projections and applying costs ratios to derive profits from projected revenues. In other instances, such as in the case of terminated franchisees, the damages analysis may involve employing business valuation techniques to place a value on a terminated franchisee which no longer exists.

Contracts to Provide Services

Other types of contract-related damages can arise from a failure to provide the contractually agreed-upon services. When these cases involve major figures in high-profile businesses, they tend to attract media attention. For example, movie stars who walk out on film agreements or authors who do not provide manuscripts both are failing to honor their contractual obligations. Publishers may simply demand the return of an advance. In the film industry, however, the analysis may be substantially more complicated, involving loss of invested capital or lost projected profits.

Construction-Related Contract Cases

Another common type of contract cases are construction cases. These often involve lawsuits for failure to complete construction on time or according to the specifications of the contract. Other construction cases have to do with who pays for certain costs and whether cost overruns can be passed on to the builder. Still another type of construction case is one which involves damages related to the loss of bonding capacity. The loss of such capacity may limit the volume of work that a contractor can bid for. This may generate a claim for lost profits on the additional work that the plaintiff claims he would have been awarded had he had a certain bonding capacity.

Noncompete Agreement Cases

Still another common form of contract-related damages cases are those that involve covenants not to compete. This can come from provisions in a business sales agreement where an owner of a business agreed not to compete with the buyer for a period of time. Other cases involve professional service firms where individuals agreed not to compete for a certain period of time with an employer in exchange for certain consideration. The damages analysis can sometimes be complicated as it may involve measuring the damages that result exclusively from the illegal competition. An important part of this analysis is isolating these specific damages. Cases may be more straightforward where a personal service provider—such as an attorney or a broker—competed by stealing specific clients or customers than in a situation where a firm improperly competes and is one competitor among several in the market. In such cases, the industry analysis may be quite important in assessing the change in the level of competition and the resulting damages.

Lost Profits Arising from Personal Injury

As noted earlier, economists play a prominent role in measuring damages in personal injury. These often involve projections of lost earnings over a work-life expectancy or a valuation of the services that an injured party or a decedent would have provided.[49] In a personal injury lawsuit, a business generally cannot claim damages due to the injuries of an employee. However, in cases where the employees were largely responsible for the profits of the business, such as in a small business with few employees and where the plaintiff was the prime force behind the generation of the business' profits, the profits of the business may become an important part of the damage measurement process.[50] An example: a president of a small business is involved in an accident which causes him not to be further involved in the business and this, in turn, results in the closure of the business. Here, the projected profits, along with other forms of compensation that the individual derived from the business (such as officer's compensation or other perks), might be relevant.[51]

The courts have usually drawn a distinction between cases where the profits of a business are a function of an individual's efforts and returns which are the product of the invested capital. In the latter case, where returns are more passive, the law of torts is less relevant.

---

[49]Thomas Ireland, Stephen M. Horner, and James Rodgers, op. cit.

[50]*Ginn v. Penobscot Co.*, 334 A. 2d 874 (Me. 1975).

[51]Patrick Gaughan and Henry Fuentes, "Minimization of Taxable Income and Lost Profits Litigation," *Journal of Forensic Economics* IV (1) (winter 1990): 55–64.

Personal Injury and Corporate Damages Due to Loss of "Key Man"

It is not unusual that a company's success can be largely attributed to the efforts of one individual. This is sometimes referred to as the role of the *key man* in corporate finance. Corporate America is filled with examples of companies whose growth and success can be attributed to an individual who makes a far greater contribution than any other member of the company. It is logical, then, that a company can be significantly damaged if that individual dies or is impaired as a result of injury—he can no longer participate in the activities of the business. The courts have come to recognize this. Although the company itself may not be able to recover its lost profits, the injured party, who may be a controlling shareholder, may be able to individually recover such lost profits.[52]

Damages Resulting from Other Business Torts

A variety of tortious behaviors can cause recoverable damages in the form of lost profits. These can include tortious interference with business, fraud, and unfair competition. The varieties of each of these categories of business torts can be virtually limitless. While the case law is correspondingly voluminous, the methodology used to measure damages (such as lost profits) can be found within the chapters that follow. However, courts have found that "lost profits in a tort action are limited to those damages proximately caused by the defendant's wrongful conduct."[53] Such profits usually can be measured through a projection of *but for* profits and a comparison of such projected profits with the actual and "projected actual" profits. This will be described in detail in the chapters that follow.

SUMMARY

This chapter introduces the use of an expert to measure damages in commercial litigation. One of the first steps in this process is selecting the right expert. Given the diverse nature of business interruption cases, this expert needs to have a well-rounded background in the fields of economics, econometrics, and finance. This expert may also need to have knowledge of accounting. Because a wide range of

---

[52]*Lundgren v. Whitney's Inc.*, 94 Wash. 2d 91, 614 P. 2d 1272 (1980).

[53]*Horan v. Klein's-Sheridan, Inc.*, (1965) 62 Ill. App. 2d 455, 459, 211 N.E. 2d 116.

expertise is often needed, it may be necessary to have a team of experts from which one expert testifies but relies on the work of other experts. In some cases, more than one expert may testify.

There are many sources of experts. The most common of which is referrals from colleagues. If that is not a fertile source of experts, then other sources such as local universities or referral agencies may be needed. Particularly in cases where the expert is not referred by a colleague, attorneys need to carefully review the expert's credentials. These credentials should include a terminal degree in the field, a Ph.D. degree, and publications in the field. Publications may include books and refereed journal articles. Care must be applied when reviewing experts' CVs to ensure that they are accurate. For example, what is listed as a publication should be verified as a published work.

There are several ways to use damages experts. One is to have the expert author a report and serve as a witness. Another is to use the expert purely as a consultant but not as a testifying witness. This latter strategy is often used by defendants who do not want to give credence to the plaintiff's damages claims. Instead, they may want to use the expert to help cross-examine the plaintiff's expert. Research results, as well as the experience of several notable cases, raise serious questions about this strategy. In some cases it works well and in others it does not. The strategy for each case will vary and should be determined based on close consultation with the expert.

REFERENCES

Alcan Aluminum v. Carlton Aluminum of New England, Inc., 35 Mass. App. 161, 617 N.E. 2d 1005 (1993), *review denied*, 416 Mass. 1105, 621, N.E. 2d 685 (1993).

Aluminum Products Enterprises v. Furhmann Tooling, 758 S.W. 2d 119, 112 (Mo. Ct. App. 1988).

Associated Indemnity Co. v. CAT Contracting, Inc., 918 S.W. 2d 580 (Tex. App. 1996).

Babitsky, Steven, and James J. Mangraviti, Jr., *Writing and Defending Your Expert Report*. Falmouth, MA: Seak, 2002.

Bachmier, Lanie, Patrick Gaughan, and Norman Swanson, "The Volume of Litigation and the Macroeconomy." *International Review of Law and Economics*, forthcoming.

Baker, W. Gary, and Michael K. Seck, *Determining Economic Loss in Personal Injury and Death Cases*. Shephard's/McGraw-Hill. 1987.

Bank Brussels Lambert v. Credit Lyonnais, 2000 WL 1762533 (S.D.N.Y.).

Brookshire, Michael, and Frank Slesnick, "A 1990 Survey Study of Forensic Economists." *Journal of Forensic Economists* IV (2) (spring/summer 1991).

Brookshire, Michael L., and Stan V. Smith, *Economics/Hedonic Damages, The Practice Book for Plaintiff and Defense Attorneys.* Anderson Publishing, 1990.

Cerillo, William, *Proving Business Damages,* 2nd ed. New York: Wiley, 1991.

Daubert v. Merrill Dow, 509 U.S. 579 (1993).

Delcastor, Inc. v. Vail Assoc., Inc., 108 F.R.D. 405 (D. Colo, 1985).

Digital & Analog Design Corporation v. North Supply Company, 44 Ohio St. 3d 36; 540 N.E. 2d 1358, 1989.

Dillman, Evert, "Punitive and Exemplary Damages," in *Litigation Economics,* Patrick Gaughan and Robert Thornton, eds. Greenwich, CT: JAI Press, 1993.

Dunn, Robert, *Expert Testimony: Law and Practice.* Westport, CT: Lawpress, vol. I, 1997.

Dunn, Robert, *Recovery of Damages for Lost Profits,* 5th ed. Kentfield, CA: Lawpress, 1998.

Eastern Auto Distributors, Inc. v. Peugeot Motors of America, Inc., 795 F2d 329, 338 (4th Cir. 1986); *American Key Corp. v. Cole National Corp.,* 762 F2d 1569, 1581 (11th Cir. 1985); and *Merit Motors, Inc. v. Chrysler Corp.,* 187 U.S. App. D.C. 11, 569 F2s 666, 673 (D.C. Cir. 1977).

Empire Gas Company v. American Bakeries Co., 840 F2d 1333, 1342 (7th Cir. 1988).

Frye v. United States, 293 F1013 (D.C. Cir. 1923).

Frymire-Brinati v. KPMG Peat Marwick, 2 F3d 183 (7th Cir. 1993)

Garcia v. Columbia Medical Center, 996 F. Supp 617, 621 (E.D. Tex 1998).

Gaughan, Patrick A., "Economics and Financial Issues in Lost Profits Litigation," in *Litigation Economics,* Patrick A. Gaughan and Robert Thornton, eds. Greenwich, CT: JAI Press, 1993.

Gaughan, Patrick A., and Henry Fuentes, "Minimization of Taxable Income and Lost Profits Litigation." *Journal of Forensic Economics* IV (1) (winter 1990).

Ginn v. Penobscot Co., 334 A. 2d 874 (Me. 1975).

Hadley v. Baxendale, 156 Eng. Rep. 145 (1854).

Harold Larsen et al., Respondents v. Walton Plywood Company et al., Appellants, Washington Plywood Company, Inc. No. 36863, Supreme Court of Washington, Department One, 65 Wash. 2d 1; 390 P.2d 677; Wash.

Hartford Fire Ins. Co. v. Pure Air on the Lake Ltd., 154 F.R.D. 202 (N.D. Ind. 1993).

Hein v. Merck & Co., 868 F. Supp 203 M.D. (Tenn 1994) and *Ayers v. Robinson,* 887 F. Supp. 1049 (N.D. Ill. 1995).

Horan v. Klein's-Sheridan, Inc., (1965) 62 Ill. App. 2d 455, 459, 211 N.E. 2d 116.

In Re Brand Name Prescription Drugs Antitrust Litigation, 1999 U.S. Dist. Lexis 550, January 19, 1999 *(decided and docketed).*

Ireland, Thomas, Stephen M. Horner, and James Rodgers, "Reference Guide for Valuing Economic Loss in Personal Injury, Wrongful Death and Survival Actions," in *Economic Expert Testimony: A Guide for Judges and Attorneys.* Tucson, AZ, 1998.

Liccardi, 140 F3d at 364.

Liu v. Korean Airlines Co., 1993 Westlaw 478343 (S.D.N.Y.).

Lundgren v. Whitney's Inc., 94 Wash. 2d 91, 614 P. 2d 1272 (1980).

Martin, Gerald, *Determining Economic Damages.* James Publishing, October, 1995.

Mattot v. Ward, 48 N.Y. 2d 455, 423 N.Y.S. 2d 645 (1979).

Newport Ltd. v. Sears Roebuck & Co., 1995 Westlaw 328158 (E.D. La.).

Nutrasweet Company v. X-L Engineering Company, 227 F3rd 776 (7th Cir. 2000).

Piette, Michael, "Economic Methodology and the Analysis of Employment Discrimination." *Journal of Forensic Economics* IV (3) (fall 1991).

Plummer, James, and Gerald McGowan, "Ten Most Frequent Errors in Litigating Business Damages," *Association of Business Trial Lawyers (ABTL) Northern California Report,* November, 1995.

Sons of Thunder, Inc. v. Borden, Inc. 148 N.J. 396; 690 A.2d 575, 1975.

Speiser, Stuart, *Recovery for Wrongful Death and Injury: Economic Handbook,* 2nd ed. The Lawyer's Cooperative Publishing, 1988.

Spizman, Lawrence, and John Kane, "Defending against a *Daubert* Challenge: An Application in Projecting the Lost Earnings of a Minor Child." *Litigation Economics Digest* III (1) (spring 1998).

Story Parchment Co. v. Paterson Parchment Co., 282 U.S. 555, 563 (1931)

Technical Advisory Service for Attorneys, Blue Bell, PA.

Texaco Inc. v. Pennzoil Co., 729 S.W. 2nd 768 (Tex. App. 1987), *cert. dismissed,* 485 U.S. 994 (1988).

Trout, Robert R., "Does Economic Testimony Affect Damage Awards?" *Journal of Legal Economics* 41 (March 1991).

Ullman-Briggs, Inc. v. Salton/Maxim Housewares, Inc., 1996 Westlaw 535083 (N.D. Ill).

United Phosphorus, Ltd. v. Midland Fumigant, Inc., 173 F.R.D. 675; 1997.

Verdict Search, Moran Publishing Company, East Islip, NY.

Vickers v. Wichita State University, 213 Kan. 614, 620, 518 P.2d 512, 517 (1974).

Wright v. Williams, 47 Cal. App. 3d 802, 121 Cal Rptr. 194 (1975).

2

ECONOMIC FRAMEWORK FOR THE LOST PROFITS ESTIMATION PROCESS

This chapter discusses two preliminary and fundamental aspects of commercial damages analysis: causality and the methodological framework for measuring damages. The first section of this chapter examines the ways in which economic analysis can be used to provide evidence of causality in commercial damages litigation. Economists employ certain statistical techniques to determine whether or not the plaintiff was responsible for the alleged damages of the defendant. Having established causality, the next step is determining the loss period. The loss period can be determined by many factors, including whether the losses have ended as of the trial date. Following this discussion, the methodological framework for measuring damages is introduced.

FOUNDATION FOR DAMAGES TESTIMONY

An expert may be provided with factual assumptions that serve as a basis for testimony. This is set forth in Rule 703 of the Federal Rules of Evidence, which states "The facts or data in the particular case upon which an expert bases an opinion or inference may be those perceived by or made known to the expert at or before the hearing." In the context of commercial damages analysis, this may involve various facts, such as the assumed actions of the opposing party in the litigation. However, the expert is not a fact witness. Rather, the expert may be asked to compute the damages that result from certain data and assumed facts. This gives rise to a systematic method by which the assumptions utilized by the expert are analyzed.

ROLE OF ASSUMPTIONS IN DAMAGES ANALYSIS

Economic damages testimony is typically based upon a series of assumptions. It is important for the attorney retaining the expert to know all of the key assumptions as well as what the basis for each is. It is equally important for the opposing counsel to understand the role of these assumptions and to know how the damages would differ if other assumptions were employed. There are three categories of assumptions an expert may rely upon: factual assumptions, assumptions involving the opinions of other experts, and economic assumptions.

Factual Assumptions

These are the facts that the expert is asked to assume. Depending on the particular circumstances of the case, the expert may do some investigation of these facts to ascertain whether any differences exist between what the expert is *told* occurred and what, in fact, *did* occur. However, the expert is not a private investigator and will not necessarily verify all of the facts that he is asked to assume. These facts may be made known to the expert either by the retaining attorney or through documents that the expert reviews. These documents include deposition testimony as well as trial testimony that may precede the expert's own testimony.

Assumptions Involving the Opinions of Other Experts

Additional experts are sometimes employed to analyze other aspects of the damages claim. These include appraisers, who will determine the value of equipment or real estate assets, and industry experts, who may testify on industry practices and standards or the existence of certain industry trends. The use of other experts' opinions as a predicate for a damages calculation is very common in types of damages analysis other than commercial damages. For example, in personal injury analysis, an economist may employ the findings of a vocational expert who opines on the expected future employability and earnings potential of an injured party. In business interruption cases, when supportive experts are used in conjunction with the damages expert, industry experts are often such witnesses. When the characteristics of the industry are unique, an industry expert is helpful.

Economic Assumptions

These are the assumptions that the economic expert brings to the analysis. Examples of these assumptions include the rate of inflation and the discount rate that are applied to a projection of future lost profits. Such assumptions are usually the product of the expert's knowledge and of the analysis that has been done for the case in question.

In cross-examining an opposing expert, it is important to focus on the above categories of assumptions. The expert can be asked how the analysis would differ if the assumptions of the opposing party were employed. In some cases, it is possible for the expert to indicate how the damage value would be different if alternative assumptions were used. In other cases, the analysis may be complicated and opposing counsel may have to settle for a basic response on the approximate magnitude of the revised loss. If this happens, opposing counsel will have to bring an expert into court to provide more specific answers to such questions. Obviously, opposing counsel's expert may be asked some of the same questions. That is, the expert brought in by the defendant may be provided some of the factual assumptions that were provided to the plaintiff's expert and asked how this would affect his opinion. If defense counsel is concerned about what the answers might be to such questions, then defense counsel may want to simply have an expert work with him to conduct an effective cross-examination of the plaintiff's expert. On the other hand, if defense counsel is confident that the jury would accept the factual assumptions provided by the defendant, then he may not be concerned about loss values that would result from an adoption of the defendant's assumptions—he may believe that the jury would find such assumptions irrelevant.

HEARSAY

One of the ironies of trial testimony is that the expert is often able to testify by relying on written or oral statements that in other contexts would be considered hearsay.[1] This often frustrates trial attorneys. Evidence that otherwise would not be admissible can be introduced through the expert, who might simply say that he has heard or reviewed certain items, items which the attorney normally would not have been able to introduce. Obviously, opposing counsel is still able to challenge the contents of the documents or statements upon which the expert is relying.

Not all courts, however, allow experts to introduce what would otherwise be considered hearsay. For example, in *Target Market Publishing, Inc. v. ADVO, Inc.*, the court heard the testimony of a "deal maker" who was relying on a valuation analysis done by others at his former employer; the court considered the testimony to be nothing more than hearsay and thus was inappropriate.[2] One of the

---

[1] Robert L. Dunn, *Expert Witness: Law & Practice* (Westport, CT: Lawpress, vol. I, 1997), 160.

[2] *Target Market Publishing, Inc. v. ADVO, Inc.*, 136 F3d 1139; 1998 U.S. App. Lexis 2412.

issues that the U.S. Appeals Court for the Seventh Circuit found objectionable was that the "expert" did not do the analysis about which he was testifying and apparently was not able to adequately clarify it. It is not unusual for one expert to testify about analysis that another expert conducted, but the former must be able to respond on cross-examination about issues concerning this analysis. When the testifying expert is relying on an analysis outside his own expertise, the counsel presenting the expert may want to consider having both experts testify—one establishes the predicate for the other.

Opinions That Are Inconsistent with the Evidence

Opinions based upon assumptions that are not based upon the evidence, and which are inconsistent with it, are speculative. Theoretically, this is problematic for the expert who relies on facts that are not in evidence or hearsay. One instance, however, which is clearer is one where there are certain facts in evidence that are totally inconsistent with the expert's assumptions and analysis. When an expert's analysis relies on facts that are contrary to the evidence, the expert risks having the analysis termed speculative. It is here that the counsel who retained the expert—who may know the record, and the body of materials, and testimony that has been developed in discovery better than the expert—can be helpful in guiding the expert. Counsel who knows of facts and evidence that are inconsistent with the assumptions upon which the expert is relying should alert the expert to these inconsistencies. In researching the case, the expert needs to be mindful of any records and testimony that could contradict his assumptions. In complex litigation, it often happens that certain testimony conflicts. In such cases, it is not unusual for a decision to be made as to which evidence and testimony should be utilized and which should be ignored. In some instances, this decision is made by counsel, who will retain an expert to base his analysis upon specific assumptions that counsel feels confident will be accepted by the jury. Unless the record is clearly to the contrary, the expert will normally provide such analysis. For the sake of clarity, it may be helpful for the expert to delineate which assumptions he is using and what the sources of those assumptions are.

Expert Reports

Under the Federal Rules and the rules of certain states, expert reports must be exchanged. However, as discussed in Chapter One, the rules are not very specific regarding the level of detail required in such reports. Presumably, the expert is required to indicate what he relied upon in formulating his opinion. Nonetheless, this is still a gray area in litigation; the expert has a wide degree of latitude in deciding what to include in the report and what to omit.

Many expert reports are quite terse. Some are even intentionally cryptic so as to make it difficult for opposing counsel to challenge the analysis. It is difficult to challenge something that one does not understand. When faced with an incomprehensible analysis, it is important for the attorney to have his own damages expert carefully dissect it. Attorneys should be aware that this work can be very time-consuming. Experts may have to devote many hours to "reverse engineer" the opposing expert's calculations. Once this is done, however, and the relationship between the computations and their underlying assumptions is established, cross-examining attorneys can quantitatively assess the ramifications of adjusting the existing assumptions and substituting more favorable ones.

Some attorneys wait until after the opposing expert's deposition has been taken to employ the services of their own expert. If they don't understand the opposing expert's report, the attorneys may try to have the expert educate them on his analysis during the deposition. This is usually a mistake. The deposing attorney should have his own expert dissect the report and prepare deposing counsel prior to the deposition.

APPROACHES TO PROVING DAMAGES

Courts have accepted two broad approaches to proving damages. They are the *before and after method* and the *yardstick approach*. The methods are widely cited in the case law on damages; finding precedents in support of their application is not difficult.

Before and After Method

This method compares the revenues and profits before and after an event—in this case, a business interruption. A diminution in revenues or profits may be established based upon the difference between the before and after levels. This method assumes that the past performance of the plaintiff is representative of its performance over the loss period. It also assumes that sufficient historical data are available from which to construct a statistically reliable forecast. In addition, it assumes that economic and industry conditions during the loss period are similar to what they were during the before period so that the data are comparable. If they are not, the expert should either attempt to make adjustments to account for these differences or abandon this approach (if he decides that the differences are significant enough to make the analysis unreliable).

While the before and after method has a certain appeal, it cannot be blindly applied without sufficient analysis, such as that which is presented in this book. If some of the factors upon which its successful application is dependent are not available—sufficient historical data, for example—then the expert must utilize another methodology.

Failing to Give Consideration to Before and After Factors

In many types of business interruption cases, it is logical to compare the pre-interruption period with the post-interruption period. Failing to do so implies that the expert assumes the two periods are the same. If they are not, a major error can result. An example of the court's recognition of such oversight by an expert is found in *Katskee v. Nevada Bob's Golf.* In this case, a lessee sued a lessor for lost profits on sales of merchandise resulting from the failure of the lessor to allow the lessee the right to renew a lease.[3] The expert assumed that the location in question and the replacement location were the same in all relevant aspects except for their square footage.

> The witness called as an expert on the topic by Nevada Bob's testified that Nevada Bob's lost $130,455 in profits because it was not permitted to expand into the adjacent L.K. Company Space. The witness computed this figure by computing the yearly revenue produced per square foot at the location to which Nevada Bob's moved after vacating the L.K. Premises and multiplying that figure by the square footage of the adjacent space. . . . He then next multiplied this computation by gross profit margin and subtracted therefrom his estimate of the additional expenses incident to the increased square footage. He then divided this figure by 12 to obtain what he designated as lost profits per month and multiplied that figure by the number of months Nevada Bob's stayed at the premises after L.K. breach . . .

In its criticism of this methodology the court stated:

> No studies and comparisons were made as to differences in customer bases, relative accessibility of the facilities, proximity to recreation areas or other shopping areas, parking or other external factors. *The witness also used sales figures from a different time period and made no study as to any changes in the relative market* (emphasis added). He did not evaluate whether there was any change in the number of competitors, whether there was any change in customer interest in the relevant products, or whether there was any changes in the products sold by Nevada Bob's.

Katskee v. Nevada Bob's Golf is a good example of the court's rejection of an overly simplistic method and one which ignores differences in the before and

---

[3]*Katskee v. Nevada Bob's Golf,* 472 N.W. 2d 372 (November 1991).

after time periods. The court indicated that many important changes may have occurred and the expert simply ignored this possibility. The case is instructive in that it requires that a sufficiently detailed analysis, including an application of the before and after method, should be conducted when relevant.

Challenges to the Use of the Before and After Method

One of the ways a defendant can challenge the use of the before and after method is by trying to prove that the after period is different from the before period. The defendant may want to show that there is a good reason for such a difference and that this difference is not based upon any actions of the defendant. For example, the defendant may try to prove that other factors, such as the plaintiff's own mismanagement, were responsible for a poorer performance in the after period. A weaker economic demand in the after period, such as one caused by a recession, is another explanation that the defense may try to use. Under such circumstances, it might be reasonable to expect that firms like the plaintiff's would do as well as before. In order to effectively make this argument, the defense needs to present its own analysis showing how the plaintiff performed in the past relative to the performance of the economy. Having established this association, the defense can then present an analysis of the economic conditions during the after period and show how it was a weaker economic environment.

The weaker economic environment is only one of many reasons why a plaintiff's performance during the after period could be expected to decline. Presumably, this is fully explored through the economic analysis that the expert conducts (see Chapter Three). The circumstances of each case differ and each may bring its own relevant economic factors. Examples could be poor management decisions, changed industry conditions, etc. In order to find such alternative explanations, defense counsel and the expert may need to devote sufficient time to learning the plaintiff's business and understanding how the business, or the actions of the plaintiff, have changed over time.

Defense counsel may find that the time and resources required for doing a thorough analysis are greater than those that the plaintiff's expert devoted to his work. This most often occurs when one of the drawbacks of the plaintiff's analysis is its simplistic nature which did not research and consider certain relevant factors.

Yardstick Approach

The yardstick approach involves a comparison with *comparable* businesses to see if there is a difference between the level of the plaintiff's performance after an event and that of comparable businesses. It is a method that can be used if there is insufficient justification for applying the before and after method. It also can be used to buttress the findings of the before and after method.

One of the key issues in applying the yardstick method is comparability. Each case is different, and comparability may be defined differently depending on how the yardstick approach is being used. If the performance of other firms in the industry is being used to estimate how the plaintiff would have performed, then the expert needs to do an analysis of these other firms to determine that they are truly comparable. This may involve determining that they service similar markets and sell similar products or services as the plaintiff's.

Challenges to the Use of the Yardstick Method

The defendant can challenge the use of this method by asserting that the so-called comparable firms are not truly comparable and that there is a reasonable basis to expect these companies to perform differently than the plaintiff. This may involve an analysis of the comparable group to see if they are similar. In doing this analysis, the services of an industry expert who works with the damages expert can be particularly helpful. An industry expert may be able to quickly alert the damages expert to important differences between the plaintiff and the comparable group, thus explaining differences in performance.

Lack of comparability can derive from many sources. It could be that the industry definitions used by the plaintiff's expert are inappropriate. Industries can have important subcategories and these subcategories can differ significantly from one another. For example, there may be a high-end or high-margin luxury category and there may be a low-end category that features significant discounting and price competition. If the competitive pressures have intensified in the low-end category but not in the luxury category, then using one category to measure the profitability in the other may not be helpful. The high-end category will have different profit margins than the low end, its lower margins depending on volume to generate its profitability.

Another difference between the comparable group of companies selected by an expert and the plaintiff is the size of the respective firms. If the comparable group is far larger than the plaintiff, this size difference may bring with it important differences. For example, if some of the so-called comparable firms are larger and, by virtue of that size, are involved in other business areas beyond what the plaintiff is involved in, then this may make them less comparable. Size differences alone, as measured by revenues and assets, may not mean a lack of comparability, however, they may lead to imbalances that allow the expert to conclude the firms are sufficiently different and should not be included as comparables.

Using the Yardstick Approach
for Newly Established Businesses

The before and after method often cannot be used effectively for a newly established business—it has not been around long enough to have sufficient before period data to compare with data from the after period. In these cases, a plaintiff may be restricted to using a yardstick approach. An example of the application of the yardstick method for a newly established business is provided by *P.R.N. of Denver v. A. J. Gallagher*. The Florida Court of Appeals recognized that a standard before and after method would not be possible.[4]

> Denver concedes that the usual predicate for a commercial business's claim of lost profits is a history of profits for a reasonable period of time anterior to the interruption of the business. . . .

In citing the reasoning of another case involving a wrongfully evicted hotel coffee shop, the court stated:

> The operator of a hotel coffee shop who is wrongfully evicted after a mere two weeks of operation may prove his loss of profits by establishing the profits of his business whose fifteenth month operation of a coffee shop was similar in every respect then, a fortiori, PRN of Denver, Inc. a successor whose operation and operators are the same as its predecessor, may prove its loss in the same manner, without running afoul of the rule prohibiting the recovery of purely speculative damages.

The issues related to measuring damages for unestablished and newly established business are revisited later in this book.

Concluding Comments on the Before
and After and Yardstick Methods

While these two methods are continually cited in the case law, they only outline two alternative ways of proving damages. This book attempts to go beyond these two methods and provide a broader methodological framework that the expert can adapt to a variety of damage circumstances. As the court said in *Pierce v. Ramsey Winch Company*, a "plaintiff is not limited to one of these two methods.

---

[4]*P.R.N. of Denver v. A.J. Gallagher & Co.*, 521 So 2d 1001 (Fla. Dist. Ct. App. 1988).

A method of proof specially tailored to the individual case, if supported by the record, is acceptable."[5]

The methodology presented herein is one that encompasses both methods but goes beyond the bounds of either one to present a more complete methodological framework. The approach in this book can be more flexibly applied to a broader array of circumstances than either the before and after method or the yardstick approach.

CAUSALITY AND DAMAGES

The issue of causality is fundamental to commercial damages litigation. If the losses of the plaintiff are substantial, but it is not conclusive that the losses were caused by the actions of the defendant, the litigation may be pointless. This occurred in *McGlinchy v. Shell Chemical Co.*[6] Here the court excluded an expert's testimony as his loss analysis could not be traced to the actions of the defendant.

When liability is questionable, the courts and both parties may save resources through bifurcation of the proceedings. The liability phase of the trial may, for example, focus on the obligations of the defendant under a contractual agreement. However, even in the liability phase, there can also be important economic and financial issues for which the expert may provide evidence.

Economists have long been used to present evidence on liability in employment litigation. For example, economists are used in age, gender, or racial discrimination cases to ascertain if a defendant's employment policies are biased.[7] The economist might use statistical techniques, such as logit and probit analysis, to determine if age is a statistically significant explanatory variable in a equation in which employee terminations is the dependent variable. The courts have long accepted such statistical or econometric testimony to help the trier of the facts make these kinds of liability determinations in bias-related litigation.[8] Interestingly, the level of these courtroom presentations can be sophisticated, employing complicated techniques normally reserved for advanced research, for an audience that generally lacks statistical training. This disconnect, however, has not hindered the acceptance of, or the reliance on, such evidence.

---

[5]*Pierce v. Ramsey Winch Co.,* 753 F. 2d 416 (5th Cir. 1985).

[6]*McGlinchy v. Shell Chemical Co.,* 845 F2d 802 (9th Cir. 1988).

[7]Dolores A. Conway and Harry V. Roberts, "Regression Analysis in Employment Discrimination Cases," in *Statistics and the Law,* Morris H. DeGroot, Stephen E. Feinberg, and Joseph B. Kahane, eds. (New York: Wiley, 1986), 107–168.

[8]*Vuyanich v. Republic National Bank of Dallas,* (D.C. Tex. 1980).

Under certain circumstances, statistical analysis is applied to investigate liability in a commercial lawsuit. On the simplest level, statistics can be employed to bolster economic theory used to establish how the sales of the plaintiff would have varied had it not been for a specific event, such as the actions of the defendant. This can be done by establishing the closeness of association between the sales of the plaintiff and various economic variables. For example, correlation or regression analysis could be used to show the historical degree of association between the plaintiff's sales and broad economic aggregates, such as national income, GNP, retail sales, as well as more narrowly defined economic variables, such as industry sales.

Understanding Correlation Analysis in a Litigation Context

A basic step in applying correlation analysis is the computation of the correlation coefficient (r). In equation form, this is expressed as follows:

$$r = \frac{n(\Sigma XY) - (\Sigma X)(\Sigma Y)}{[n(\Sigma X^2) - (\Sigma X)^2][n(\Sigma Y^2) - (\Sigma Y)^2]}$$

n	is the number of observations
ΣX	is the X variable summed
ΣY	is the Y variable summed
(ΣX^2)	is the X variable squared and the squares summed
$(\Sigma X)^2$	is the X variable summed and the sum squares summed
(ΣY^2)	is the Y variable squared and the squares summed
$(\Sigma Y)^2$	is the Y variable summed and the sum squares summed

The correlation coefficient can take on values between -1 and $+1$. A perfect negative correlation exists when there is a one-to-one negative relationship between two variables. Here the correlation coefficient is -1. (See Exhibit 2.1 (a).) The opposite is the case when there is a perfect one-to-one positive relationship between two variables, giving a correlation coefficient of $+1$. (See Exhibit 2.1 (c).) If there is absolutely no relationship between two variables, then the correlation coefficient equals 0. (See Exhibit 2.1 (b).)

In the real world, however, such perfect relationships rarely exist. That is, when there is some relationship between two variables, it will show up in correlation coefficient values between -1 and $+1$. The closer the coefficient is to $+1$, the more positive the relationship. In other words, when one variable increases, the other tends to increase as well. This is depicted in Exhibit 2.2 (a). The closer the corre-

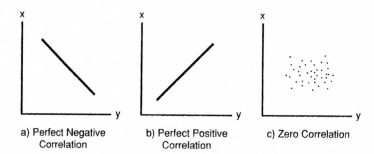

a) Perfect Negative
Correlation

b) Perfect Positive
Correlation

c) Zero Correlation

Exhibit 2.1   Different correlation examples.

lation coefficient is to −1, the more inverse the relationship. That is, when one variable increases, the other decreases. This is shown on Exhibit 2.2 (b).

Correlation Scale

The degree of association between two variables can be put into perspective through the use of a *standard correlation scale.* This is a mapping of the range of values for the correlation coefficient where the various values are represented as being indicative of the strength of association—be it positive or negative. This mapping technique is useful because it translates the strength of the association into verbal terms that may be easier to understand.[9] Correlations greater than 0.5 are considered to be higher than moderate (see Exhibit 2.3).

In addition to the correlation coefficient, economists also express the strength of the association in terms of the *coefficient of determination,* which is simply the squared value of the correlation coefficient. This measure, r^2, shows how much of the variation in one variable can be explained by variation in the associated variables.

One of the advantages of using the correlation coefficient is that it provides a numerical measure of the *degree* of association, rather than simply saying that there is a good association between the variables in question. For example, the expert may be trying to examine the relationship between the sales of a company and certain deterministic factors, such as macroeconomic aggregates like national manufacturing shipments and industrial production. The economist may know that when the economy is expanding, as reflected by upward movements in these macroeconomic aggregates, a company's sales are expected to increase. The

[9]Robert D. Mason and Douglas A. Lind, *Statistical Techniques in Business and Economics,* 10th ed. (New York: Irwin/McGraw Hill, 1999), 426.

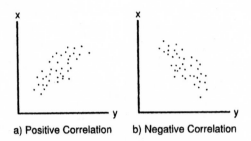

a) Positive Correlation   b) Negative Correlation

Exhibit 2.2 Strong positive and negative correlation.

expert may also testify that such a co-varying pattern is observable in the data. However, the strength of this testimony may be bolstered by mathematically measuring this association and stating that the correlation coefficient between the company's sales and total U.S. manufacturing shipments is 0.87 while the coefficient of determination is 0.76. The latter measure means that 76 percent of the variation in the company's sales is explained by variation in manufacturing shipments, an indicator used to measure the broad macroeconomic influence of the economy as a whole.

It is important to remember that finding a relatively high correlation coefficient does not *prove* causality. A high positive or negative correlation coefficient tells us there is a high direct or indirect degree of association between two different series of data which, in turn, implies that changes in one of the series *may* cause changes in the other. In our example of the manufacturer, an increase in demand from an expanding economy, as reflected by growth in national manufacturing shipments and increased industrial production, may increase the demand for a company's product which, under normal circumstances, would cause the company's sales to rise. It could be the case, however, that the plaintiff's sales have fallen and the

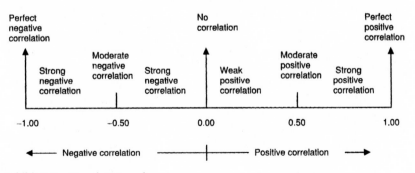

Exhibit 2.3 Correlation scale.

expected increase failed to materialize. If all other factors can be ruled out, this economic analysis may lend credence to the claim that the actions of the defendant caused the sales of the plaintiff to decline.

Even a high correlation could simply be *spurious*—without any causality. For example, there is a high correlation between the number of firemen at fires and the severity of fires. This correlation is spurious; one cannot conclude that it is the number of firemen that is causing the severity of the fire. However, a high correlation coefficient can provide a strong suspicion of causality. Even without establishing causality among the associated variables, it may be useful to show that these variables have tended to move together in the past and that something has since caused this association to cease.

In economic research, economists sometimes employ econometric tools to analyze causality. *Econometrics* is the field of economics that applies statistical analysis to economic issues. Within econometrics there is a subfield called *time series analysis* that investigates causality.[10] However, although these techniques are sometimes used in econometric research, they are not as often used in commercial damages analysis and are not an accepted part of the standard methods in this field. Other more basic methods are usually employed. These include the aforementioned correlation analysis as well as graphical analysis in which plots of relevant variables are graphically depicted. For example, in Exhibit 2.4, a graph of a hypothetical national company's sales and U.S. retail sales is shown. Such graphs are sometimes referred to as scatter diagrams.

The expert may find that giving the jury the opportunity to visually inspect a plot of the observations over time may reinforce the contention that there is a causal relationship. This is based upon the belief that a "picture is worth a thousand words." In a courtroom, where demonstrative evidence helps win cases, such exhibits can be quite useful.

---

[10]The statistical technique in the econometric field of time series analysis called Granger Causality can be used in a regression of a dependent variable time series $\{y_t\}$ against an independent variable time series $\{x_t\}$. One can conclude that series $\{x_t\}$ fails to *Granger cause* $\{y_t\}$ if a regression of y_t on lagged x_i's reveals that the coefficients of the x_i's are zero. The validity of the Granger test comes from the basic premise that the future cannot cause the past. "If event A occurs after event B, we know that A cannot cause B. At the same time, if event A occurs before B, it does not necessarily imply that A causes B." It is important to bear in mind that Granger causality is not causality in the legal sense. For further discussion of this technique see C.W.J. Granger, "Investigating Causal Relations by Econometric Models and Cross Spectral Models," *Econometrica* 37 (January 1969): 24–36, and G.S. Maddala, *Introduction to Econometrics* (New York: Macmillan, 1988).

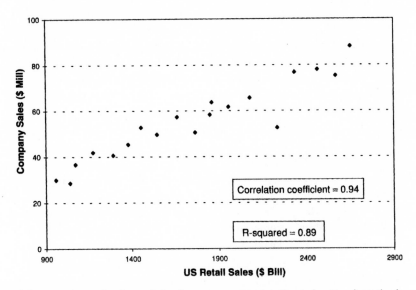

Exhibit 2.4 Example of correlation between company sales and national retail sales. *Source:* U.S. Department of Commerce, Bureau of Economic Analysis, Washington, D.C.

The example above shows a joint plot of the dependent variable (i.e., the plaintiff's sales) and the probable causal variables. In cases of a historical business interruption, the graph can be extended beyond the interruption date at trial to help show what sales of the plaintiff would have been absent the interruption. This extension of the "but for" stream of plaintiff's revenues can be constructed using regression analysis. This statistical technique is further discussed later in this module. However, putting the correlation analysis together with forecasting techniques allows one to see what happens if the historical relationship that was measured using the correlation coefficient is extrapolated over the loss period.

In conclusion, it is important to note that correlation analysis and graphical demonstration can be very useful but not necessarily conclusive. They can be an important first step in the analytical process. If the results are promising, this may yield a need to continue the analysis further.

USING DEMONSTRATIVE EVIDENCE TO HELP THE CLIENT UNDERSTAND ITS LOSSES OR LACK OF LOSSES

Normally we think of preparing graphical and statistical exhibits as part of the pre-trial preparatory process. However, such analysis and exhibits can be helpful early in the expert's work on the case. It is often the case that the plaintiff has a biased or emotional view of his losses. For example, the plaintiff may think he has incurred a "seven figure loss." This feeling may be inflamed by the animus the plaintiff bears towards the defendant for whatever actions precipitated the suit. The plaintiff may attribute a downturn in sales exclusively to the actions of the defendant when other events, such as changes in the degree of competition in the plaintiff's market, may have played a more important causal role. As another example, a plaintiff's sales pattern may have remained essentially unchanged, possibly because of the efforts that the plaintiff has exercised to mitigate his damages by substituting other sales for those that were lost. Some basic statistical analysis, presented in the form of graphical exhibits, can efficiently demonstrate the impact of these factors. Even when there is a real loss, it is important for the plaintiff to see that he may have to refute the implication of the sales pattern in an exhibit prepared by the opposing expert. This indicates that he and his attorney will have an uphill evidentiary battle ahead of them.

The initial statistical and graphical analysis can give the client an advance word on whether they have a convincing liability case and shows them the approximate magnitude of their losses. It allows the client to give explanations for what may have caused the trends that are readily apparent in the graphs. Armed with this information, the client can make a more enlightened decision on how much to invest in the litigation. If the true losses are, for example, less than $100,000, but legal and expert fees through trial would be far greater than this amount, the client may decide to withdraw the suit. For this reason, it is useful to do some early analysis and allow the client to react to this first step in the analytical process.

One drawback of doing such initial analysis is that it does not reflect the thorough final analysis that the expert would present in a final report. Given that this may be discoverable at some point, the attorney has to weigh the possibility of being confronted with the analysis and exhibits at a later date. This is another reason why it is important to have an expert who is aware of the ramifications of putting work in writing which may later be discovered. This does not mean that the expert should try to conceal analysis that is not favorable. Rather, the expert should simply be mindful of what is written down and how it can be manipulated to mean something other than what was originally intended.

CAUSALITY AND LOSS OF CUSTOMERS

One instance in which causality is clear is when economic losses can be attributed to the loss of particular customers. This could occur in several ways. An example is a business interruption in which customers are lost because the ability of the plaintiff to supply products or services to its customers was compromised. Another scenario might be that specific customers were stolen through illegal actions of the defendant.

The establishment of causality in the case of the loss of specific customers is more straightforward. Liability may be established through testimony and other means. However, even when liability is established without economic analysis, the economist still has to conduct an analysis of the plaintiff's sales. This usually involves a breakdown of sales-by-customer over a historical period. This sales breakdown naturally goes together with the usual steps the attorney would take to legally establish liability.

A model has recently been developed for measuring sales of lost customers in litigation.[11] This model takes into account an important factor—the historical rate of *customer attrition*. It is normal for firms to lose some of their customers over time. This can occur for many reasons, including competitive forces, service quality, etc. Some firms are able to keep a very high percentage of their customers; others may experience more rapid rates of customer loss. If a plaintiff states that he lost certain customers as a result of the defendant's actions, a simple projection of the sales of those lost customers without attempting to factor in an anticipated rate of customer loss may overestimate the true losses.

The analysis of the historical attrition rates may be limited by the availability of data. However, if sufficient data are available, the economist may be able to measure the average length of time that a firm retains its customers or, conversely, the average number of customers that leave in a given year. This is analogous to what is done in employment litigation where the average number of years that a worker would remain in the employ of a particular company is measured using statistics such as tenure with the company, education levels, and other variables.[12]

GRAPHICAL SALES ANALYSIS AND CAUSALITY

In its simplest form, the effects of a business interruption are clearest when there is a dramatic change in the plaintiff's revenues. For example, if the plaintiff's revenues fell sharply after the defendant took certain actions, then the counsel for the

---

[11]Laura Bonanomi, Patrick A. Gaughan, and Larry Taylor, "A Statistical Methodology for Measuring Lost Profits Resulting from a Loss of Customers," *Journal of Forensic Economics* 11 (2) (1998): 103–113.

[12]Robert R. Trout, "Duration of Employment in Wrongful Termination Cases," *Journal of Forensic Economic* 8 (2) (1995): 167–177.

plaintiff may find it easier to convince the trier of the plaintiff's loss and the defendant's culpability. Earlier in the chapter, the issue of co-variability between certain economic variables and the sales of the plaintiff was defined and examined. If suddenly co-variability is interrupted, as would be the case if the economic variables continued to rise while the plaintiff's revenues started declining, the defendant's actions may be a possible explanation.

Another way in which graphical analysis may be used to issue a statement on causality is by examining the trends in the plaintiff's historical revenues. If, as in Exhibit 2.5, there is a significant break in the plaintiff's revenues that coincides with the actions of the defendant (assumed to have occurred at time t_0), then a causal link between the two events may exist. The defendant, of course, may try to proffer alternative explanations for the break in the plaintiff's revenue trend. If, for example, it can be shown that another event occurred at time t_0 (see Exhibit 2.5), such as an adverse change in the competitive environment, and the actions of the defendant did not occur until later, at time t_1, with little change in the downward trend in revenues, then the plaintiff may face an uphill liability battle. If, however, the actions of the defendant made the plaintiff's revenues decline more rapidly than they would have otherwise, an argument may be made for some of the plaintiff's losses being attributable to the actions of the defendant.

Simply examining and graphically depicting the plaintiff's revenues may not conclusively establish causality, but it may be an integral part of the liability portion of a commercial damages case. One should be mindful, however, that graphical analysis, while a useful first step, is only one part of a more involved analytical process. Merely noticing that the revenue trend varies consistently with the actions of the defendant does not prove that the defendant caused the plaintiff's losses. On the other hand, if the graphical analysis provides promising results, the

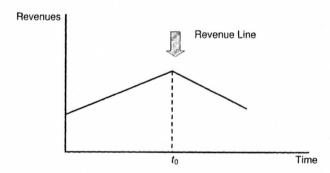

Exhibit 2.5 Revenues over time with break in trend at t_0.

plaintiff may be further equipped to convince the trier of the facts that the defendant is liable.

Economists and Other Damage Experts: Role of Causality

One of the advantages of using an economist to address causality, rather than using another type of damages expert, is that the economist has training in and regularly uses statistical analysis in his work. Statistical and econometric analysis are normal components of the economist's toolbox. Ignoring causality may be a fatal flaw in the damages presentation. It is pointless to measure damages if they cannot be linked to the actions of the defendant. This issue, and the selection of the correct expert, was clearly demonstrated in *Graphic Directions, Inc. v. Robert L. Bush* in which an accountant testified on damages but did not analyze the causal link between the actions of the defendant and the damages.[13] The Court of Appeals of Colorado rejected the damages argument involving a lost customer's analysis because it did not address this important issue.

> Additionally, it is axiomatic that before damages for lost profits may be awarded, one who seeks them must establish that the damages are traceable to and are the direct result of the wrong to be redressed. (citation omitted) GDI's accountant testified that he did not have an opinion as to whether the losses were caused by Bush and Dickinson's conduct and stated that he had not related calculation of lost net taxable profits to the lost customers. Nor is there evidence establishing a causal link between all of the lost sales and Bush and Dickinson's solicitation of customers. At least four of the "lost" customers continued to do business with GDI, and GDI presented no evidence that eight other lost customers did any business with Concepts 3.
>
> Based upon our review of the evidence, we conclude that GDI did not present substantial evidence from which the jury could compute its loss of net profits.

CAUSALITY AND THE SPECIAL CASE OF DAMAGES RESULTING FROM ADVERSE PUBLICITY

Another type of case in which causality is important is one in which damages arise from adverse publicity, whereby a defendant makes defamatory statements

---

[13]*Graphic Directions, Inc. v. Robert L. Bush*, 862 P. 2d 1020 (Colo. App. 1993).

about the plaintiff which cause the plaintiff to incur losses. Here, the economist can utilize basic quantitative techniques commonplace in the field of public relations to measure the dollar value of the adverse publicity which caused the damages.[14]

Public relations professionals often measure the dollar value of the publicity they generate for their clients by treating it as though it were an advertisement. In other words, if a favorable half-page article touting the positive attributes of a business was placed in a local newspaper, the public relations firm would contend that the market value of that publicity is equivalent to the cost of purchasing that advertising space.

The methodology used by public relations firms to measure the market value of the positive publicity they generate also can be used to measure the market value of adverse publicity. Adverse media publicity is viewed as an advertisement that cites negative attributes of an individual or business. When there is a series of such stories in the media, it is viewed as a negative advertising campaign. Its market value can be determined using the market value of the print space (or advertising time, if the medium is radio or television). The cost of the space or time is available from the various media sources who provide their "rate cards" upon receiving a request.

It is well known that advertising can increase sales. Attempts to quantify the "advertising elasticity of demand" have shown that it can be a difficult exercise.[15] Nonetheless, while an exact measurement of the quantitative impact of advertising on sales is difficult to measure, the positive relationship between the two variables is widely accepted. Quantifying the market value of the adverse publicity can be helpful to a trier of the facts by arriving at a measure of its significance. This may be helpful in assessing the causal relationship between the adverse publicity and the alleged losses of the plaintiff.

LENGTH OF LOSS PERIOD: BUSINESS INTERRUPTION CASE

In a business interruption case, losses are measured until such time as the sales or profits of the plaintiff's business have recovered. In a growing business, this

---

[14]Patrick A. Gaughan, "An Application of Exposure Measuring Techniques to Litigation Economics," paper presented at the Eastern Economics Association Annual Meetings.

[15]Leonard Parsons and Randall L. Schultz, *Marketing Models and Econometric Research* (New York: North Holland Publishing, 1978), 82–85.

may not necessarily be the time when the plaintiff's revenues reached the pre-interruption level. If it can be established that the plaintiff's revenues would have grown absent the actions of the defendant, then the recovery period may be when the post-interruption actual revenues reach the forecasted "but for" revenues.

Closed, Open or Infinite Loss Periods

The loss period is characterized as *closed, open* or *infinite*.[16] In a closed business interruption, the loss period has ended and actual sales, both before and after the interruption, are available. Such a loss period is demonstrated in Exhibit 2.6. The graph shows that not only has the sales decline ended, the post-interruption revenues have increased beyond the pre-interruption level of R_1. At time t_1, the revenues are consistent with the level that would be forecasted (R_2) if we were to extrapolate a simple linear trend from the downturn point.

The loss period is "open" when the losses continue into the future. It can be seen in Exhibit 2.7 that the forecasted revenues are continually above the actual post-interruption revenues and that, although the plaintiff surpasses the pre-interruption revenue level of R_1, it never returns to its previous growth path. As a result, the plaintiff is continually below where it would have been had it not been

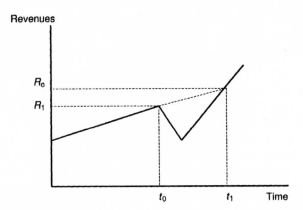

Exhibit 2.6   Closed loss period.

[16]This categorization of loss periods is derived from Robert R. Trout and Carroll B. Foster, "Business Interruption Losses" in *Litigation Economics,* Patrick A. Gaughan and Robert Thornton, eds. (Greenwich, CT: JAI Press, 1993).

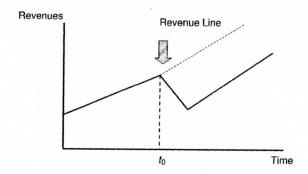

Exhibit 2.7   Business interruption with incomplete recovery.

for the interruption. An examination of Exhibit 2.7 shows that the firm is grow-ing at the same rate as it did prior to the interruption but that it has "lost ground" during the interruption period. Growth in the post-interruption period at the same rate as pre-interruption will never be sufficient to offset the downturn that occurred in the interruption period. Only a higher post-interruption rate of rev-enue growth would be sufficient to offset the effects of the downturn.

It is important for the reader to bear in mind, however, that these examples are simplistic and feature constant pre- and post-interruption growth, so that conven-ient conclusions, such as full recovery (in Exhibit 2.6) or the inability to ever reach full recovery (in Exhibit 2.7), can be easily attained. In the real world, how-ever, revenues do not behave so conveniently. In such cases, the expert may have to conduct a more sophisticated analysis to determine the actual loss period.

Case of Post-Interruption Growth
Exceeding Pre-Interruption Growth

Is it possible for a plaintiff to recover damages if its growth after the business interruption exceeded the pre-interruption growth? Just as in the case of a new or unestablished business (see Chapter Five), the analytical and evidentiary burdens of proving such damages beyond a reasonable doubt are greater than when there is dramatic negative growth after the interruption date. However, a plaintiff could indeed be damaged by the fact that it was not able to realize a higher-than-actual growth due to the actions of a defendant.

An example of how difficult this is to prove occurred in *Bendix Corp. v. Balax, Inc.* The defendant-counterclaimant argued that its growth was less than what it would have enjoyed had it not had to incur the financial pressures brought on by the plaintiff's patent infringement suit.[17] The defendant's case was made difficult by the fact that its revenues grew from 8 percent to 26 percent over this time period. The defendant argued that its growth would have been even higher. Its president testified that their business was only 60 percent of what it would have been and its sales manager said it was only half as large. However, the defendant-counterclaimant's proofs—in the form of testimony from members of its management—were unconvincing to the court.

In commenting on the fact that Balax's revenues increased after the actions of the defendant, the U.S. Court of Appeals for the 7th Circuit stated:

> In the ordinary situation of proving damages allegedly caused as a result of certain action of another, the injured person or corporation shows how its sales declined during the pertinent period but even that is not deemed sufficiently probative . . .
>
> Here, where Balax's revenues increased very substantially, the evidence of damages consists of (1) Val Vleet's testimony that he thinks that "one of the reasons for Balax's Detroit representative discontinuing representing Balax was because a Ford Motor Company plant to which he hoped to sell tapes had learned of the infringement suit"; (2) VanVleet's testimony that "I believe that our business amounted to something like 60% of what it would have amounted to had this action not been brought" and (3) Balax's sales manager's testimony that but for the lawsuit sales would be "I would say at least twice as much as we are currently selling." . . .
>
> In other words Balax's business has steadily increased and would have increased more if it had carried cutting tapes, which it does not, through no reason proved to be attributable to the plaintiff.

Disaggregating Revenues by Product Line to Prove Causality

When the defendant's actions cause a loss in profits for one of a business's product lines or business segments, it is necessary to disaggregate total revenues and examine the trends in the revenues of the relevant product line or business segment separately. In cases where total revenues for the entire business have increased after the interruption, the defendant may want to examine only the trend in total revenues and thus argue that the plaintiff was not hurt. However, on a disaggregated basis, the plaintiff may be able to show that the product line or business segment's revenues fell after the interruption.

An example in which the plaintiff made just such a convincing demonstration occurred in *Pierce v. Ramsey Winch Co.*[18] A terminated distributor brought suit

---

[17]*Bendix Corp. v. Balax, Inc.*, 471 F2d 149 (7th Cir. 1972).

[18]*Pierce v. Ramsey Winch Co.*, 753 F2d 416 (5th Cir. 1985).

against the manufacturer and other distributors. The plaintiff did a standard loss computation in which he projected "but for" revenues, deducted revenues from sales of substitute products, and applied a profit factor to the lost incremental revenues. The defendant argued that the plaintiff could not have experienced a loss since its post-termination gross profits were higher than before. The plaintiff responded that these elevated gross profits came from other goods it sold—truck beds and trailers—not from the winches which were the subject of this litigation. The plaintiff was able to segregate its total revenues and profits which, when combined with other segments of the business, masked its true losses. The relevant trend was the trend in the product at issue—winches that the manufacturer would have sold to the plaintiff—not in the total revenues and gross profits from the sale of other products unrelated to the case.

The U.S. Court of Appeals for the Fifth Circuit recognized the problems of proving damages when revenues increase after a business interruption, but it also recognized that there are circumstances when damages exist even when revenues and profits have increased.

> Pierce Sales, however, cannot show declining sales. As noted Pierce Sales's gross profits have risen sharply since termination. For this reason Ramsey's argument that Pierce Sales was not in fact injured by termination indeed has surface appeal.
>
> Improvement in a distributor's business following termination, it seems to us necessarily flows from (1) a diversion of the resources that were previously devoted to selling products that were previously devoted to selling products supplied by the defendant; (2) successes in an aspect of the business unrelated to the expenditure of resources freed up by the termination; or (3) a combination of these two sources.
>
> If the distributor's successes flow from the utilization of resources other than those previously devoted to selling the defendant's products, post-termination profits would have no bearing on the fact of damage flowing from termination. If the evidence shows, on the other hand, that post-termination profits exceed pre-termination profits, and that they are attributable to the use of resources diverted because of termination to other endeavors, it would seem at least possible that post-termination endeavors are more profitable for plaintiff than operation of the defendant's distributorship. We do not think, however, that a plaintiff is necessarily precluded from showing fact of damage in this latter situation. He may demonstrate fact of damage by showing that (1) he lost sales or revenues during the lag period between termination and completion of his efforts to divert resources to substitute endeavors and (2) although substitute endeavors proved more profitable than distribution of defendant's products did immediately prior to termination, to a level sufficient to earn him greater profits than his substitute endeavors did. He cannot, however, make this showing through speculation or through reliance on unfounded assumptions.

Pierce v. Ramsey Winch Co. is instructive in that it shows that analyzing and graphing total revenues may not capture the relevant trends if only a portion of the business is affected by the defendant's actions. If this occurs, it is necessary to first disaggregate the revenues by business segment and graph these trends separately. It may also be wise to do a separate statistical analysis of the relationship between the revenues of the various segments and their causal factors.

Disaggregating Revenues to Show Spill-Over Losses

A defendant's actions that were directed at one part of the plaintiff's business may have "spill-over" effects onto other parts of the plaintiff's business. In cases like this, it may not be possible to credibly prove damages by merely disaggregating revenues. It may be necessary to disaggregate costs as well. This is sometimes difficult, particularly when inputs are used for a variety of products. An example in which a plaintiff claimed losses on related products resulting from a cutoff of beer supply is found in *Cooper Liquor Inc. v. Adolph Coors Co.* The plaintiff claimed that beer sales were a loss leader and were used to bring in customers who would buy other products that generated positive profits. The court rejected the plaintiff's loss analysis because it was based upon gross bank deposits with no product-by-product breakdown.[19] The lesson from this case is that when claiming interrelated spill-over effects, a product-by-product revenue analysis must demonstrate these effects. This means constructing a table which analyzes not only the trends in historical total revenues but also in disaggregated components.

LENGTH OF LOSS PERIOD: PLAINTIFF GOES OUT OF BUSINESS

When a plaintiff has gone out of business, the loss period is termed "infinite." This is shown in Exhibit 2.8 where a business interruption occurred at time t_0, causing the plaintiff so much damage that by time t_1, it went out of the business. Actual sales may only be available for the period from when the interruption began to when the company went out of business. It is important to note that although the loss period may have no definite termination date, this does not imply that the losses are infinite. Through the process of *capitalization* it is pos-

---

[19]*Cooper Liquor Inc. v. Adolph Coors Co.*, 509 F2d 758 (5th Cir.) Denying petition for rehearing, 506 F2d 934 (5th cir. 1975).

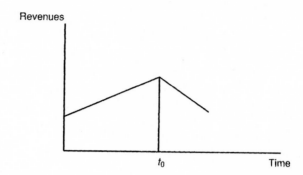

Exhibit 2.8   Infinite loss period: revenues ends as business goes out of existence.

sible to determine the present value of such losses. The determination of present value places increasingly lower values on amounts that are further into the future. This process will be discussed later in this module.[20]

A number of cases involving firms that went out of business due to the actions of the defendant have held that the value of the damages is equal to the market value of the business on the date the operations ceased. In cases where the company operates for a period of time before going out of business, the plaintiff may be able to recover lost profits for the interim period between the wrongful acts of the defendant and the date that the plaintiff went out of business, at which time the remaining value of the loss is the value of the business on that date. The valuation of businesses, which is one way that such losses may be measured, is discussed in Chapter Eight.[21]

LENGTH OF LOSS PERIOD: BREACH OF CONTRACT

In the case of an alleged breach of contract, losses are typically projected until the end of the contract period. While this seems fairly straightforward, sometimes it is not. The actual length of the contract period also may be an issue of dispute. This occurs when there are early termination clauses or option periods. In the event of an early termination clause, the loss may be shorter than the end of

---

[20]While it may be obvious, a business that is not profitable, or more importantly does not generate positive operating cash flows, may not be able to show lost profits (although it may have incurred other losses) even if it goes out of business. This is a general statement, however, and each case is different.

[21]*Aetna Life and Casualty Co. v. Little,* 384 So. 2d 213 (Fla. App. 1980).

the contract, while an option period may allow for losses to extend beyond the normal end of the contract. In such cases, the expert may be retained to project losses until an assumed end of the contract period based upon the client's legal interpretation of the contract. The expert will have to look for legal guidance from the retaining attorney.

Long-Term Contracts

For long-term contracts, some courts have been reluctant to award damages for the full length of the loss period due to concerns over the degree of certainty associated with long-term projections. The courts have correctly concluded that the further into the future one forecasts, the greater the uncertainty surrounding the forecast. In his review of the case law in this area, Robert Dunn has concluded that although courts have not clearly articulated their reasoning, they have chosen to award damages for periods that are significantly shorter than the actual number of remaining years on the contract.[22] In *Palmer v. Connecticut Railway & Lighting Co.*, for example, the court awarded damages for only eight years even though the remaining time on the contract was 969 years and the plaintiff itself conceded that it could not project damages beyond 40 years due to the uncertainty of such a projection.[23] In another example of the court's simply truncating the remaining years of a contract, the court in *Sandler v. Lawn-a-Mat Chemical & Equipment Corp.* allowed damages for only 3 years although the contract had a term of 50 years with an option to renew for another 50 years.[24]

One issue that the court has not addressed is the implicit estimate of no losses that this truncation process places on the remaining years of contract. By terminating the losses at a certain date, the court is substituting its own estimate of $0 for losses after the truncation period. On the other hand, the court's position that only damages which can be projected with reasonable certainty are allowed is affirmed in these and other decisions. The courts are simply saying that there may be losses, but that at some point in the future such losses may not be measurable with reasonable certainty. In addition, after some passage of time, it becomes more reasonable that the plaintiff would be able to pursue other mitigating activities.

---

[22]Robert L. Dunn, *Recovery of Damages for Lost Profits* (Westport, CT: Lawpress, 1992), 402–404.

[23]*Palmer v. Connecticut Railway & Lighting Co.*, 311 U.S. 544 (1941).

[24]*Sandler v. Lawn-a-Mat Chemical & Equipment Corp.*, 141 N.J. Super. 437, 358. A. 2d 805 (1976).

METHODOLOGICAL FRAMEWORK

The methodological framework is a step-by-step process that combines various components that should be part of the entire damages analysis. Though each case has unique aspects, it is common that the components presented below are integral parts of the overall loss measurement process. The components are:

A. Macroeconomic Analysis: Analysis of the condition and role of the national and possibly international economy
  - Regional Economic Analysis (if relevant): Analysis of the condition of the regional economy
B. Industry Analysis: Analysis of the plaintiff's industry and any changes in relevant conditions within it which might affect the alleged loss
C. Firm-Specific Analysis
  - Revenue Forecasting
  - Cost Analysis
  - Financial Analysis
D. Measurement of Lost Profits: This brings together the different elements of C to arrive at a measure of profits per period, such as annual periods
E. Adjustment for the Time Value of Money: This step converts the projected future amounts to present value terms through the process of discounting. Past losses may possibly also be adjusted to convert them to current values.

A. Macroeconomic Analysis

Using a top-down due diligence process, this methodology first examines the overall macroeconomic environment within which the alleged loss took place. This examination considers the condition of the overall economy as measured by several relevant macroeconomic aggregates. The performance of the macroeconomy is then compared to the performance of the plaintiff before and after the event/events in question. The expert will determine, based upon the analysis of the company's historical performance compared to macroeconomic aggregates, what role such variables play in determining the success of the plaintiff. In doing so, the expert will also consider the role that the cyclical variation in the economy has played in the company's performance and the alleged losses.

Regional Economic Analysis
In some instances, the macro-economy may be less relevant than a more narrow economic environment. This is the case for firms who are exclusively regional.

Here a more narrowly focused group of economic aggregates, such as state economic data rather than national data, are used to measure the performance of a relevant regional economic environment. The expert will have to decide which macroeconomic and which regional economic data to utilize. As is discussed in Chapter Three, the quality of the regional data may differ from the macroeconomic data.

B. Industry Analysis

An analysis of the plaintiff's industry provides valuable information about the performance and profitability of the business area within which the plaintiff operates. This, in turn, can give clues as to how the plaintiff should have performed and what level of profits it should have derived absent the alleged wrongdoing. It allows the expert to see if the trends that are at issue in the litigation, such as the plaintiff's losses, are specific to it or are part of a wider industry phenomenon that has nothing to do with the actions of the defendant. In order to do this, though, the expert needs to analyze the industry and to determine to what extent that plaintiff is similar to its industry peers. In many cases, there are subcategories within an industry and the expert may end up comparing the plaintiff with a subgroup as opposed to a broader collection of companies that make up the industry.

Several different data sources are used to measure this industry performance. They tend to vary in quality across industries. Some industries gather abundant and reliable data; others have limited data available and they may not be collected in a reliable manner. This needs to be explored by the expert. Industry analysis is discussed in Chapter Four.

C. Firm-Specific Analysis

Having established the macroeconomic, regional, and industry environment within which the firm operates, the next step in the top-down process is to analyze the performance of the firm itself. This includes an analysis of the firm's historical and current performance as measured by several variables (revenue growth and a number of profitability measures). Depending on the type of case, this firm-specific analysis may include an analysis of the firm's financial statements. Such analysis may differ depending on the reliability of the data contained in the plaintiff's financial statements. Such statements may be audited or merely compiled. Nonetheless, the analysis of these financial statements may employ the standard tools of corporate finance, such as financial ratio analysis. It also may involve analysis of the financial trends of the business such as those apparent in its historical revenues and profits. This analysis may also be considered in light of the aforementioned economic and industry data.

D. Loss Measurement Process

Having analyzed the performance of the plaintiff in relation to the macroeconomic, regional, and industry economic environments, the expert can begin the actual loss measurement process. This typically involves a two-part process whereby revenues are first forecasted and a relevant profit margin is then applied to the forecasted revenues. The economic, industry, and firm-specific analyses may all be considered when determining the growth rates to be used in the forecasting process. Once the revenues and lost revenues are estimated, the lost profits on these revenues need to be measured. To do this, a profit margin needs to be established. In order to derive the appropriate profit margin, a cost analysis must be conducted to determine the incremental costs associated with the lost incremental revenues. This loss measurement process combines the forecasting skills of an economist with the costs measurement abilities of either an economist or an accountant to derive lost profits.

E. Adjusting for the Time Value of Money

The estimated loss measures have to be converted to present value terms so that both historical and future loss amounts are brought to terms that are consistent with the date of the analysis or the trial date. A pre-judgment return may be applied to pre-trial amounts to make them current. Whether or not this is done, and what rate is used, depends on the relevant law. Similarly, the projected future losses need to be brought to present value through the use of a relevant discount rate. This rate should reflect the perceived risk of the lost earnings stream.

SUMMARY

Two broad methods for measuring damages are continually cited in the case law. They are the before and after method and the yardstick approach. The before and after method involves comparing the plaintiff's performance before the actions of the defendant with its performance after these actions. The plaintiff may attribute differences, such as lower revenues and profits, to the actions of the defendant. The yardstick approach involves finding comparable business and attributing the performance of these similar businesses to the plaintiff. Both methods are merely general outlines of an approach to measuring damages. This book provides a broad methodological framework which is consistent with both methods but is more intricate and more flexible.

The economic loss analysis includes an analytical component that helps establish the allegation of causality linking the actions of the defendant to the alleged losses of the plaintiff. The determination of causality involves some basic statistical analysis to assess the link between relevant economic time series and certain performance measures of the plaintiff. Such an analysis may establish, for example, that prior to the business interruption there was a close statistical relationship between the growth in the plaintiff's revenues and the growth in general economic activity and in the plaintiff's industry, in particular. The deviation from the normal and expected relationship between these variables in the post-interruption period may be one component, along with other fact-based evidence, of a demonstration of causality.

The loss period varies by type of case. Loss periods can be closed if a business has fully recovered. Open loss periods exist when a business continues to experience losses. Loss periods are infinite when the business ceases to exist. An infinite loss period, however, does not imply that the losses themselves are infinite.

The methodological framework for economic loss analysis is a top-down process that begins with a macroeconomic analysis of the overall economy. This establishes the macroeconomic environment in which the damages are alleged to have occurred. In most circumstances, the weaker the macroeconomic environment, the more conservative the projection of damages.

Following the macroeconomic analysis, the focus narrows to the regional level. This occurs only if the alleged damages are confined to a specific region or geographical sector. Many of the same economic time series used at the national level are employed in this analysis but they are narrowed to a specific region.

The next step in the process is to conduct an analysis of the industry in which the losses are alleged to have occurred. This usually involves collecting industry data which are then compared to the macroeconomic and regional data as well as to firm-specific data. As part of this process, the growth, level of competition, pricing, and other industry factors are analyzed.

The next step in the commercial damages loss framework is to conduct a firm-specific analysis. This will involve an analysis of the trend in the firm's historical revenues and performance measures such as gross and net profits as well as cash flows. Pre-loss trends are contrasted with post-loss trends as part of a loss projection process.

The next step typically involves a "but for" revenue projection from which actual revenues are deducted to derive lost revenues. Having established lost revenues, a cost analysis is conducted to measure the incremental costs associated with the lost incremental revenues. The lost profits are then measured as the difference between the incremental lost revenues and their associated costs.

REFERENCES

Aetna Life and Casualty Co. v. Little, 384 So. 2d 213 (Fla. App. 1980).

Bendix Corp. v. Balax, Inc., 471 F2d 149 (7th Cir. 1972).

Bonanomi, Laura, Patrick A. Gaughan, and Larry Taylor, "A Statistical Methodology for Measuring Lost Profits Resulting from a Loss of Customers." *Journal of Forensic Economics* 11 (2) (1998): 103–113.

City of Greenville v. W.R. Grace & Co., 640 F. Supp, 559 (D.S.C. 1986).

Conway, Dolores A. and Harry V. Roberts, "Regression Analysis in Employment Discrimination Cases," in *Statistics and the Law,* Morris H. DeGroot, Stephen E. Feinberg, and Joseph B. Kahane, eds. New York: Wiley, 1986.

Cooper Liquor Inc. v. Adolph Coors Co., 509 F2d 758 (5th Cir.) Denying petition for rehearing, 506 F2d 934 (5th Cir. 1975).

Custom Automated Machinery v. Penda Corp., 537 F. Supp. 77 (N.D. Ill. 1982).

Dunn, Robert L., *Expert Witness: Law & Practice.* Westport, CT: Lawpress, vol. I, 1997.

Dunn, Robert L., *Recovery of Damages for Lost Profits.* Westport, CT: Lawpress, 1998.

Gaughan, Patrick A., "An Application of Exposure Measuring Techniques to Litigation Economics," paper presented at the Eastern Economics Association Annual Meetings.

Granger, C.W.J., "Investigating Causal Relations by Econometric Models and Cross Spectral Models." *Econometrica* 37 (January 1969).

Graphic Directions, Inc. v. Robert L. Bush, 862 P. 2d 1020 (Colo. App. 1993).

Katskee v. Nevada Bob's Golf, 472 N.W. 2d 372 (November 1991).

Maddala, G. S., *Introduction to Econometrics.* New York: Macmillan, 1988.

Mason, Robert D. and Douglas A. Lind, *Statistical Techniques in Business and Economics.* 10th ed., New York: Irwin/McGraw Hill, 1999.

McGlinchy v. Shell Chemical Co., 845 F2d 802 (9th Cir. 1988).

Palmer v. Connecticut Railway & Lighting Co., 311 U.S. 544 (1941).

Parsons, Leonard and Randall L. Schultz, *Marketing Models and Econometric Research.* New York: North Holland Publishing, 1978.

Pierce v. Ramsey Winch Co., 753 F2d 416 (5th Cir. 1985).

P.R.N. of Denver v. A.J. Gallagher & Co., 521 So 2d 1001 (Fla. Dist. Ct. App. 1988).

Sandler v. Lawn-a-Mat Chemical & Equipment Corp., 141 N.J. Super. 437, 358. A. 2d 805 (1976).

Target Market Publishing, Inc. v. ADVO, Inc., 136 F3d 1139; 1998 U.S. App. Lexis 2412.

Trout, Robert R., "Duration of Employment in Wrongful Termination Cases." *Journal of Forensic Economic* 8 (2) (1995): 167–177.

Trout, Robert R. and Carroll B. Foster, "Business Interruption Losses" in *Litigation Economics,* Patrick A. Gaughan and Robert Thornton, eds. Greenwich, CT: JAI Press, 1993.

Vuyanich v. Republic National Bank of Dallas (D.C. Tex. 1980).

3

ECONOMIC ANALYSIS IN BUSINESS INTERRUPTION LOSS ANALYSIS

As noted in Chapter Two, there are several different forms of economic analysis that may enter into a business interruption loss analysis. In the top-down framework presented in that chapter, a broad-based macroeconomic analysis is used to assess the overall economic environment. Following that, the focus is narrowed to the regional level if the business at issue is a regional one. The focus then gets progressively narrowed further where the firm-specific analysis is conducted. However, this chapter starts the process by developing the macroeconomic and regional economic tools that are necessary for a thorough business interruption loss analysis. The analytical process for macroeconomic analysis and regional analysis is similar although some of the data used is different. The macroeconomic and regional economic analysis then sets the stage for industry analysis, covered in Chapter Four.

MACROECONOMIC ANALYSIS

Macroeconomics is the study of the overall economy; microeconomics focuses on subunits of the overall economy, such as specific industries or firms. Within the field of macroeconomics, there is a subfield called business fluctuations which analyzes the various factors in the economy that cause it to grow and contract. These business fluctuations are referred to as "business cycles." The term "cycles" is unfortunate since it implies a periodicity such as that of a sine curve. Exhibit 3.1 features the usual textbook presentation of a business cycle; it shows an expansion phase that reaches a peak followed by a downturn, usually referred to as a recession. However, the economy does not behave in such a predictable

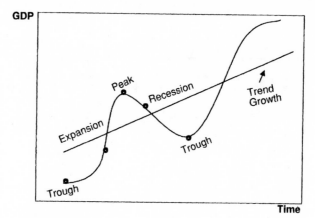

Exhibit 3.1   The business cycle.

manner. Moreover, the economics profession has not been very successful in predicting the turning points of business cycles.

DEFINITION OF A RECESSION

When the economy turns down and exhibits negative growth, this is termed a *recession.* Exhibit 3.2 depicts the 1990–91 and 2001 recessions. As mentioned earlier, recessions are generally defined as periods when economic growth is negative. The more recent 2001 recession started in March 2001, and ended in November 2001.

A simple definition of a recession, one which is often used by the media, is a period when there are two consecutive quarters of negative growth. Recessions, however, are defined on a case-by-case basis by the Business Cycle Dating Committee of the National Bureau of Economic Research (NBER) using a variety of economic data to make this determination.[1] This is an entity of six economists who essentially make a "judgement call" based upon their review of a variety of economic data. They look at more than simply real gross domestic product (GDP) growth; they also consider factors such as employment, personal income, manufacturing and industrial production.[2]

---

[1]See *www.nber.org/cycles.*
[2]The NBER's Business Cycle Dating Procedure, June 7, 2002.

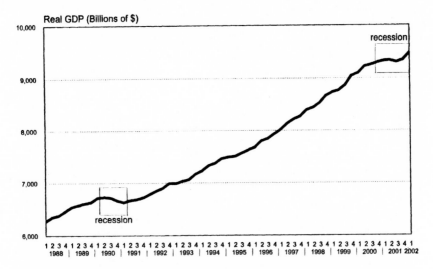

Exhibit 3.2 Examples of the 1990–91 and 2001 recessions.
Source: U.S. Department of Commerce, Bureau of Economic Analysis, Washington, D.C.

Table 3.1 shows the recessions that occurred in the U.S. economy between 1948 and 2001. The average duration of a recession is 10.7 months. The severity of recessions decreased in the U.S. economy of the twentieth century. In fact, recessions have become increasingly shorter and milder over the last two decades. Exhibit 3.3 graphically depicts the various recessions over the period 1948–2001.

Table 3.1 Recession Comparisons

Period	Real GDP Change			Recessions (Months)	Period	Recoveries (Months)
	Peak	Trough	% change			
1948–49	1,571.40	1,546.50	−1.6%	11	1949–53	44
1953–54	1,992.20	1,941.00	−2.6%	10	1954–57	38
1957–58	2,198.90	2,129.70	−3.1%	8	1958–60	23
1960–61	2,379.20	2,366.50	−0.5%	10	1961–69	105
1969–70	3,571.40	3,566.50	−0.1%	11	1970–73	94
1973–75	4,151.10	4,010.00	−3.4%	16	1975–80	23
1980	4,958.90	4,850.30	−2.2%	6	1980–81	57
1981–82	5,056.80	4,915.60	−2.8%	16	1982–90	12
1990–91	6,719.40	6,631.40	−1.3%	8	1991–01	91
2001	9,229.90	9,186.40	−0.5%	8	2001	
Average	4,182.92	4,114.39	−2.0%	10.4		

Source: National Bureau of Economic Research.

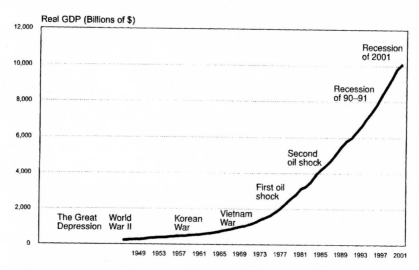

Exhibit 3.3   Examples of recessions between 1948–2001.
Source: U.S. Department of Commerce, Bureau of Economic Analysis, Washington, D.C.

MEASURING ECONOMIC GROWTH AND PERFORMANCE

Many different economic statistics are used to measure the performance of the overall economy and its subunits. The broadest measure of economic perform-ance is gross domestic product (GDP). GDP is the market value of all newly pro-duced goods and services in a country over a period of time such as one year. When this value is not adjusted for inflation, it is called *nominal* GDP (see Exhibit 3.4). When it is adjusted for the effects of inflation, which causes the value to increase due to price inflation, rather than greater production, it is called *real GDP* (see Exhibit 3.5).[3] Real GDP grows at a lower rate than nominal GDP. This is reflected in the flatter slope of Exhibit 3.5 relative to Exhibit 3.4. The Bureau of Economic Analysis of the U.S. Department of Commerce publishes both real and nominal GDP data.

GDP is subdivided into four broad components. They are personal consump-tion expenditures, investment, government expenditures, and net exports (defined as the difference between exports and imports). The relative contribution of each component is shown in Table 3.2. The real equivalents of the nominal data shown

[3]Karl E. Case and Ray C. Fair, *Principles of Macroeconomics,* 6th ed. (Upper Saddle River, NJ: Prentice-Hall, 2002), 393–400.

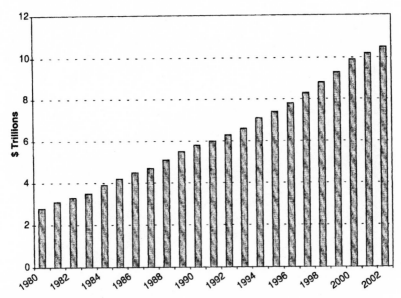

Exhibit 3.4   Nominal GDP.
Source: U.S. Department of Commerce, Bureau of Economic Analysis, Washington, D.C.

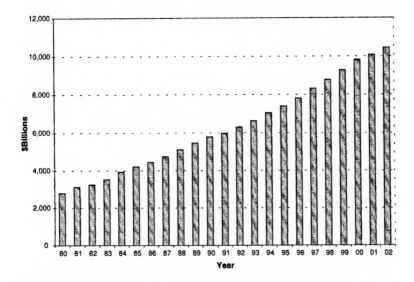

Exhibit 3.5   Real GDP.
Source: U.S. Department of Commerce, Bureau of Economic Analysis, Washington, D.C.

Table 3.2 Nominal GDP and Its Components (billions of dollars)

Year	GDP	Percent Change (%)	Personal Consumption Expenditures	Percent Change (%)	Gross Private Domestic Investment	Percent Change (%)	Net Exports of Goods and Services	Percent Change (%)	Government Expenditures	Percent Change (%)
1980	2,795.6		1,762.9		477.9		-14.9		569.7	
1981	3,131.3	12.01	1,944.2	10.28	570.8	19.44	-15.0	0.67	631.4	10.83
1982	3,259.2	4.08	2,079.3	6.95	516.1	-9.58	-20.5	36.67	684.4	8.39
1983	3,534.9	8.46	2,286.4	9.96	564.2	9.32	-51.7	152.20	735.9	7.52
1984	3,932.7	11.25	2,498.4	9.27	735.5	30.36	-102.0	97.29	800.8	8.82
1985	4,213.0	7.13	2,712.6	8.57	736.3	0.11	-114.2	11.96	878.3	9.68
1986	4,452.9	5.69	2,895.2	6.73	747.2	1.48	-131.9	15.50	942.3	7.29
1987	4,742.5	6.50	3,105.3	7.26	781.5	4.59	-142.3	7.88	997.9	5.90
1988	5,108.3	7.71	3,356.6	8.09	821.1	5.07	-106.3	-25.30	1,036.9	3.91
1989	5,489.1	7.45	3,596.7	7.15	872.9	6.31	-80.7	-24.08	1,100.2	6.10
1990	5,803.2	5.72	3,831.5	6.53	861.7	-1.28	-71.4	-11.52	1,181.4	7.38
1991	5,986.2	3.15	3,971.2	3.65	800.2	-7.14	-20.7	-71.01	1,235.5	4.58
1992	6,318.9	5.56	4,209.7	6.01	866.6	8.30	-27.9	34.78	1,270.5	2.83
1993	6,642.3	5.12	4,454.7	5.82	955.1	10.21	-60.5	116.85	1,293.0	1.77
1994	7,054.3	6.20	4,716.4	5.87	1097.1	14.87	-87.1	43.97	1,327.9	2.70
1995	7,400.5	4.91	4,969.0	5.36	1143.8	4.26	-84.3	-3.21	1,372.0	3.32
1996	7,813.2	5.58	5,237.5	5.40	1242.7	8.65	-89.0	5.58	1,421.9	3.64
1997	8,318.4	6.47	5,529.3	5.57	1390.5	11.89	-89.3	0.34	1,487.9	4.64
1998	8,781.5	5.57	5,856.0	5.91	1538.7	10.66	-151.7	69.88	1,538.5	3.40
1999	9,274.3	5.61	6,246.5	6.67	1636.7	6.37	-249.9	64.73	1,614.0	4.91
2000	9,824.6	5.93	6,683.7	7.00	1755.4	7.25	-365.5	46.26	1,751.0	8.49
2001	10,082.2	2.62	6,987.0	4.54	1586.0	-9.65	-348.9	-4.54	1,858.0	6.11
2002	10,446.2	3.61	7,303.7	4.53	1593.2	0.45	-423.6	21.41	1,972.9	6.18

Source: U.S. Department of Commerce, Bureau of Economic Analysis, Washington, D.C.

in Table 3.2 are shown in Table 3.3. However, within each broad component there are still more narrowly defined subcomponents. For example, within total personal consumption expenditures one finds expenditures on durables, non-durables, and services. Depending on the business of the plaintiff, one may want to know the overall economic performance as reflected by GDP and personal consumption expenditures; however, if the plaintiff is a marketer of durables, the durable component of personal consumption expenditures may be more relevant. In addition, if the plaintiff is a retailer, one may want to also review the trend in retail sales in addition to these consumer expenditure data (see Table 3.4). By narrowing the focus of the broad macroeconomic aggregates to better fit the nature of the plaintiff's business, it is possible to obtain additional information on the state of the economy specific to the case in question.

Releases of GDP Data

GDP is the most frequently cited measure of economic performance. Near the end of every month, articles appear in the media about the latest release of GDP data. Given that this indicator is used so regularly to measure the performance of the overall economy, it is useful to know more about it.[4] GDP statistics are released on a quarterly basis. Each quarterly value that is released is subsequently revised twice. These revisions can sometimes change the value significantly. Although the GDP numbers are released each quarter and apply to production in that quarter, they are quoted in terms of an annual rate. This allows the values to be comparable to other periods. In addition, the GDP values are adjusted to negate seasonal influences like the fourth-quarter increase in production that occurs in preparation for the holiday season.

International Business Cycles

Business cycles are as relevant to other economies as they are in the United States. Indeed, the increasing globalization of the economy means that economic weakness in one nation's economy can lead to economic slowdowns in other nations. Economic shocks, such as the increases in oil prices in 1973, had damaging effects on the economies of several countries—the United States, Japan,

---

[4]John Taylor, *Economics*, 3rd ed. (New York: Houghton Mifflin, 2001), 415–416.

Table 3.3 Real GDP and Its Components [billions of chained (1996) dollars]

Year	GDP	Percent Change (%)	Personal Consumption Expenditures	Percent Change (%)	Gross Private Domestic Investment	Percent Change (%)	Net Exports of Goods and Services	Percent Change (%)	Government Expenditures	Percent Change (%)
1980	4,900.9		3,193.0		655.3		10.00		1,020.9	
1981	5,021.0	2.45	3,236.0	1.35	715.6	9.20	5.20	-48.00	1,030.0	0.89
1982	4,919.3	-2.03	3,275.5	1.22	615.2	-14.03	-14.60	-380.77	1,046.0	1.55
1983	5,132.3	4.33	3,454.3	5.46	673.7	9.51	-63.80	336.99	1,081.0	3.35
1984	5,505.2	7.27	3,640.6	5.39	871.5	29.36	-128.40	101.25	1,118.4	3.46
1985	5,717.1	3.85	3,820.9	4.95	863.4	-0.93	-149.10	16.12	1,190.5	6.45
1986	5,912.4	3.42	3,981.2	4.20	857.7	-0.66	-165.10	10.73	1,255.2	5.43
1987	6,113.3	3.40	4,113.4	3.32	879.3	2.52	-156.20	-5.39	1,292.5	2.97
1988	6,368.4	4.17	4,279.5	4.04	902.8	2.67	-112.10	-28.23	1,307.5	1.16
1989	6,591.8	3.51	4,393.7	2.67	936.5	3.73	-79.40	-29.17	1,343.5	2.75
1990	6,707.9	1.76	4,474.5	1.84	907.3	-3.12	-56.50	-28.84	1,387.3	3.26
1991	6,676.4	-0.47	4,466.6	-0.18	829.5	-8.57	-15.80	-72.04	1,403.4	1.16
1992	6,880.0	3.05	4,594.5	2.86	899.8	8.47	-19.80	25.32	1,410.0	0.47
1993	7,062.6	2.65	4,748.9	3.36	977.9	8.68	-59.10	198.48	1,398.8	-0.79
1994	7,347.7	4.04	4,928.1	3.77	1,107.0	13.20	-86.50	46.36	1,400.1	0.09
1995	7,543.8	2.67	5,075.6	2.99	1,140.6	3.04	-78.40	-9.36	1,406.4	0.45
1996	7,813.2	3.57	5,237.5	3.19	1,242.7	8.95	-89.00	13.52	1,421.9	1.10
1997	8,159.5	4.43	5,423.9	3.56	1,393.3	12.12	-113.30	27.30	1,455.4	2.36
1998	8,508.9	4.28	5,683.7	4.79	1,558.0	11.82	-221.10	95.15	1,483.3	1.92
1999	8,859.0	4.11	5,964.5	4.94	1,660.5	6.58	-320.50	44.96	1,540.6	3.86
2000	9,191.4	3.75	6,223.9	4.35	1,762.9	6.17	-398.80	24.43	1,582.5	2.72
2001	9,214.5	0.25	6,377.2	2.46	1,574.6	-10.68	-415.90	4.29	1,640.4	3.66
2002	9,439.9	2.45	6,576.0	3.12	1,589.6	0.95	-488.50	17.46	1,712.8	4.41

Source: U.S. Department of Commerce, Bureau of Economic Analysis, Washington, D.C.

82

Table 3.4 GDP, Retail Sales, and Personal Income

	Gross Domestic Product (Billions of $)				Retail Sales (Billions of $)				Personal Income (Billions of $)			
Year	Nominal	Percent Change (%)	Real (Chained 1996 $)	Percent Change (%)	Nominal	Percent Change (%)	Real (Chained 1996 $)	Percent Change (%)	Nominal	Percent Change (%)	Real (Chained 1996 $)	Percent Change (%)
1980	2,795.6		4,900.9		957.4		946.5		2,323.9		4,208.7	
1981	3,131.3	12.01	5,021.0	2.45	1,038.7	8.49	1,060.1	12.00	2,599.4	11.86	4,326.0	2.79
1982	3,259.2	4.08	4,919.3	-2.03	1,069.4	2.96	1,103.4	4.08	2,768.4	6.50	4,361.5	0.82
1983	3,534.9	8.46	5,132.3	4.33	1,170.2	9.42	1,196.8	8.46	2,946.9	6.45	4,452.3	2.08
1984	3,932.7	11.25	5,505.2	7.27	1,286.9	9.98	1,331.4	11.25	3,274.8	11.13	4,771.8	7.18
1985	4,213.0	7.13	5,717.1	3.85	1,375.0	6.85	1,426.3	7.13	3,515.0	7.33	4,951.5	3.77
1986	4,452.9	5.69	5,912.4	3.42	1,449.6	5.43	1,507.6	5.70	3,712.4	5.62	5,105.3	3.11
1987	4,742.5	6.50	6,113.3	3.40	1,541.3	6.33	1,605.6	6.50	3,962.5	6.74	5,248.7	2.81
1988	5,108.3	7.71	6,368.4	4.17	1,656.2	7.45	1,729.4	7.71	4,272.1	7.81	5,446.8	3.77
1989	5,489.1	7.45	6,591.8	3.51	1,759.0	6.21	1,858.4	7.46	4,599.8	7.67	5,619.2	3.17
1990	5,803.2	5.72	6,707.9	1.76	1,844.6	4.87	1,964.7	5.72	4,903.2	6.60	5,726.1	1.90
1991	5,986.2	3.15	6,676.4	-0.47	1,855.9	0.61	2,026.7	3.16	5,085.4	3.72	5,719.7	-0.11
1992	6,318.9	5.56	6,880.0	3.05	2,054.6	10.71	2,139.3	5.56	5,390.4	6.00	5,883.1	2.86
1993	6,642.3	5.12	7,062.6	2.65	2,194.1	6.79	2,248.4	5.10	5,610.0	4.07	5,980.4	1.65
1994	7,054.3	6.20	7,347.7	4.04	2,372.8	8.14	2,388.3	6.22	5,888.0	4.96	6,152.1	2.87
1995	7,400.5	4.91	7,543.8	2.67	2,492.5	5.04	2,505.5	4.91	6,200.9	5.31	6,334.1	2.96
1996	7,813.2	5.58	7,813.2	3.57	2,645.2	6.13	2,645.2	5.58	6,547.4	5.59	6,547.3	3.37
1997	8,318.4	6.47	8,159.5	4.43	2,767.4	4.62	2,816.2	6.46	6,937.0	5.95	6,804.9	3.93
1998	8,781.5	5.57	8,508.9	4.28	2,906.7	5.03	2,973.0	5.57	7,426.0	7.05	7,173.5	5.42
1999	9,274.3	5.61	8,859.0	4.11	3,149.2	8.34	3,137.9	5.55	7,777.3	4.73	7,429.8	3.57
2000	9,824.6	5.93	9,191.4	3.75	3,388.8	7.61	3,342.5	6.52	8,319.2	6.97	7,713.2	3.81
2001	10,082.2	2.62	9,214.5	0.25	3,476.0	2.57	3,456.0	3.40	8,723.5	4.86	8,621.0	11.77
Average	6,096.7	6.38	6,831.6	3.13	2,020.5	6.36	2,064.1	6.38	5,126.5	6.52	5,844.4	3.50

Source: U.S. Department of Commerce, Bureau of Economic Analysis, U.S. Census Bureau, Washington, D.C.; U.S. Department of Labor, Bureau of Labor Statistics, Washington, D.C.

and European nations. However, different economies may react differently to such shocks; not all economies move together.[5] Each economy has its own cycles, but over time, the cycles have become more interrelated. The role on international economic data in the analysis of damages related to non-U.S. economies is discussed later in this chapter.

BUSINESS CYCLES AND ECONOMIC DAMAGES

One factor that can cause a firm to experience losses is an overall slowdown of activity in the economy. When the economy is in recession, many companies slow down and generate losses. Such economy-induced declines need to be differentiated from ones caused by the actions of the defendant. The analysis can become more complicated when both events are occurring at the same time. That is, it may be more challenging for the economist to filter out the losses caused by an economic downturn which were coincident with the damaging actions of the defendant. In some cases, the economy may be solely responsible for the losses of the plaintiff. In other cases, an economic downturn may explain some but not all of the plaintiff's losses. When the economy-wide influences are not considered, the defendant may be wrongly blamed for the losses of the plaintiff. In order to understand this, we need to learn more about business cycles.

There are varying theories on for the causes of business cycles. For example, one theory that is currently popular in the economics profession is the Real Business Cycle Theory.[6] This theory sees the causes of the employment and output variations that occur in business cycles in terms of variations in technology and supply shocks.[7] An example of an adverse supply shock is the increase in oil prices in the 1970s which slowed the economy and contributed to the recessions of 1974–75 and 1980.

Though the role that supply shocks can play in causing a recession is well established, there is not one accepted theory that can convincingly explain all business cycles. Most economists agree that there is no single cause of all economic downturns; further, the cause of such declines in the performance of the economy can vary depending on the particular circumstances of the economic downturn in ques-

---

[5]Joseph Stiglitz and Carl E. Walsh, *Economics,* 3rd ed. (New York: W.W. Norton, 2002), 608–609.

[6]Finn E. Kydland and E. C. Prescott, "Time to Build and Aggregate Fluctuations," *Econometrica* 50 (November 1982): 1345–1370.

[7]Robert Gordon, *Macroeconomics,* 6th ed. (New York: HarperCollins, 1993), 189–196.

tion. The forensic economist, however, is not as concerned about the cause of a recession as she is about the reality of recessions and their recurring yet unpredictable pattern. One way to assess this pattern is to consider certain trends that are common to the cyclical variation of the national economy. These are the frequency of recessions and the average duration of recessions and recoveries.

During the years 1945–2002, there were ten recessions in the U.S. economy. The average duration of these recessions was 10.4 months while the average duration of the recoveries that followed was 54 months (see Table 3.1). A recovery is defined as the number of months between the trough of the downturn and the peak of the following upturn. There is some evidence that recessions have been getting milder and perhaps that recoveries have started more slowly and have been weaker at first. While they may have started slowly, especially the 1990s expansion, the U.S. economy has had two very impressive back-to-back-expansions in the 1980s and the 1990s.

Firms' Reactions to Business Cycles

Cyclical fluctuations need to be explicitly taken into account in a business interruption loss analysis. That is, the loss analysis and its associated revenue projection need to be placed in an overall macroeconomic context. Most firms are procyclical, meaning they do better when the economy is expanding. When the economy grows, demand for many goods and services increases. In a recession, however, demand may be stagnant or even declining. For companies that face a very cyclical demand, such as automobile or steel manufacturers, the overall cyclical variation of the economy can have great influence on company sales. This is an important factor if the plaintiff faces a very cyclical demand and is claiming lost profits for a time period that included a recession, such as in the recent 2001 recession. A declining sales level could possibly be explained, in part or even in total, by the declining level of demand in the economy. In order to assess the relationship between the overall economy and the plaintiff's sales, the economist needs to analyze the historical pattern of sales in this industry relative to the overall economy. In effect, the expert needs to filter out the influence of the economy's fluctuations and isolate the variation in the plaintiff's sales that is specifically attributable to the actions of the defendant.

Generally, the greater the rate of growth in GDP, the better the economic conditions. The better the economic conditions, the more likely it is that firms will enjoy an increase in sales. However, this is a very general statement; even when GDP is growing, many companies are declining or going bankrupt. The opposite is also the case. That is, even when the economy is in recession, many companies grow rapidly. Therefore, an examination of the trends in the overall economy, as measured by GDP, is merely a starting point in the macroeconomic analysis.

USING MORE NARROWLY DEFINED
ECONOMIC AGGREGATES

The expert should select specific economic aggregates that are closely related to the performance of the plaintiff's business. For example, if the plaintiff is a retailer, the expert could look at the variation in consumption expenditures and retail sales (see Exhibit 3.6 and 3.7). If the retailer sells only consumer durables, such as appliances, then more defined aggregates, such as the consumer durable component of consumption expenditures, can be selected (see Exhibit 3.8). Depending on the nature of the plaintiff's business, various economic aggregates can be selected to determine overall macroeconomic environment. The economist needs to examine the historical trends of the selected aggregates and the company's sales to make sure that the hypothesized relationship between the overall level of economic activity, as reflected in the trends in the selected aggregates, is consistent with the variation in the plaintiff's sales. That is, the economist needs to verify that when the economy was expanding, as evidenced by the variation of

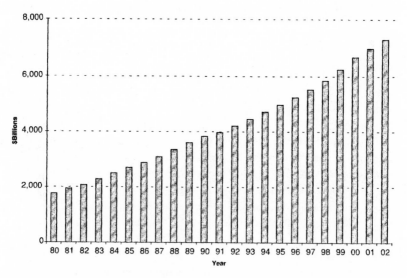

Exhibit 3.6   Consumption expenditures.
Source: U.S. Department of Commerce, Bureau of Economic Analysis, Washington, D.C.

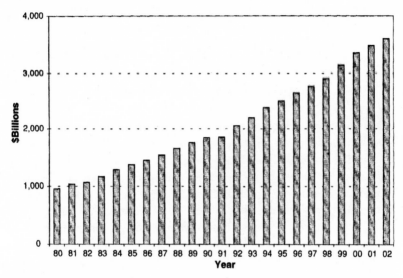

Exhibit 3.7   U.S. retail sales.
Source: U.S. Department of Commerce, Bureau of Economic Analysis, Washington, D.C.

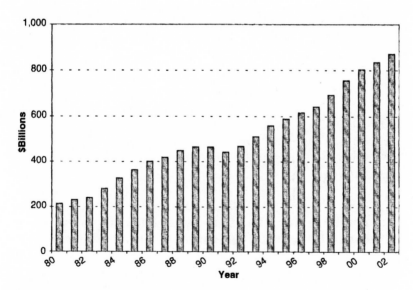

Exhibit 3.8   Durable goods.
Source: U.S. Department of Commerce, Bureau of Economic Analysis, Washington, D.C.

the selected aggregates, the plaintiff's business was also expanding. If that co-variation is not apparent, then a further investigation needs to be conducted to make sure that there is a satisfactory explanation for what caused the differences.

Sources of Economic Aggregates

There are numerous sources of economic data. Most of the frequently used ones are published by the U.S. Government. The two most prolific sources are the Bureau of Economic Analysis (BEA) of the U.S. Department of Commerce, and the U.S. Department of Labor. The BEA provides data on GDP and the various components that make up the GDP. The U.S. Department of Labor publishes a variety of labor market data, such as total employment and the unemployment rate, as well as various measures of inflation including the consumer price index (CPI) and producer price index (PPI). The labor market data can be a useful complement to the data published by the BEA. It reveals the impact on economic activity of the number of workers in a given area. The labor market data are often available in narrowly defined regional segments which will be helpful when narrowing the analysis to the regional level. In addition, labor market data are released monthly and are often some of the most current data available.

Another source of economic data is the Federal Reserve Bank. This institution, through its 12 district banks, produces its own data, such as its capacity utilization series. In addition, the Federal Reserve banks disseminate economic data provided by other governmental entities.

Useful Web Sites for Macroeconomic Data

A wide variety of macroeconomic data are available for free on various federal government Web sites. Other macroeconomic data are available through private Web sites. Table 3.5 provides a list of relevant Web sites and the data that can be acquired from them.

Quantifying the Strength of the Relationship between Selected Economic Aggregates and Firm Performance

The closeness of the association among these economic aggregates and the revenues of the plaintiff can be quantitatively measured using the correlation analysis discussed earlier. This is important to consider because it bolsters the

Table 3.5 Sources for Macroeconomic Data

	Web Site	Type of Data Available
Government Sources		
Bureau for Labor Statistics	http://www.bls.gov	Inflation, consumer spending, wages, un/employment, demographics
Federal Reserve	http://www.federalreserve.gov/	Monetary, banking, payment system
Federal Reserve Districts	http://federalreserve.gov/otherfrb.htm	Link to the twelve federal reserve districts
Census Bureau	http://www.census.gov	U.S. census, demographic profiles, searchable by states & counties
Office of Management and Budget, Executive Office of the President	http://www.whitehouse.gov/omb/	U.S. budgets, policies
FEDSTATS	http://www.fedstats.gov/	Gateway to various statistic sources, by states & counties.
Committee on Finance, United States Senate	http://www.ssa.gov/policy/	Annual Statistical of Social Security Benefits
AmeriStat	http://www.ameristat.org/	Various topics on U.S. population data
U.S. International Trade Commission	http://www.usitc.gov/	International trade statistics and agreements
Institute for Economic Analysis	http://www.iea-macro-economics.org/	Policy issues, unemployment, economic indicators
FRED of Federal Reserve	http://www.stls.frb.org/fred/	Macroseries data
Economic Trends by FR of Cleveland	http://www.clev.frb.org/research/index.htm#trends	Monthly, national, regional, international series data
GPO Access	http://www.access.gpo.gov/su_docs/index.html	Access to all federal government information
Economic Statistics of the White House	http://www.whitehouse.gov/fsbr/esbr.html	President's economic reports, federal statistics.
Department of Commerce	**http://www.doc.gov/**	
Bureau of Economic Analysis	http://www.bea.doc.gov/	A GDP-related data, balance of payments, state and local area data
STAT-USA	http://www.stat-usa.gov/	Business, economic, and trade statistics
Globus and NTDB of STAT-USA	http://stat-usa.gov/tradtest.nsf	National trade estimate reports (by country)
Bureau of Export Administration (Industry and Security)	http://www.bxa.doc.gov/	U.S. trade regulations updates
International Trade Administration	http://www.ita.doc.gov/td/industry/otea/	U.S. trade statistics

(continued)

Table 3.5 Sources for Macroeconomic Data *(continued)*

	Web Site	Type of Data Available
International Organization		
Worldbank's Macroeconomic data and statistics	*http://www.worldbank.org/data/databytopic/ /macro.html*	Data by country, by topics (incl. finance, GNP, PPP, Macroeconomics growth
United Nations' Statistics Division	*http://unstats.un.org/unsd/*	Statistical Yearbook, Country Profile, Monthly Bulletin
Academic Articles		
JSTOR	*http://www.jstor.org*	(subscription) articles of various journals
NBER	*http://www.nber.org*	(subscription) articles of various journals
News		
The Economist Intelligence Unit	*http://www.eiu.com/*	Country reports, news analysis
The Economist	*http://www.economist.com*	Finance, economic, business news, economic indicators
The Financial Times	*http://news.ft.com/home/us/*	Business, market, industries news
New York Times	*http://nytimes.com/*	Business, market, industries news
Wall Street Journal	*http://online.wsj.com/public/us*	Business, market, industries news
Other Private Vendors		
Haver Analytics	*http://www.haver.com/*	Economic, financial, and statistics from government economic agencies
Dismal Scientist	*http://www.economy.com/dismal/*	Macroeconomic, industry, financial, and regional trends
DRI-WEFA	*http://www.dri-wefa.com/main.cfm*	Economic and industry analysis/data, incl. historical macroeconomic indices
Economagic	*http://www.economagic.com/*	Economic timeseries data
Economic Statistics Data Locator		
B&E DataLinks	*http://www.econ-datalinks.org/*	
OFFSTATS	*http://www2.auckland.ac.nz/lbr/stats/offstats/ OFFSTATSmain.htm*	
Statistical Data Locators	*http://www.ntu.edu.sg/library/stat/statdata.htm*	
Survey Research Center	*http://members.bellatlantic.net/~abelson/*	
Statistical Resources on the Web	*http://www.lib.umich.edu/govdocs/stats.html*	
Government Info Sharing Project	*http://govinfo.kerr.orst.edu/*	
Demography & Population	*http://demography.anu.edu.au/VirtualLibrary/*	
FEDSTATS	*http://www.fedstats.gov/*	

economic theory that the economist presents. For example, the expert can say that a retail firm's revenues for the years 1998–99 should have risen because the economy was expanding: national income, consumer expenditures, and retail sales were all rising. The economist can go on to elaborate that the economy was in the longest postwar expansion in U.S. history. It may be even more compelling, for example, to state that 48 percent of the variation in the sales of the plaintiff could be explained by variation in national retail sales. A correlation analysis allows such percentages to be derived through the computation of what is known as the *coefficient of determination*. This is the square of the correlation coefficient. It represents the proportion of the total variation in the dependent variable, such as the plaintiff's sales, that is explained by variations in selected independent variables such as the national retail sales depicted in Exhibit 3.9. This further establishes the importance of considering these specific economic aggregates.

Nominal versus Real Values

Economists are typically more concerned about variations in real values as opposed to nominal values. When the inflationary component of an increase in an economic variable, such as GDP, is filtered out, the resulting value is called a real variable. Although real values are the appropriate measures to use when trying to assess the economic progress of an economy, they may not always be the appropriate measures when conducting a business interruption loss analysis. The plaintiff may have lost the actual unadjusted values and the real values may be less relevant to the loss measurement process. If a comparison is being made to the growth of the plaintiff's revenues relative to selected economic variables, then the nominal macroeconomic aggregates will be the more relevant ones to compare with revenues. In an inflationary environment, the growth rates derived from an analysis of the variation in these nominal values will also reveal higher growth rates than what would be derived from an analysis of a real time series.

If the expert, however, is merely trying to assess the level of economic activity, then an analysis of real values, such as real GDP, is more relevant since the National Bureau of Economic Research uses such real variables to determine business cycle dating. Merely looking at unadjusted nominal values may obfuscate the real decline in the economic time series. Both real and nominal values have a place in an economic loss analysis. The real values are used to isolate the time periods when demand is slowing. In such time periods, even though a firm may experience an increase in sales, costs may rise such that the company loses ground or experiences an erosion in its margins.

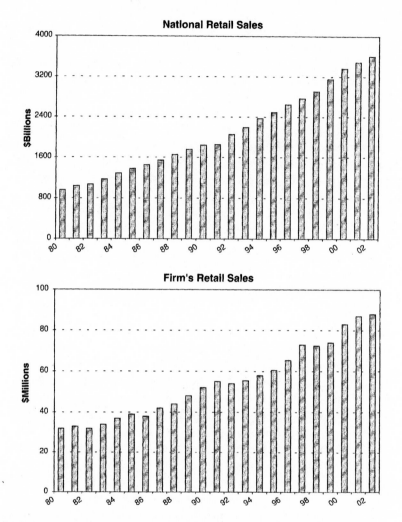

Exhibit 3.9   Retail sales: comparison between national and firm.
Source: U.S. Census Bureau, Washington, D.C.

When constructing a projection of revenues during an affected loss period, greater weight is placed on the rates of growth in the nominal values of the selected macroeconomic aggregates. When the plaintiff has lost nominal profits and is attempting to be compensated in nominal terms, growth rates in nominal series are what must be used in forecasting; real values need to be considered in conducting an analysis of economic fluctuations.

OVERSTATEMENT OF INFLATION STATISTICS

Economists have believed for some time that the inflation statistics issued by the Bureau of Labor Statistics may overstate the true rate of inflation. These statistics are constructed using what is known as a Laspeyres Index. This type of index compares the value of a variable in a specific year with that of a preselected base year. In the case of the consumer price index, the most frequently cited inflation measure, the dollar value of a market basket of goods and services is compared to the dollar value in the selected base year. At time of writing, the year 1992 is used as the base year to convert nominal amounts into real terms.

The consumer price index is only one of several price indices used by economists. Another index is the producer price index, which is designed to deflate goods that producers, as opposed to consumers, buy. In addition, different CPIs are used to deflate a more narrow group of products and services (such as the CPI for wages). Many categories of goods and services have their own specific deflators that are available from the Bureau of Labor Statistics.

One of the drawbacks of the CPI is that it does not take into account the substitution effect whereby consumers switch to less expensive substitutes when prices of certain goods rise. The CPI keeps the market basket the same in both years, so the true market basket, after some substitution to less expensive products, costs less than what the CPI reports. Another flaw of the CPI is that it does not take into account qualitative differences in products over time. Products such as computers improve substantially over time—a computer bought today for $3,000 may be of significantly greater quality than one sold five or six years earlier for the same price. Other factors ignored in the traditional CPI are discount buying trends that result in lower prices for certain products.

The report of the Advisory Commission to Study the Consumer Price Index—headed by Michael Boskin, chairman of the Council of Economic Advisors—concluded that the consumer price index, which was approximately 3 percent in 1996, the year of the report, may be overstated by as much as 1.1 percent per year.[8] This implies that the inflation rate in that year might be below 2 percent. The authors of the *Boskin Report* have admitted that many of the adjustments they made were subjective judgments on factors such as qualitative improvements. In making such judgments they have, in effect, created more of a cost-of-living index than a true price index.

---

[8]Michael Boskin, Ellen R. Dulberger, Robert J. Gordon, Zvi Griliches, and Dale Jorgenson, "Toward a More Accurate Measure of the Cost of Living," *Final Report of the Advisory Commission to Study the Consumer Price Index to the Senate Finance Committee*, December 4, 1996.

Table 3.6   Inflation Using the Unadjusted CPI—1970–2002

Year	Inflation Rate (%)	Year	Inflation Rate (%)	Year	Inflation Rate (%)
1970	5.72	1980	13.50	1990	5.40
1971	4.38	1981	10.32	1991	4.21
1972	3.21	1982	6.16	1992	3.01
1973	6.22	1983	3.21	1993	2.99
1974	11.04	1984	4.32	1994	2.56
1975	9.13	1985	3.56	1995	2.83
1976	5.76	1986	1.86	1996	2.95
1977	6.50	1987	3.65	1997	2.29
1978	7.59	1988	4.14	1998	1.56
1979	11.34	1989	4.82	1999	2.20
				2000	3.40
				2001	2.80
Averages				2002	1.60
1970–80	7.67				
1980–90	5.54				
1990–2002	2.91				
1970–2002	4.98				

Source: U.S. Department of Labor, Bureau of Labor Statistics, Washington, D.C.

The overstatement of the CPI is important because once the correction to the true rate of inflation is made, the difference between nominal and real values becomes less significant. This, combined with the anti-inflation policy begun by the Federal Reserve in 1980, has kept the inflation rate at approximately three percent as of the start of 2002 prior to the adjustment for the overstatement (see Table 3.6).

The *Boskin Commission Report* led to changes in the way that the CPI is computed. Many economists believe that the upward bias may vary between 0.8 and 1.6 percent.[9] It seems that the overstatement still exists but has been reduced to a lower and knowable level.[10]

Other Measures of Inflation

Although it is the most often cited, the consumer price index is not the only measure of inflation. Two other frequently cited measures are the *producer price index*

---

[9]N. Gregory Mankiw, *Macroeconomics* (New York: Worth Publishers, 2003), 32–33.

[10]Readers interested in this issue may want to review Matthew Shapiro and David Wilcox, "Mismeasurement in the Consumer Price Index: An Evaluation," *NBER Macroeconomics Annual*, 1996.

and the *GDP deflator*.[11] The producer price index shows the average level of prices for goods sold by producers. It is sometimes used as an indicator of what is going to happen to consumer prices based upon the idea that increases in producer prices may, to varying degrees, be passed on to consumers.

REGIONAL ECONOMIC TRENDS

The fact that there are unique regional differences within a national economy is a well established proposition within the field of regional economics—also called urban economics.[12] However, while there are many practitioners in the field of regional economics, the published literature is limited.[13] Nonetheless, the field is an established one with reliable data sources.

When the economy expands, not all regions of the country participate equally in this expansion. For example, California entered the 1990–91 national recession after many other parts of the country. However, the recession in California and the Northeast lasted longer than it did in other regions of the country (the Midwest, for example). While the economy entered a recession prior to September 11, 2001, the regional economic impact of this terrible event was particularly pronounced in New York City, especially lower Manhattan.

For companies whose markets are mainly regional, where firms derive most or all of their sales from a particular region, the difference between regional and national economic climates is important. The macroeconomic analysis needs to focus on the economic activity within a particular region.

Many of the data sources available on the national level are also available on a regional level. State governmental agencies, as well as private sources, supply a variety of regional data. Using such data, the economist can observe the trends in regional economic aggregates and investigate the relationship between the plaintiff's sales and the variation in the regional aggregates. Regional aggregates, such as state retail sales (see Exhibit 3.10 and 3.11), should be included in the overall macroeconomic framework; this puts the variation in the plaintiff's

---

[11]For a good introductory explanation of the use of various price indices see Joseph Stiglitz and Carl E. Walsh, *Economics*, 3rd ed. (New York: W.W. Norton, 2002), 472–474.

[12]Edwin S. Mills and Bruce W. Hamilton, *Urban Economics*, 5th ed. (New York: HarperCollins College Publishers, 1994).

[13]One such book which seeks to apply a Keynesian approach to regional economic modeling is George Treyz, *Regional Economic Modeling: Economic Forecasting and Analysis* (Norwell, MA: Kluwer Academic Publishers, 1993).

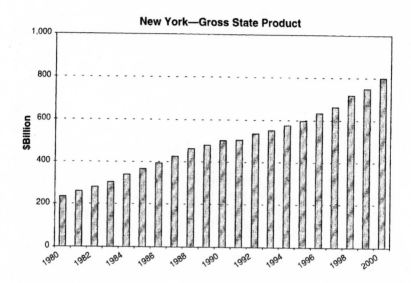

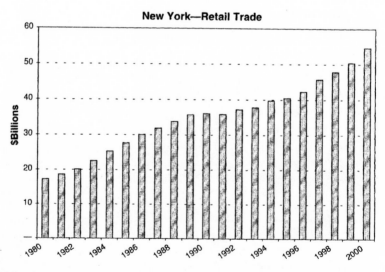

Exhibit 3.10   New York's gross state product and retail sales.
Source: U.S. Department of Commerce, Bureau of Economic Analysis, Washington, D.C.

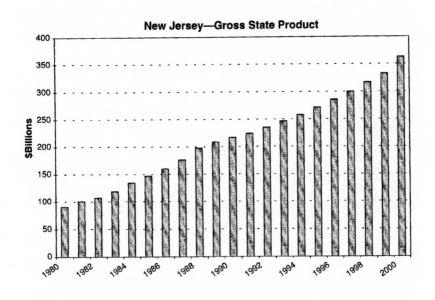

Exhibit 3.11 New Jersey's gross state product and retail sales.
Source: U.S. Department of Commerce, Bureau of Economic Analysis, Washington, D.C.

sales during the alleged loss period in the proper macroeconomic context. For example, if all of the national and regional aggregates were expanding during the loss period, and the plaintiff's sales (which normally move with the variation in these aggregates) moved sharply in the opposite direction, then an explanation other than the level of economic demand needs to be explored. However, when dealing with a more regional business and when there is a significant difference between the performance of the regional and the national economy, there may be cause to place more weight on the regional economic data and less on the national data.

Quality and Timeliness of Regional Economic Data

As the geographic region narrows, the availability and quality of the economic data may decline. Some data, such as gross state product, are not readily available from the Commerce Department and may be several years behind their national counterparts. Lacking access to aggregates such as consumption expenditures, the economist may substitute other closely varying time series such as retail sales, which are available on a more timely basis. This substitution process must be handled on a case-by-case basis and is often influenced by factors such as the nature of the product at issue.

Certain regional economic data are readily available. These include employment data produced by the U.S. Department of Labor. Typically, employment data are the most timely and are even available for certain industry subcategories. They also can be used as an indicator of the performance of certain other sectors for which timely data are not available. For example, construction employment data are available on a timely basis for specific regions such as states. This can be used in the analysis of the performance of the construction industry. Although employment is a variable that lags the business cycles, it may provide useful information on the trends in a given industry. For plaintiffs in an industry such as construction, such a data series adds information that the economist can consider when analyzing the alleged damages of a plaintiff.

Regional Data Sources

There are certain governmental agencies that publish regional economic data. For example, the New Jersey Department of Labor issues a publication called *Economic Indicators*; it includes a variety of economic data for the State of New

Jersey and its counties. These data include labor market data as well as other economic data that the New Jersey Department of Labor gathers from other vendors. Other state departments of labor publish data related to their respective regions, although most are not as detailed as this publication.

The Federal Reserve banks publish monthly reports and newsletters on the condition of the regional economy and on other economic issues, such as monetary policy. For example, the Federal Reserve Bank of Boston publishes the *New England Economic Indicators* which reports on the condition of the economy in the New England region. The Federal Reserve Bank of Kansas City publishes a similar report called *Regional Economic Digest*. The Federal Reserve banks also have Web sites that can be useful sources of timely data.[14] However, the multiple sources of data notwithstanding, the quantity of timely data is significantly less at the regional level than it is on the national level.

Subregional Analysis

Regional economic analysis is usually done for a broad economic region: a geographic area like the Northeast, multistate areas such as the tristate region of New York, New Jersey, and Connecticut, or specific states. However, economic data are also often analyzed according to standard metropolitan statistical areas (SMSAs).

In the case of losses of small businesses, regional analysis can be further narrowed within the state economy to focus on cities, counties, towns, or even neighborhoods. It is often possible to get some economic data, such as retail sales and employment data, on the county level (see Exhibit 3.12). This is important, since the national and state economy could be booming while a town's economy could be depressed due, for example, to the exit of key businesses. In this case, using state data rather than more narrowly focused economic data could present a misleading picture.

The aforementioned September 11th tragedy is a case in point. While the New York state economy was suffering the effects of a national recession exacerbated by the disaster, the adverse effects of the tragedy were more pronounced in New York City, especially in lower Manhattan. If one is analyzing the losses of a business that derives the bulk of its demand from the lower Manhattan region, then these economic conditions need to be specifically addressed. State data alone will not tell the complete economic story.

---

[14]*www.ny.frb.org.*

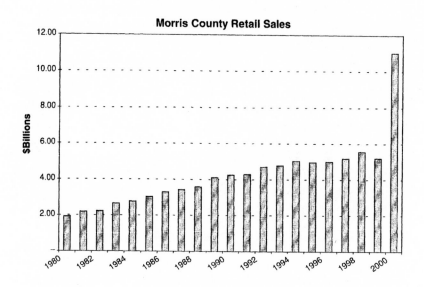

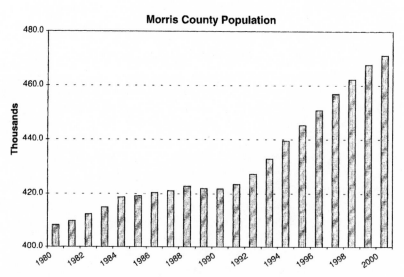

Exhibit 3.12   Morris County economic data.
Source: New Jersey Department of Labor.

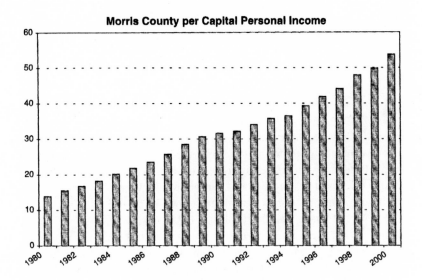

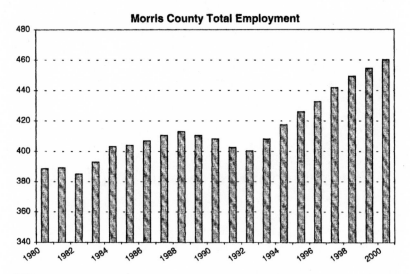

Exhibit 3.12 *(continued)*

The problems of quality and timeliness tend to increase as the region under study narrows. This is ironic since much of the aggregate data are compilations of the various disaggregated components. Nonetheless, the more disaggregated the data, the more problems arise.

Caution on Using
Economic Growth Rate Data Too Directly

It is important to know what the growth of the economy and its more narrowly defined segments, were during the loss period. These growth rates should be measured and compared to the historical growth of the revenues or profits of the plaintiff. One must be careful, however, not to blindly attribute the growth of the relevant segment of the economy to the growth of the plaintiff. That is, it does not necessarily follow that if the segment of the national or regional economy was growing at 3 percent per year during the loss period, then the plaintiff's revenues should also have grown at a 3 percent annual rate during the loss period. One may want to prepare a table showing the relevant variables, the changes in their absolute values, and the percent changes. These percent changes can then be averaged over different time periods. Only when the expert has quantitatively established that the association between the plaintiff's business and the economy is so close that the economic growth rates can be used to estimate the growth of the plaintiff can they be used in this manner. Conversely, it may be easier to simply say that when the economy was growing, the plaintiff's revenues, for example, also grew. Then, if during the loss period the economy continued to grow but the plaintiff's business fell significantly, the plaintiff may be closer to effectively proving its damages.

INTERNATIONAL ECONOMIC ANALYSIS

For some types of commercial damages analysis, the focus of the economic analysis may need to be widened, rather than narrowed, even beyond the national level. If the plaintiff derived its demand from an international source, then an international area may require scrutiny. For example, if a U.S. plaintiff derives its sales from a specific country or group of countries outside the United States, the performance of those economies may need to be analyzed. A review of the performance of different national economies can quickly reveal that not all countries grow at the same rate. For example, when the United States economy started to recover and grow after the 1990–91 recession, the Japanese economy, the international economic star during the 1980s, was stagnant and experienced the pains of a recession. The same occurred again in the 1990s and early 2000s as the Japanese economy repeatedly went in and out of recession. This is shown in Exhibit 3.13. One can see from an examination of the respective growth rates of the U.S., British, and Japanese economies that growth rates are somewhat similar; however, there are important differences. For example, in 1990, the U.S. and British economies slowed and then entered a recession in 1991, while the Japanese economy exhibited strong growth in 1990 but began to slow in 1991 and 1992. Japan's growth turned negative in 1998; growth, however, remained strong in the United States and England. What is clear is that if the conditions of one nation's economy are relevant to the losses of a plaintiff, such as when a nation or company in another nation is responsible for a significant amount of the lost sales of the plaintiff, a separate economic analysis of that country's economy is required.

For companies that have lost sales that would have been generated in a currency other than U.S. dollars, a currency conversion may be necessary. For historical losses, the historical conversion rates need to be used to convert the foreign currency into dollars. These statistics are readily available from several sources. For projection of future losses, the value of the respective currencies needs to be taken into account.

Countries which have converted to the euro no longer have currency conversion available for their older currencies; their conversion rates were "frozen" at the prior conversion rates. Therefore, only the euro will be relevant to these countries.

The field of international economics is a separate subfield within economics. Economists who work in the field of international economics, and who publish in the field's specific journals, may not work in other areas. It is common for economists in the field of international economics to specialize in the economies of a specific country or group of countries. In cases that involve international economics, it may be useful to bring in an international economics specialist whose concentration is the economies of the countries in question. However, given that litigation economics is a separate subfield of economics, it is likely that the international economist lacks experience in litigation and the techniques of measuring damages. Therefore, such a specialist is an expert who is brought on to the litigation support team and who works at the direction of the economist conducting the loss analysis. That economist will stipulate the method of measuring damages and the damages loss model. As part of that process, certain tasks may be delegated to the international economist who will "hand off" his or her output to the primary litigation economist. Depending on the issues involved, it may be useful to have both an economist and an accountant use the interdisciplinary approach advocated in this book. It may also be wise to involve international counterparts, each of whom deals with relevant international economic and accounting issues.

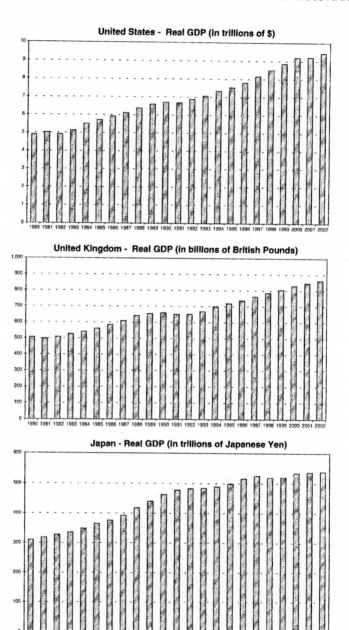

Exhibit 3.13   Real GDP levels for U.S., Japan, and the U.K., and their respective growth rates.

Source: Annual National Accounts, Organisation for Economic Co-operation and

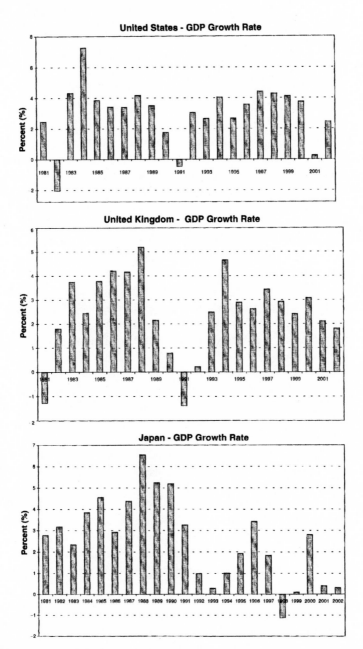

Exhibit 3.13 *(continued)*
Development, Paris, France. U.S. Department of Commerce, Bureau of Economic
Analysis, Washington, D.C.

Obviously, the size of the case and the international orientation of the issues have to justify involving such a group of experts.

MACROECONOMIC AND REGIONAL ECONOMIC ANALYSIS AND THE BEFORE AND AFTER METHOD

A macroeconomic and regional economic analysis can be an invaluable ingredient to an application of the before and after method. The macroeconomic and regional analysis (when relevant) establishes the economic environment during the before period and compares it to the after period. Differences in the economic environment may explain why the before period should be different from the after period. For example, if the economy was booming during the before period and the plaintiff's revenues also grew rapidly during this period but during the loss period the economy fell into a recession, then the declining performance of the economy may explain some or all of the losses of the plaintiff. The expert should have done some statistical analysis, or at least an analytical comparison of the relevant time series, to assess the historical co-movement of the plaintiff's revenues and profits relative to the economy. If there was a significant amount of cyclical co-variation between the economy and the plaintiff, then one might expect declining performance when the economy falters.

When there is reason to believe that the plaintiff's losses are jointly attributable to both the economic decline and the actions of the defendant, the analysis becomes more complicated. The expert has to filter out the influence of the economy and discern what portion of the losses is attributable to the economy and what portion is attributable to the defendant. The defendant may argue that all of the plaintiff's losses are attributable to the economy. In cases such as this, the joint application of the before and after method along with the yardstick approach may be helpful. The yardstick approach may enable the expert to see how similar businesses have declined during the economic downturn. If similar businesses only experienced a mild downturn while the plaintiff experienced a precipitous decline, then there may be a basis for determining what part of the total falloff in the plaintiff's business was attributable to the actions of the plaintiff. The average decline of similar firms *may* serve as a guide to what component is attributable to the economy.

SUMMARY

This chapter introduced the first step in the methodological due diligence process of measuring business interruption loss analysis. This first step is the analysis of the macro-economy. In doing this analysis, the expert assembles a variety of macroeconomic aggregates starting with gross domestic product and then concentrates on the part of the macro-economy that most directly relates to the business of the plaintiff. In doing this analysis, the expert analyzes the strength of the relationship between changes in the selected macroeconomic aggregates and the plaintiff's revenues and profits. Statistical measures such as the correlation coefficient can be used to measure the association between the performance of the macro-economy and the performance of the plaintiff.

One reason for doing the macroeconomic analysis is to determine the extent to which the performance of the economy was responsible for the losses of the plaintiff. Conversely, if the economy was doing well, past experience, as assessed by the aforementioned statistical analysis, may create an expectation that the plaintiff should have realized a certain level of revenue and profit growth, while instead it incurred losses. In this case, macroeconomic analysis is an important first step in the economic damages analysis. The term *first step* is important because the macroeconomic analysis is but one part of the overall loss estimation process. Further investigation may show that the role of the economy was not that significant compared to other factors.

After having done the broad-based macroeconomic analysis, the focus may be narrowed to the regional level if the plaintiff was mainly a regional business or if the losses at issue are restricted to a specific region of the country. In this part of the analysis, regional economic aggregates are used in a similar manner as they were for the macroeconomic analysis. The regional aggregates may be state-level data or more narrowly focused economic statistics. Unfortunately, the quantity and timeliness of regional economic data is not as good as it is on the macro level.

Sometimes the economic analysis may need to be broadened rather than narrowed. This is the case when the losses have an international element. In such an instance, the economist may need to conduct a macroeconomic analysis of other relevant economies. This may involve the expertise of international economists depending on the relevant issues.

The macroeconomic framework defines the overall economic environment within which the plaintiff and defendant were operating at the time of the alleged losses. It can be used to find other possible causes of the plaintiff's losses, such as an economic downturn. It can also be used to create an expectation of gains instead of losses as the focus of the litigation, when the economy was doing well in the loss period and when the macroeconomic analysis has shown that the plaintiff has done well in such economic conditions. The macroeconomic analysis is an important first step in the overall damages process. Once it has been done the next step is to do an analysis of the industry within which the plaintiff was operating.

REFERENCES

Boskin, Michael, Ellen R. Dulberger, Robert J. Gordon, Zvi Griliches, and Dale Jorgenson, "Toward a More Accurate Measure of the Cost of Living," *Final Report of the Advisory Commission to Study the Consumer Price Index to the Senate Finance Committee,* December 4, 1996.

Case, Karl E., and Ray C. Fair, *Principles of Macroeconomics,* 6th ed. New Jersey: Prentice-Hall, 1999.

Gordon, Robert, *Macroeconomics,* 6th ed. New York: HarperCollins, 1993.

Kydland, Finn E., and E. C. Prescott, "Time to Build and Aggregate Fluctuations." *Econometrica* 50 (November 1982).

Mankiw, Gregory N., *Macroeconomics.* New York: Worth Publishers, 2003.

Mills, Edwin, S., and Bruce W. Hamilton, *Urban Economics*, 5th ed. New York: HarperCollins, 1994.

The NBER's Business Cycle Dating Procedure, June 7, 2002.

Shapiro, Mathew, and David Wilcox, "Mismeasurement in the Consumer Price Index: An Evaluation," *NBER Macroeconomics Annual,* 1996.

Stiglitz, Joseph, *Economics,* 2nd ed. New York: W.W. Norton, 1997.

Stiglitz, Joseph, and Carl E. Walsh, *Economics,* 3rd ed. New York: W.W. Norton, 2002.

Taylor, John, *Economics,* 3rd ed. New York: Houghton Mifflin, 2001.

Trcyz, George, *Regional Economic Modeling: Economic Forecasting and Analysis* Norwell, MA: Kluwer Academic Publishers, 1993.

www.nber.org/cycles.

www.ny.frb.org.

4

INDUSTRY ANALYSIS

An industry analysis is often an integral part of the overall business interruption loss analysis. As part of the due diligence process in measuring such losses, the expert may need to research and analyze the economics of the plaintiff's industry. However, there may be cases where the issues are so straightforward and narrowly defined that such an analysis is not necessary. Typically, the economic expert does not specialize in the plaintiff's industry. Depending on the facts and nature of the case, the expert may have to do research on the trends in the industry as well as other factors relevant to the litigation. This process may involve gathering of relevant industry data and statistics. Standard tools of economic analysis are employed to conduct this industry analysis.

Industry analysis draws on the subfield within microeconomics known as *industrial organization*. Industrial organization is the study of the structure of an industry and the interaction of companies within that industry. Among the topics studied in this field are the level of competition and the determination of prices and quantities in a given industry. While industrial organization is a broad field and covers many issues that are not relevant to a litigation-oriented industry analysis, the field does provide some useful tools of analysis that may be relevant depending on the nature of the case.

SOURCES OF INDUSTRY DATA

There are two main sources of industry data: government sources and private sources. Depending on the industry being studied, these data sources can vary significantly in terms of their quality and availability. It is important for the expert to research the specific data source and determine how the data was gathered and whether or not they are reliable.

Government Data Sources

One main government data source is the U.S. Department of Commerce. Much of the Commerce Department's data is gathered by the U.S. Bureau of the Census. Unfortunately, there have been significant expenditure cutbacks at the Commerce Department, as a result of which data are not as readily available, and some data sources have been discontinued. One often cited data source is the *U.S. Industry & Trade Outlook*. This useful publication was temporarily discontinued by the Commerce Department after the 1994 edition appeared. However, it is now being published by DRI/McGraw-Hill and Standard & Poor's and U.S. Department of Commerce/International Trade Administration.[1] The *U.S. Industry & Trade Outlook* is an annual publication which contains detailed data on shipments, revenues, and employment by industry category along with a narrative discussion on recent trends in the industry. Where relevant, a breakdown by subindustry categories is also available. Most industries that are covered contain the names and telephone numbers of staff at the Commerce Department who regularly study that particular industry. This can be most valuable to the expert as the individuals listed may specialize in this industry and can provide the expert with useful additional information beyond what appears in the *U.S. Industry & Trade Outlook*. In addition, each industry section ends with a bibliography which usually indicates the names of industry associations or other industry publications where one can go for further information.

Table 4.1 is a sample of some of the data that appears in the *U.S. Industry & Trade Outlook*. While the *U.S. Industrial Outlook* is no longer published in hard copy form, the data that are shown in this table are still available online from the U.S. Commerce Department.

Two alternatives to the *U.S. Industry & Trade Outlook* are two other Commerce Department publications: the *Statistical Abstract of the United States* and *Business Statistics of the United States*.[2] Unlike the *U.S. Industry & Trade Outlook,* the *Statistical Abstract of the United States* only includes data and does not have any narrative discussion. The experienced analyst, however, can use these data along with other available data sources to conduct a thorough industry analysis. The *Statistical Abstract of the United States* contains valuable statistical data on a wide variety of topics not limited to industry data. Among the other useful categories of

---

[1] *U.S. Industry & Trade Outlook,* annual, U.S. Department of Commerce/International Trade Administration, Washington D.C.

[2] *Statistical Abstract of the United States,* annual, U.S. Department of Commerce, Washington D.C. and *Business Statistics of the United States,* annual, Courtenay M. Slater, ed. (Lanham, MD: Bernan Press). The latter is based on another Commerce Department publication, *Business Statistics,* which is also no longer available.

Table 4.1 Sample of Data in *U.S. Industrial and Trade Outlook*

Paper Manufacturing (NAICS 322)—Trends and Forecasts (millions of dollars except as noted)

	1997	1998	1999	2000	2001	Percent Change			
						97–98	98–99	99–00	00–01
Industry data									
Value of shipments	150,296	154,984	156,915	166,099		3.1	1.2	5.9	
Value of shipments (1997$)	150,296	151,767	153,164	150,632		1.0	0.9	(1.7)	
Total employment (thousands)	574	572	561	552		(0.3)	(1.9)	(1.6)	
Production workers (thousands)	440	439	432	427		(0.2)	(1.6)	(1.2)	
Capital expenditures	8,595	8,547	7,081	8,100		(0.6)	(17.2)	14.4	
Product data									
Value of shipments	144,674	149,191	151,160	159,911		3.1	1.3	5.8	
Value of shipments (1997$)	144,674	146,332	147,877	144,891		1.1	1.1	(2.0)	
Trade data									
Value of exports	14,417	13,632	13,839	15,539	14,045	(5.4)	1.5	12.3	(9.6)
Value of imports	14,662	15,598	16,424	19,080	18,170	6.4	5.3	16.2	(4.8)

Source: U.S. Department of Commerce: Bureau of the Census; International Trade Administration (ITA) http://www.ita.doc.gov/td/industry/otea.

information are demographic and economic data which may be used in other parts of a commercial damages analysis. A sample of how the data included in the *Statistical Abstract of the United States* appear is shown in Table 4.2.

Business Statistics of the United States is actually a private data source that features government data. It has some limited narrative and does not have the industry-by-industry description of recent trends that the *U.S. Industry & Trade Outlook* has. Much of the data in *Business Statistics of the United States* is general economic data, although there are some broad categorized industry data such as those shown in Table 4.3.

The government data sources are good starting points from which to begin an industry analysis. However, the detail needed to complete a thorough industry analysis may not be sufficient for the litigation expert to submit a reliable and nonspeculative opinion on damages. The expert may then have to go beyond the published data sources and gather more detailed data. This can often be done by contacting the U.S. Department of Commerce directly. Often the expert will want to get copies of the relevant sections of the *Annual Survey of Manufactures* which is gathered by the U.S. Bureau of the Census.[3] The *Annual Survey of Manufactures* is designed to provide industry data for those periods that occur between the surveys that the Bureau of the Census takes every five years. Data are gathered from a representative sample of approximately 55,000 manufacturing establishments. These data include statistics on employment, hours, payroll, value added by the manufacturer, capital expenditures, materials costs, end-of-year inventories, and value of industry shipments. The last variable, value of industry shipments, is usually the most useful of the data that are included in the survey. A sample of how the data are displayed in the *Annual Survey of Manufactures* is shown in Table 4.4.

Industry data in the *Annual Survey of Manufactures* are organized using Standard Industrial Classification (SIC) codes. This is often the case for both government and private data sources. Knowing a business's SIC code can enable the expert to more quickly locate industry data. It is therefore useful to have an understanding of this classification system.

STANDARD INDUSTRIAL CLASSIFICATION CODES

SIC codes are assigned to specific industries and product lines according to a classification system that was designed by the Federal Government's Office of Management and Budget.[4] The system was first developed in the 1930s and has

---

[3]*Annual Survey of Manufactures*, U.S. Bureau of the Census, Washington, D.C.
[4]*SIC Code Manual*, U.S. Government Printing Office, 1987, Washington D.C.

(Text continues on page 118)

Table 4.2 Sample of *Statistical Abstract of the United States* Data

Tobacco Products—Summary: 1990 to 2001

Item	Unit	1990	1994	1995	1996	1997	1998	1999	2000	2001
Production										
Cigarettes, total	Billions	710	726	747	758	720	680	607	580	580
Nonfilter tip	Billions	23	15	15	14	12	12	8	7	NA
Filter tip	Billions	687	710	732	744	708	669	599	573	NA
Cigars	Billions	1.9	1.9	2.1	2.4	2.3	2.8	2.9	2.8	2.8
Tobacco[1]	Mil. Lb.	142	132	131	131	134	131	133	133	131
Smoking	Mil. Lb.	16	14	12	12	11	13	15	14	13
Chewing Tobacco	Mil. Lb.	73	63	63	61	58	53	51	49	47
Snuff	Mil. Lb.	53	60	60	62	64	66	67	70	71
Exports										
Cigarettes	Billions	164.3	220.2	231.1	243.9	217.0	201.3	151.4	147.9	133.9
Cigars	Billions	72	74	94	84	86	93	84	113	120
Smoking Tobacco	Billions	0.8	0.5	0.3	0.7	0.8	1.1	1.6	0.5	5.3
Imports										
Cigarettes	Billions	1.4	3.5	3.0	2.8	3.2	4.3	8.7	11.3	14.7
Cigars	Billions	111	146	195	320	576	582	463	497	489
Smoking Tobacco	Billions	2.9	3.9	4.2	4.2	4.3	4.3	4.3	4.2	4
Consumption										
Consumption per person[2]	Lb.[3]	5.6	4.9	4.7	4.5	4.5	4.5	4.3	4.2	4.1
Cigarettes	1,000	3	3	3	3	2	2	2	2	2
Cigars[4]	Number	13	12	15	18	18	18	19	19	19
Expenditures										
Consumer expenditures, total	Bil. Dol.	43.8	47.7	48.7	50.4	52.2	57.3	72.1	77.5	NA
Cigarettes	Bil. Dol.	41.6	44.5	45.8	47.2	48.7	53.2	68.3	72.9	NA
Cigars	Bil. Dol.	0.7	0.9	1.0	1.0	1.2	1.6	1.8	1.8	NA
Other	Bil. Dol.	1.5	2.3	2.5	2.2	2.2	2.4	2.7	2.7	NA

Note: NA Not available.

[1]Smoking and chewing tobaccos and snuff output.

[2]Based on estimated population 18 years old and over, as of July 1, including Armed Forces abroad.

[3]Unstemmed processing weight equivalent.

[4]Weighing over 3 pounds per 1,000.

Source: Statistical Abstract of the United States: 2002, U.S. Department of Commerce, p. 620.

Table 4.3 Sample of *Business Statistics of the United States*

| | Manufacturers' Shipments ($Millions, seasonally adjusted) | | | | | | | | | |
| | | | | NAICS nondurable goods industries | | | | | | |
Year	Total[1]	Food products	Beverage & Tobacco[3]	Textiles	Textile products	Apparel	Paper products	Basic chemicals	Petroleum & coal products	Plastics & rubber products
SIC Basis[2]										
1970	295,787	98,353	5,350	22,614		⋮	24,573	49,195	24,200	16,754
1971	311,788	103,637	5,528	24,034		⋮	25,182	51,681	26,198	18,409
1972	348,477	115,054	5,919	28,065		⋮	28,004	58,130	27,918	21,662
1973	399,552	135,585	6,341	31,073		⋮	32,495	66,003	33,903	25,191
1974	487,403	161,884	7,139	32,790		⋮	41,514	85,387	57,229	28,828
1975	515,887	172,054	8,058	31,065		⋮	41,497	91,710	67,496	28,128
1976	578,088	180,830	8,786	36,387		⋮	47,939	106,467	80,022	32,880
1977	648,399	192,913	9,051	40,550		⋮	51,881	120,905	94,702	40,944
1978	710,082	215,969	9,951	42,281		⋮	56,777	132,262	100,967	44,823
1979	816,110	235,976	10,602	45,137		⋮	64,957	151,887	144,156	48,694
1980	923,662	256,191	12,194	47,256		⋮	72,553	168,220	192,969	49,157
1981	1,012,819	272,140	13,130	50,260		⋮	79,970	186,909	217,681	55,178
1982	1,009,673	280,529	16,061	47,516		⋮	79,698	176,254	203,404	57,307
1983	1,044,794	289,314	16,268	53,733		⋮	84,817	189,552	187,788	62,870
1984	1,112,908	304,584	17,473	56,336		⋮	95,525	205,963	184,488	72,938
1985	1,119,104	308,606	18,559	54,605		⋮	94,679	204,790	176,574	75,590
1986	1,097,022	318,203	19,146	57,188		⋮	99,865	205,711	122,605	78,379
1987	1,178,374	329,725	20,757	62,787		⋮	108,989	229,546	130,414	86,634
1988	1,273,931	354,084	23,809	64,627		⋮	122,882	261,238	131,682	95,485
1989	1,362,475	380,160	25,875	67,265		⋮	131,896	283,196	146,487	101,236
1990	1,426,915	391,728	29,856	65,533		⋮	132,424	292,802	173,389	105,250
1991	1,426,169	397,893	31,943	65,440		⋮	130,131	298,545	159,144	105,804
1992	1,462,861	406,964	35,198	70,753		⋮	133,201	305,420	150,227	113,593

Table 4.3 *(continued)*

Manufacturers' Shipments ($Millions, seasonally adjusted)

Year	Total[1]	Food products	Beverage & Tobacco[3]	Textiles	Textile products	Apparel	Paper products	Basic chemicals	Petroleum & coal products	Plastics & rubber products
					NAICS nondurable goods industries					
NAICS Basis										
1992	1,385,162	358,494	85,687	52,923	24,763	61,535	127,122	319,501	150,095	113,827
1993	1,415,953	373,612	79,227	55,375	25,623	63,210	126,982	330,760	144,731	122,807
1994	1,474,051	379,786	83,434	58,607	27,233	64,894	136,922	350,098	143,339	134,288
1995	1,576,862	393,204	88,945	59,885	27,976	65,214	166,051	376,995	151,431	145,084
1996	1,618,591	404,173	94,033	59,796	28,515	64,237	152,860	385,919	174,181	149,773
1997	1,687,315	421,737	96,971	58,707	31,052	68,018	150,296	415,617	177,394	159,161
1998	1,668,225	428,479	102,359	57,416	31,137	64,932	154,984	416,742	137,957	163,736
1999	1,716,520	429,054	107,437	54,854	32,642	62,798	157,491	419,674	168,096	172,397
2000	1,845,859	438,913	112,366	53,282	32,947	65,097	170,217	442,832	232,581	182,303
2001	1,797,588	453,218	116,788	44,932	34,434	57,678	153,378	434,150	220,959	174,556

[1]Includes categories not shown separately.

[2]Data are for roughly similar categories in SIC classification system.

[3]SIC tobacco only, 1970–1992.

... = Not available.

Source: Business Statistics of the United States, Eighth Edition, 2002, p. 260. Published by Bernan Press, a division of the Kraus Organization Limited.

Table 4.4 Sample of Annual Survey of Manufactures

		Manufacturers' New Orders (Net, $millions, seasonally adjusted)											
		NAICS durable goods industries								Transportation equipment			
			Primary metals						Electrical				
Year	Total	Total	Total	Iron & steel mills	Aluminium and nonferrous metal products	Fabricated metal products	Machinery	Computers and electronic	equipment, appliances & components	Total	Motor vehicles and parts	Non-defense aircraft and parts	Defense aircraft and parts
SIC Basis													
1970	624,541	328,079	51,793	25,521	…	43,990	…	99,312		67,380	…	17,417	…
1971	671,134	358,856	51,284	25,571	…	44,305	…	100,191		89,900	…	22,459	…
1972	770,056	420,455	61,447	30,996	…	52,879	…	123,820		96,501	…	20,963	…
1973	912,279	511,525	78,395	39,413	…	64,733	…	153,895		118,194	…	26,669	…
1974	1,047,811	562,339	98,831	51,047	…	74,281	…	180,382		114,081	…	29,934	…
1975	1,022,133	503,485	75,034	38,611	…	64,349	…	157,212		109,050	…	26,869	…
1976	1,194,759	615,680	94,491	47,212	…	76,372	…	183,967		143,502	…	31,851	…
1977	1,382,309	732,422	105,689	52,103	…	92,028	…	218,263		175,446	…	40,625	…
1978	1,579,715	867,335	124,471	62,648	…	105,182	…	259,233		213,539	…	54,600	…
1979	1,771,603	953,796	139,783	66,968	…	117,428	…	292,088		223,226	…	67,818	…
1980	1,877,053	952,701	134,416	62,473	…	116,195	…	295,945		202,584	…	72,514	…
1981	2,015,982	1,003,845	137,286	67,457	…	123,245	…	324,821		203,482	…	63,530	…
1982	1,944,671	936,764	98,445	43,013	…	113,399	…	282,673		209,325	…	73,365	…
1983	2,106,726	1,057,677	113,884	49,123	…	122,760	…	301,639		261,359	…	86,952	…
1984	2,314,256	1,201,964	118,354	50,719	…	141,650	…	353,759		295,202	…	91,620	…
1985	2,346,410	1,228,268	112,276	49,079	…	142,300	…	360,695		311,482	…	100,889	…
1986	2,340,899	1,243,761	108,218	46,408	…	143,541	…	352,108		327,541	…	107,993	…
1987	2,510,890	1,329,712	125,989	54,763	…	150,716	…	371,887		348,224	…	114,835	…
1988	2,737,716	1,464,916	152,578	64,002	…	158,170	…	408,225		389,635	…	137,443	…
1989	2,872,514	1,512,664	152,814	62,752	…	160,037	…	417,088		411,434	…	153,430	…

Table 4.4 *(continued)*

Manufacturers' New Orders (Net, $millions, seasonally adjusted)

Year	Total	NAICS durable goods industries Total	Primary metals Total	Iron & steel mills	Aluminium and nonferrous metal products	Fabricated metal products	Machinery	Computers and electronic	Electrical equipment, appliances & components	Transportation equipment Total	Motor vehicles and parts	Non-defense aircraft and parts	Defense aircraft and parts
1990	2,931,275	1,507,001	149,338	63,369	....	163,285		422,179		395,737	....	150,329	
1991	2,866,841	1,438,187	134,657	56,366	....	158,401		401,851		363,366	....	132,645	
1992	2,977,116	1,515,694	136,849	58,002	....	165,793		424,401		377,147	....	110,830	
NAICS Basis													
1993	2,995,788	1,579,835	128,895	62,580	53,733	175,990	202,848	283,877	88,263	427,966	311,928	38,427	32,569
1994	3,246,790	1,772,739	146,503	67,619	64,594	196,567	232,226	321,880	96,919	487,253	367,306	39,309	31,524
1995	3,495,515	1,918,653	159,957	72,600	72,264	214,488	251,307	380,287	101,409	508,133	378,886	57,454	27,736
1996	3,638,149	2,019,558	158,066	71,301	70,657	227,447	258,405	398,053	104,837	552,024	385,712	72,094	32,520
1997	3,859,016	2,171,701	171,407	78,577	74,974	247,839	272,998	442,816	113,411	581,780	422,427	85,797	23,280
1998	3,884,868	2,216,643	160,743	72,378	71,274	253,847	278,100	449,158	115,711	600,205	440,934	84,150	23,854
1999	4,062,133	2,345,613	158,580	70,703	70,819	257,983	278,625	490,834	122,497	659,855	498,366	82,614	25,973
2000	4,349,672	2,503,813	160,770	70,001	73,842	259,406	305,598	558,875	135,889	706,834	479,432	116,242	36,391

Source: U.S. Census Bureau: Annual Survey of Manufacturers
http://www.census.gov/econ/www/ma0300.html.

117

Table 4.5   Standard Industrial Classification Codes

Numerical Range	Industry Category
0000–0299	Agriculture
0300–0699	Not Assigned
0700–0999	Agricultural Services, Forestry & Fishing
1000–1499	Mining
1500–1799	Construction
1800–1999	Not Assigned
2000–3999	Manufacturing
4000–4999	Transportation, Communications & Utilities
5000–5199	Wholesale Trade
5200–5999	Retail Trade
6000–6699	Finance, Insurance & Real Estate (FIRE)
6700–6999	Not Assigned
7000–8999	Service Sector
9000–9099	Not Assigned
9100–9799	Public Administration
9800–9899	Not Assigned
9900–9999	Nonclassifiable Establishments

been periodically revised since that time, the last revision took place in 1987. Industries are classified broadly using 2-digit groups or more narrowly using 3- or 4-digit groups. The 4-digit numbers range from 0000–9999; the range 2000–3999 is reserved for the manufacturing sector. A "9" appearing in the third or fourth position of the classification code usually designates miscellaneous industry groups that are not otherwise classified. Table 4.5 provides a breakdown of the various SIC categories.

NEW NORTH AMERICAN INDUSTRY CLASSIFICATION SYSTEM

Given the many structural changes that have taken place in the U.S. economy, including the growth of the service sector relative to the manufacturing sector, a new industry classification has been developed. This system, called the North American Industry Classification System (NAICS), features 350 new industries and 9 service industry sectors.[5] Federal government agencies implemented the system in 1999 using data from the 1997 economic census. It uses a six-digit system to categorize specific industries; the first two digits designate the sector, the

---

[5]*North American Industry Classification System*, Executive Office of the President, Office of Management and Budget, Washington, D.C., 1997.

Table 4.6   North American Industry Classification System

Numerical Range	Industry Category
11	Agriculture, Forestry, Fishing & Hunting
21	Mining
22	Utilities
23	Construction
31–33	Manufacturing
41–43	Wholesale Trade
44–46	Retail Trade
48–49	Transportation & Warehousing
51	Information
52	Finance and Insurance
53	Real Estate and Rental & Leasing
54	Professional, Scientific & Technical Services
55	Management of Companies and Enterprises
56	Administrative, Waste Management & Remediation Services
61	Educational Services
62	Health Care and Social Assistance
71	Arts, Entertainment, and Recreation
72	Accommodation and Food Services
81	Other Services (except Public Administration)
91–93	Public Administration

third the subsector, the fourth the industry group, and the fifth and sixth digits designate the NAICS and the national industries. The system focuses on the economies of the United States, Canada, and Mexico. The sectors in the NAICS system are shown in Table 4.6.

Private Data Sources

Government industry data are available through the Commerce Department (such as through the Census of Manufacturers) and also through private vendors. One such source which was often used was *Predicasts Basebook*.[6] It contains data organized according to SIC codes, as well as detailed subcategories within broad industry groupings. Both unit and dollar volumes, as well as other relevant data, such as employment, are available. Thanks to the rapid growth of many online sources, most of these data are available through the Internet. Researchers can easily access data sources such as the U.S. Department of Commerce or the Internal Trade Administration. The data that are available on such governmental

---

[6]For example, *Predicasts Basebook,* annual, Information Access Company, Foster City, CA.

data sources can often be accessed in downloadable forms. This greatly facilitates industry analysis.

Private sources of useful industry data often include industry associations. One source containing lists of industry associations is the *Encyclopedia of Associations.*[7] Many industries, even some obscure ones, have an industry association that compiles data and may publish such data in a report. Care must be taken in the use of such data. The analyst should contact the association and learn how the data were gathered. It is often the case that data are gathered in a questionnaire from association members with little verification of data accuracy. If many of the members are closely held firms, the association may have limited ability to verify the data.[8]

Associations differ in how they gather their data. Some employ professional survey companies who try to gather and analyze the data in a more reliable and scientific manner. Some associations employ their own professionals in these areas and may be able to competently gather and analyze the data. Other associations do not gather the data in a reliable manner; the use of such data may be more open to challenge. Later in this chapter some examples are provided in which courts have rejected the use of industry data due to their questionable reliability.

Certain private vendors prepare industry reports on specific industries. These vendors include Business Data Analysts, Packaged Facts, and the Freedonia Group. The Freedonia Group claims to have published over 1,000 studies since 1985.[9] Packaged Facts is one of three brands of market intelligence and industry studies disseminated by Find/SVP.[10] Like most of these vendors, Find/SVP publishes a catalog listing their various industries.[11] The benefit of such reports is that they often include a variety of data which are broken down by relevant subcategories. In addition, such reports usually include a narrative discussion of the industry. This can be helpful to an expert who lacks a prior background in the industry. The testifying expert still needs to do an industry analysis but the use of such reports can be a benefit. The costs of such reports vary; many are in the $1,000–$3,000 range. While it may appear to raise the costs of the expert's services, it may actually save money, for the expert is then not required to "reinvent the wheel." By using such studies, the expert can draw on the work of others who have devoted considerable time to studying the particular industry.

---

[7]*Encyclopedia of Associations,* annual (Detroit, MI: Gale Research).

[8]See later discussion in this chapter on the court's position on the use of data from industry associations and problems with their reliability.

[9]*Freedonia Industry Study Catalog* (Cleveland, OH: The Freedonia Group).

[10]*Packaged Facts* (New York: Find/SVP).

[11]*The Information Catalog* (New York: Find/SVP).

Another source of private industry data on consumer goods is one that is very often used in the field of marketing. This is the data made available by A.C. Nielsen on fast moving consumer-goods (FMCG). This data set includes information compiled from scanner data that is, in turn, gathered at supermarkets, drug stores, and other outlets.[12] However, most of these data are cross-sectional rather than time series. Being cross-sectional, the data set is more useful for determining market shares and size of markets as of the survey date. Therefore, the data set is not as useful for determining trends. Nonetheless, it may play a role in a commercial damages analysis for certain consumer goods. One way in which such data can be helpful is in analyzing what market shares are implied by various forecasts. The data can be used to determine what percent of total market revenues are implied by a plaintiff's revenue projection. The reasonableness of such market shares can then be considered. Market share analysis may be useful in a basic industry analysis and may be invaluable in doing an antitrust analysis.

Industry Publications

Many industries have their own publications. Some have several which may be directed at various segments of the overall industry. These contain industry data which may be produced by some associations covering the industry. The expert can learn about important developments and trends that affect the performance of the industry. Published articles on the plaintiff may provide useful information on the company's performance; they may yield alternative explanations for a downturn in the plaintiff's performance, performance that it is attributing to the defendant. These publications can often be accessed through online data sources such as *Nexis*. If the expert does not have an account with *Nexis* he may be able to access it through publicly available sources such as the local library. Other industry publications may be marketed by private vendors. In the tobacco industry, for example, one such publication is *The Maxwell Report,* which publishes data in sales of specific brands by specific manufacturers.[13] In addition, private vendors also gather data on tobacco sales by brand and manufacturer for specific markets (such as sales by states). Other industries, however, may not be as closely studied. Each industry is different and presents different data sets for the expert.

---

[12]Douglas P. Handler, "Business Economist at Work: Linking Economics to Market Research: A.C. Nielsen," *Business Economics,* vol. XXXI, no. 4 (October 1996): 51–52.

[13]*The Maxwell Report,* Richmond, VA.

Online Data Sources

Numerous online data sources are available to augment an industry analysis. The volume of data sources available on the Internet is ever-expanding. This source can often provide useful information for an industry analysis. A simple query using a search engine such as Google can yield useful information on the industry and the plaintiff's position within it. Another source is the *Wall Street Journal* online.

Annual Reports

In cases where a significant percent of the industry includes public firms, the analyst can take advantage of the public filing requirements of securities laws by gathering data from the annual reports and other filings such as 10Ks. Annual reports generally have more information than 10Ks since they contain some verbiage which may include management's "spin" on the facts. If the analyst can isolate some major companies that comprise a large percent of industry sales, then such reports, and the data they contain, like revenue and total costs data, may allow for some useful disaggregation of the total industry revenue data. Annual reports may be used to establish what some typical margins, such as the gross, operating, and net margins, are. This may give some indication as to what average industry profitability is and what the magnitude of the major cost areas is. These data are summarized in other publicly available sources such as *Value Line*.[14] Sometimes, however, this avenue does not prove fruitful. This is due to the fact that major companies are diversified and are not required to provide significant detail on divisions. Therefore, total reported revenues and costs may include many industries that are not the object of the analysis. In addition, larger segments of the industry may be private or non-U.S. firms who do not have to abide by the same U.S. securities laws.

Securities Markets Analysts Reports

In cases where a significant component of the industry is comprised of public companies, it is often possible to find industry analysts at brokerage firms who study the firms and the industry in general. For example, the tobacco industry is followed by several securities firms which issue reports and make them available

---

[14]See Value Line Investment Survey, *www.valueline.com.*

for clients. New developments that are of interest to investors are summarized by such analysts. Tobacco is such a large industry that several major brokerage firms—Salomon Smith Barney, Merrill Lynch, Goldman Sachs, and Morgan Stanley—have issued reports on it.[15] Their reports include discussions on important recent trends in the industry as well as other valuable data such as market share and industry growth data. The reports contain specific data that can be helpful in conducting an industry analysis. They provide other information such as a discussion of the plaintiff's other problems which may be unrelated to the defendant's actions but could be the cause of the plaintiff's losses. The expert may be able to follow-up on such reports by contacting the market analysts who wrote the report. Such investigations may unearth the true cause of the plaintiff's losses. Once again, how available and useful such reports may be varies widely from case-to-case.

RETAINING AN INDUSTRY EXPERT

An industry expert can be of great assistance in the analysis of damages. This may be a testifying expert or a consultant who works with the damages expert. The damages expert may be able to rely on the industry expert's knowledge without this expert having to testify. While this might be considered hearsay if a fact witness attempted to rely on such information, courts often conclude that if it is a source on which experts customarily rely, the expert may be able to incorporate such information into his analysis and ultimate opinions. Having an industry expert is particularly important if the industry in question is technical in nature or is one in which there has been significant changes affecting the comparability of historical data. One example of both is the telecommunications industry, which has several highly specialized and technical subcomponents; it has also undergone significant changes in recent years. If the industry expert does testify, it makes sense that his testimony precedes that of the damages expert as the latter would most likely rely on some of the analysis and opinion expressed by the industry expert. In this manner, the industry expert sets forth a foundation of the damages expert's testimony.

Attorneys sometimes try to limit monies spent on damages experts; one way they do this is in the retaining of another expert who supports the damages expert. When the industry expert is not expected to testify, attorneys or their clients may be reluctant to pay the fees of such an expert, especially considering that these

---

[15]See *www.smithbarney.com, www.morganstanley.com, www.gs.com.*

fees, on a hourly basis, may be similar to those of the damages expert. However, such reasoning has been included in the *The Ten Most Frequent Errors in Litigating Business Damages* list.[16] Having an industry expert relieves the damages expert of bearing the full burden of being an expert on the industry as well as an expert on damages. It also eliminates some of the impact of cross-examination directed at the damages expert's knowledge of the industry. When the damages expert works in conjunction with the industry expert, he may be able to respond to such questions by saying that he has done a certain amount of his own industry analysis but has also relied upon the expertise of the industry expert. Having such an expert to rely on can also lower the fees of the damages expert, who might otherwise have to do additional industry research to acquire the information that the industry expert already has.

CONDUCTING AN INDUSTRY ANALYSIS

One of the first steps in conducting an industry analysis is to determine the industry growth rate. The growth rate is often computed for units, such as shipments, as well as revenues, although revenues may be more useful since one of the initial steps in a lost profits analysis is to construct a lost revenues projection. The industry revenue growth rate may be more relevant to the lost revenues projection. This growth is depicted graphically in Exhibit 4.1.

The growth rate computation is usually done for historical time periods such as the past five or ten years. The longer the loss projection, the more historical years are considered. This is not to imply that all historical years have equal importance. Generally, the more remote the years of data the less weight is placed on them. However, each case has unique factors requiring the expert to address the specifics for each assignment on a case-by-case basis.

A review of shipment data for the corrugated box industry shows that over the period 1992–2001 these data exhibit an average annual growth rate equal to six percent. The cyclical nature of this industry can be readily seen in the negative growth rate that occurred in 2001—a year which featured and eight month recession. This could be relevant to a plaintiff claiming losses due to a business interruption during such time periods. The damages expert would expect that lower sales might have occured without any actions on the part of the defendant.

---

[16]James Plummer and Gerald McGowin, "The Ten Most Frequent Errors in Litigating Business Damages," *Association of Business Trial Lawyers (ABTL) Northern Califormia Report* (November 1995).

Value of Shipments for Corrugated Boxes: 1992–2001

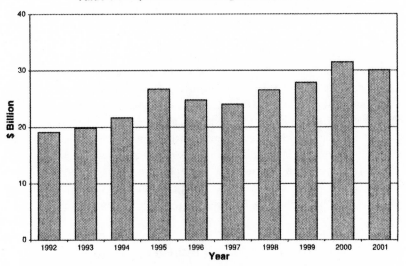

Percent Change in Value of Shipments of Corrugated Boxes

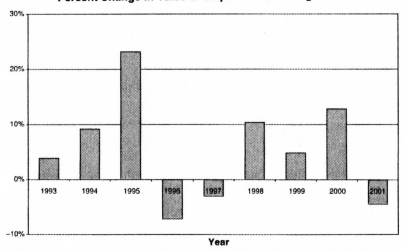

Exhibit 4.1 Value and percent change of value of shipments of corrugated boxes.
Source: Annual Survey of Manufactures, 1966, 2001. U.S. Census Bureau, Washington, D.C.

Regional Industry Data

If the plaintiff's is a regional business, then the expert may want to try to gather industry data on a regional basis. This is dependent upon the availability of such data. Many industry associations do not publish regional data, but instead merely aggregate all of the data they gather across the nation. If there are significant differences across the nation for the industry, this may be a problem. When such regional data are available, they can be added to the presentation.

Exhibit 4.2 depicts the value of shipments of computer and electronic products in the Southwest of the United States. Using the Southwest value data, an 8 percent growth rate is computed for the year 1998 and 7 percent for 1999. In 1998, the nation as a whole only showed a 1 percent growth rate and 5 percent in 1999. If the hypothetical plaintiff were located in the Southwest, we would be aware that the industry's growth in that region of the nation was higher in 1998 and 1999 than the rest of the country. This would be relevant for companies that were mainly regional but it might be less relevant to national companies

Industry Growth and Industry Life Cycles

High industry growth implies higher firm sales. However, to simply apply the industry growth rate to a firm's revenue projection is simplistic and possibly erroneous for a couple of reasons. The industry growth rate cannot be blindly applied to the firm involved in the litigation since the industry might be at a different stage of growth than the injured firm. For example, the industry could be in a mature state while the firm is a new entrant. Such new firms would be expected to experience high rates of growth initially and then experience a lower growth rate as they mature. In addition, in cases where the plaintiff is an established firm but is marketing a new product line, the industry growth rate may understate the expected growth rate of such new products.

Various firm-specific factors, in addition to industry factors, may explain the firm's historical sales trends. That is, the firm's growth may follow a life cycle such as that shown in Exhibit 4.3. Stage I is the early part of a firm's life. In this stage, growth rates often are high. In Stage II, a company's growth rate slows as the firm becomes more mature. In Stage III, the firm's growth has leveled off and may even be in decline. Where a plaintiff is in its life cycle affects the growth rate that an expert uses for the loss projection. Companies in Stage I may warrant higher growth rates than those in Stages II and III. It is important, however, to understand that this is a generality. Not all companies go through such staged growth, although many do. Each case and plaintiff is different and the expert

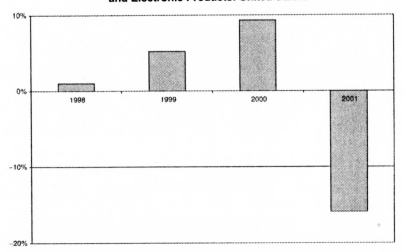

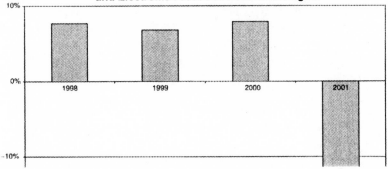

Exhibit 4.2   Percent change in value of shipments for computers and electronic products for the United States and Southwest Region: 1998–2001.
Source: Geographic Area Statistics: 2001, Annual Survey of Manufactures, U.S. Census Bureau, Washington, D.C.

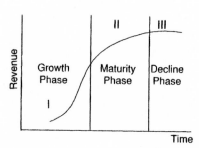

Exhibit 4.3   Firm's growth life cycle.

needs to consider many factors other than simply the stage that the company is in its life cycle.

RELATING INDUSTRY GROWTH TO THE PLAINTIFF'S GROWTH

There are several ways that the expert can relate the growth of the industry to that of the plaintiff. Two common ways are to create a Firm-Industry Growth table where the revenues, and possibly shipments, of the industry and the firm are shown side-by-side. An example is shown in Table 4.7; the national and regional industry data from the corrugated box industry are compared with the performance of a hypothetical company in that industry. The average growth rates of the industry and the firm are computed for selected historical time periods. The firm experienced similar growth to that of the industry until 1993, when the industry continued to rebound from the 1990–91 recession and the company's revenues fell sharply. The falloff in the company's revenues was short-lived and the company's revenues quickly recovered. These trends are shown in Exhibit 4.4. An examination of Table 4.7 and Exhibit 4.4 seems to imply that whatever afflicted the plaintiff in 1993 was not an industry-wide phenomenon and that the answer to the plaintiff's declining performance can be found in firm-specific factors.

Measuring the Strength of Association: Industry versus Firm

Statistical analysis, such as using correlation analysis, can be used to assess the closeness of association between the historical industry performance and that of the firm. This is the same type of analysis as was used to establish the strength of association between the performance of the national or regional economy and the

Table 4.7 Industry/Firm Corrugated Box Revenues

Year	Value of Industry Shipments ($Billions)	Percent Change (%)	Firm Revenues ($Millions)	Percent Change (%)
1980	9.010		10.01	
1981	9.957	10.5	10.95	9.4
1982	9.279	−6.8	10.575	−3.4
1983	9.778	5.4	10.945	3.5
1984	11.491	17.5	11.945	9.1
1985	11.413	−0.7	12.2	2.1
1986	11.673	2.3	12.25	0.4
1987	14.015	20.1	14.65	19.6
1988	15.539	10.9	16.125	10.1
1989	16.067	3.4	17.35	7.6
1990	15.695	−2.3	17.25	−0.6
1991	15.265	−2.7	17	−1.4
1992	16.447	7.7	17.95	5.6
1993	18.609	13.1	13.64	−24.0
1994	23.264	25.0	17.95	31.6
1995	20.675	−11.1	21.25	18.4
1996	19.150	−7.4	22.5	5.9
1997	20.184	5.4	21.45	−4.7
1998	21.709	7.6	22.48	4.8
1999	24.468	12.7	25.30	12.5
2000	23.029	−5.9	25.95	2.6
2001	23.179	0.7	21.35	−17.7

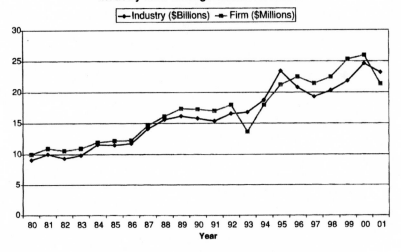

Exhibit 4.4 Comparative firm–industry trends for corrugated box revenues.

performance of the firm. In order for such analysis to yield fruitful results, sufficient historical data must be available to allow the results to be statistically reliable.

OTHER INDUSTRY FACTORS

It is important for the expert researching an industry to be aware of important recent trends that might affect the performance of the plaintiff over the loss period. These factors vary by industry and the time when the analysis is being conducted is also a factor. They also vary from case to case but some of the more common ones are discussed below.

Changing Level of Competition

These include competitive factors such as the degree of competition in the industry. There are several different market structures in microeconomics (also called price theory) that vary in terms of the level of industry profitability and in how price and output are determined. These structures are briefly reviewed in the Table 4.8.

Table 4.8 Alternative Market Structures

Market Structure	Description
Pure Competition	Many small independent companies, each producing a very small percent of total market output thereby making these firms price takers. Assume no product differentiation and perfect information. Companies operating in this type of industry earn what economists term normal profits and no economic rent in the long run.
Monopolistic Competition	Many small independent companies which produce a very small percent of total market output. Assume there is some product differentiation.
Oligopoly	A market where there are a few sellers. As a rule of thumb this can be between 3–12 sellers. There is product differentiation and usually price is interactively determined by competitors' responses.
Monopoly	This is where there is one seller in the market. The monopolist determines either price or output, depending on the structure of the demand curve. Such firms may have market power as reflected by the difference between price and marginal cost. However, just because a firm is a monopolist does not guarantee that it will generate a profit. A company can monopolize the sales of a product where its costs exceed revenues.

If new entrants have increased the level of competition, then profit margins derived from a historical period may no longer apply. In such a case, the new level of competition should be considered when computing the plaintiff's new profitability; greater competition often implies lower profitability.

New Product Innovations

Some industries are very volatile. The computer and telecommunications industry are good examples. Historical data derived from an environment that was unaffected by important new product introductions may not be as relevant to projections made for a period that will include such products. New product introductions in an industry may increase the future sales within that industry. However, new product introductions in other industries could enhance or reduce the sales of the company in question. If more attractive product substitutes have been introduced in another related industry, the future performance of the plaintiff may be adversely affected. Many of the issues that relate to measuring the sales of new businesses, discussed in Chapter Five, are also relevant to discussions of new product introductions.

Structural Changes in an Industry

The expert needs to be cognizant of any important structural changes in an industry. If these changes are significant, they could have an impact on the future of firms in that industry. They may include regulatory change or changes in the distribution channels within an industry. For example, numerous changes have occurred in the carpet industry over the past several decades. The changes affect all levels of the industry. There has been great horizontal consolidation among the larger carpet manufacturers; the market shares of many of the surviving companies have increased greatly. In addition, the industry is now a vertically-integrated industry, meaning manufacturers sell directly to retailers. This has caused the industry position and profitability of middlemen or distributors to deteriorate. Many such firms have gone out of business as manufacturers went direct as part of their expansion process. An expert projecting losses for a carpet distributor would have to be aware of this trend; it limited the market and profit potential of such firms. While losing business to manufacturers who are going direct, revenues may fall and retailers, who now have the option of buying direct, would not be willing to pay the same prices for products. Distributors might have to provide better and more costly service to keep revenues from falling while accepting lower margins on the revenues they maintain.

The 1990s and early 2000s witnessed the fifth merger wave in U.S. economic history.[17] Many industries consolidated as companies merged with others. Some of these corporate restructuring transactions resulted in many efficient companies competing more aggressively.[18] Smaller companies that were not able to take such efficiency-enhancing steps could find it difficult to maintain prior levels of profitability in such a competitive environment. Such changes could be important when trying to extrapolate future results from historical data.

An example of such restructuring occurred in the banking and telecommunications industries. Partly induced by a changing regulatory environment, these industries are undergoing dramatic changes. Both industries consolidated as competitors merged to form larger companies. The structural changes in these industries are manifested on both the national and regional level. The expert needs to be aware of such structural changes and know what impact, if any, they have on the plaintiff and its claim of losses.

YARDSTICK APPROACH AND INDUSTRY ANALYSIS

An industry analysis is a major component of a properly implemented yardstick approach to measuring damages. As described in Chapter 2, the yardstick approach involves finding comparable firms, sometimes called *proxy firms,* which are similar in most respects except for the fact that the proxy firms are not affected by the actions of the defendant. As part of the process of finding such firms, one needs to do some analysis of the industry so as to be able to correctly determine which firms are truly comparable. In fact, it is difficult to apply the yardstick approach without doing some industry analysis. In most cases, the industry analysis is a precursor to implementing the yardstick approach.

Court's Position on the Use of Industry Averages

Courts have favorably accepted the use of industry averages when such use was clearly appropriate. For example, in *Bob Willow Motors, Inc. v. General Motors Corp.,* the court held that the use of industry sales trends was a useful guide to

---

[17]Patrick A. Gaughan, *Mergers, Acquisitions, and Corporate Restructurings,* 3rd ed. (New York: Wiley, 2002), 51–55.

[18]Unfortunately, as with prior merger waves, many of these deals failed to yield true economic benefits.

help project the lost sales of the plaintiff, who was an automobile dealer.[19] In this case, the averages served as guides in selecting the appropriate growth rate to use to project "but for" revenues. In commenting on the expert's reliance on industry data to project lost revenues and profits of Bob Willow Motors, the court stated:

> Strachota (the plaintiff expert) relied on actual sales by the plaintiff during periods when sufficient vehicles were delivered to the plaintiff's dealership by the defendant manufacturer. Strachota further relied on national and regional sales to determine sales trends and market conditions in his efforts to determine those sales which the plaintiff should have experienced for the pertinent periods. . . .
>
> To arrive at a lost profits figure, Strachota took a baseline figure (e.g., for Chevrolet he used 1980 when Willow sold 309 cars) and adjusted it by national sales trends. This assumed that Willow would do at least as well as the national sales trends. (This was not without good reason. From 1979 to 1980, sales declined nationally by 18 percent while Willow's sales increased 83 percent.) . . .
>
> Damages of course may not be speculative or conjectural, but neither are they required to be calculated with scientific precision or mathematical certainty. To calculate damages, Willow had to estimate the number of cars it would have sold—and thus what its profits would have been—had GM not engaged in unconscionable practices.

Courts' Rejection of the Applicability of Industry Averages

Courts have rejected the flawed use of averages when the data were not comparable. For example, in *Midland Hotel Corp. v. Reuben H. Donnelly Corp.*,[20] one of many cases involving alleged losses caused by erroneous telephone listings and incorrect or omitted advertisements, the Illinois Supreme Court rejected the use of data on industry hotel occupancy rates because the time period being used was not relevant to the loss analysis to which they were being applied. However, in this case it was not the use of industry averages that was the problem. Rather, it was the use of averages from one time period to explain losses in another time period; the court determined other explanatory variables had an impact during the loss period and that the industry averages did not reflect these factors. This is clear from these excerpts from the opinion:

---

[19]*Bob Willow Motors, Inc. v. General Motors Corp.*, 872 F2d 788 (7th Cir. 1989).

[20]*Midland Hotel Corp. v. Reuben H. Donnelly Corp.*, 118 Ill 2d 306, 515 N.E. 2d 61 (1987).

The plaintiff sought $1,359,857 in lost net profits from July of 1981 to July of 1984. Net profits from July of 1982 to July of 1984 were sought as the consequence of the residual effect of being omitted from the 1981 Guide. John Jaeger, an accountant and plaintiff's expert witness, testified that the damages figure was arrived at by measuring the variance between the plaintiff's occupancy percentage and the average occupancy percentage of other downtown Chicago hotels as derived from a trade publication entitled, *Trends in the Hotel Industry* (Trends). Jaeger's calculation of lost occupancy assumed the plaintiff's occupancy percentage would have equaled the downtown trends average for the three year period. Jaeger then added the lost revenue from the food and beverage sales as well as lost telephone revenue and deducted from this the plaintiff's variable expenses to arrive at the total lost net profits.

Defendant's expert witness, James Adler, an accountant, testified that Jaeger's calculation of damages was invalid since it incorrectly assumed that plaintiff's occupancy percentage would have otherwise equaled the downtown Trends average. Adler noted that for numerous months prior to July of 1981, plaintiff's occupancy percentage was trailing the Trends average and that therefore there was no basis for the assumption that the plaintiff would otherwise have equaled the Trends average after July of 1981. . . .

Defendant maintains that as the plaintiff's occupancy rate had been consistently trailing the Trends average prior to the issuance of the Guide in July of 1981, there was therefore no basis upon which to conclude that the plaintiff would have otherwise performed as well as the Trends average.

Defendants can learn a lesson from *Midland Hotel Corporation v. The Reuben H. Donnelly Corporation*: a useful defense to a lost profits analysis based upon industry averages may be to challenge the relationship between the industry average and the historical revenue and/or profits (depending on what industry data are being used: revenue or profits). If the defendant can statistically show that there was no historical relationship, then it may be able to challenge the use of the industry data as a predictor of lost revenues. This means that the plaintiff's expert must make sure that such a historical relationship really does exist. If possible, the closeness of association should be measured statistically, and demonstrated graphically through the use of exhibits.

Court's Position on the Reliability of Industry Association Data

The courts have also been sensitive to data quality issues particularly when the data-gathering methods employed by industry associations are suspect. An example of this sensitivity is found in *Polaris Industries v. Plastics Inc*—a case in which a manufacturer of snowmobiles (Polaris) sued a manufacturer of plastic fuel tanks (Plastics). In this case, the Supreme Court of Minnesota rejected the use of data culled from a snowmobile industry association because there was little assurance that the data reported by the association was accurate.[21] In agreeing with the trial court, the appeals court pointed out that some members did not report data, thus making the data a partial sample containing information of questionable reliability.

> Of crucial importance to the plaintiff's proof was the testimony of Joseph Buchan, the director of management services with the accounting firm of Touche, Ross & Co., who had considerable experience with calculating lost profits caused by business interruptions. Mr. Buchan's testimony was excluded almost in its entirety after an extensive offer of proof, in which the witness was examined and cross examined before the court in the absence of the jury. The trial court found the testimony, exhibits, and conclusions of the witness to lack foundation.
>
> The principal objection made to some exhibits used by Buchan and the conclusions drawn from them was they utilized data from International Snowmobile Industry Association surveys which were found unreliable after it was determined that it was not known how many snowmobile manufacturers were ISIA members, how many members reported to ISIA, or whether those who did report did so with some degree of accuracy. Since the exclusion of the ISIA reports was proper, the exclusion of the exhibits that graphically displayed the ISIA data was proper.

The above excerpt reveals another opportunity for defendants who face a plaintiff's damages analysis based upon the use of industry data. Defendants may want to explore the reliability of the data being used for the projection. In addition to measuring the strength of the association between the historical data and the plaintiff's revenues/profits, the plaintiff's expert must make sure that the data are reliable. It may not be reasonable for the plaintiff to embark on an extensive analysis of the industry association data. However, some research should be done to determine that the data were gathered and analyzed in a reliable manner. If the defendant can find, as it did in *Polaris Industries v. Plastics, Inc.*, that the data are unreliable, then the projection itself may be preempted.

The court's position in *Polaris Industries v. Plastics, Inc.* highlights the problems that can occur in using industry association data. The reliability of such

---

[21]*Polaris Industries. v. Plastics, Inc.* 299 N.W. 2d 414 (Minn. 1980).

data can vary greatly. As noted earlier, some associations pay greater attention to the quality of the data-gathering and analysis than others. Some are able to enlist the support and compliance of their members more than others. Sometimes the associations contract out the surveying process to competent firms that specialize in such work. When specialized firms have conducted the surveying and analysis of the data, there *may* be higher comfort level with the data and results. When the association does this work itself, the expert should make sure that it was done competently.

One solution is to have more than one source of industry data. If there is more than one industry association, such as when there are different components of the industry and each has its own data, then these data can be compared. Larger industries, such as the automobile industry, may have several industry subcomponents; some of these have their own data. The trends in these data can be compared for consistency.

SUMMARY

Industry analysis is the second step in the methodological due diligence process. Having assessed the condition of the macro-economy, the focus is narrowed to the industry in which the plaintiff operates. The analysis considers the performance of the industry, which is compared to that of the macro-economy and to that of the firm. As part of this analysis, the growth of the industry is measured and compared to that of the plaintiff. The historical interrelationship between the two can be assessed using some of the same statistical analysis as was used in the macroeconomic analysis. Once again, if the industry is growing and performing well, the expectation exists that the plaintiff would have also done well. However, this is a very general and simplistic conclusion and there may be important factors at play that could cause the plaintiff's experience to differ from the overall industry. This is why industry analysis, like macroeconomic analysis, is but one step in the methodological due diligence process.

In using industry data, the expert needs to make sure that the industry data are reliable. The whole analysis is undermined if the data themselves are determined to be unreliable. One way this can be done is to do some research into how the data were gathered and analyzed. Another form of assurance is to have more than one source of industry data. In addition, if the trends in the industry data are consistent with trends in other variables, such as the macroeconomic and regional (if relevant) data, then this may provide some limited degree of assurance that the industry data are reliable.

REFERENCES

Annual Survey of Manufactures, U.S. Bureau of the Census, Washington, D.C.

Bob Willow Motors, Inc. v. General Motors Corp., 872 F2d 788 (7th Cir. 1989).

Business Statistics of the United States, annual, Courtenay M. Slater, ed. Lanham, MD: Bernan Press.

Encyclopedia of Associations, annual. Detroit, MI: Gale Research.

Freedonia Industry Study Catalog. Cleveland, OH: The Freedonia Group.

Gaughan, Patrick A., *Mergers, Acquisitions, and Corporate Restructurings,* 3rd ed. New York: Wiley, 2002.

Goldman Sachs Web site, *http://www.gs.com.*

Handler, Douglas P., "Business Economist at Work: Linking Economics to Market Research: A.C. Nielsen." *Business Economics,* vol. XXXI, no. 4 (October 1996): 51–52.

The Information Catalog. New York: Find/SVP.

The Maxwell Report, Richmond, VA.

Midland Hotel Corp. v. Reuben H. Donnelly Corp., 118 Ill 2d 306, 515 N.E. 2d 61 (1987).

Morgan Stanley Web site, *http://www.morganstanley.com.*

North American Industry Classification System, Executive Office of the President, Office of Management and Budget, Washington, D.C., 1997.

Packaged Facts, various industry reports. New York: Find/SVP.

Plummer, James, and Gerald McGowin, *"The Ten Most Frequent Errors in Litigating Business Damages."* Association of Business Trial Lawyers (ABTL) Northern California Report (November 1995).

Polaris Industries. v. Plastics, Inc. 299 N.W. 2d 414 (Minn 1980).

Predicasts Basebook, annual. Foster City, CA: Information Access Company.

SIC Code Manual, U.S. Government Printing Office, 1987, Washington, D.C.

Smith Barney Web site, *http://www.smithbarney.com.*

Statistical Abstract of the United States, annual, U.S. Department of Commerce, Washington, D.C.

U.S. Industry & Trade Outlook, annual, U.S. Department of Commerce/International Trade Administration, Washington, D.C.

U.S. Industry & Trade Outlook '98, DRI/McGraw-Hill and Standard & Poor's and U.S. Department of Commerce/International Trade Administration, 1998.

Value Line Investment Survey, http://www.valueline.com/support.html.

5

PROJECTING LOST REVENUES

In most cases, lost profits resulting from a business interruption can be measured by first projecting lost incremental revenues and then applying a relevant profit margin to the projected lost revenues. This margin should reflect all the incremental costs that would have been incurred in an effort to achieve the forecasted incremental revenues. This chapter focuses on the first step of this process—the revenue projection. It covers the various projection techniques that can be used to create a "but for" revenue stream over the relevant loss period. These techniques vary from basic methods to more sophisticated ones. This chapter discusses the court's position on the use of these methods. In addition to the techniques of forecasting, other related issues, such as the data upon which the forecast is based, are discussed. Finally, the chapter details the special cases of forecasting "but for" revenues when there are very limited data, as in the case when the plaintiff is a newly established or unestablished business.

PROJECTIONS VERSUS FORECASTS:
ECONOMIC VERSUS ACCOUNTING TERMINOLOGY

Economists tend to use the terms *projections* and *forecasts* interchangeably. This was purposely done in the introduction to this chapter. Accountants, however, attach very different meanings to these two terms. When preparing prospective financial statements, accountants consider a financial forecast their best judgment of what is going to happen. This forecast can be a range or a point estimate.[1] In projections, however, accountants consider "what if" events and put forward financial data based upon hypothetical assumptions.[2] Several possible scenarios

---

[1]*AICPA Guide.*

[2]Don Pallais and Stephen D. Holton, *A Guide to Forecasts and Projections* (Fort Worth, TX: Practitioners Publishing, 1993), 1-10–1-11.

can be considered in projections. Only the most likely, however, are included in an accountant's financial forecast.

When trying to establish a nonspeculative measure of damages, courts are more interested in what accountants term forecasts rather than projections. Forecasts carry a greater degree of certainty than the more hypothetical projections. However, in economics, the distinction between the two terms is significantly less meaningful. Because damages expert witnesses may be either economists or accountants, it is important for attorneys to know that these two groups of practitioners use these terms differently.

USING GRAPHICAL ANALYSIS AS AN AIDE IN THE FORECASTING PROCESS

The construction of graphs can be quite helpful in detecting the relationship between a business interruption and the performance of a plaintiff, as reflected in variables such as revenues. Graphical analysis can be particularly useful for simplistic business loss scenarios in which an event occurs and revenues diminish around the event date. Such graphs can be visually compelling in court. An example of such a graph is Exhibit 5.1. It shows that around time t_0 an event took place which caused the company's revenues to turn downwards sharply. Forecasting is used when extending the revenue curve beyond t_0 to construct a "but for" revenue projection.

The use of graphical analysis can be very helpful early on in the interaction between the damages expert and the attorney who retained the expert. This is especially true when the damages expert has been retained by a plaintiff's counsel who relates a scenario of damages that is very inconsistent with the pattern of revenues. For example, in Exhibit 5.2, the plaintiff's revenues continue to exhibit

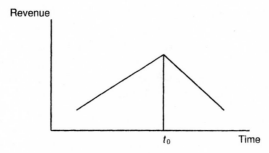

Exhibit 5.1   Sharp downward revenue trend caused by a business interruption.

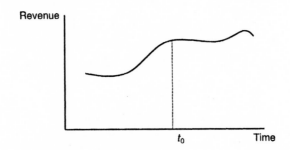

Exhibit 5.2 No clear business interruption.

a very similar growth pattern after the interruption as they did prior to that date. It is often the case that the plaintiff's counsel simply relies upon the client's verbal representations without investigating the numbers. If the damages expert is brought in early enough in the litigation process, he can advise counsel on the strength of the damages claims. Unless there are compelling reasons to believe that the post-interruption growth should have been significantly higher, Exhibit 5.2 may be an example of a situation where proving damages may be difficult.

The previous section applies to very simplistic business interruptions in which revenues are growing at a nearly constant rate when an interruption causes revenues to turn downwards sharply. In the case of growing businesses, however, where an interruption may cause a decline in the growth rate but not in the absolute value of revenues, the impact of the interruption may be more difficult to discern using graphical analysis. In these cases, one can graph the growth rate along with the absolute revenue values. The fall-off in the growth rate is then clearly depicted in graph form (see Exhibit 5.3).

Graphical analysis can also be used to get a quick picture of a possible interrelationship between one series, such as the plaintiff's revenues, and another rel-

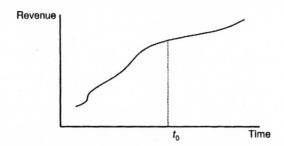

Exhibit 5.3 Fall-off in the revenue growth rate.

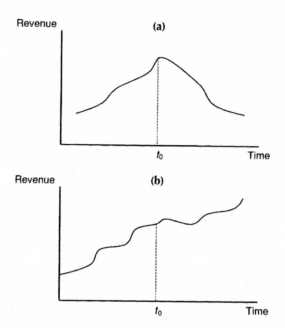

Exhibit 5.4 **(a)** Plaintiff's revenues, **(b)** Industry revenues.

evant series, such as the revenues of the industry in which the plaintiff operates or those of a proxy firm. In Exhibit 5.4 the industry continued to grow before and after the plaintiff's business interruption date of t_0 (see 5.4b); the plaintiff's revenues abruptly declined after that date (see 5.4a).

Graphical analysis is a simple first step that does not necessarily confirm the impact of a business interruption. However, such analysis may be used as part of the expert's demonstrative analysis; it can serve as an exhibit in the expert's initial meeting as well as an exhibit in a report and at trial.

Selecting the Appropriate Revenue Base for Forecasting

It is important that the damages expert focus on the relevant revenue base prior to starting a forecast of lost revenues. This is particularly important when the plaintiff has several different product lines or operates in different geographic markets and when the actions of the defendant only affected certain products or certain geographic markets. Using total sales, as opposed to a more specific component of total sales, was one of several flaws that the court exposed in *William J. McGlinchy et al. v. Shell Chemical Co.*

Worse, appellants causes of action specify that Shell Oil defendants breached obligations and tortiously interfered with appellants contracts and business opportunities involving particular product lines and in particular overseas countries and territories. Jizmagian, however, compiled his report and was prepared to testify on the basis of the appellant's gross sales. He stated that he did not know which of the appellant's product lines had declined in sales, or in which geographic areas—even as between the United States and the rest of the world. Jizmagian's report and testimony would pose a great danger of misleading a jury into believing that appellant's losses associated with a decline in gross sales were the amount of damages to appellants from "lost profits" in particular product lines and territories.[3]

The flaws in the simplistic analysis of the plaintiff's expert could be remedied by disaggregating revenues by product line and by geographical location. The expert could then isolate the relevant revenues and use these for the forecasting process. This does not mean that the expert ignores the rest of the plaintiff's business. Such information may be useful to the expert in his overall understanding of the business. However, when it comes time to forecast losses, only those revenues directly affected by the actions of the defendant should be considered.

Product Line "Spillover" Effects

The discussion in the previous section emphasized that the expert should base his analysis on the relevant product lines and geographical areas that were affected by the actions of the defendant. An exception to this is when there is a business link between the revenues of one product line and the others. For example, if a company uses one product to generate sales for other products, then focusing on just one product line does not capture the sales that were lost for the other products. When this is the case, the expert needs to convincingly demonstrate the link between the different products. This type of argument was made by the plaintiff's expert in *Cooper Liquor, Inc. et al. v. Adolph Coors Company*. He argued that the Coors beer product line served as a loss leader to bring in traffic into the business and thereby led to the purchase of other products. Although the plaintiff's expert argued this, he did not provide any support for this assertion.

The uncertainty surrounding virtually every aspect of the earlier attempt to prove injury and damages led us to remand for further proceedings. Moreover, as we understand it, the theory of the plaintiff's damages expert relied upon by the jury, was largely premised on the effect on overall sales of all products of no longer having Coors as a loss leader. The primary difficulty we have alluded to in this com-

---

[3]*William J. McGlinchy et al. v. Shell Chemical Co.* 845 F2d 802; 1988.

putation (although there were many others) was that it was wholly based upon a decline in bank deposits of about $7,000 between the months of June and July of 1966. We said: "[The expert's] assumption that these deposits accurately reflected gross sales of all products for the period in question is unsupported. Even if they accurately reflected a decline in gross sales, we noted, there was no showing that this decline was attributable to the loss of the Coors account. In other words, regardless of whether Lechter sold Coors at an overall profit or loss, the root assumption of the damage calculation did not demonstrate the necessary causal relationship between the loss of Coors and the purported decline in gross sales. Demonstration of such a causal relationship is vital to a showing of actual injury."[4]

The flaws in the analysis of the plaintiff's expert could have been remedied by a more detailed analysis of the interrelationship between the sales of the different product lines. The degree of rigor required to demonstrate this is dictated by the circumstances of each case. A basic table showing the variation in the sales might be helpful. In some cases, the expert may do a correlation analysis to show the covariation.

METHODS OF PROJECTING LOST REVENUES

The revenue forecasting process can vary from basic historical growth rate extrapolation methods to more sophisticated statistical curve-fitting techniques. Several factors influence the decision of what level of sophistication to employ. The two most important factors are *accuracy* and *simplicity*. Because the methods used must be explained to a judge or jury, who most likely do not have a background in statistical analysis, simple methods have certain advantages. Only if it can be demonstrated that the sophisticated methods are significantly more accurate should they be contemplated. However, the damages expert should bear in mind that sophisticated econometric and statistical analysis are commonly used with success in various types of litigation, such as employment litigation. One can argue, though, that the analytical requirements in such litigation are such that simple methods will not produce the required results and that this is not the case in many business interruption matters. As with many decisions in business interruption loss analysis, the answer is dependent upon the case.

One factor that determines whether sophisticated curve-fitting techniques can be pursued is the availability of historical data. These techniques require sufficient historical data in order for the expert to produce accurate forecasts. If such data are not available, then basic techniques, such as simple growth rate extrapolations, should be used.

---

[4]*Cooper Liquor, Inc. et al. v. Adolph Coors Company,* 509 F2d 758; 1975.

Basic Growth Rate Extrapolation

This is the simplest and most frequently used revenue forecasting method. This revenue projection process can be divided into two parts. The first part is the determination of the appropriate revenue base. In the second part, growth rate is selected and applied to the chosen revenue base to project what are referred to as "but for" revenues. These are the revenues that the plaintiff would have realized had it not been for the events at issue in the litigation.

Selection of the Revenue Base

An analysis of the plaintiff's revenue history must be conducted in order to determine the appropriate revenue base. If the plaintiff has enjoyed a steady stream of positive annual revenue growth, then the appropriate base for the revenue projection may be the last year of pre-interruption revenues. When the plaintiff has experienced both positive and negative growth, the expert needs to apply judgment in selecting the appropriate base. One possible alternative is the use of average revenues computed over prior years, such as the past three years.

Table 5.1 shows the revenue stream of two companies. Company A is a firm that has had a history of uninterrupted and steady growth prior to the interruption year (2000). It seems reasonable that, but for the interruption, revenues would have grown beyond the pre-interruption level. Therefore, it would be inappropriate to use the average revenues for the last, say, three years. Rather, the revenues associated with the last year prior to the interruption—$3,620,500—should be used as the base for the projection.

Table 5.1 Selection of Base for Revenues Forecasts

Year	Company A		Company B	
	Revenues	Growth Rate	Revenues	Growth Rate
1990	2,057,000		2,157,650	
1991	2,270,300	10.4%	2,668,700	23.7%
1992	2,320,000	2.2%	2,920,100	9.4%
1993	2,568,000	10.7%	2,757,950	−5.6%
1994	2,720,800	6.0%	3,059,600	10.9%
1995	2,850,300	4.8%	3,268,900	6.8%
1996	3,087,000	8.3%	3,100,900	−5.1%
1997	3,296,900	6.8%	3,585,620	15.6%
1998	3,596,800	9.1%	3,459,420	−3.5%
1999	3,620,500	0.7%	3,689,600	6.7%
Base Revenues	3,620,500		3,578,213	
Average Growth Rate		6.5%		6.6%
Compounded Growth Rate		6.5%		6.1%

Table 5.2   An Example of a Weighted Average

Company B Revenues	
1997	3,585,620
1998	3,459,420
1999	3,689,600

1. Simple Average (equal weights)
   $R = 3,585,620(\frac{1}{3}) + 3,459,420(\frac{1}{3}) + 3,689,600(\frac{1}{3}) = 3,578,213$

2. Weighted Average (different weights)
   $R = 3,585,620(0.25) + 3,459,420(0.3) + 3,689,600(0.45) = 3,594,557$

Company B, however, fails to exhibit a clear trend in its revenue history, which is of the same length as Company A's. Given the lack of any apparent trend in the revenue data, the simple average of the last three years of revenues—$3,578,213—seems an appropriate base for the projection.

In selecting the base for the projection, the expert may have to choose between the revenues from the last pre-interruption year and an average of historical revenue data. For example, if the expert concludes that the more recent year's revenues contain a greater amount of relevant forecasting information than the more remote years, then a weighted average (which places progressively greater weight on the more recent years) can be used. Weighting schemes may differ depending on how much weight one wants to assign to various years. An example of a weighted average is shown in Table 5.2.

As Table 5.2 shows, the weighted average places greater significance on the more recent year's value which, because it is higher than the others, causes the weighted average to be higher than the simple average. The rationale for placing more weight on more recent years is that the years closer to the interruption date are likely to be more similar to the "but for" years than prior years. Once again, though, each case brings its own set of facts which may not necessarily make this judgment appropriate.

The above discussion is framed in the context of companies that have a long history of annual revenues. For newer businesses, which have shorter histories, other forecasting methods should be used. These methods are discussed in the context of the losses incurred by new businesses.

Selection of the Projected Revenue Growth Rate

One method of projection is to simply extrapolate the historical revenue growth rate. In doing so, it is useful to select a historical period that is similar in length

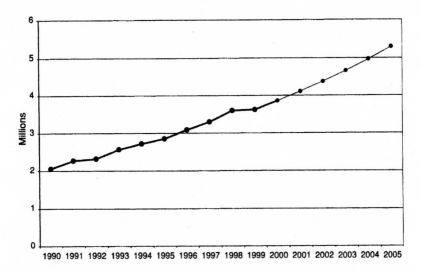

Exhibit 5.5   Actual versus forecasted revenues.

to that of the forecast period. For example, if one is forecasting six years into the future, it is useful to determine the historical revenue growth rate using the revenues for the six years preceding the business interruption.

The compounded annual growth rate can be calculated using the following formula:

$$g = \left(\frac{Y_n}{Y_0}\right)^{1/n} - 1 \tag{5.1}$$

where g = the compounded growth rate
Y_0 = the first period's sales level
Y_n = the last period's sales level
n = the number of periods

Although it is acceptable to use the compounded sales growth rate as an alternative to the arithmetic mean (average) of the historical annual growth rates, beginning and ending points must be chosen with care. There is no assurance that a historical period of the same length as the forecast period is the best predictor of growth over the forecast period (see Exhibit 5.5). Although this rule of thumb is sometimes used, each case is unique; the rule of thumb may not apply. Table 5.3 shows the revenue projection for Company A using the average growth rate (6.5 percent) for the historical period available.

Table 5.3   Revenues Forecast Using Average Growth Rate

Year	Annual Forecasted Revenues
2000	3,857,109
2001	4,109,182
2002	4,377,728
2003	4,663,824
2004	4,968,617
2005	5,293,330

Selecting the Proper Data Upon Which to Compute a Growth Rate

In deriving a growth rate to forecast lost revenues, it is important to make sure that the correct data are used. If, for example, a company has several different divisions or products, using the total company growth rate may be an inaccurate estimate of the historical growth of one particular division or product. It may be difficult to know if the company grows at a different rate than a division if the historical data are not disaggregated and analyzed. This type of challenge was made by the defendant in *Hobart Brothers Co. v. Malcolm T. Gilliland, Inc.* The defendant claimed that the plaintiff's economist used a growth rate for the overall company rather than a growth rate relevant to the business operations that were the subject of the lawsuit, a General Electric plant in Rome, Georgia. The court agreed that this was a legitimate criticism but was satisfied that the expert had adjusted his growth rate sufficiently:

> Hobart fails in its contention that Dr. Deitz used in his calculations to determine damages an 8% annual growth rate as applied to the entire General Electric Company instead of using a growth rate applicable to the General Electric plant in Rome, Georgia. The record clearly shows that Dr. Deitz in his calculations winnowed the growth rate to the General Electric plant at Rome, Georgia.[5]

CURVE-FITTING METHODS AND ECONOMETRIC MODELS

This method requires the expert to define an equation for a line or a polynomial curve which *best fits* the historical data. This line of best fit is placed within the plot of points representing the historical data. The statistical technique known as regression analysis positions the line in the "middle" of these points. From the two

---

[5]*Hobart Brothers Co. v. Malcolm T. Gilliland, Inc.*, 471 F2d 894; 1977 U.S. App.

Table 5.4   Revenue Forecast Using Two-Variable Model

Year	Annual Forecasted Revenues	
2000	3,836,360	
2001	4,017,742	
2002	4,199,123	
2003	4,380,505	
2004	4,561,887	
2005	4,743,269	
Variable	Coefficient	T-Statistic
Constant Term	1,841,160	41.45
Time	181,382	25.34
R-squared	0.9877	
Durbin–Watson	2.0425	
F-Statistic	641.92	

parameters derived from this line—the intercept and the slope—one can project values beyond the available historical data. Regression analysis needs a minimum number of data points to produce a reliable estimate of the slope coefficient, however. Sometimes such data are not available. Therefore, because of a lack of data, the expert may simply decide to use a historical growth rate extrapolation. If sufficient data are available, though, the regression method may either be exclusively employed or used in conjunction with simpler methods. Table 5.4 and Exhibit 5.6 show the revenues projection for Company A, using a simple regression model

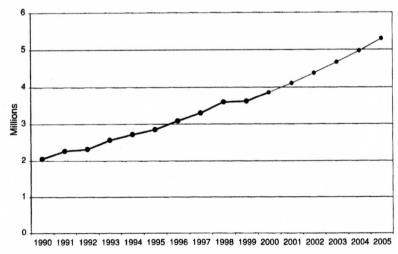

Exhibit 5.6   Actual versus forecasted revenues—using two-variable regression.

which postulates that revenues are a function of time. This form of regression analysis, which uses time as the independent variable, is called *time series analysis*. It is important to note that this example is somewhat simplistic and the forecast that an expert would make would involve the consideration of more factors and a more detailed analysis. However, the simplistic regression analysis considered here, along with a limited but conveniently picked data set, does illustrate the relevant points.

The forecasted values are derived using the estimated regression equation:

$$Y = 1,841,160 + 181,382 \text{ (Time)}$$

When the historical revenue data do not form a clear pattern, simple time series curve-fitting methods do not work as well. A statistical alternative is to construct an econometric model that uses selected independent variables to explain the variation in a dependent variable, which in this case is revenue.[6] However, using a more expansive model may increase the data requirements. Table 5.5 and Exhibit 5.7 shows the revenue projection for Company A, using a more sophisticated model which postulates that revenues are both a function of time and of the industry shipments in the previous year.[7]

Table 5.5 Revenue Forecast Using a Multivariable Model

Year	Annual Forecasted Revenues	
2000	3,873,537	
2001	4,065,415	
2002	4,258,929	
2003	4,454,123	
2004	4,651,039	
Variable	Coefficient	T-Statistic
Constant Term	51,197.70	5.16
Time	151,526.50	12.76
Indshp (−1)*	43,064.38	2.8
R-squared	0.9942	
Durbin–Watson	2.4630	
F-Statistic	600.87	

*In this example, Company A is in the retail appliance business.

---

[6]Carroll B. Foster, Robert R. Trout, and Patrick Gaughan, "Losses in Commercial Litigation," *Journal of Forensic Economics* VI (3) (fall 1993).

[7]This example, with its limited historical data points, is very simplistic. While it simply demonstrates how regression analysis may be used, the contrived numbers we have picked produce results that are "too good" such as the R^2 of 0.99. However, for the purpose of the goals of this section we chose to ignore this.

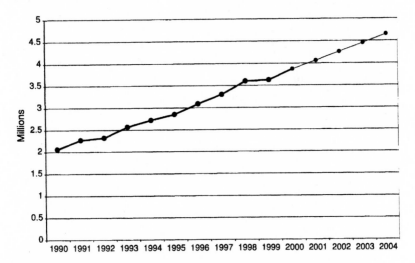

Exhibit 5.7   Actual versus forecasted revenues—using multivariate regression.

UNDERSTANDING REGRESSION OUTPUT AND DIAGNOSTICS

A complete explanation of regression analysis and its diagnostic statistics is clearly beyond the scope of this book. However, a brief review of some of the more frequently cited statistics that are generated by the major regression computer programs is provided below:

R^2 As noted earlier, this statistic measures the degree to which two variables move together. The adjusted R^2 is more often cited. This version makes an adjustment for the number of independent or explanatory variables included in the model or equation. This adjustment is made because adding even irrelevant variables causes the unadjusted R^2 to increase. Users should be aware that while higher R^2s are certainly a good sign, a high R^2 from sample data does not necessarily mean that the model will generate accurate forecasts out-of-sample. The high R^2 may simply reflect that within the sample the regression line fits the data well.

t statistic When a regression output is produced, such as the one reproduced in Table 5.5, the reliability of the co-

	efficients' values is judged by their t scores. Scores greater than or equal to 2 are considered good—meaning that there is a relationship between this particular explanatory variable and the dependent variable.
F score	This score measures the overall significance of the complete model including all the explanatory variables. If the value computed is above a certain critical value, then we reject the hypothesis that all the explanatory variables have coefficients of zero and that the model has no explanatory power.
Durbin–Watson Statistic	This score tells us whether the data are inflicted with serial correlation. This statistic can vary between 0 and 4 with values close to 2 being considered good. Values close to 4 indicate the presence of negative serial correlation; values close to 0 are indicative of the presence of positive serial correlation.

COMMON PROBLEMS AFFECTING REGRESSION MODELS

It is not unusual to see a practitioner blindly use the regression analysis functions of spreadsheet programs to generate forecasts without knowing the reliability of the model and of the resulting forecasts. A review of some common problems that occur in regression analysis is provided below:[8]

Serial Correlation	Also referred to as autocorrelation, serial correlation sometimes occurs in time series analysis when there is some systematic relationship between the error terms or residuals of a regression model. The presence of serial correlation can cause the t scores to be higher than what they would be without serial correlation. This can cause the user to believe that the determined relationship is better than what it really is.
	The presence of simple serial correlation can be detected by the Durbin–Watson statistic. Once detected,

---

[8]For a good, pragmatic discussion of these issues see A.H. Studenmund, *Using Econometrics: A Practical Guide*, 4th ed. (Boston: Addison Wesley, 2001), 389–408.

	various techniques, such as Generalized Least Squares, can be used to correct the problem.
Heteroskedasticity	This problem occurs when the variance of the data changes over the range of the data being considered. The consequences of heteroskedasticity are the same as for serial correlation, in that the t statistics may be higher than what they might be if this phenomenon were not present. Several tests, such as the Park test and the Goldfeld test, exist to detect this phenomenon. Heteroskedasticity can be corrected using certain methods including Generalized Least Squares.
Multicollinearity	This problem occurs when some explanatory variables in the model are correlated. Regression analysis assumes that the variables are not correlated. The presence of multicollinearity creates a problem in the interpretation of the coefficients, as the magnitude of a coefficient could be a reflection of not just the variable to which it refers but of other variables as well. Sometimes the solution is the elimination of the redundant variables. In other cases, however, econometricians simply leave the model untouched as the coefficients are still "unbiased" estimators of the "true" coefficients.
Omitted Variables	This problem occurs when the model leaves out an important variable. The estimates of the coefficients are not as reliable as they are biased. An estimator is inconsistent if, as the sample used for developing an estimate gets larger, the mean of the sample does not approach the population mean.

Lack of Stationary Time Series

Many of the series that we discussed in the macroeconomics chapter were nonstationary time series. Examples included GDP, personal consumption expenditures, and retail sales. A *stationary* time series is one that has a constant mean and variance and a covariance between any two values in the series which only depend on the distance (lag) between the values. A nonstationary time series occurs when there is a shift in the average value of the series over time. This could be the case when dealing with variables that increase over time due to the overall growth of the economy. This is also the case with GDP and the aggregates that represent its components.

This discussion sounds technical, so in order to make it relevant to a litigation audience, it is useful to consider applications that might arise in litigation. One of the problems that occurs in regression when faced with a multiple nonstationary time series is that one may get a seemingly good model when, in fact, the regression model is *spurious*. Consider the following example. Assume that an expert is interested in measuring the losses associated with a group of employees who allegedly breached a contract by leaving their employer. Using historical sales (prior to the departure of any employees), the expert constructs an estimated mathematical relationship between the sales of the "leavers" and "stayers." This mathematical relationship is then used to forecast lost sales post–departure date. In doing so, the expert is assuming that the unrealized sales of the leavers are meaningfully correlated with the actual sales of the stayers. Unfortunately, if during the historical period the sales of the leavers and stayers were both growing (that is, trending upward) due to an overall favorable economy and industry, then the mathematical relationship between the sales of the leavers and stayers may be meaningless. The good fit of the model may be due to the upward trend in both sales series during the historical period, while the sales of the stayers have little intrinsic ability to track the sales of the leavers. This reflects a potential problem associated with nonstationary time series. The problem is insidious in that, at first glance, one might get some impressive regression diagnostics, such as a high R^2 and a high t-statistic for the explanatory variable (actual sales of the stayers in the above example). Yet, the high R^2 simply reflects the fact that both series are growing during the sample period and not that the two are related beyond it. A sign that one may be dealing with a spurious regression is a high R^2 coupled with a low value of the Durbin–Watson test statistic.[9]

The reason why a spurious regression occurs is that the two time series are growing independently of each other; however the high R^2 may suggest a close relationship between the two series that can be exploited for the purpose of forecasting one of the series from the other. A full discussion of the problems of nonstationary time series and spurious regression is not given in this book. However, if spurious regression exists, it can render a seemingly impressive regression as

---

[9]One rule of thumb that has been put forward by Granger and Newbold is that when R^2 is greater than the Durbin–Watson statistic, then there is a decent chance that you have a spurious regression. See C.W.J. Granger and P. Newbold, "Spurious Regressions in Econometrics," *Journal of Econometrics* 2 (1974): 111–120.

seriously flawed. Various tests are employed to detect nonstationary time series and spurious regression. One test for nonstationarity is the *unit root test*, which examines the relationship between successive values in a given series.[10] A related test is the *tau test*, or *Dickey–Fuller test*, which compares the value of a test statistic, τ, to some critical value in order to determine if the series is stationary.[11]

The goal of this section is to make attorneys and users of these techniques aware that the potential problems can make a damages forecast based upon regression analysis invalid. Experts who want to use time series analysis should make sure they consult a skilled econometrician. Attorneys who have retained an expert who uses econometric techniques should inquire as to whether the proper testing was done and whether a consulting econometrician was used (assuming the expert is not an econometrician). Cross-examining attorneys should retain a firm that has a good econometrician on staff. Chances are the expert may not even be aware of the potential flaws inherent in his analysis. When this is exposed on cross-examination, the analysis given by the plaintiff's expert may fall apart.

Example of Other Problems Encountered in the Use of Regression Analysis to Measure Damages in Litigation

As noted above, several problems can occur when regression analysis and other econometric techniques are used to project lost revenues by an expert who lacks specialized expertise in econometrics. Naive users of regression analysis may be unaware of the presence of large forecast errors resulting from limited data or data which are so variable that they do not contribute to accurate forecasting. This happens when the users rely on the regression functions of basic spreadsheet software packages that may not even contain a full set of diagnostic test results which would reveal the presence of a problem, if one existed. Even if the user employed a sophisticated software package, he would need the expertise to properly interpret the diagnostic statistics and implement a statistical solution to any potential problem.

The lack of specialized expertise on the part of the user of the econometric techniques creates an opportunity for opposing counsel to challenge both the expertise and the analysis of the expert. Econometrics is a very specialized and challenging

---

[10]Damodar Gujarati, *Basic Econometrics*, 3rd ed. (New York: McGraw-Hill, 1995), 718–719.

[11]D.A. Dickey and W.A. Fuller, "Distribution of the Estimators for Autoregressive Time Series with a Unit Root," *Journal of the American Statistical Association* 74 (1979): 427–431.

field. It has a rich body of literature and requires a strong background in the field to be properly understood and used. A well-coached opposing counsel can use the rigor of this field against the naive user. The opposing counsel may also use his own expert to explain to the court the flaws of the opposing expert's analysis.

This was successfully done in *Worldcom, Inc. v. Automated Communications, Inc. et al.* In this case, *Worldcom* presented a damages analysis which created a lost revenues projection using basic regression analysis produced by a spreadsheet package. The plaintiff's expert was not an econometrician and his analysis was simplistic and unreliable, in the opinion of the defense's expert, Dr. Larry Taylor, of Economatrix Research Associates, Inc. and Lehigh University. The case involved the projection of lost revenues resulting from an alleged breach of a noncompete agreement and claims of employee pirating. Excerpts from Dr. Taylor's testimony, which are included in the Appendix of this chapter, are quite instructive; they describe a situation in which the plaintiff's analysis was done using a simplistic spreadsheet regression program. This analysis was fraught with some of the econometric problems discussed above, including heteroskedasticity and spurious regression result.

USING BREAK POINT OR CHOW TESTS
TO DETERMINE BREAK POINTS

A statistical technique known as the Chow test can be used to determine if a statistically significant change in a data series, such as a plaintiff's annual revenues, occurred around a particular time period.[12] Although when applied to determine break points the Chow test is used, it is really just an application of the commonly used F test which is a mainstay in statistical analysis.[13]

When testing for a structural change in a time series, which is sometimes also referred to as searching for structural breaks, researchers are trying to determine if the relationship between a dependent and an independent variable has changed over time. In the more common application of the Chow test, the researcher divides the sample into two or more groups, estimates the model separately for each period, and then estimates the model by combining the data for the entire sample.

---

[12]Gregory C. Chow, "Test of Equality Between Sets of Coefficients in Two Linear Regressions," *Econometrica* 28 (3) (1960): 591–605.

[13]Damodar Gujarati, *Basic Econometrics*, 3rd ed. (New York: McGraw-Hill, 1995), 263.

To apply the Chow test, let's assume that we want to test whether there was a structural change at time t_0. We divide the same data into two groups: the data before t_0 (group one), and the data after t_0 (group two). We then estimate the model separately for each of the two groups of data and compute the sum of the squared residuals for each group: ESS_1 and ESS_2. We then can get the unrestricted sum of squares whereby $ESS_u = ESS_1$ and ESS_2. This will have a chi-square distribution when divided by σ^2. It will have $n_1 - k + n_2 - k = n - 2k$ degrees of freedom. It is $n - 2k$ because we estimate the model separately for each group; each equation has k regression coefficients. The next step is to assume that the regression coefficients are the same in the periods before t_0 and after. We then estimate the model again using the entire sample to obtain ESS_R. The relevant F statistic is then:

$$F_c = \frac{(ESS_R - ESS_1 - ESS_2)\,/\,k}{(ESS_1 + ESS_2)\,/\,(n - 2k)}$$

We then apply the Chow test by trying to determine we can reject the null hypothesis that there is no structural change if F_c is greater then $F_{k,\,n-2k}$.

When applying the Chow test to business interruption cases, we may choose to consider the revenue series before and after an interruption date of t_0. We then have to compute the F statistic using revenues before and after this date. We are trying to determine if there is a statistically measurable structural change in the relationship between revenues and the independent variable in the time series model—time. Such a test result may lend credence to the plaintiff's assertion that "something" changed at that time. It is important to remember that the Chow test may lend only indirect support (or may fail to support) the plaintiff's version of events, as it is not capable of proving that the specific actions of the defendant caused the plaintiff's loss of revenues. However, a properly applied Chow test may be one link in an investigation of liability.

CASE STUDY: HOW THE CHOW TEST CAN BE MISAPPLIED

In a case in which a plaintiff distributor sued the developer of software for the pharmaceutical industry, the plaintiff's economic expert applied a Chow test to a time series of the plaintiff's gross profits. Gross profits are the difference between revenues and the costs of sales. The allegation in the case is that the defendant software developer failed to make necessary changes in the program and thus the demand for the software declined. When examining the plaintiff's

Table 5.6   Plaintiff's Revenues and Gross Profits

Year	Gross Sales	Cost Goods Sold	Gross Profits
1986	1,047,001	639,056	407,945
1987	886,563	447,893	438,670
1988	701,733	287,834	413,989
1989	891,484	253,783	637,701
1990	842,312	302,807	539,505
1991	893,109	314,229	578,880
1992	700,420	186,038	514,382
1993	728,792	170,354	558,438
1994	587,241	98,214	489,027
1995	542,241	112,787	429,454
1996	550,909	97,370	452,720
1997	512,991	76,731	436,260
1998	451,169	71,026	380,143
1999	469,307	110,694	358,613
2000	351,766	37,250	314,516

revenues, however, one sees that sales had been declining before and after the alleged breach which was asserted to have occurred in approximately 1994 (see Table 5.6).

When running a regression on the gross profits series, the plaintiff's economist computed a Chow statistic of 9.2126 and concluded that there was a structural shift in 1994 (see Table 5.7).

Given that gross profits are defined as the difference between revenues and the costs of sales, the structural shift could be in revenues, costs of sales or both. Since revenues are driven by demand-side factors and the costs of sales are affected by supply-side factors, it would be quite a coincidence that both are simultaneously causing the shift. Given the nature of the plaintiff's allegation, one would expect the statistical evidence of the shift to manifest itself in revenues—not the

Table 5.7   Regression Output for Gross Profits, 1986–1993

Ordinary Least Squares Estimation			
Dependent variable is PROFIT 8 observations used for estimation from 1986 to 1993			
Regressor	Coefficient	Standard Error	T-Ratio [Prob]
CONSTANT	−4.28E + 07	2.14E + 07	−2.0018[0.92]
YEAR	21769.5	10746.6	2.0257[0.089]
R-Squared	0.40615	Chow Test $F(2,11) =$	9.2126[0.004]

Source: Dr. Larry Taylor's econometric report, Economatrix Research Associates, Inc.

Table 5.8 Regression Output for Gross Sales, 1986–1993

Ordinary Least Squares Estimation			
Dependent variable is SALES 8 observations used for estimation from 1986 to 1993			
Regressor	Coefficient	Standard Error	T-Ratio [Prob]
CONSTANT	6.32E + 07	3.07E + 07	2.0577[.085]
YEAR	−31349.3	15439.6	−2.0305[.089]
R-Squared	0.40727	Chow Test	$F(2,11) = 0.77613[.484]*$

Source: Dr. Larry Taylor's econometric report, Economatrix Research Associates, Inc.

cost of sales. To test this, the economist retained by the defendant ran a regression on revenues and then costs of sales. The results for the revenue regression are shown in Table 5.8

We see that the Chow statistic (F test) for revenues is 0.77613 while the critical value is 3.98. This provides no support for the assertion that there is a structural change. However, the Chow test on gross profits did support the structural change theory. Since revenues are not the cause of the shift, one examines the costs of sales. The regression results for costs of goods sold are shown in Table 5.9.

The costs of goods sold regression reveals a Chow statistic of 4.0260, which does support the assertion of structural instability. Since the actions of the defendant should not affect the plaintiff's costs, we see that the statistical phenomenon detected by the plaintiff's economist is irrelevant to the allegations of the defendant's liability. This result is not surprising and should have been obvious to the plaintiff's economist. Moreover, a review of the plaintiff's revenue history shows that revenues were declining both before and after the alleged interruption date (see Exhibit 5.8). A regression forecast with the limited data shows that perhaps revenues declined more rapidly after the interruption date. The limited number of

Table 5.9 Regression Output for Cost of Goods Sold, 1986–1993

Ordinary Least Squares Estimation			
Dependent variable is COST 8 observations used for estimation from 1986 to 1993			
Regressor	Coefficient	Standard Error	T-Ratio
CONSTANT	1.06E + 08	2.67E + 07	3.9647[.007]
YEAR	−53118.8	13439.1	−3.9526[.008]
R-Squared	0.72251	Chow Test	$F(2,11) = 4.0260[.049]*$

Source: Dr. Larry Taylor's econometric report, Economatrix Research Associates, Inc.

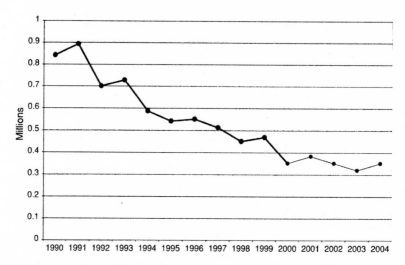

Exhibit 5.8   Actual and forecasted sales.

pre-interruption observations does allow us to place much weight on the regression forecast. However, further industry research does help explain the declining trend in the plaintiff's sales. The software in question was sold to independent pharmacies whose share of industry sales was declining significantly as they lost market share to chains, mail-order businesses, and other marketers of pharmaceutical products. If the plaintiff's economist had done a thorough industry analysis, he may have questioned the results of the statistical analysis. In both respects the plaintiff's analysis was flawed.

Chow tests are occasionally used in business interruption analysis. Such tests alone will not conclusively prove casualty but may be part of an overall analysis. As evidenced by this case study, it is important for users to be aware of how Chow tests can be misused.

CONFIDENCE IN FORECASTED VALUES

Statistical tools exist which allow the economist to introduce evidence on the level of confidence of a forecast. This helps establish that damages are projected within a *reasonable degree of economic certainty*. One method is to construct *confidence intervals*. These are statistical bands that are placed around forecasted values. The bands allow the economist to show a range around the forecasted values which contain a predetermined percentage of the "true values" line.

Within the context of a simple two-variable regression model, the use of confidence intervals can be demonstrated as follows:

Let   Y = the explained variable
     $\hat{Y}$ = the forecasted values of the explained variable
      X = the explanatory variable
      α = intercept term
      β = slope coefficient

$$Y_t = \hat{\alpha} + \beta X_t + \varepsilon_t \qquad (5.2)$$

This relationship can be used to forecast future values of Y. Specifically:

$$\hat{Y}_{t+1} = \hat{\alpha} + \beta X_{t+1} \qquad (5.3)$$

The forecast error is then:

$$\hat{\varepsilon}_{t+1} = \hat{Y}_{t+1} - Y_{t+1} = (\hat{\alpha} - \alpha) + (\hat{\beta} - \beta)X_{t+1} - \varepsilon_{t+1} \qquad (5.4)$$

There are several sources of error in a regression forecast. The first comes from the random nature of the error process, causing the forecast to deviate from the actual values even when the model is correctly specified and when the parameters are known. The second source of error is the use of sample estimates which are different from the true values. When we start forecasting, we add new error elements. We now have to forecast the explanatory variable in addition to the dependent variable. If we relax the assumption that the model is correctly specified, we add still another potential error—misspecification.[14]

The economist in litigation can show that the errors in the forecast are a function of the sample size and the variance of X. The confidence band constructed around the regression line (see Exhibit 5.9) will have a smaller prediction interval when X is closer to its mean (average) value. A 95 percent prediction interval can be constructed from the following expression:

$$\hat{Y}_{t+1} - t_{0.05}s_f \le Y_{t+1} \le \hat{Y}_{t+1} + t_{0.05}s_f \qquad (5.5)$$

(Note: s_f is the estimated standard deviation of the forecast error)

The estimated standard deviation of the forecast error is the square root of the estimated variance of the forecast error, which is defined by the following equation:

$$s_f^2 = s^2 \left[1 + \frac{1}{t} + \frac{\left(X_{t+1} - \overline{X}\right)^2}{\sum \left(X_t - \overline{X}\right)^2} \right] \qquad (5.6)$$

---

[14]Robert Pindyck and Daniel Rubinfeld, *Econometric Models and Economic Forecasts*, 5th ed. (New York: McGraw-Hill, 1998), 204–206.

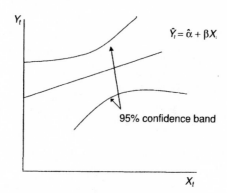

Exhibit 5.9   Confidence band around a regression line.

Equation (5.5) shows that the distance between the regression line and either confidence band is approximately twice the standard error (given that $t_{0.05}$ is approximately equal to 2). Thus, the standard errors of the forecast serve as a guide to the confidence the economist has in the forecast. The further in the future the economist forecasts, the lower the reliability of the forecast. The benefit of this type of presentation is that the reduction in reliability is quantified for each time interval in the future. The confidence band approach, however, is applicable only when the economist has decided to utilize regression analysis to measure lost profits.

Other More Sophisticated Measures of Forecast Accuracy

Two econometric measures exist which allow the analyst to assess the accuracy of a forecast more carefully than when simply applying confidence bands around the forecasted values. These measures are the *Akaike Information Criterion* (AIC) and the *Schwartz Information Criterion* (SIC).

Akaike Information Criterion
The Akaike Information Criterion measures the out-of-sample error variance. However, this measure applies a penalty for the degrees of freedom (the number of parameters to be estimated).

$$AIC = \exp^{\left(\frac{2k}{T}\right)} \frac{\sum\limits_{t=1}^{T} e^2}{T} \tag{5.7}$$

Schwartz Information Criterion
This is a similar measure to the Akaike Information Criterion, except that it assesses an even harsher penalty for the degrees of freedom.

$$SIC = T\left(\frac{k}{T}\right)\frac{\sum\limits_{t=1}^{T} e^2}{T} \tag{5.8}$$

FREQUENCY OF THE USE OF ECONOMETRICS TECHNIQUES IN COMMERCIAL LITIGATION

Although sophisticated measures of forecast accuracy, such as confidence bands, AIC, and SIC are mentioned here, they are *not* normally a standard part of commercial damages projections. This is partly because regression analysis itself is not used frequently. Simple projections using historical growth rates are more commonly used. One of the reasons regression analysis is not used very often is that this type of statistical analysis requires many historical data points in order for the expert to construct forecasts that have statistical reliability. Such data are often not available. These data-related constraints limit the confidence in the regression coefficients and produce very wide confidence bands that would indicate a less reliable forecasting process. Another reason why regression analysis is not used is that the user often lacks expertise.

Multiple Regression Analysis in Litigation

We have mainly focused on time series analysis. However, multiple regression analysis may also be used in loss analysis in the appropriate situations. This statistical technique relates a dependent variable to a group of independent variables in a model that needs to be well-specified. Equation 5.9 shows that the sales of a company, denoted by S, are a function of several variables X, Y, and Z. These variables could include a broad-based economic aggregate, such as GDP, as well as other variables (those which reflect industry-specific factors). The expert econometrician must perform the necessary testing to ensure that the model is well-specified and reliable. An opposing expert also needs to do the necessary analysis to ensure that the model is correctly specified and does not leave out important variables.

$$S = \beta 1X + \beta 2Y + \beta 3Z + \varepsilon \tag{5.9}$$

The issue of the appropriate tests and the reliability of the model can be a source of great controversy as Daniel Rubenfeld notes:

> When courts require experts to utilize "standard statistical practice," such as reporting t tests with multiple regression models, courts have not yet begun to require new techniques that test the robustness of a regression model with respect to some of its assumptions. Assuming that the standard regression model is correct, t tests can help determine statistical significance, but when the assumptions of the model are inaccurate, t tests can substantially overstate the significance of statistical results.[15]

Analyzing Econometric and Statistical Analysis

When a plaintiff or defendant submits a statistical or econometric analysis in support or in challenge of a business interruption loss claim, it is often useful to conduct an independent econometric analysis of the data to determine if the results are accurate and reliable. The econometrician can apply a diagnostic test to determine how confident one can be in the results that the other side has presented. Sometimes, the side originally presenting the results in support of their position does not show certain diagnostic test results that would undermine the position advanced. When being presented with such an analysis, it is useful to redo the analysis and make an independent determination of the validity of the results. It also may be that the analysis of the data presented was accurate but not all relevant data were considered. If such relevant data are added to the analysis, a very different picture is presented.

Court's Position on the Use of Econometric Analysis in Lost Profits Analysis

Regression analysis and other econometric techniques are mainstays in employment litigation involving claims of bias. For example, in *Vuyanich v. Republic National Bank of Dallas,* the court includes an extensive discussion of statistical and regression models with several problems that can occur in applying these techniques, such as misspecification and multicollinearity.[16] While relied upon less frequently, econometric techniques in general and regression analysis in particular have been determined by a number of courts to be an acceptable method to project revenues. Such was the case in *White v. Southwestern Bell Telephone*

---

[15]Daniel Rubinfeld, "Econometrics in the Courtroom," *Columbia Law Review* 85 (June 1985): 1048–1097.

[16]*Vuyanich v. Republic National Bank of Dallas* (D.C. Tex 1980).

Co. where an accountant used regression analysis to project what the revenues would have been in 1978 (the only year in which the plaintiff suffered a loss) based upon the revenue history presented to the court which covered the years 1974 through 1980.[17] The plaintiff claimed a loss due to an incorrect Yellow Pages advertisement. The plaintiff's presentation was buttressed by the fact that he showed that sales through wire services, which should not be affected by Yellow Pages advertising, increased in 1978. The defense tried to show that the purported functional relationship underlying the regression analysis did not exist.

The acceptability of regression analysis in business interruption litigation has not been universal. For example, in *ABC Trans National Transport Inc. v. Aeronautics Forwarders, Inc.* the court rejected the use of regression analysis. This court found that the results of such forecasts were not *conclusive proof of legal damages.*[18] However, in this case, which involved claims that the defendant diverted employees and customers from the plaintiff to itself, the court was troubled by some of the simplistic assumptions of the analysis. Specifically, the analysis, which was performed by a "chartered financial analyst" assumed with a 100 percent probability that, but for the diversion, the employees and customers would have remained with the plaintiff. While statistical techniques exist to compute the attrition rates, these were not employed. Therefore, *ABC Trans National Transport Inc. v. Aeronautics Forwarders, Inc.* should not be seen as a rejection of econometric techniques, but rather as a rejection of statistical methods based upon flawed and overly simplistic assumptions. More advanced statistical techniques have now been introduced into the field which directly address the court's concerns regarding attrition rates and customer tenure.[19] Courts have recognized that the reliability of a regression forecast is a function of the number of historical data points available. In *In re Oil Spill by Amoco Cadiz,* the court stated that the limited number of data points renders the regression analysis unreliable.[20] Other courts have recognized that a misspecified equation or a regression analysis that estimates parameters by relying on data not relevant to the plaintiff's business has *little probative value.*[21]

---

[17]*White v. Southwestern Bell Telephone Co.,* 651 S.W. 2d 260 (Tex. 1983).

[18]*ABC Trans National Transport, Inc. v. Aeronautics Forwarders, Inc.* 90 Ill. App. 3d 817 413 N.E. 2d 1299 (1980).

[19]Laura Bonanomi, Patrick Gaughan, and Larry Taylor, "A Statistical Methodology for Measuring Lost Profits Resulting from a Loss of Customers," *Journal of Forensic Economics* 11 (2) (spring/summer 1998):103–113.

[20]*In re Oil Spill by the Amoco Cadiz,* 1988 U.S. Dist. Lexis 16832 (N.D. Ill., Jan, 11, 1988).

[21]*Micro Motion, Inc. v. Exac Corp.,* 761 F. Supp. 1420 (N.D. Cal. 1991).

Reasonableness of Econometric Results

Courts try to reconcile the results of an econometric analysis using general reason. Judges are not often trained in statistical analysis, but usually possess much knowledge of the law but also a great deal of common sense and experience in evaluating a wide variety of damage claims. For them, the results must make intuitive sense. If not, sound reasons for a counterintuitive result must be given. This was the case when the court, in *Polaroid Corporation v. Eastman Kodak Company*, rejected the econometric analysis of the-well known economics professor, Dr. William Baumol. As the following excerpt from the opinion reveals, the court rejected his econometric analysis and found the conclusions he derived from it to be unreasonable.

> Professor Baumol freely admits that any model is colored by the assumptions upon which it is based and by influences the model builder chooses to include or omit. Although Professor Baumol chose to include market expansion, I have found with few exceptions, that there was no market mechanism unique to Kodak which the facts show could have expanded the market. Although I cannot paint a perfect picture of the market from the testimony of fact witnesses, contemporaneous documents and market research, *I find that evidence much more reliable than even the best econometric model* [emphasis added]. The direct evidence is, after all, the factual basis of the case, not some approximation built on facts. Besides being contrary to the facts, the extreme results of Professor Baumol's model, that Polaroid would have captured none of Kodak's sales between 1976–1978 and only a small percentage from 1979–1983—add to my conviction that it is unreliable. I, therefore, reject its conclusions as contrary to other evidence which I find more credible. . . .
>
> While I do not accept these models in this case, I am not critical of the field of econometrics as a whole. I believe that it can provide valuable insight into complicated matters. However, in this case the models contain assumptions contrary to the facts and achieve extreme results which by their very nature are suspect. Perhaps the inner working of the models, which I cannot comprehend, are biased. Perhaps the instant photography markets does not lend itself to mathematical interpretation. Whatever the reason, I cannot adopt Professor Baumol's model as evidence of market expansion.

SEASONALITY AND THE FORECASTING PROCESS

The issue of seasonality may not be relevant when constructing projections of annual values. However, when there is a need to forecast values within a given year, it is necessary to make adjustments for the fact that businesses often experience seasonal variation. Some businesses have a very distinct and significant pattern of seasonal variation. For example, in the United States retail sales are typically 24 percent higher in the month of December than in any other month.[22] This pattern may be even more pronounced in certain types of businesses, such as toy stores, which conduct a very significant percent of their annual sales in the year-end holiday season. It would, therefore, be inaccurate to annualize a toy store's first five months of revenues simply by dividing the revenues by five and multiplying them by 12. Other more sophisticated techniques should be applied.

Seasonal adjustment is regularly done in statistical and econometric analysis for one of three reasons:

1. For comparison of different values that appear at different points in time to be influenced by seasonal variation
2. For better use of regression analysis without being concerned that the results are being influenced by seasonality
3. For more accurate short-term forecasting[23]

One way to handle the seasonal variation is to use a *seasonal decomposition technique*. With this technique, the historical sales pattern is smoothed or averaged out to eliminate the seasonal variation. This process is sometimes referred to as *filtering*. The seasonally adjusted revenue values are then used to construct a smoothed forecast. The economist can then reintroduce the seasonal pattern to obtain revenue values that pertain to each seasonal period.[24]

One of the most basic ways of smoothing out seasonal variation is to use some type of moving average process. For example, assume that we have quarterly revenue data for a plaintiff and that we want to use the pre-interruption data to forecast the post-interruption revenues. The greater the quarterly variation, the greater the chances that the forecasts are going to be biased by seasonal variation. The expert could try to ignore the quarterly variation by using annual data, thinking that annual revenues associated with the year of the interruption should have some relationship with the prior years—a given level of growth, for example. Unfortunately, an annual analysis is not always workable. One reason is that there

[22]Olivier Blanchard, *Macroeconomics* (Upper Saddle River, NJ: Prentice-Hall, 1997), 159.

[23]W.R. Bell and S.C. Hillmer, "Issues with the Seasonal Adjustment of Economic Time Series," *Journal of Business and Economic Statistics* 2 (1984): 291–320.

[24]For a basic discussion of the seasonal adjustment process see William S. Brown, *Introducing Econometrics* (St. Paul, MN: West Publishing, 1991), 255–256.

may be only a few annual pre-interruption data points and, therefore, the use of quarterly values may add more historical pre-interruption data. Another reason is that the loss period could be confined to some short time span, such as a quarter. In this case, the focus on quarters instead of years may have an obvious advantage.

There are a number of different smoothing techniques that can be used. We have already mentioned the use of simple moving averages. Data on seasonal weighting factors for a wide variety of industries are available from the U.S. Department of Commerce through their Census II program. Other sophisticated techniques, such as *exponential smoothing*, are also available.[25] These methods, unlike simple moving average models which weigh all pre-interruption values equally, apply more weight to the values that are closer to the interruption date. If the expert believes that more recent values have greater information content than more remote values, then an exponential smoothing process may work better than a simple moving average adjustment method. One of the most commonly used exponential smoothing methods is the *Holt-Winters exponential smoothing technique*. All of these methods allow the economist to smooth out the seasonal variation and see the underlying pattern in the data more clearly.[26] The economist is better able to discern the underlying trend in the data, having filtered out the component of the total variation in the sales that was caused by seasonal influences. This pattern can then be used to forecast "but for" revenues.[27]

CAPACITY CONSTRAINTS AND FORECASTS

A common error made in the projection of commercial damages is to project revenues beyond the capacity constraints of the plaintiff's firm. It is not sufficient to merely show that there would have been sufficient demand to support the projected revenue levels. Unless it can be established that the plaintiff had the ability to generate such revenues, perhaps through the use of subcontractors, this projection may be inappropriate. If the ability of the plaintiff to produce the projected revenues is uncertain, then a capacity analysis needs to be conducted. Although such

---

[25]Spyros Makridakis and Steven C. Wheelwright, *Forecasting Methods for Management*, 5th ed. (New York: Wiley), 71–76.

[26]See Paul Newbold and Theodore Bos, *Introductory Business Forecasting* (Cincinnati, OH: South Western Publishing, 1990), 158–218.

[27]Applications of these methods are shown in Robert R. Trout and Carroll B. Foster, "Business Interruption Losses," in *Litigation Economics,* Patrick A. Gaughan and Robert Thornton eds. (Greenwich, CT: JAI Press, 1993).

an analysis may be within the expertise of an economist, it requires an understanding of the plaintiff's business in relation to its facilities and their usage levels.

If it can be shown that in the past the plaintiff manufactured products or provided services at the projected revenue levels, then capacity may not be an issue. If not, other analytical justifications should be provided. This can be done by analyzing the plaintiff's production function. This is the functional relationship between the inputs that the plaintiff utilizes and the output (goods or services) that he produces. Once this relationship has been established, the maximum production attainable, given the plaintiff's fixed inputs, can be established. This production level represents, at least in the short run, the ceiling for projected revenues. When a sufficient time period has passed, long enough for the fixed inputs to vary, then the production associated with the projected revenues may exceed this ceiling.

Each case is unique, so the presence of capacity constraints may not automatically preclude a forecast beyond the plaintiff's current capacity level. To forecast beyond such constraints, however, the costs and availability of greater capacity need to be taken into account. In capital-intensive industries, capacity constraints may present a formidable barrier which cannot be crossed without the investment of significant capital and the passage of the requisite time period needed to expand capacity.

SENSIBILITY CHECK FOR THE FORECASTED VALUES

It is important that the forecasted values be within a reasonable range attainable by the plaintiff. The economist can use industry data to test the reasonability of the forecast. For example, a standard measure of sales productivity in the retail industry is sales per square foot. The average sales levels for retail establishments are provided by the National Retail Merchants Association's Merchandising Operating Results in what are called MOR reports. When the projected sales are divided by the total square footage or the square footage of the selling space, the projected sales levels can be compared with the industry average. If the projected sales levels are significantly above the levels for even "superior stores," then the projected levels should be reconsidered.

Another sensibility check may be to evaluate the *market share* of the plaintiff at the projected sales levels. This involves making assumptions about the rate of growth in the total market which is done through an examination of the industry growth rate. If, for example, the plaintiff had a 2 percent market share at the time of the business interruption but the projections show that the plaintiff would have had a 40 percent market share at the end of the loss period, the reasonableness of the projection needs to be carefully revisited.

One recurrent theme of this chapter is that the uniqueness of each case provides varying opportunities to conduct a sensibility test of the forecasted values. Where possible, such a test should be used.

Forecasting Lost Sales for Breach of a Distributor Agreement

When a plaintiff distributor is claiming lost sales and profits for termination of a distribution agreement, one of the first damages questions that must be addressed is "What are the alleged lost sales of the plaintiff?" In cases where the position of the plaintiff has been taken over by a replacement distributor, the plaintiff may assert that the sales of the replacement distributor would have been the plaintiff's sales. Similar issues arise in intellectual property cases in which an infringer has generated sales and profits which a plaintiff asserts would have been its own. The plaintiff needs to provide some economic basis when supporting the contention that it would have generated these sales. In cases where the replacement distributor had a greater capacity to generate sales than the plaintiff, it could be that the replacement distributor generated greater sales than what the plaintiff would have generated. (Perhaps this is the reason why the defendant hired the replacement distributor.) If this is the case, there are two different sales measures: the sales that the distributor would have made and the higher sales that the replacement distributor made. The plaintiff's losses are the former. When both the original and the replacement distributor have similar capabilities, simply knowing at time of trial the sales that the replacement distributor made assists with the projection of lost sales.

Another type of lawsuit involving a breach of a distribution agreement is a case in which a defendant manufacturer or other marketer diverts sales to itself in violation of an agreement which allegedly entitles the plaintiff to those sales. Sometimes this occurs when a company asserts that certain accounts are "house accounts." One area of legal dispute may be whether the agreement between the parties allows the defendant to do this. If the plaintiff's argument is that the defendant's sales would have been its sales, the lost sales estimation process may involve measuring the relevant sales of the defendant, unless the defendant can show that if it did not make these sales, the plaintiff would otherwise not have been able to complete them. This was the conclusion of the court in *Willred Co. v. Westmoreland Metal Manufacturing Co.*—the plaintiff was able to successfully argue that it would have enjoyed the same sales as the defendant manufacturer of furniture for schools.[28]

---

[28] *Willred Co. v. Westmoreland Metal Manufacturing Co.*, 200 F. Supp. 59 (E.D. Pa. 1961).

PROJECTING LOST SALES FOR A NEW BUSINESS

The losses of a new business may be more difficult to project. However, if the expert responds to this higher level of difficulty by not projecting any loss, he is implicitly assigning a value of zero to the loss. This itself is a projection, and probably one that is substantially less accurate than the best projection an economist may construct.

The cause of the higher level of difficulty in projecting losses of new or unestablished businesses is the fact that such businesses lack a track record. The courts have been very aware of this difficulty—what one court termed a "paucity of proofs."[29] However, the economist may use *proxy firms*, firms similar in many relevant respects to the plaintiff, such as product line, size, capitalization, etc., to derive a growth rate and some information about sales volume and profitability. One has to be careful when ascribing the characteristics of a proxy firm to a plaintiff, however, because it needs to be established that the plaintiff would have truly been like the proxy firms. It is also important to note that the proxy firms are a biased sample of the total population of businesses that were also new at one time. This sample, in fact, includes only those firms which survived some minimum period, including what may be the risky years of initial operation. The risk of failure, which is estimated by using statistics (if available) showing the number of similar firms that have failed, needs to be incorporated into the analysis.

Industries which feature many similar firms selling nearly identical products are better candidates for a failed new business analysis. Franchises, such as fast food chains, are good examples of this. Their product lines are designed to be as consistent as possible and they often have a large number of franchisees whose data may be useful in determining the expected sales across different time periods. Data available from the franchiser may enable the expert to construct a model which explicitly includes regional and demographic factors.

Use of Business Plans and Other Prelitigation Projections

Particularly in the case of unestablished businesses or products not brought to markets, plaintiffs often give projections that are set forth in business plans and other prelitigation business planning. Sometimes these documents are prepared for the purposes of raising capital. As such, they may include more optimistic

---

[29]*Hunters Int'l Mfg. Co. v. Christiana Metals Corp.*, 561 F. Supp. 614 (E.D. Mich. 1982) aff'd, 725 F2d 683 (7th Cir. 1983)

assumptions that help the plaintiff raise capital. They are not necessarily based upon standards that are customarily required by courts—measurable within a reasonable degree of economic certainty and not speculative. The authors of such reports do not prepare them thinking that they may have to go to court and give sworn testimony on the issue. Some courts, however, have accepted prelitigation proposals. This was the case in *Upjohn Co. v. Rachelle Laboratories, Inc.* where the court found a proposal prepared by one of the plaintiff's own executives to be credible for the purposes of measuring damages.[30] Among the factors that convinced this court that the proposal's analysis was credible were the forecasting expertise of those who prepared the projections and the fact that millions of dollars were invested based upon the proposal.

> The amount of Upjohn's lost profits could not have been established with absolute certainty. There is inevitably an element of uncertainty in determining the future profitability of an enterprise which only existed briefly. Our role is to determine where reasonable minds could disagree as to the adequacy of the proof of Upjohn's lost profits.
>
> We agree with the District Court's assessment of the lost profits assessment of the lost profits evidence. Upjohn's proof was based upon marketing forecasts prepared well before litigation was anticipated, by employees specializing in economic forecasting. Riggs had clearly qualified as an expert by reason of his marketing and strategic planning experience. The accuracy of the projections was extensively litigated, and Rachelle presented its own proof concerning the proper calculation of lost profits. The trial court instructed the jury that the law does not permit pure guesswork or speculation as to damages. As for the expenses saved by the breach, the jury was instructed that Upjohn "had the burden of proving that its has deducted its costs from the sales forecasts to arrive at projected profit or to prove that it could not have saved any of these costs." Finally, the jury's award was well within the range established by the evidence. This indicates, as the trial court pointed out, that the jury made its own assessment of the weight of the evidence.[31]

Legal Precedent for Damages for a New Business: Prior New Business Rule

The court's position on new businesses has evolved dramatically over the years. Under the old rule, the courts concluded that damages for a new business were

---

[30]*Upjohn Co. v. Rachelle Laboratories, Inc.,* 661 F2d. 1105 (6th Cir. 1981).

[31]*The Upjohn Company v. Rachelle Laboratories, Inc. and International Rectifier Corporation,* 661 F2d 1105; 1981. U.S. App. Lexis 16698.

"simply too speculative and incapable of being ascertained with the requisite certainty."[32] The courts had great difficulty getting around the fact than there is too much uncertainty when the cost structure and resulting profitability of new businesses are unknown.[33] In summarizing the prior new business rule, this court stated:

> The usual method of proving lost profits is from profit history. It is argued that when a plaintiff is conducting new business with labor, manufacturing, and marketing costs unknown, prospective profits cannot be awarded.

Modern New Business Rule

Under the prior new business rule it was very difficult to prove damages for a newly established business. This changed in favor of the plaintiff with the adoption of an easier standard that is known as the Modern New Business Rule. This rule allows plaintiffs to establish damages as long as these damages are within a reasonable degree of economic certainty. The plaintiffs still face an uphill battle in proving such damages, but under the Modern New Business Rule successful damage claims are achievable.

Franchiser with Limited Track Record

There have been many cases in which damages have been awarded to a new business with a limited track record. In *Lightning Lube, Inc. v. Witco Corp.*, a jury awarded the plaintiff, a franchiser of "quick lube" businesses, $2.5 million in past damages for breach of contract and $7 million in future damages for tortious interference, even though none of the franchisees had been in existence for even one of their ten-year franchise agreements.[34] In reaching its decision, the jury took into account that the plaintiff had entered into 170 franchisee contracts; however, less than 40 franchisees had actually opened business. They used the fact that the plaintiff had received a total of over $330,000 in royalties from these initial franchisees to make a conservative projection of damages over the ten-year contract period. This decision is instructive in that the jury used a limited data

---

[32]William Cerillo, *Proving Business Damages* (New York: Wiley, 1997), 46.

[33]*Larsen v. Walton Plywood Co., Wash,.* 2d 1, 16, 390 P.2d 677, 687 (1964), 396 P. 2d 879.

[34]*Lightning Lube, Inc. v. Witco Corp.*, 4 F3d 1153 (3rd Cir. 1993).

history to project damages for a significantly longer, contractually determined loss period. The standard used by the court was less stringent than what would have resulted if confidence bands had been used to determine whether the projection was speculative.

Construction Litigation Involving a Newly Established Business

Litigation is a common occurrence in the construction industry. Projects can remain suspended in a partially completed state for a significant period of time due to conflicts between participants or subcontractors. One example is when financing providers do not provide the financing necessary to continue a project. Courts have been willing to award damages in cases like this even though a project may have only been partially completed. In *South Carolina Federal Savings Bank v. Thornton-Crosby Development Co.*, the South Carolina Supreme Court upheld an award of damages based upon testimony of what revenues and profits would have been generated from a developer's eventual sale of condominiums.[35] The court relied on the actual records of precompletion sales (the project was one-half sold), anticipated sales (the remainder of the project was projected to be completely sold in another nine months), records of various expenses that would have been incurred, and testimony that the project would have been fully sold as of a certain date.

Another instructive lost profits case in the construction industry is *S. Jon. Kreedman & Co. v. Meyers Bros. Parking-Western Corp.*—a California court awarded damages to a lessor due to the failure of a lessee to build a parking garage and lease it to the plaintiff. In this case, the court awarded damages, even though the construction was never completed, after a consideration of the experience and track record of the plaintiff in this field.[36] In particular, the court relied upon the combined testimony of an economist and a long-term employee as well as partial financial histories and performance records of the parties involved to reach the conclusion that the estimates of damages were not speculative. The employee of Meyers, the cross-complainant and appellant, testified as to the performance and profitability of a similar underground garage operated by Meyers. This is another example of the use of proxy firms to fill the void of a financial history.

---

[35] *South Carolina Federal Savings Bank v. Thornton-Crosby Development Co.*, 423 S.E.2d 114 (S.C. 1992)

[36] *S. Jon. Kreedman & Co. v. Meyers Bros. Parking-Western Corp.*, 58 Ca. App. 3d 173, 130 Cal. Rptr. 41 (1976).

Using Expert Testimony in Newly Established Business Cases

While expert testimony may be invaluable in establishing commercial damages in general, it is particularly useful in cases involving newly established businesses. This is because it is inherently difficult to project damages when only a limited business history is available. In addition to the normal lost profits methodology, the expert may want to present research on the existence and applicability of data of proxy firms. In articulating its reasoning for a departure from the prior New Business Rule, the court, in *Larsen v. Walton Plywood Company,* used expert testimony to bridge the gap caused by the limited data available for newly established businesses. The court stated:

> Experts in the area are competent to pass judgement. So long as their opinions afford a reasonable basis for inference, there is a departure from the realm of uncertainty and speculation. *Expert testimony alone is a sufficient basis for an award for loss of profits.*

In this case, the plaintiff used a combination of damages and industry experts who weaved together a collection of statistical evidence to establish lost profits. This inclusion of an industry expert to buttress the analysis of the damages expert can be a wise decision.

PROJECTING LOSSES FOR AN UNESTABLISHED BUSINESS

Measuring losses for an unestablished business can be even more difficult than it is for a new business. With a new business, there are some data available on the actual performance of the business. It may be possible to compare this performance to other established businesses with a longer track record to try to determine comparability. Even these limited data, however, are not available for an unestablished business.

Legal Precedent for an Award of Damages for an Unestablished Business

There are abundant legal precedents for the awarding of damages to an unestablished business as a result of a defendant's actions. An established track record in the field in which the business is operating is beneficial in convincing the court that the estimated profits are not speculative.[37] This can be greatly enhanced when there are numerous other proxy businesses which share many of the same characteristics as the plaintiff's and which can be used to reliably approximate how the plaintiff would have performed. Franchisees, such as those in the fast food industry, are good examples of the ability to use such proxy firms. This was successfully done in *Smith Development Corp. v. Bilow* where data on the performance of existing McDonald's franchisees was used to show how a McDonald's restaurant which never opened would have performed.[38] In the case of major franchises, such as McDonald's, there are abundant data available on the performance of similar businesses. Moreover, since fast food franchises are designed to be very similar in the products and services that they offer, establishing comparability is not difficult. A final note on this case: up until the trial date, no McDonald's franchisee had ever failed, a fact that helped remove an element of speculation that might have otherwise been present with an unestablished business.

Defendants' Successful Challenges to Lost Profits Claims for Unestablished Businesses

A plaintiff may have to rely on convincing evidence through various sources like proxy firms in order to remove the element of speculation surrounding the projection of lost profits for an unestablished business. Further, a defendant may be able to focus on other factors to show just the opposite—that a projection cannot be relied upon with a reasonable degree of economic certainty. Just like in *Smith Development Corp v. Bilow,* statistical evidence on the success rate of similar businesses was used to show that the projection was within the realm of economic certainty in *Rancho Pescado v. Northwestern Mutual Life Insurance Co.*[39] Statistical evidence, including data on failure rates as high as 95 percent, was used to show the level of risk in the plaintiff's business—catfish farming. Other risk factors were explored by the defendant, including the defendant's inability to distribute the high quantities of the product projected by the plaintiff. In this case, it was shown that only a small minority of firms like the plaintiff actually survive. In such industries, the burdens of proof on the plaintiff may be insurmountable, particularly when the defendant can supply statistical evidence to support the risk

---

[37]*Short v. Riley*, 150 Ariz. 583, 724 P. 2d 1252 (Ariz. Ct. App. 1986).

[38]*Smith Development Corp. v. Bilow*, 308 A. 2d 477 (R.I. 1973).

[39]*Rancho Pescado v. Northwestern Mutual Life Insurance Co.*, 140 Ariz. 174, 680 P. 2d 1235 (1984).

level of the business. If this evidence is not sufficient to void the plaintiff's lost profits projection, it may still be used to show that the high level of risk should at least be incorporated into a risk premium and added to the discount rate.

CASE STUDY: *LIGHTNING LUBE, INC. V. WITCO*

Between 1985 and 1989, Lightning Lube, Inc., a New Jersey corporation, was a quick lube franchiser. This is a business where customers can have the oil in their cars changed or have other minor services done within a short period of time. The owner of the business, Ralph Venuto, negotiated with Witco to purchase Kendall motor oil and to have Witco assist Lightning Lube in the purchase of lubrication dispensing equipment. Lightning Lube, Inc. would then sell oil directly to customers while providing them with the equipment that it represented to its franchisees that it owned. Venuto testified that he turned down another oil purchase and equipment financing deal with Valvoline in order to deal with Witco.

The relationship deteriorated when Witco did not provide Lightning Lube, Inc. with the equipment repayment schedule it requested and when Lightning Lube fell behind on its payments for oil purchases by more than 90 days. Witco placed Lightning Lube, Inc.'s purchases on hold, although it allowed Lightning Lube, Inc.'s franchisees to purchase oil directly from Witco at the same price it sold to Lightning Lube, Inc.

Between 1985 and 1987 Lightning Lube, Inc. sold over 170 franchisees but only 35–40 of them actually opened for business. The failure of these franchisees to open or to continue with Lightning Lube led to cash flow problems for Lightning Lube and to its eventual demise. The reason why the franchisees either failed to open or to continue with Lightning Lube was a major point of debate at the trial. However, the jury was eventually convinced that Witco's actions, such as offering the franchisees free equipment and cheaper oil than what Lightning Lube gave them, constituted tortious interference and helped cause the failure of Lightning Lube.

At trial, Lightning Lube founder and CEO Ralph Venuto was allowed to testify on his revenue and profits projections for the business. Prior to the trial, Witco objected to such lay testimony being admitted; they did not prevail, though, as the court was persuaded of Venuto's knowledge of the business. However, Venuto was not allowed to offer opinion testimony of the kind that an expert might give. Venuto's projection was based upon 117 contracts that he sold for $17,500 each. He stated that each franchise would generate $28,000 in annual royalties. The record reflects that there were 34 franchisees in the first year and that they averaged $140,000 in annual revenues. Using a 7 percent royalty rate, this translated to $9,800 in revenues for Lightning Lube for each of these 34 franchisees. Venuto went on to testify that the first year's performance was 40 percent higher than what he expected. This played an important role in persuading the jury to accept Venuto's projections of the future performance of Lightning Lube.

The defense challenged Venuto's projections stating that he did not account for economic factors, such as the effects of the recession. Venuto responded that the recession might reduce the purchase of new cars but that the declining demand should not affect car service for existing vehicles. The jury was also impressed by Venuto's testimony that Lightning Lube was one of the fastest-growing franchisees in the country.

In the end, Lightning Lube prevailed even though it was a relatively new business with a limited track record. With respect to damages, its success can be attributed to a combination of factors, including its performance during the first-year period and the track record and credibility of its CEO.

SUMMARY

A common first step in the damage measurement process is to forecast "but for" revenues. The methods used to forecast revenues range from very simple to sophisticated techniques. The simple methods, which are the most frequently used, often involve the selection of a base level to which a growth rate is then applied. The growth rate may come from an analysis of the plaintiff's historical growth. Factors that influence the selection of the growth rate include the growth of the economy, the region (if relevant), and the industry. By applying the growth rate to the selected base, a series of "but for" revenues is derived. These are then compared to actual revenues in cases where the business continued at a lower level than in the "but for" revenues projection.

More sophisticated methods of forecasting involve the use of regression analysis to project "but for" revenues. The statistical projection may be based upon a time series analysis, where historical revenues are used to forecast future revenues, or may involve the estimation of an econometric model, whereby future revenues are forecasted based upon a functional relationship between historical revenues and other selected explanatory variables.

If the forecasting process relies on econometric methods, the users must fully understand the intricacies involved in such analysis. This requires having the necessary expertise in using such methods. Attorneys should make sure that their experts either have this expertise or are relying upon other experts who have it. When faced with an expert who uses regression analysis, attorneys need to consult an econometrician, as the analysis can be useful fodder for cross-examination.

This is because these methods sometimes result in deceptive results when misused. A skilled econometrician may be able to determine if the analysis is reliable.

APPENDIX

Shown below are various excerpts from the testimony of Dr. Larry Taylor of Econometrix Research Associates, Inc. and Lehigh University in *Worldcom v. Automated Communications*.[40]

Q. In the context of Mr. X's written analysis—and I think you referred to his testimony.[41] Were you able to determine from the words of the analysis and the figures that he created and so on whether or not he had done any testing? Did it say so one way or another?

A. It was clear to me that Mr. X was relying solely on the goodness of fit measure—that is, the R^2—from each of the models in order to determine whether or not they are good or bad models. And it is well known in econometrics, especially in the time series literature, that you cannot do that. You are not allowed just simply to look at the goodness of fit measure to determine whether or not a model is valid or invalid. He did not go beyond that.

Q. The goodness of fit measure is a statistic that's generated before any testing is done?

A. It is generated from the estimation stage. And it is intended—as a matter of fact, I have developed goodness of fit measures for more complicated models than the one that is being used here. And in all cases, the goodness of fit measure is simply a first glance.

If your goodness of fit measure is low, then you have to question your model. But if the goodness of fit measure is high, well, that's great, but that's only one of the necessary conditions that must be met in order for the model to be considered valid.

The testimony goes on to explain what more rigorous testing would reveal. One of the problems that more rigorous testing revealed to Dr. Taylor was a con-

---

[40]It should be noted that very minor editing has been applied to this testimony to remove perceived typographical errors by the stenographer and to enhance readability.

[41]Given the critical nature of the comments, the name of the plaintiff's expert is not revealed.

dition called nonstationarity that was present in the data. This was not taken into account by the plaintiff's expert and that was one of the reasons why his analysis was flawed.

The Court. Are you saying that you can't make any projections from a non-stationary group?

A. It's very difficult, Your Honor. That's exactly right. There is a big issue in econometrics as to whether or not a series could be estimated or predicted by a strong law like a time trend. So that no matter how far you get off the trend line, there is a law that says you will come back to the trend line. And so no matter, you know, if you work really hard and you network and you, say, increase your account levels to a larger number and are really on a roll, the trend line—the deterministic trend line says that you will automatically—you will just tend to go back to that line.

And the assumption here is that as a group, these 13 individuals will go back toward that line. Now, clearly, you know, in a number of economic situations, including, for example, if we had gross national product and we were trying to estimate gross national product and predict gross national product. We don't think that that is going to be independent of the past.

So with a nonstationary series, what it says is that what you did yesterday and the day before yesterday and the day before that could have a very strong influence on what path you take in the future. And so, therefore, what we are saying is there might be some tendency, for example, to increase your number of accounts by, say, ten or five—just making up these numbers—say five a month. But I cannot actually tell you which direction you're going to be off from that. It could be one month or so that you're up two accounts, another month or so you're down two accounts.

But the whole idea is that I know it's growing, but it's growing in a very unpredictable manner. And that's what we mean by nonstationary. There is no set path. There is no attractor (phonetic) line, say, that this series tends back towards. And that's one of the reasons why with respect to a deterministic trend line like Mr. X has assumed here for the projections from March 1993 onward seems so untenable to me. And it certainly seems to me that in light of what we've learned in the past 20 years in econometrics, that that is something that any serious econometrician would look at.

The Court. All right.

Q. Thank you. Going back, I think you had just said that you found strong evidence of inertia?

A. That's right.

Q. What did you mean by that?

A. Well, exactly what I was saying with regards to the unpredictability of the line. In other words, past errors tend to accumulate. So if I made an error in forecasting the first month, then chances are I'm going to have an error on the positive side. Say if I have a positive error in the first month I am forecasting, I'm going to have a positive error in the second month. There is strong correlation over time. These series are correlated. And that's just simply another way of saying that there is strong inertia in the system. This inertia actually is in the errors. But because of that strong inertia in the errors of the model, what that is telling me is that that inertia perhaps could be better brought back into the model. Let's model this inertia in a better way. And so, therefore, I'm saying that it's made me suspect that we had a problem here in the sense that these two series could have been growing independently of each other.

One of the symptoms or one of the clues in this is that, yes, we did see a higher R square for the first model, .94. As Mr. X indicates, that's very close to one. But I know that if there is strong inertia in the errors, that that tends to bias my R square upwards toward one. Not only do I have an R square that's very high, but I have a low Durbin–Watson statistic.

Well, Granger and Newbold in the *Journal of Econometrics* back in 1974 had a very famous paper on spurious regression, which said just this: That if you have strong inertia in the system in the errors, then you had better look to make sure that inertia could not be brought into the model itself. And this high R square, low Durban–Watson clued me in on that to make me think that maybe this regression was spurious. That, yes, the reason I'm getting this high R square within the estimation period is because both series are growing and it's picking it up. It's picking up the fact they're both growing. But yet are they growing independently?

So I saw this problem. And I investigated it further. And indeed what I found that there is strong evidence that indeed there is a problem here. I think, you know, to best illustrate it, I know based upon these series, I'm getting the sales—the sales of the departing group, and I'm trying to predict that by looking at the control. And what I'm seeing here is that for every account that the control group adds, I should be adding about ten accounts for the departures.

So, therefore, if I just simply look at the growth in accounts and look from period to period to see how many accounts the departing group grows by versus how much the control group grows by—if I just simply regress the growth rates on each other, I should get around ten. For every—for every one unit in the control group, if the control group increases its sales by, the departing group should increase its sales by ten.

However, when I run the regression that I just simply said here on the growth rates in the accounts, what I find is, very interestingly, the coefficient on the control group for this growth model is not anywhere near ten, but rather it's negative .4930, which is extremely close to zero.

Q. Which means what?

A. Which means that it really does not influence the growth rate of sales. Okay?

Q. What doesn't?

A. The growth rate of the control group does not influence the growth rate in the sales group. Even though I would expect that for every one unit increase in the control group, I get ten units over here in the sales group. I'm getting close to zero. There appears as though there is no relationship—no set relationship between the growth in the sales of the control group versus the growth in the sales of the departing sales group. The R square, far from being .94 for this model, which follows logically from the preceding model that Mr. X estimated—

Q. Now, which model are we talking about?

A. Model 1. Okay? Where we've got control group on the right-hand and got departing sales group on the left-hand side. Instead of getting an R square of .94 for this regression, which should have a high R square, if the logic of the first model is correct, I'm getting an R square of .0040072. That's about as close to zero as you're going to find.

Q. And what does that lead you to conclude?

A. That leads me to believe more strongly that these two series are growing independently of each other. And therefore, projecting the sales of the departing group by using the sales of the control group does not make sense. There is also—there are also some other errors.

Q. Are you still in the testing of the Model 1?

A. Just Model 1. There are other issues. There is an issue here with respect to the functional form.

Q. What is that?

A. Functional form just is—let me give you an example. You could have Y is equal to A plus B times X. Or you could have the model, the square root of Y is equal to A plus B times X. Or some other functional form. In other words, you are just simply changing the mathematical relationship between the dependent variable Y and the independent variable X. It entails no new information here. Oh, and by the way, I want to make it clear that in reading Mr. X's testimony, it is absolutely clear to me that he does not understand this issue.

Q. Why do you say that?

A. Because his statement there is to the effect that the reason we do a misspecification test is to check for omitted variables. That's essentially what he is saying, is there should be other variables in the equation that we do not find. Well, clearly, a functional form test is not a test for omitted variables, not at all.

We're just simply saying whether or not the mathematical relationship between the two variables has been specified properly. The test for inertia in the disturbances is not a test for omitted variables. We just simply have to correct for the inertia in the system. The normality test is the same way. The heteroskedasticity—

The Court. Not too fast now?

A. I'm sorry.

The Court. Okay.

A. The heteroskedasticity test suggests that the spread of the disturbances is changing over time, either increasing or decreasing. That involved absolutely no additional information than what you already have at your disposal in order to attempt to correct the problem. The test for normality is similar. We can actually use techniques to correct that particular problem, again without trying to go and search for additional information.

The only thing then that I am pointing out is that conditional upon your information set, conditional upon the variables that you have in your model, there are problems that you can correct without actually trying to access additional data. And Mr. X clearly does not understand this issue from his testimony.

Q. How did you—I am sorry. Were you going to say something else?

A. Well, I can go on and point out some other tests that Mr. X's models fail, but—in particular a structural change test. But I think I will delay that because the same criticism applies to the second model in the business as usual framework. So I think I will delay.

Q. How did you detect this strong evidence of inertia in Model 1 you mentioned before?

A. There are two tests. First is the low Durbin–Watson test. Durbin–Watson is a very standard test that has been around since about, I would say, in the mid-fifties, maybe the early sixties. And it's a test that we inform all of our undergraduates to look at when they are trying to decide whether or not their model is correctly specified and whether or not they can interpret the regression output correctly.

And that was one of the biggest clues was that this Durbin–Watson value was clearly in the unacceptable region. And for that reason, I thought about looking at the inertia issue. There is also another test which directly tests for serial correlation. And this test rejected at the 10 percent significance level.

So, again, there was evidence that I should be looking in this particular regression direction in order to determine whether or not the information that Mr. X had had been used in an optimal fashion.

Q. Are you saying that there were some preliminary tests that you performed that generated results that caused you, as an expert econometrician, to know that you needed to look further and perform additional—

A. That's right. This is the same iterative process that we discussed before. That when you get to the testing stage, that regardless of what model you have in the conceptual stage, that if you are in your testing stage and you realize that something is wrong, then you have to iterate back and think through the conceptual stage again as to what might be wrong—how might you correct the model so that it does pass the necessary conditions for it to be a good econometric model.

Q. Based on the testing you performed, did Model 1 pass the necessary tests for it to be a good econometric model?

A. Not at all.

Q. Now, you did some testing with respect to Model 2?

A. Model 2, I had some similar issues. This gets back to the idea of whether or not I could have a deterministic time trend so that I have this law which says that regardless or how far I get away from the trend line, that I will always go back to it eventually versus this idea of a nonstationary process where I have strong inertia and such that I know that if I had done well last month, this might help me to do well this month in term of my sales.

And clearly, it's something worthy of testing. And again, I found that under the business as usual second model, that there is very, very strong evidence of serial correlation in the disturbances even more so than in Model 1. There is strong evidence of a functional form problem. And moreover, there is evidence that there is a structural break in the time series model itself.

In other words, we have a time series line with a variable slope. There is evidence that even within the estimation period, that first period that we see from January 1992 up to February 1993, that the trend line is actually changing its slope. And the way that I did that was I actually estimated the trend line based upon the first 11 observations, the first 11 months. And then I used the last three months in order to construct the test.

Essentially what it's telling me is that there is some sort of structural break; and therefore, the model does not predict well even within the estimation period. So if the model does not predict well even within the estimation period—that is, January 1992 to February 1993—then it's very, very hard to understand how in the world we could rely on these predictions thereafter.

Q. Did you do any other tests with respect to Model 2 besides the ones you've described so far?

A. Just the Chow (phonetic) test, the one—the structural shift, the serial correlation test and functional form test. I did do other tests. The normality and the heteroskedasticity tests actually passed. And so I wasn't particularly concerned about those issues.

Q. Is the fact that Model 2 passed a couple of tests significant?

A. It doesn't work that way. If one of these tests rejects, then you need to investigate further. It's not—it's not one of these issues where it passed three out of four tests or it passed two out of four tests. So, therefore, I'm doing pretty well. You need to at least investigate as to why the test is failing.

And as I said, I think that I discovered—and I do have the supporting evidence to indicate that I do not have a deterministic time trend, but I have more of a nonstationary process. Or at least if not a nonstationary process, at least a process where I can say that my current sales depends upon my previous sales and/or accounts. Okay? And that's important. That is a very important issue because it gets back to the idea of projection and the reliability of my projections.

In its opinion, the court accepted Dr. Taylor's analysis. The court's opinion was stated as follows:

Dr. Taylor's testimony persuaded this court that there are problems with Mr. X's models which render the models inadequate for the determination of lost profits argued by the plaintiff. Overall this court is troubled by Mr. X's models being based in part supposedly upon Mr. X's personal experiences. For instance, Mr. X explained that he first calculated lost profits for a period of two years because this was the remaining duration of the noncompete agreements. Then, says Mr. X, the period was changed to three years based upon his personal estimate of the situation.

Furthermore, Mr. X failed to follow econometric principles when setting up his models. On cross-examination, Mr. X admitted that he simply has extended the historic trend of Y's operations as the "business as usual" line without taking any other factors into account such as market saturation, competition, or the ordinary attrition and replacement of Y's sales representatives. The court had difficulty accepting

Mr. X's presumption that the approximately six-month period in which it took Worldcom to recover must be translated into a three year period of damages based on the speculative upward trend of the "business as usual" line in the second and third charts presented.

Finally, Mr. X's models fail econometric tests for consistency, allow for changes in methodology, and ignore market factors crucial to their integrity.

REFERENCES

ABC Trans National Transport, Inc. v. Aeronautics Forwarders, Inc. 90 Ill. App. 3d 817 413 N.E. 2d 1299 (1980).

AICPA Guide.

Bell, W.R., and S.C. Hillmer, "Issues with the Seasonal Adjustment of Economic Time Series," *Journal of Business and Economic Statistics* 2 (1984): 291–320.

Blanchard Olivier, *Macroeconomics.* Upper Saddle River, NJ: Prentice-Hall, 1997.

Bonanomi, Laura, Patrick A. Gaughan, and Larry Taylor, "A Statistical Methodology for Measuring Lost Profits Resulting from a Loss of Customers," *Journal of Forensic Economics* 11 (2) (spring/summer 1998): 103–113.

Brown, William S., *Introducing Econometrics.* St. Paul, MN: West Publishing, 1991.

Cerillo, William, *Proving Business Damages.* New York: Wiley, 1997.

Chow, Gregory C., "Test of Equality Between Sets of Coefficients in Two Linear Regressions," *Econometrica* 28 (3) (1960).

Cooper Liquor, Inc. et al. v. Adolph Coors Company, 509 F2d 758; 1975.

Dickey, D.A., and W.A. Fuller, "Distribution of the Estimators for Autoregressive Time Series with a Unit Root," *Journal of the American Statistical Association* 74 (1979): 427–431.

Foster, Carroll, B., Robert R. Trout, and Patrick A. Gaughan, "Losses in Commercial Litigation." *Journal of Forensic Economics* VI (3) (fall 1993).

Granger, C.W.J., and P. Newbold, "Spurious Regressions in Econometrics, *Journal of Econometrics* (2) (1974): 111–120.

Gujarati, Damodar, *Basic Econometrics*, 3rd ed. New York: McGraw-Hill, 1995.

Hobart Brothers Co., v. Malcolm T. Gillilard, Inc., 471 F2d 894; 1977 U.S. App.

Hunters Int'l Mfg. Co. v. Christian Metals Corp., 561 F. Supp.614 (E.D. Mich. 1982) aff'd 725 F2d 683 (7th Cir. 1983).

In re Oil Spill by the Amoco Cadiz, 1988 U.S. Dist. Lexis 16832 (N.D. Ill., January 11, 1988).

Larsen v. Walton Plywood Co., Wash. 2d 1, 16, 390 P. 2d 677, 687 (1964), 396 P. 2d 879.

Lightning Lube, Inc. v. Witco Corp., 4 F3d 1153 (3rd Cir. 1993).

Makridakis, Spyros, and Steven C. Wheelwright, *Forecasting Methods for Management*, 5th ed. New York: Wiley.

Micro Motion, Inc. v. Exac Corp., 761 F. Supp.1420 (N.D. Cal 1991).

Newbold, Paul, and Theodore Bos, *Introductory Business Forecasting*. Cincinnati, OH: South Western Publishing, 1990.

Pallais, Don, and Stephen D. Holton, *A Guide to Forecasts and Projections*. Fort Worth, TX: Practitioners Publishing, 1993.

Pindyck, Robert, and Daniel Rubinfeld, *Econometric Models and Economic Forecasts*, 5th ed. New York: McGraw-Hill, 1998.

Rancho Pescado v. Northwestern Mutual Life Insurance Co., 140 Ariz 174, 680 P. 2d 1235 (1984).

Ramanathan, Ramu, *Introductory Econometrics*. Fort Worth, TX: Dryden Press, 1995.

Rubinfeld, Daniel, "Econometrics in the Courtroom," *Columbia Law Review* 85 (June 1985).

S. Jon. Kreedman & Co. v. Meyers Bros. Parking-Western Corp., 58 Ca. App. 3d 173, 130 Cal. Rptr. 41 (1976).

Short v. Riley, 150 Ariz. 583, 724 P. 2d 1252 (Ariz. Ct. App. 1986).

Smith Development Corp. v. Bilow, 308 A. 2d 477 (R.I. 1973).

South Carolina Federal Savings Bank v. Thornton-Crosby Development Co., 423 S.E.2d 114 (S.C. 1992)

Studenmund, A.H., *Using Econometrics: A Practical Guide*, 4th ed. Boston: Addison Wesley, 2001.

Trout, Robert R., and Carroll B. Foster, "Business Interruption Losses," *Litigation Economics*, Patrick A. Gaughan and Robert Thornton eds. Greenwich, CT: JAI Press, 1993.

Upjohn Company v. Rachelle Laboratories, Inc., 661 F2d 1105 (6th cir. 1981).

The Upjohn Company v. Rachelle Laboratories, Inc. and International Rectifier Corporation, 661 F2d 1105; 1981. U.S. App. Lexis 16698.

Vuyanick v. Republic National Bank of Dallas, (D.C. Tex 1980).

White v. Southwestern Bell Telephone Co., 651 S.W.2d 260 (Tex. 1983).

William J. McGlinchy et al. v. Shell Chemical Co., 845 F2d 802; 1988.

Willred Co. v. Westmoreland Metal Manufacturing Co., 200 F. Supp 59 (E.D. Pa. 1961).

6

COST ANALYSIS AND PROFITABILITY

In the typical lost profits analysis, certain costs are deducted from projected revenues. This analysis often employs a combination of skills and may involve the interaction of economists and accountants. A common area of analysis for economists working in the field of microeconomics is the relationship between revenues and costs. Much economic research has been done on the various types of costs analysis, including the separation of variable and fixed costs, how costs vary over time, and the relationship between average and marginal costs. For most economists, this analysis is a theoretical exercise, although practicing litigation economists working on commercial damages necessarily deal with these issues on a regular basis.

Accountants, particularly cost accountants, are regularly involved in the pragmatic measurement of costs and how they vary with the operations of the firm. Accountants who report on financial statements for public use must understand issues involving consolidation of financial entities, the components of various costs in financial statements, and various costing methods, all of which have a significant influence on the reported profitability of the firm.[1] Therefore, the services of accountants can be invaluable in computing the costs associated with lost incremental revenues.

---

[1]For a discussion on the role of accountants in commercial damage analysis which emphasize the strengths of accountants see Elizabeth Evans, "Interaction Between Accountants and Economists," in *Litigation Services Handbook: The Role of the Financial Expert*, 3rd ed., Roman Weil, Michael Wagner, and Peter B. Frank, eds. (Wiley, 2001), 3.1–3.20.

PRESENTATION OF COSTS ON THE COMPANY'S FINANCIAL STATEMENTS

An examination of the appropriate expenses to be deducted from projected revenues begins with a review of the company's financial statements—especially the income statements, which list gross revenues and the various cost deductions necessary to arrive at net income. An example of a typical consolidated income statement is presented in Table 6.1. It shows the total revenues and costs of Philip Morris Companies during the calender year 2002.

In the right-hand column of Table 6.1, the cost components of the income statement are expressed as a percentage of revenues. Such an expression is often used in financial analysis for what is known as *percentage of sales forecasting*.[2]

Table 6.1 Consolidated Statement of Income of Altria Group

(in millions of dollars) for the year ended in December 31,	2002	% of Sales
Net Revenues	$80,408	100.00
Cost of Sales	32,748	40.73
Excise Tax on Products	18,226	22.67
Gross Profit	29,434	36.61
Marketing, administration, and research costs	12,282	15.27
Gains on sales of businesses	(80)	−0.10
Integration costs and a loss on sale of a food factory	111	0.14
Separation programs and asset impairments	223	0.28
Provision for airline industry exposure	290	0.36
Amortization of intangibles	7	0.01
Operating Income	16,601	20.65
Gain on Miller Brewing Company transaction	(2,631)	-3.27
Interest and other debt expenses, net	1,134	1.41
Earnings before income taxes, minority interest, and and cumulative effect of accounting change	18,098	22.51
Provision for income taxes	6,424	7.99
Earnings before minority interest and cumulative effect of accounting change	11,674	14.52
Minority interest in earnings and other, net	572	0.71
Earnings before cumulative effect of accounting change	11,102	13.81
Net earnings	$11,102	13.81

[2]Eugene Brigham and Philip R. Davies, *Intermediate Financial Management*, 7th ed. (New York: Thomson South-Western, 2002), 262–273.

The expression of costs as a percent of revenues can be very helpful for quickly discerning the average relationship between a company's revenues and its specific costs. This, in turn, can be useful when attempting to apply a cost percentage to projected revenues. However, considerable care needs to be used when employing such percentages, as they imply that all costs are variable; in reality, though, some are variable and some are not. A "percentage of sales" representation merely shows all costs as a percent of revenues regardless of whether they are fixed or variable. As is discussed later in this chapter, the distinction between fixed and variable costs depends on the time interval being considered.

MEASURES OF COSTS

A preliminary step in understanding cost analysis is defining some basic terms. Often these terms are used interchangeably although they can have different meanings in different contexts. To avoid confusion, these basic terms are defined in Table 6.2.

Table 6.2   Cost Definitions

Fixed Costs	These are costs that do not vary with output. As the time interval under consideration varies, as when moving from the market period to the short-run and to the long-run, costs that were once considered fixed become variable.* Examples are plants and equipments which are fixed in the short-run but can be variable in the long-run.
Variable Costs	These are costs that vary with output. Examples include labor or materials.
Total Costs	The sum of fixed and variable costs.
Average Costs	Total costs divided by output. This value will vary depending on how total costs change as output changes.
Marginal Costs	These are the added costs of producing an additional unit of output. This concept is used more by economists than by accountants. Marginal cost is a key concept in microeconomic theory where it is used in conjunction with marginal revenue to derive the profit maximizing output level of a firm.
Incremental Costs	These are costs incurred over a certain range of output caused by a change in business activity.
Out-of-Pocket Costs	These are costs for which there has been a cash outlay.
Sunk Costs	These are costs that have already been expended. This concept has particular significance in economics in that sunk costs should not affect decision making as such decisions should be made at the margin. An example could be research and development expenditures.

*The market period is an economic concept. It is a time period so short that there can be no change in output. The length of the various time periods, such as the market period, the short-run, and the long-run vary by industry.

PROFIT MARGINS AND PROFITABILITY

There are several different profit margins which are regularly used in financial analysis. Among the most frequently cited are the *gross margin,* defined as sales minus costs of sales divided by sales, the *operating margin*, defined as earnings before interest and taxes (EBIT) divided by sales, and the *net margin,* defined as earnings after taxes divided by sales. These margins differ from each other in that they incorporate different cost components. The gross margin includes the fewest costs (costs of goods sold only) while the net margin incorporates all costs including taxes. Although these margins are the ones most often cited in financial analysis, none of these coincides with the precise margin that is used in a business interruption lost profits analysis.

APPROPRIATE MEASURE OF PROFITABILITY FOR A LOST PROFITS ANALYSIS

The true economic losses of a firm are its *lost incremental revenues minus the incremental costs associated with these revenues.* The margin associated with these lost incremental revenues is usually less than or equal to the *gross margin,* but is greater than or equal to the *net margin.* In effect, the lost incremental revenues minus the associated incremental costs becomes the definition of net profits appropriate to commercial damages litigation.[3] There are abundant legal precedents to support the proposition that gross incremental revenues without a deduction for the costs that would have been incurred to achieve these revenues are an invalid measure of damages.[4]

> In order to prove lost profits a party must prove income and expenses of the business for a reasonable time prior to the alleged breach [cites omitted]. If the party present evidence only of gross receipts or fails to prove expenses with some specificity, an award of damages relating to lost profits will be reversed [cites omitted]. While an inability to prove an exact or precise amount will not preclude recovery

---

[3]See Robert L. Dunn, *Recovery of Damages for Lost Profits,* 4th ed., vol. II (Westport, CT: Lawpress, 1992), 354–383; and William A. Cerillo, *Proving Business Damages* (Santa Ana: CA, James Publishing, 1989), 1-18–1-19.

[4]*Clayton v. Howard Johnson Franchise Systems, Inc.,* 954 F2d 645 652 (11th Cir. 1992) and *General Devices v. Bacon,* 888 S.W. 2d 497 (Tex. App. 1994).

[cites omitted], the evidence must establish lost profits with reasonable certainty such that an impartial and prudent mind would be satisfied.[5]

Other cases show that even gross profits, which do not include all the relevant costs associated with the lost incremental revenues, are also an inaccurate measure of damages.[6] The court wording in *Lee v. Durango Music* is instructive.

> . . . the word profits has a definite meaning. It means the net earnings, or the excess of returns over expenditures, and relates to any excess which remains after deducting from the returns the operating expenses and depreciation of capital, and also, in the proper case, interest on the capital employed. "Profit" in the ordinary acceptation of the law, is the benefit or advantage remaining after all costs, charges, and expenses have been deducted from the income, because, until then, and while anything remains uncertain, it is impossible to say whether or not there has been a profit.[7]

In cases involving a breach of contract, lost profits are the lost revenues from the contract minus the costs of performance. These costs may in general be considered as "savings" to the plaintiff in that the plaintiff did not have to expend them. This, however, is not always the case. If the plaintiff incurred certain costs for items which could not be utilized for other revenue-generating activities, then this may be another element of loss.

CASE STUDY:
COST ANALYSIS IN BUSINESS INTERRUPTION*

The measurement of economic damages in a business interruption lawsuit requires that there be a determination not only of the potential lost gross revenue but the related incremental costs of supporting that revenue. Incremental costs in this context mean the variable costs of the company. Variable costs are costs which, by definition, vary in direct proportion to a certain level of activity, usually defined as sales revenue.

The cost structure of most companies includes both variable and fixed costs. Fixed costs are costs that remain relatively constant (within a certain range) regardless of changes in the level of activity. Since fixed costs do not change with

---

*Case study developed by Professor Henry Fuentes.

[5]*Clayton v. Howard Johnson Franchise Systems, Inc.* 954 F2d 645 652 (11th Cir. 1992) and *General Devices v. Bacon*, 888 S.W. 2d 497 (Tex. App. 1994).

[6]*Graphics Directions, Inc. v. Bush*, 862 P.2d. 1020 (Colo. Ct. App. 1993).

[7]*Lee v. Durango Music*, 355 P. 2d, 1083, 1088, (Colo. 1960.)

variations in sales volume, such costs usually are not considered when measuring lost incremental profits. Although some costs lend themselves fairly easily to classification as either variable or fixed, others do not. Rental expense is an example of a fixed cost: it stays the same regardless of sales activity unless there is a dramatic increase in production or new product lines requiring new facilities. In this case, old cost structures are probably not appropriate.

Similarly, costs such as the material used in a product are easily identified as variable costs. However, there are some costs that have fixed and variable elements, and these may present some difficulty in being classified as either fixed or variable. An example of this type of cost would be repair and maintenance staff. In order to maintain and repair machinery a repairman must be kept on staff even if the machinery does not require repairs in a given time period. As the number of machines or the number of shifts that they run increases, however, it becomes too much work for one person and additional repairmen are needed.

There are also occasions where variable costs may not apply to an entire customer base but only to specific customers. For example, a business may pay commissions on sales to specific customers but pay no commissions on sales to other customers. In determining losses for specific customers, it may be necessary to isolate those variable costs which pertain to specific customers.

As a final comment on the issue of fixed versus variable costs, it should not be assumed that costs classified as cost of goods sold are all variable costs. Although many of the direct costs in cost of goods sold (material and direct labor) are considered variable, there are a number of costs in manufacturing overhead which are fixed. Conversely one cannot consider all other operating costs as fixed, as there may be both fixed and variable costs in other operating expenses (selling, general, and administrative).

Example 1 shows the allocation of the cost structure of a company into its fixed and variable components. The first column represents the revenue and costs per the financial statements. Columns two and three are allocations of all costs that are variable, and column four lists the fixed costs. At the bottom of the exhibit are a variable cost percentage and an incremental profit percentage which can be applied to lost revenue data. The exhibit reiterates the following issues.

- Some variable costs are attributable only to specific customers. In the illustration, commissions and freight (both variable costs) are only attributable to Customer X
- There are certain costs in cost of goods sold that contain both fixed and variable elements such as salaries, payroll taxes, and benefits
- Allocating salaries between fixed and variable will also necessitate allocating related charges such as payroll taxes, pension, etc.

Example 1   ABC Management Services Statement of Operations

	Per Financial Statements	Variable Customer X	Variable Other Customers	Fixed Costs
Sales	3,675,669	3,675,669	3,675,669	
Cost of Goods Sold				
Salaries	973,526	417,000	417,000	556,526
Commissions	568,602	568,602	0	0
Programming & Support	251,054			251,054
Service Center Fees	229,790	229,790	229,790	0
Agency Fees	227,065	227,065	227,065	0
Consulting Fees	76,638	76,638	76,638	0
Freight	61,750	61,750	0	0
Operating Expenses				
Officer Salaries	243,000	0	0	243,000
Professional Fees	142,721	0	0	142,721
Travel & Entertainment	126,305	126,305	126,305	0
Telephone, Telex, Courier Data Transmission, etc.	108,867	102,867	102,867	6,000
Rent	108,552	0	0	08,552
Employee Benefits	97,764	33,511	33,511	64,253
Payroll Taxes	84,827	29,077	29,077	55,750
Depreciation	64,736	0	0	64,736
Advertising	63,752	63,752	63,752	0
Employees Auto Allowance	50,700	17,379	17,379	33,321
Insurance	33,003	0	0	33,003
Office Expense	25,080	0	0	25,080
Pension	18,164	6,226	6,226	11,938
Other Taxes	7,746	0	0	7,746
Equipment Rental & Maintenance	6,283	0	0	6,283
Bad Debts	4,098	0	0	4,098
Miscellaneous	51,396	0	0	51,396
Other Income	(7,607)	0	0	(7,607)
Total Expenses	3,617,812	1,959,962	1,329,610	1,657,850
Net Profit per Financials	57,857			
Incremental Profit		1,715,707	2,346,059	
Variable Cost Percentage		53.3%	36.2%	
Incremental Profit Percentage		46.7%	63.8%	

Source: Case study authored by Professor Henry Fuentes of Economatrix Research Associates, Inc. and Fairleigh Dickinson University.

BURDEN OF PROOF FOR DEMONSTRATING COSTS

As part of its lost profits presentation, the plaintiff must prove its lost revenues as well as the costs associated with these revenues. That is, the plaintiff bears the burden of proving what expenses it would have incurred while generating the lost revenues. Plaintiffs may try to argue that proving expenses is similar to a mitigation of damages (which may be considered the responsibility of the defendant to prove). However, courts have rejected this reasoning. The plaintiff must focus as closely on the costs associated with the projected lost revenues as on the projected revenues themselves.

FIXED VERSUS VARIABLE COSTS

Fixed costs are those costs which do not vary with output. Variable costs, on the other hand, do vary as output changes. Courts have recognized this simple definition which is standard in economics. For example, in *Autotrol Corp. v. Continental Water Systems, Corp.*, the court adopted this definition when providing the distinction between fixed costs and variable costs.

> Economists distinguish between a firm's fixed and variable costs. The former, as the name implies, are the same whether or not the firm does anything; a good example is the fee that a state charges for a corporation charter. The fee is paid before the firm begins operations and is utterly invariant to the firm's fortunes. It would be an improper item of damages for the breach of contract because the breach could not have caused the expense to be incurred.
>
> Variable costs are those that vary with the firm's activity—more precisely they are caused by fluctuations in that activity.[8]

In many cases, the distinction between fixed and variable costs is straightforward. For example, rent, lease payments, and other overhead are often treated as fixed costs. Other costs, such as costs of materials or commissions on sales, are categorized as variable costs because they vary according to output. The expert will often enhance the data contained in the financial statements with other information gathered directly from the company to determine which costs vary with output. After the fixed inputs are separated from the variable ones, the percentage relationship between the variable costs and the revenues is used to compute a *variable costs percentage*.

---

[8]*Autotrol Corp. v. Continental Water Systems Corp.*, 918 F2d 689 (7th Cir. 1990).

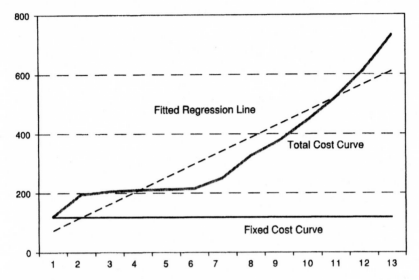

Exhibit 6.1   Fitting a regression line to cost data.

In economics, the typical cost function expresses various categories of costs as a function of output.[9] The initial presentation of the method used to differentiate between fixed and variable costs also uses such a functional relationship. Regression analysis can again be used to separate those costs which vary with sales from those which do not. A regression of costs against revenues will produce a fitted relationship and an equation describing this relationship. This is depicted in Exhibit 6.1.

The regression analysis allows the estimation of a fitted regression line based on the following equation:

$$C_t = F + vQ_t + u_t \qquad\qquad (6.1)$$

where C_t = Total cost
   F = Fixed cost
   v = Variable cost percentage
   Q_t = Quantity of output
   u_t = Error term

---

[9]Stephen A. Mathis and Janet Koscianski, *Microeconomic Theory: An Integrated Approach* (Upper Saddle River, NJ: Prentice-Hall, 2002), 261–262.

It would be expected that v varies between 0 and 1. That is:

$$0 < v < 1$$

The value v captures the relationship between costs and revenues.[10]

USING REGRESSION ANALYSIS TO ESTIMATE COSTS AS OPPOSED TO MORE BASIC METHODS

Although regression analysis can be used to measure the relationship between fixed and variable costs, it is more common in a litigation context for the expert to present such costs as a percent of revenues. In corporate finance, one of the more frequently used financial forecasting techniques, *percentage of sales forecasting*, predicts costs and the resulting profits as a percent of a separately forecasted sales level.[11] However, if the expert can use both approaches and arrive at similar results, the analysis is even more impressive.

When the damages analysis is conducted both by an economist and an accounting expert, the work is divided according to the respective expertise of the team's members. Typically, the economist conducts an analysis of the economy and of the firm's relevant industry and constructs a projection of "but for" revenues. This projection is then "handed off" to the accountant who computes the costs associated with the incremental lost revenues. This latter exercise falls within the domain of cost accounting. When the analysis is done in this manner, the accountant typically does not use regression analysis to measure costs but instead relies on more traditional accounting methods.

PITFALLS OF USING REGRESSION ANALYSIS TO MEASURE INCREMENTAL COSTS

Regression analysis can be a powerful tool in estimating relationships among variables and in creating projections. However, it has certain limitations and its usefulness varies from case-to-case. It is very important that the user of this tool understand both its potential complexity and limitations. As noted in Chapter Five,

---

[10]Robert R. Trout and Carroll B. Foster, "Economic Analysis of Business Interruption Losses," in *Litigation Economics,* Patrick A. Gaughan and Robert Thornton, eds. (Greenwich, CT: JAI Press, 1993), 151–174.

[11]Eugene Brigham and Philip R. Davies, *Intermediate Financial Management,* 7th ed. (New York: Thomson South-Western, 2002), 262–273.

too often, experts with little training in statistical analysis and econometrics blindly use the regression analysis features built into spreadsheet software packages without any appreciation of the complexity or limitations of the techniques employed.

The section below briefly discusses some issues which may arise when using regression analysis to estimate costs and cost functions. Experts and attorneys should be aware of these issues and make sure that, where relevant, they are discussed in advance of the report's submission.

POSSIBLE NONLINEAR NATURE OF TOTAL COSTS

If a company's production function is characterized by economies of scale over a certain range of output, then the per-unit costs of production decline over that range. Certain industries, particularly capital intensive industries like public utilities, may have significant ranges of output over which per-unit costs decline. This occurs when a company leverages its fixed costs. In financial analysis, this is referred to as *operating leverage*.[12] In other industries, the range over which economies of scale are realized may be small. At some point, however, per-unit costs stop declining and may even increase resulting in diseconomies of scale. The relationship between total costs and per-unit costs is shown in Exhibit 6.2. For output levels up to $x = 8$, per-unit costs decline. This implies that total costs increase at a decreasing rate. However, beyond the output level of 8, the firm begins to experience diseconomies of scale with a resulting increase in per-unit costs. This causes total costs to increase at an increasing rate.

If the cost function exhibits declining followed by increasing per-unit costs, the relationship between total costs and output is nonlinear. Exhibit 6.3 depicts two costs functions. The cost function on the top shows a linear relationship between costs and output; the cost function on the bottom shows a nonlinear relationship.

Over a range of output where per-unit costs are either declining or increasing, the cost function may be better estimated using nonlinear regression analysis rather than the more standard linear regression. The equation underlying a nonlinear cost function is shown in Equation 6.2.

$$C = {}_{.0} + {}_{.1}X_t + {}_{.2}X_t^2 + {}_{.3}X_t^3 \tag{6.2}$$

---

[12]Arthur Known, John D. Martin, J. William Petty, and David F. Scott, *Financial Management: Principles and Applications*, 9th ed. (Upper Saddle River, NJ: Prentice-Hall, 2002), 482–486.

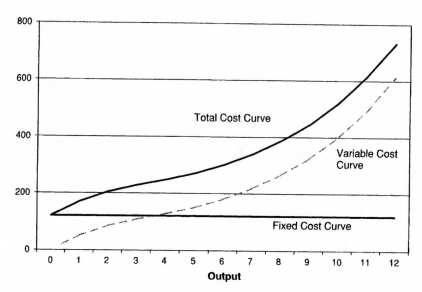

Exhibit 6.2a Total costs.

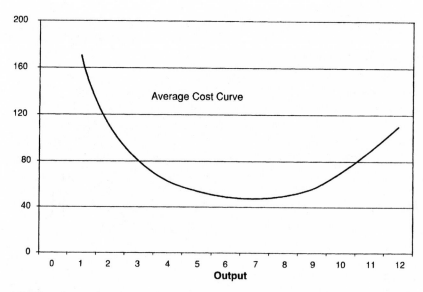

Exhibit 6.2b Average costs.

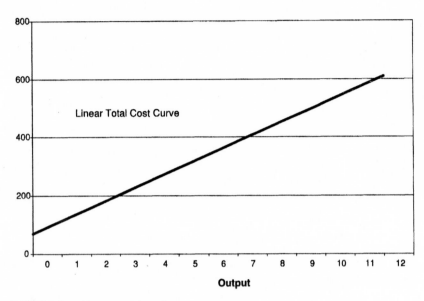

Exhibit 6.3a Linear cost functions.

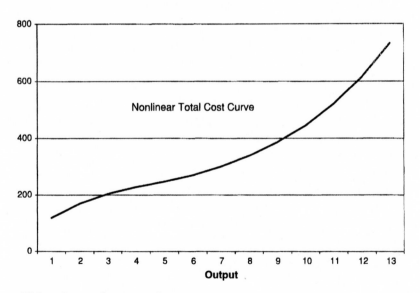

Exhibit 6.3b Nonlinear cost functions.

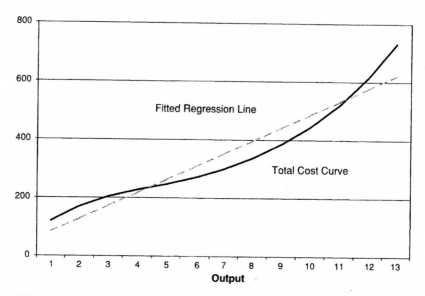

Exhibit 6.4   Linear regression forecast versus nonlinear actual cost function.

Costs may be inaccurately estimated if the expert uses linear regression when the true cost function is nonlinear. This is shown in Exhibit 6.4: linear regression analysis is used to estimate the cost function, thereby implicitly assuming that costs increase at a constant rate as output increases. In this example, however, the true cost function first exhibits economies and then diseconomies of scale. Because of the misspecification of the relationship between output and costs, the true costs are higher than the estimated ones for low and high levels of output, whereas they are lower than the estimated ones for intermediate levels of output. The solution is to use nonlinear regression analysis to estimate costs.

As noted earlier, care must be exercised in reviewing the regression analysis that is included in many economic damages reports. Some "experts" have had very little exposure to regression analysis and may not even know of nonlinear regression models. It is not uncommon for users to simply utilize the linear regression functions included in most spreadsheet packages without even being aware of the existence of other more sophisticated methods that result in more accurate costs estimates. This is why it is useful to have either an economist with a background in econometrics or an econometrician review any regression analysis included in an opposing expert's report.

Further Complications Involving Nonlinear Costs

If a plaintiff is prevented from generating sufficient sales to enjoy a reduction in per-unit costs, then it is possible that the costs associated with the projected lost revenues are lower than the level inherent in the historical relationship between costs and units produced. To a certain extent, this was previously explored where a solution involving the use of nonlinear costs estimation was recommended. The situation becomes more complicated if the cost reduction is such that it applies to not only the projected lost revenues but also to actual revenues. This can occur in the case of volume discounts. Here, the measure of loss would be not only the lost profits on the lost revenues, but also the difference in costs of the units affected by the volume discount.

Other Concerns about Using Regression Analysis to Measure Costs

While there are many instances in which courts have endorsed regression analysis and have found it to be of great probative value, they have been quick to reject a regression analysis that is based upon flawed assumptions. Regression analysis simply measures the relationship between the variables in question, a relationship that is inherent to the historical data used for the estimation process. If, however, there is reason to believe that the relationship would be different over the loss period, then the estimated coefficients from the regression analysis may not be useful. Such was the case in *Micro Motion, Inc. v. Exac Corp.* in which the court stated the following:

> The Court finds Mr. Holdren's historical and regression analyses to be of little probative value. An historical or regression analysis may be quite useful in a case involving a well-established firm with relatively constant costs and sales. But it is less useful where, as here, the firm can incur substantial nonrecurring costs, which because they can vary from year-to-year may appear to be, but are not, incremental costs. Moreover, the database Mr. Holdren used for his historical and regression analyses included data not at issue in this case, such as costs and revenues associated with international sales, and sales of meters not affected by Exac's infringement.[13]

---

[13]*Micro Motion, Inc. v. Exac Corp.*, 761 F. Supp. 1420 (N.D. Ca)

LIMITATIONS OF USING UNADJUSTED ACCOUNTING DATA FOR MEASURING INCREMENTAL COSTS

It may not be accurate to include all of the costs shown on the company's financial records when measuring incremental costs. Certain costs, such as depreciation, may be important for the computation of taxable income but may not be an accurate measure of costs of the depreciable assets in the period for which the depreciation is measured. The Delaware Supreme Court confirmed this when it reversed a lower court finding that depreciation was an appropriate costs measure to include in a lost profits computation.[14] The court stated:

> In this loss-of-profits case, we conclude that Barcroft is entitled to recover for any actual loss caused by Cannon's breach, including any actual decline in value or "depreciation" of the plant while it was out of production. But Barcroft's obligation is to establish that loss by showing what, in fact, the decline was. In our judgement, decline (measured by before and after values) cannot be established entirely by reference to an accounting technique, no matter how reliable it is for other purposes.

> We recognize that the straight-line method is commonly used in financial statements, tax returns, and other similar documents, but it is an improper basis for computing damages in this case, which is not concerned with the recovery of costs over useful life, nor with an equitable allocation of use costs over their shutdown period. In short, proof by reference to an arbitrary accounting rule is not an acceptable way of establishing actual loss resulting from depreciation in this litigation which seeks to compensate for lost profits.

This inaccuracy of using depreciation as a cost measure may be even more pronounced in cases where the depreciation charge is unusual, such as when there is accelerated depreciation. This highlights the artificial nature of depreciation as a measure of actual costs.

Other examples of accounting data deficiencies include the case when one is trying to measure losses over a less-than-one-year period but the data on employee compensation do not vary evenly with output or revenues.[15] This can occur when the firm pays year-end bonuses which may reflect work per-

---

[14]*Oliver B. Cannon & Son v. Dorr-Oliver, Inc.*, 394 A. 2d 1160 (Del. 1978).

[15]William Wecker and Roman L. Weil, "Statistical Estimation of Incremental Cost Data from Accounting Data," in *Litigation Services Handbook*, 2nd ed., Roman L. Weil, Michael J. Wagner, and Peter Frank, eds. (Wiley, 1995).

formed over a much longer period—possibly an entire year. In this case, the compensation data should be adjusted to more accurately reflect the time period under consideration.

Appropriate Profit Margin in Breach of Distributor Agreement Cases

The previous chapter discusses the methods that can be used to measure lost sales in cases of a breach of distribution agreement where the plaintiff distributor has been terminated. Once the dollar value of lost sales has been established, one must then determine what is the appropriate profit margin to apply to these lost sales. The methods discussed earlier in this chapter apply here as well, but a few comments are needed. In cases where a defendant has diverted sales to itself instead of to the plaintiff, once the lost sales are known, one determines the appropriate profit margin based upon the plaintiff's own costs structure rather than the defendant's. That is, courts have determined that the losses of the plaintiff are not the profits enjoyed by the defendant but, rather, the profits that the plaintiff would have made on these lost sales. In *Willred Co. v. Westmoreland Metal Manufacturing Co.* the court, after determining the diverted sales, awarded profits based upon the plaintiff's net profits experience over the five-year period prior to the breach.[16]

> Having found the amount of business which the plaintiff lost as a result of the defendant's breach of the contract, our next problem is to find the profit which it would have made on that volume of business. Williston on Contracts, Section 1346A, points out various methods of proving (cited with approval in *Massachusetts Bonding and Ins Co. v. Johnston & Harter, Inc.*, 343 Pa, 270, 279, 22 A.2d 709) evidence of past profits in an established business (may) furnish a reasonable basis of estimating future profits. The methods are not mutually exclusive, and the court may consider more than one in arriving at a conclusion, nor do they exclude from the court's consideration any other evidence which may throw light upon the question. In the present case, the plaintiff, having had an established business covering a five year period extending both before and after the breach, the percentage of profit which it actually realized will be the chief consideration. The figure can be obtained by referring to the plaintiff's income tax returns for the fiscal years 1953, 1954, 1955, 1956, and 1957. These returns should give a better picture of what profit was received on the business done than any method of accounting devised for the purpose of this lawsuit. They are as follows:

---

[16]*Willred Co. v. Westmoreland Metal Manufacturing Co.*, 200 F. Supp. 59 (E.D. Pa. 1961).

Fiscal Year Ending May 31,	Cost Goods Sold	Net Profit
1953	$116,260.82	$11,447.28
1954	$229,612.33	$ 6.095.28
1955	$306,973.59	$ 2,290.34
1956	$199,433.45	$17,220.72
1957	$529,781.99	$ 2,090.53

The figures show that, in the five year period covered, upon a volume of business measured by the total cost of goods sold, a total net profit of $39,144.15 was realized.

Some of the above figures must be adjusted because, as a result of the defendant's other breach (defective merchandise, late deliveries, etc.) the plaintiff's expenses during part of the five year period were substantially increased, resulting in a smaller percentage of profit for that part. Since these expenses were abnormal and were incurred as a necessary result of the defendant's defaults, they should be eliminated from any calculation of a percentage on which to base an estimate of lost profits. As allowable, they amount to $15,455.92. They should be subtracted from the expenses for the fiscal year 1956 and will increase the net profit in that year to $32,676.64. As a result of this adjustment, the percentage of profit of the total good sold during the five years will be 3.95%. The lost profit is, therefore, 3.95% of $1,759,512.75 or $69,500.75.[17]

The court's reasoning in *Willred* is interesting. The court seemed to place much weight on tax returns and valued them more than any other analysis presented in the litigation. The court also used several historical years of data to come up with an average profit percentage. In doing so, the court recognized, without explicitly stating it, that such percentages derived from several historical years would be more representative of the plaintiff's business than data for just one year. In doing so the court wanted to utilize more than one year so as to have a more representative average.

TREATMENT OF OVERHEAD COSTS

There is some confusion in commercial damages analysis regarding the treatment of overhead costs. This is evident when reviewing the case law and attempting to reconcile certain decisions with basic economic principles. The economic theory, however, is clear on the issue. For example, in the case of contract litigation, the costs of performance should be deducted from the incremental revenues to be derived from such performance. If overhead costs in the

---

[17]*Willred Company and Professional Metal Manufacturing Company v. Westmoreland Metal Mfg. Co.*, 200 F. Supp. 59; 1961.

form of fixed costs (such as rent and administrative expenses) were incurred anyway by the ongoing business, it would make little sense to deduct even a portion of these expenses that were already paid. However, if the business closed due to the acts of the defendant, then some or all of the overhead costs may not have been incurred. In this case, the net margin, which includes all expenses including overhead, is a more appropriate measure of cost to apply to projected lost revenues.

If a deduction for overhead is deemed appropriate, then it can be measured in a number of ways. One of the simplest is to compute overhead costs as a ratio of some output measure, such as production. This is shown below:

$$\text{Overhead Ratio (Revenues)} = \text{Total Overhead Costs/Revenues} \qquad (6.3)$$

$$\text{Overhead Ratio (Output)} = \text{Total Overhead Costs/Output} \qquad (6.4)$$

The ratio form is convenient in that it can be mathematically applied to various performance measures, such as revenues, that are projected to occur according to events that are the subject of the litigation. One danger in using such ratios, is that they make overhead costs look like variable costs; in fact, over a large range of output they are usually fixed. As output increases, overhead may be fixed until some relevant capacity constraint is reached. Some or all the components of overhead may then increase. If the expert is seeking to measure the increase in overhead, the ratios expressed in Equations 6.3 and 6.4 may not be very relevant, as they reflect total overhead including those portions which are fixed over the range considered.

It is helpful to compute the overhead ratios over several ranges of output to see how they vary as output varies.[18] This allows us to see how the ratio changes as output increases (see Exhibit 6.5). A plot of the trend in this ratios reveals how stable they are over multiple output ranges. The more stable these ratios are, the easier it is to use them over several projected output ranges.

Legal Authority on Deduction of Overhead

Ample legal authority supports the economic reasoning that in business interruption loss analysis, overhead should not be included in the measurement of costs

---

[18]Jeffrey H. Kinich, "Cost Estimation" in *Litigation Services Handbook*, 2nd ed. Roman Weil, Michael Wagner, and Peter Frank, eds. (Wiley, 1995), 7.7–7.8.

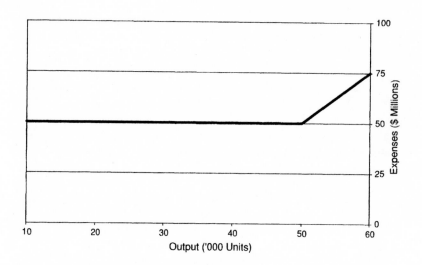

Exhibit 6.5   Overhead expenses versus output.

to apply to lost incremental revenues. In his review of the case law in this area, as well as in the debate on this issue in *Speidel and Clay* and in *Childres and Burgess*, Robert L. Dunn concludes that "The few cases that analyze the one place in the Uniform Commercial Code, Section 2-708, which addresses overhead 'tends to support their (Childres and Burgess) conclusion that overhead costs are not to be deducted from damages under the code',"[19] Indeed, in *Universal Power Systems, Inc. v. Godfather's Pizza, Inc.*, the court concluded that "variable overhead costs" should be deducted while "fixed overhead costs" should not be deducted.[20] Given that overhead is often considered fixed, this seems a contradiction. The designation of overhead as a fixed rather than a vari-

---

[19]Robert L. Dunn, *Recovery of Damages for Lost Profits*, vol. 2 (Westport, CT: Lawpress, 1992), 6.6; Richard E. Speidel and Kendall O. Clay, "Sellers Recovery of Overhead Under UCC Section 2-708 (2): Economic Costs Theory and Contractual Remedial Policy," 57 *Cornell Law Review*, 681 (1972); Robert Childres and Robert K. Burgess, "Sellers Remedies: The Primacy of UCC 2-708 (2) 48 *N.Y.U.L.*" Rev. 831 (1973).

[20]*Universal Power Systems, Inc. v. Godfather's Pizza, Inc.*, 818 F2d 667 (8th Cir. 1987).

able cost was also confirmed in *Scullin Steel Co. v. PACCAR, Inc.*[21] Here the court defined reasonable overhead as:

> Fixed costs, which dominate "reasonable overhead," commonly include property taxes, salaries, rent, utilities, depreciation, insurance, and other costs not directly affected by fluctuations in productivity.

As is discussed later in this chapter, however, some costs are fixed over a certain range of output but become variable as output expands. Such costs are semi-fixed or semi-variable, depending on the vantage point. In *Universal Power Systems v. Godfather's Pizza, Inc.,* the defense objected that the plaintiff's expert who computed lost profits failed to make any deduction for overhead including depreciation and warehouse expenses. The court, however, failed to accept this argument and concluded that expenses such as depreciation should not be deducted because they did not vary with output.

Overhead is a legitimate cost element to include in a loss computation if the plaintiff goes out of business due to the action of the defendant. If the business does not continue to operate and pay certain overhead expenses while experiencing lower revenues, then the sum of the revenues and all costs should be included in the loss computation.

Overhead as a Recoverable Component of Damages: Cost-Plus Contracts

Some contracts are cost-plus contracts—ones that allow for the addition of some profit component to some definition of costs. *"The cost-plus contract concept in which the contract price is the contractor's estimated costs plus 6% of cost for his overhead and profit is legitimate."*[22] The inclusion of overhead costs as an element of damages depends on whether the agreement provides for recouping of overhead costs. In such contracts, the measure of profits is usually a straightforward function of the level of overhead expenses and can be readily computed. In *Juengel Construction Co., Inc. v. Mt. Etna Inc.,* the court computed the lost profits as follows:

---

[21]*Scullin Steel Co. v. PACCAR*, Inc., 748 S.W. 2d 910 (Mo. App. 1988).
[22]*Juengel Construction Co., Inc. v. Mt. Etna, Inc.* 622 S.W. 2d 510, 1981.

In its cost-plus contract with Mt. Etna, Juengel's profit was to equal 6% of costs. By totaling the low subcontractor bids, Juengel rationally estimated costs to equal $759,442.00, 6% of which is $45,566.52. The latter amount is clearly Juengel's lost profits.

Unabsorbed Overhead as an Element of Damages

Unabsorbed overhead is a litigation issue arising out of government contracts. It is defined as the loss derived from an underrecovery of fixed overhead costs due to less work being performed by a contractor. The reduced amount of work can be attributed to a variety of reasons including suspension of work or some form of delay or interruption. In analyzing damages from unabsorbed overhead, one should focus on a period longer than what the plaintiff indicates to be the period during which work was insufficient to absorb the required overhead. This may be the case when work is shifted to another period so that it is overabsorbed in another time period.[23]

Uncertainty about when work may continue during a delay that is not the fault of the plaintiff may cause the plaintiff to restrain from taking on alternative work to mitigate his damages. The principles governing to what extent such overhead is a compensable element of damages is sometimes referred to as the *Eichleay* formula.[24] When a company can shift resources to other revenue-generating activities, there may not be a valid claim for damages. However, when the company is inhibited from doing so due to uncertainty about when work will continue or other constraints (such as limited additional binding capacity) then the plaintiff may have a more valid claim.[25]

CAPACITY CONSTRAINTS AND FIXED VERSUS VARIABLE COSTS

While economists are well-acquainted with the separation of costs into fixed and variable categories, this simple separation may not suffice for all projections of lost profits.[26] For projections of sales that go beyond the firm's capacity constraints,

[23]David G. Anderson, "Practitioner's Viewpoint: Federal Circuit Creates an Invalid Test for Determining Entitlement to Unabsorbed Overhead," *Public Contract Law Review* 26 (3) (spring 1997): 353–372.

[24]*C.B.C. Enterprises v. United States,* 978, F2d 669 (Fed. Cir. 1992).

[25]Mech-Con Corp., ASBCA No. 45105, 94-3 BCA ¶ 27,252, at 135,784.

[26]For a traditional economic discussion of fixed versus variable costs see Jeffrey M. Perloff, *Microeconomics,* 2nd ed. (New York: Addison Wesley, 2001), 181–182.

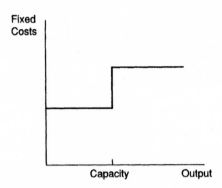

Exhibit 6.6 Fixed costs and capacity constraints.

additional fixed costs may have to be considered. This is shown in Exhibit 6.6. Fixed costs increase to a higher level in order for the company to go beyond its initial capacity constraints. This relationship is what is known in mathematics as a *step function.*

The traditional economic treatment divides costs into short-run and long-run cost functions. A more appropriate treatment of this issue for litigation analysis is to simply divide costs into three categories: *fixed, semi-variable,* and *variable.* Such a division allows the economist to reliably forecast revenues beyond the company's current constraints.

MUST A PLAINTIFF BE A PROFITABLE BUSINESS TO RECOVER DAMAGES?

It does not seem reasonable that a previously unprofitable business can recover damages. However, it could be the case that a business would have been profitable had it not been for the actions of the defendant. While actual revenues were insufficient to cover all fixed and variable costs, it is possible that if the business had reached the projected "but for" levels, total costs would have been surpassed and the company would have enjoyed positive profits. The situation becomes more complicated when it can be shown that even if the plaintiff had reached the projected revenue levels, it would still show a loss. The defendant may then try to argue that its improper actions prevented losses. It is difficult to state one catch-all rule that applies to a virtually infinite number of situations. However, the plaintiff's burden in a case such as this is significant. One way the plaintiff can recoup damages is if it can show that its loss was even greater due to the fact that the defendant's actions prevented it from generating the projected levels. For example, the plaintiff may owe monies to various parties as a result of losses incurred. The plaintiff can use the proceeds of an award to meet part of these obligations.

Another way that a plaintiff can recover lost profits, even if it were never profitable during its existence, is to show that revenues would have risen above costs but for the actions of the defendant. That is, one way to show losses is to project revenues using a nonspeculative growth rate. If that results in a revenue level in excess of costs, there would be evidence of lost profits. Certain courts have allowed such reasoning. For example, in *Heatransfer Corp.*, the court stated:

> The court does not believe that a going concern, which is the victim of an anti-competitive practice, must forego damages for sales it would have made as the result of the natural expansion of its business simply because it was victimized early in its existence before its attempts to expand could ripen into evidence of preparedness and intent to increase its output.[27]

Other courts have looked even more favorably on the ability of an unprofitable business to claim losses. In *Terrell v. Household Goods Carriers' Bureau*, the court allowed for the recovery of losses for an unprofitable plaintiff. It stated that "to deny recovery to a businessman who has struggled to establish a business in the face of wrongful conduct by a competitor simply because he never managed to escape from the quicksand of red ink to the dry land of profitable enterprise would make a mockery of the private antitrust remedy."[28]

The main issue in projection of revenues and costs for a previously nonprofitable plaintiff which show profits over some part or all of the loss period is that of speculation. There needs to be a basis to show that the revenue and costs projection is not speculative. This may be difficult to do, but the courts in *Heatransfer* and *Terrill* have opened the door to its use.

MITIGATION OF DAMAGES

In computing losses, any cost savings that the plaintiff enjoyed (by not having to undertake whatever activities it would have normally undertaken in order to realize the "but for" revenue stream) needs to be deducted as an offset. For example,

---

[27]*Heatransfer Corp.*, 553 F2d at 986
[28]*Terrell v. Household Goods Carriers' Bureau*, 494 F2d 16, 23.

if the plaintiff does not have to incur all of the costs needed to achieve the projected revenue stream, such as those associated with a larger workforce and facilities, this cost saving should be taken into account. The *mitigation of damages* should also include alternative opportunities to earn other profits. Using a contract litigation example,[29] if the plaintiff could mitigate its damages by substituting other business, then the profits from the alternative activities need to be considered. If, however, it was possible for the plaintiff to complete performance of both contracts, profits from the alternative contracts should not be deducted from the lost profits.

Though the plaintiff may be required to show that it has pursued other profitable opportunities, the law is less clear when the plaintiff chooses to pursue opportunities that are far riskier than the business that was lost. The plaintiff's argument may be less persuasive if it can be shown that the plaintiff could have replaced the defendant's lost business, without incurring significant search costs, with other lower risk business opportunities.

Doctrine of Mitigation as Applied to Corporations

The doctrine of mitigation that the law applies to corporations is different than what applies to individuals. For experts who are used to measuring damages of individuals, such as in personal injury or employment law contexts, they may find the law's treatment of mitigation different from what they had expected. As an example, assume that Company X incurs damages as a result of a breach of contract by Company Y, the defendant in a lawsuit brought by Company X. If, after the breach, a new company (Company Z) is formed and conducts business which generates positive profits, the law *may* consider these profits to be irrelevant to the losses of Company X. This may be the case even when the shareholders of Companies X and Z are the same. This was the court's position in *Joseph Sandler and Law-A-Mat of Penn-Jersey, Inc. v. Lawn-A-Mat Chemical & Equipment Corp. et al.*

> The trial judge rejected the mitigation argument on the ground that the earnings of Lawn King, Inc. as an independent corporate entity could not be utilized to mitigate the damages of Penn-Jersey as a separate corporate entity. Lawn-A-Mat nevertheless urges that the corporate veils should be pierced and the issue be considered in light of Sandler's individual participation in both corporations.

---

[29] *Joseph Sandler and Law-A-Mat of Penn-Jersey, Inc. v. Lawn-A-Mat Chemical & Equipment Corp. et al.*, 141 N.J. Super. 437; 358 A.2d 805; 1976

The issue becomes complicated if it is clear that the new corporate entity was formed with the express purpose of avoiding legitimate mitigation. However, this is a legal issue which, though important for the damages expert, is often controlled by legal rulings rather than just economic expertise.

Burden of Proof of Mitigation

The proof of a failure to mitigate damages is the responsibility of the defendant. However, this may be an issue of dispute if the plaintiff argues that it actually did take reasonable steps to mitigate its damages; in turn, the defendant may argue that the plaintiff had the ability to mitigate its damages beyond the measures actually taken. The plaintiff only needs to show that it took reasonable steps to mitigate its damages. It does not need to show that it took all of the steps that the defendant states he should have taken.[30] In the face of such a presentation by the plaintiff, it is up to the court to decide if the mitigation efforts of the plaintiff were reasonable and sufficient. In *Brandon & Tibbs v. George Kevorkian Accountancy Corporation*, a case involving claims of damages of an accounting practice that was not purchased as agreed to by the defendant, the court explained the law on mitigation of damages as follows:

> A party injured by a breach of contract is required to do everything reasonably possible to negate his own loss and thus reduce the damages for which the other party has become liable [cite omitted]. The plaintiff cannot recover for harm he could have foreseen and avoided by such reasonable efforts and without undue expense. However, the injured party is not precluded from recovery to the extent that he has made reasonable but unsuccessful efforts to avoid loss.
>
> The burden of proving that losses could have been avoided by reasonable effort and expense must always be borne by the party who has broken the contract [cite omitted]. Inasmuch as the law denied recovery for losses that can be avoided by reasonable effort and expense, justice requires that the risks incident to such an effort should be carried by the party whose wrongful conduct makes them necessary [cite omitted]. Therefore, special losses that a party incurs in a reasonable effort to avoid losses resulting from a breach are recoverable as damages.

Other Offsetting Profits Not Treated as Damages Mitigation

It is possible that the plaintiff lost certain revenues due to the actions of the defendant but failed to incur a loss; because it was able to substitute other busi-

---

[30]*Brandon & Tibbs v. George Kevorkian Accountancy Corporation*, 226 Cal. App. 3d 442, 227 Cal. Rptr. 40 (1990).

ness, it was not left in a less advantageous position than the one it would have been in. Under these circumstances, in order to claim a loss, the plaintiff needs to prove that it had the capacity to handle *both* the substitute business as well as the lost business. For example, in *Sierra Wine & Liquor Co. v. Heublein, Inc.,* the court found that a plaintiff who was a franchisee was only able to recover damages until he secured a replacement franchise. The reasoning was that the plaintiff could not hold two franchisees in the same industry at the same time.[31]

Tax-Related Mitigation

An expert's computation of damages is typically calculated on a pre-tax basis. This is due to the fact that the plaintiff will be taxed on the award. As the court stated in *Polaroid Corporation v. Eastman Kodak Company:*

> An award based upon after-tax amounts could result in double taxation. Any award will certainly be scrutinized by tax officials at both the state and federal levels who will determine the correctness and applicability of any rate employed.[32]

In some instances, the plaintiff may receive certain *tax benefits* from the losses incurred as a result of the defendant's actions. These benefits could be in the form of tax losses used to offset positive income in future periods. Robert L. Dunn reports that in most recent cases, the tax benefits a plaintiff enjoys are not considered in computing damages.[33] Among the reasons the courts cite are that the awarded profits are themselves taxable and that knowing what the relevant rates are going to be in the year the award is made is difficult. The reason why the relevant rates may not be known is that the full income and other tax-related factors that enter into the determination of the firm's average tax rate for the year of the award may not be known until after the year is over.

The courts even indicate that the plaintiff should receive the benefit of any lower rates it enjoys after possibly including these offsetting tax benefits. This is in opposition to the defendant's receiving the benefit of these offsetting gains that the plaintiff enjoyed in the year the plaintiff incurred the loss that was caused by the defendant. Courts seemingly want to ignore the issue of differential tax effects. Indeed, in cases where the plaintiff contended that its tax rates in the year it would

---

[31]*Sierra Wine & Liquor Co. v. Heublein, Inc.,* 626 F2d 129 (9th Cir. 1980).

[32]*Polaroid Corporation v. Eastman Kodak Company,* 16 U.S.P.Q., 2d, 1481, 1990.

[33]Robert L. Dunn, *Recovery of Damages for Lost Profits,* 5th ed. (Westport, CT: Lawpress, 1998), 465–471.

receive the damages award were higher, the court stated that this was not a valid area of damages.

It seems that the court's theory is that when an award is made, the tax effects of that award will more or less offset any tax benefits that may have been incurred since the interruption; it is, therefore, not an issue. That the amount in question may be different or that the time value of the respective amounts may exacerbate these differences does not seem to be an issue that the courts want to examine in considering the appropriate amount to award in a lost profits case.

One can challenge the court's reasoning in the cases that advocate ignoring tax issues. The argument that taxes cannot be computed due to the inherent complexity of such a computation makes little sense. Courts allow testimony on revenue estimation using complicated models, so it would only be reasonable that testimony be allowed on the projection of taxes. The tax rate involved usually is the maximum tax rate; the incremental lost income in larger commercial cases is most often taxed at the highest corporate marginal rate. The expert can then compute the incremental taxes associated with the lost incremental profits as follows:

$$IT = LITI \times t \tag{6.5}$$

where   IT = Incremental taxes
         LITI = Lost incremental taxable income
         t = Relevant marginal tax rate

Some argue that unless there is a basis for assuming a change in tax rates, future taxes can be computed using current tax rates.[34] In computing historical losses when tax rates have changed and the rates in the year of the award are different than the period of the loss, the goal of the expert is to compute an award that leaves the plaintiff whole. This involves computing the incremental taxes using t_l, the tax rate from the loss period, and determining what the net income of the plaintiff would have been had it received the projected lost profits during the loss period. The award on the trial date, which will be taxed at current rates, t_c, may have to be adjusted to equal what the plaintiff would have received but for the action of the defendant:

$$NLI = LITI - IT \tag{6.6}$$

where   NLI = Net lost income

---

[34]John Jarocz, "Considering Taxes in the Computation of Lost Business Profits," *Creighton Law Review* 25 (1991): 41–72.

Comments on the Use of Net Income versus Cash Flows

The discussion presented thus far only focuses on net earnings and not on cash flow. Over the long run, cash flow and net earnings approximate each other. However, the accrual methods of accounting allow for income to be recorded even when the cash is anticipated in the future. This timing difference allows for there to be a difference between the two amounts. Accountants regularly review such recording and make adjustments for such differences. Nonetheless, there are many instances in which a change in income is driven by pure changes in the accounting treatment; such earnings do not translate into cash flows.[35] Research studies have shown that when the market values companies, it focuses more on cash flows and less on earnings that are the product of changes in the accounting treatment and which will not translate into cash flows.[36] This work has led to a debate about earnings quality. Earning quality is defined as "the accuracy with which a company's accounting earnings reflects its true earning power."[37] This debate recognizes that all earnings are not of the same quality.[38] The earnings quality debate highlights some of the factors that affect the sustainability of earnings. Included in this debate are issues such as extraordinary or one-time items as well as the impairment of assets. To the extent that these issues affect the expert's projections of lost earnings, they need to be addressed. If there are concerns about the quality of the historial earnings that are used for future lost profits projections, the expert should explicitly address this prior to completing his lost profits analysis.

CASH FLOWS VERSUS NET INCOME: EFFECTS ON THE DISCOUNTING PROCESS

It can happen that, in order to achieve the forecasted revenue levels, the plaintiff needs to invest certain monies in capital items. These monies are treated differently depending on what the measurement is: cash flows or net income. Consider the example shown in Table 6.3. Damages are computed using incremental oper-

---

[35]Frank K. Rielly and Keith C. Brown, *Investment Analysis and Portfolio Management*, 6th ed. (Fort Worth, TX: Dryden Press, 2000), 238–239.

[36]See Michael Brennan, "A Perspective on Accounting and Stock Prices," *The Accounting Review* 66 (1) (January 1991): 67–79.

[37]Jack C. Francis and Roger Ibbotson, *Investments: A Global Perspective* (Englewood Cliffs, NJ: Prentice-Hall, 2002), 731.

[38]Clyde P. Stockney and Paul Brown, *Financial Reporting and Statement Analysis* (Fort Worth, TX: Dryden Press, 1999), 203–205.

Table 6.3 Computing Damages Using Cash Flows versus Net Income

	Cash Basis Damages			
Year	Incremental Operating Cash Flow	Capital Expenditure	Cash Basis Damages	Cumulative Cash Basis Damages
1	50,000	60,000	(10,000)	(10,000)
2	70,000	0	70,000	60,000
3	80,000	0	80,000	140,000
4	90,000	0	90,000	230,000
	Income Basis Damages			
Year	Incremental Net Income	Capital Expenditure	Income Basis Damages	Cumulative Cash Basis Damages
1	50,000	15,000	35,000	35,000
2	70,000	15,000	55,000	90,000
3	80,000	15,000	65,000	155,000
4	90,000	15,000	75,000	230,000

ating cash flows and incremental net income. The damages computations are equal over the four year loss period. The difference is a one-time capital expenditure of $60,000 which occurs in year one. This expenditure is assumed to be necessary in order to achieve the projected cash flows/net income.

If damages are computed on a cash basis, there is no loss in year one; if computed on an income basis, however, there is a loss of $35,000. The cumulative amounts are the same—$230,000. This simple example does not address the balance sheet effects of the differences in the cash versus income basis analysis. These effects are quite complex and, fortunately, are often not necessary for the damages analysis.[39]

One major difference between the cash basis and income basis analysis is in the timing of the damages—it can significantly affect the present value computation. Consider the extension in Table 6.4. A 15 percent risk-adjusted discount rate is used to convert the projected damages amounts to present value terms in year 0. In Table 6.3, the cumulative amounts were equal over the four year loss period, but the differences in the timing of the damage amounts leads to a difference in the cumulative discounted amounts. Because the full impact of the

---

[39]Michael Wagner, "How Do You Measure Damages: Lost Income or Lost Cash Flow," *Journal of Accountancy* (February 1990): 28–33.

Table 6.4 Discounted Cash Basis Damages

	Discounted Cash Basis Damages			
Year	Cash Basis Damages	Discount Factor	Discounted Damages	Cumulative Discounted Damages
1	(10,000)	0.8696	(8,696)	(8,696)
2	70,000	0.7561	52,930	44,234
3	80,000	0.6575	52,601	96,836
4	90,000	0.5718	51,458	148,293
	Discounted Income Basis Damages			
Year	Income Basis Damages	Discount Factor	Discounted Damages	Cumulative Discounted Damages
1	35,000	0.8696	30,435	30,435
2	55,000	0.7561	41,588	72,023
3	65,000	0.6575	42,739	114,761
4	75,000	0.5718	42,881	157,643

capital expenditure is felt in year one under the cash basis treatment, lower damages are projected in the early years for the cash basis treatment. This results in lower cumulative discounted damages. The opposite is true for the projection under the income basis treatment. The higher damages in the early years result in higher discounted damages for the income basis damage computation.

On a discounted basis, the damages are different depending on which accounting approach one uses. These differences are greater the higher the discount rate, the longer the loss period, and the greater the differences in the timing of the damages.

RECASTED PROFITS

In closely held corporations, the net income may not reflect the true compensation to the company's owners. For example, the company may be controlled by a small number of key shareholders, perhaps even one, who extract a significant component of the profits of the business so that taxable income and tax are minimized. These monies can be extracted in several ways, including officer's compensation, fringe benefits, and other "perks." The after-tax net income (bottom line) may show limited profitability, while the company generates very different positive returns for its owners. Unfortunately, this tax avoidance process, one that may be quite consistent with prevailing tax laws, may present problems for the plaintiff in a lost profits case.

Public versus Private Corporations[40]

When it comes to declaring income, there are significant differences in the objectives of public and private corporations. Public corporations are quite limited in the actions they can take to minimize taxable income. These limitations come partly through dividend payment constraints, requiring that income be reported and taxes paid before dividends can be paid. Companies generally pursue a policy of dividend stability by which they try to manage the company such that the payment of dividends is at least stable, if not growing.[41] Companies which announce declining or zero dividends can risk various market corrective actions, such as an ouster of management or a takeover by an outside raider who takes advantage of the decline in the company's stock price that often accompanies such announcements.[42] For these reasons, public companies are constrained in how they can manage taxable income. Private companies are more free to control taxable income through the use of expenses that are truly a form of compensation for the shareholders. The controlling shareholders in a private company can choose to take some of their return in the form of officer's compensation rather than as a distribution of post-tax income. These shareholders may also choose to incur costs that provide indirect benefits but which also reduce taxable income. A problem arises when the managed income plaintiff enters into litigation and claims lost profits. The firm's net income history may show only limited profits in a business that is actually generating sizable returns for the shareholders/ plaintiffs.

The process of reconstructing the true profitability of the business is well known to finance practitioners. The process, called *recasting* of profitability, involves defining a series of add-backs which, as the term implies, are added back to the bottom line to reconstruct the true profitability of the business. The tax effects of these add-backs must be considered when calculating the recasted income. This process is common in a number of areas in corporate finance including acquisitions planning and business valuations. In acquisition planning, the cost structure of a target

---

[40]This section draws heavily on the following article: Patrick A. Gaughan and Henry Fuentes, "The Minimization of Taxable Income and Lost Profits Litigation," *Journal of Forensic Economics* 4 (1) (winter 1990): 55–64.

[41]Stephen A. Ross, Randolph W. Westerfield, and Bradford Jordan, *Essentials of Corporate Finance,* 4th ed. (New York: Irwin, 2004), 428–429.

[42]An example was the takeover attempt of ITT Corporation by the Pritzger Group after ITT announced a reduction in its quarterly dividend. It should be noted, however, that some companies, such as those which anticipate high growth, may not pay dividends. Therefore, the comments are more applicable to cases where the lack of dividends are not anticipated by the market.

company is evaluated from the viewpoint of the bidder, who only considers the costs that the bidder would incur if the acquisition were completed. The elimination of redundant costs, such as duplicate facilities, can form the basis for the synergistic gains that are often cited in a priori acquisition planning.[43]

In the valuation of closely held businesses for nonacquisition purposes, recasting the income statement is also commonplace. Here, the true value to an owner is measured for other reasons, such as in shareholder derivative lawsuits as well as matrimonial litigation. The process is well accepted, but whether it is legally appropriate to utilize the recasted income of shareholders in a corporation as opposed to the reported income of the corporate plaintiff itself is a separate issue. This is an issue which is still open to debate. However, the legal position of the court is not one which the expert will be deciding. Rather, the expert must be presented with an assumed legal position which creates the basis for the loss analysis. It is for the legal representatives of the litigants themselves to argue which legal theory applies.

Professional Corporations

In cases involving a professional corporation, the issue of using recasted profits may be even clearer. In a professional corporation, the shareholders and the principals are the same. In order to avoid the double taxation associated with the corporate business structure, the professional corporation can distribute earnings in the form of officer's compensation so as to have a lower taxable income. Courts have treated this officer's compensation as relevant to the computation of the lost profits of the corporation.[44] They have correctly realized that very profitable entities which paid out these profits in the form of compensation could never otherwise claim lost profits.

CASE STUDY: PROFITS THAT ARE NOT REALLY PROFITS*

This case study involves a distributor of manufactured products. The company had been in existence for approximately twenty-five years. One of the points

---

*Case study prepared by Professor Heny Fuentes.

[43]Patrick A. Gaughan, *Mergers, Acquisitions and Corporate Restructuring,* 3rd ed., university ed. (New York: Wiley, 2002), 116–117.

[44]*Bettius & Sanderson, P.C. v. National Union Fire Insurance Co.,* 839 F2d 1009 (4th Cir. 1988).

which plaintiff's counsel repeatedly emphasized was the long history of steady revenue growth over the life of the company. This revenue growth was also associated with a steady, albeit weak, profitability. The plaintiff claimed that the purchase and implementation of a computer system caused such severe disruption to the company's business that it resulted in the closure of the company.

A closer examination of the company's finances revealed many long-brewing problems that were coming to a head at the same time the computer system was being installed. These problems included insufficient write-offs of uncollectable receivables, inappropriate accounting for certain costs, and the failure to write off obsolete inventory. During the company's life, certain reserves for potentially unpaid receivables had always been set aside. Inventory purchases were financed through an asset-based lending facility at a major local bank. As Table 6.5 and Exhibit 6.7 show, operating cash flow was particularly poor. When operating cash

Table 6.5   Company X: Summary of Financial Statement Information, 1966–1988 (in Thousands)

Year	Sales	Net Income	Cash Flows (used) in Opts	Increase (Decrease) in Debt	Interest Expense
1966	5,800	40	45	(20)	1
1967	6,000	50	170	(90)	0
1968	6,900	75	90	(40)	0
1969	9,100	90	(60)	70	6
1970	11,000	120	(140)	240	6
1971	12,100	130	(300)	370	10
1972	14,300	160	(250)	200	13
1973	17,600	190	(150)	120	25
1974	19,000	300	300	(250)	25
1975	18,000	125	(130)	200	22
1976	19,000	100	(1,300)	1,450	100
1977	21,800	100	200	(275)	200
1978	25,400	155	(10)	190	270
1979	27,700	115	(1,000)	1,600	450
1980	32,000	170	300	(400)	670
1981	37,000	170	(800)	1,000	1,000
1982	34,400	90	(60)	100	900
1983	41,800	500	350	(170)	700
1984	47,700	550	(900)	930	800
1985	49,700	300	(500)	1,100	900
1986	56,600	250	(350)	1,050	750
1987	60,400	150	(600)	1,020	890
1988	57,500	(185)	(4,500)	4,450	1,460
Totals 1966–88		3,745	(9,595)	12,845	

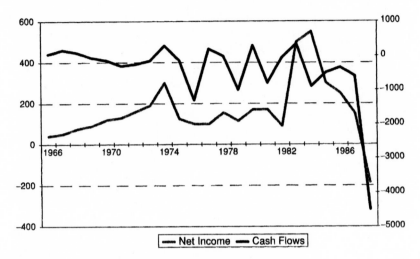

Exhibit 6.7   Cash flows versus net income.

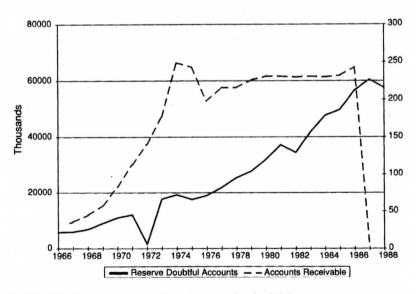

Exhibit 6.8   Accounts receivable and reserve for doubtful accounts.

flow was no longer sufficient to finance the company's activities, notably additional borrowing, presumably, no lending officer at the bank wanted to admit that the prior loans were uncollectable, and the bank continued to lend "good money after bad" and exceeded its credit limits. The company continued to extend credit to customers who were not current. It reasoned that the only way it could access the additional financing was through generating sales and extending credit even when the receivables generated from those sales might not be collectable (see Exhibit 6.8). It becomes clear that the seemingly impressive sales growth shown in Tables 6.5 and 6.6 was based on profits that did not translate into positive operating cash flows.

This case clearly shows that, if proper accounting adjustments are not made, the resulting net income is not a reliable amount upon which to base a damages computation. In such a situation, the expert may have to use other variables, such as cash flows.

Table 6.6 Company X: Historical Sales, Accounts Receivable, and Reserves for Doubtful Accounts (in Thousands)

Year	Sales	Accounts Notes Receivable	Reserve Doubtful Accounts	Ratio Reserve to Accounts Receivable(%)	A/R–N/R over 120 Days
1966	5,812	1,719	30	1.7	N/A
1967	5,978	1,748	36	2.1	N/A
1968	6,896	1,833	45	2.5	N/A
1969	9,100	2,534	58	2.3	N/A
1970	11,051	2,494	83	3.3	N/A
1971	12,106	2,623	113	4.3	N/A
1972	N/A	N/A	N/A	N/A	N/A
1973	17,726	4,021	177	4.4	N/A
1974	19,244	3,753	249	6.6	N/A
1975	17,571	3,903	243	6.2	N/A
1976	18,960	4,362	198	4.5	N/A
1977	21,848	5,342	216	4.0	N/A
1978	25,394	6,362	216	3.4	N/A
1979	27,749	7,287	226	3.1	N/A
1980	32,024	7,409	231	3.1	N/A
1981	37,162	7,472	231	3.1	N/A
1982	34,437	7,227	230	3.2	N/A
1983	41,791	8,732	231	2.6	N/A
1984	47,683	9,272	230	2.5	N/A
1985	49,715	9,304	232	2.5	N/A
1986	56,641	11,143	243	2.2	1,512
1987	60,440	11,941	0	0.0	1,603
1988	57,549	14,451	0	0.0	3,001

FIRM-SPECIFIC FINANCIAL ANALYSIS

One issue that may be relevant to a commercial damages analysis is the financial condition of the plaintiff or the defendant. There is a standard set of financial tools found in most corporate finance textbooks. Paramount among these is financial ratio analysis. This is the computation of financial ratios from data contained in the company's financial statements. A financial ratio analysis can be used to assess the financial well-being of a company. This is important in cases where it is claimed that a company would have failed anyway even if the defendant had not taken the actions the plaintiff asserts it did. However, this type of financial analysis may be unnecessary when there is a lawsuit between two companies that continue to be viable with the plaintiff alleging that it is simply less profitable due to the actions of the defendant. Each set of ratios examines a specific aspect of the company's financial well-being. The four categories of these ratios are:

1. **Liquidity Ratios:** These ratios, which include what are referred to as the *current ratio* and the *quick ratio,* describe the relationship between a company's liquid, short-term assets (such as cash, marketable securities, and inventories) and its short-term liabilities, illustrating how liquid the company is. The more liquid a business is, the lower the probability that it could be forced into receivership by not being able to pay its obligations as they come due. A more stringent version of this ratio is the quick ratio, which leaves out inventories from the computation.

2. **Activity Ratios:** These ratios measure the ability of the company to use its assets to generate sales. Certain ones, such as inventory turnover, examine how quickly a company turns its inventories into sales. Others, such as fixed asset turnover and total asset turnover measure the business's ability to use its fixed assets or all of its assets to generate sales. Generally, the higher the values of these ratios, the healthier the company; however, there are exceptions to this generalization.

3. **Leverage Ratios:** These ratios can be used to assess the level of debt, or what is called *financial leverage*, in the company's capital structure. The *debt ratio* and the *debt-to-equity ratio* are two measures that capture the amount of debt the firm has used to finance its operations. The higher

the degree of financial leverage, the greater the risk of the firm; this is because it has more fixed obligations in the form of debt to service. Other ratios such as times interest earned, examine the magnitude of operating income (earnings before interest and taxes) relative to interest payments, illustrating how much *interest coverage* the firm has.

4. Performance Ratios: Ratios such as the gross, operating, and net margins are alternative profitability measures. These ratios reflect how profitable the company is. They are also used at other times in a commercial damages analysis when computing profits associated with projected lost revenues.

The above ratios are usually compared to readily available industry norms.[45] They may be supplemented by other ratios that the analyst uses to address specific issues.[46]

CROSS-SECTIONAL VERSUS TIME SERIES ANALYSIS

In addition to comparing the firm's financial with industry averages (called a cross-sectional analysis) it may also be useful to examine the trend in these ratios over time. This is called a time series analysis of financial ratios. Such a review enables one to determine if certain components of a firm's financial condition are deteriorating or improving over time. This may indicate the start of problems that may be independent of alleged actions of the defendant.

SUMMARY

This chapter explored the steps involved in the process of measuring lost profits that commence after the "but for" revenues have been forecasted. Incremental

---

[45]A review of financial ratio analysis can be found in most corporate finance textbooks. For a clear, elementary discussion see R. Charles Moyer, James R. McGuigan, and William J. Kretlow, *Contemporary Financial Management,* 9th ed. (New York: Thomson South-Western, 2003), 64–84.

[46]*Annual Statement Studies,* Robert Morris Associates, various annual editions.

costs associated with lost incremental revenues have to be measured. These costs are usually only those that vary with output. That is, fixed costs usually are not included. The cost analysis is often done using the services of an accountant trained in measuring such costs. Typically, this expert submits either a schedule of specific costs or a simple percentage which embodies such cost schedule. Costs can also be measured using a regression analysis; it seeks to compute the variable component of costs by determining the coefficient in a estimated equation relating sales to costs. The coefficient of the cost variable in such an estimated equation then reflects to what extent costs would increase for a given increase in revenues. While regression analysis can be helpful in measuring variable costs, there are a number of factors one must consider in order to be assured that the analysis is reliable and truly quantifies what the expert is trying to measure.

In most lost profits analyses, fixed costs, such as overhead, may not be relevant. This is because much of what is covered by overhead, such as rent or equipment lease payments, may have been already incurred by the plaintiff. If that is the case, then it does not make sense to deduct such costs from incremental revenues. If, however, additional fixed costs or higher overhead would have to be incurred to reach the forecasted revenue levels, then such costs may enter into the loss computation.

In computing lost profits, net profits are the appropriate measure of the loss; the definition of net profits that is used, however, may not correspond to the net profits figure that appears at the bottom of an income statement. It may be equal to or lower than the gross margin, but often is higher than the net margin. However, when such net profits do not eventually equate to cash flows, then the focus of the damage measurement process may shift to cash flows and away from net income.

REFERENCES

Anderson, David G., "Practitioner's Viewpoint: Federal Circuit Creates an Invalid Test for Determining Entitlement to Unabsorbed Overhead." *Public Contract Law Review* 26 (3) (spring 1997).

Annual Statement Studies, Robert Morris Associates.

Autotrol Corp. v. Continental Water Systems Corp., 918 F2d 689 (7th Cir. 1990).

Bettius & Sanderson, P.C. v. National Union Fire Insurance Co., 839 F2d 1009 (4th Cir. 1988).

Brandon & Tibbs v. George Kevorkian Accountancy Corporation, 226 Cal. App. 3d 442, 227 Cal. Rptr. 40 (1990).

Brennan, Michael, "A Perspective on Accounting and Stock Prices." *The Accounting Review* 66 (1) (January 1991).

Brigham, Eugene, and Philip R. Davies, *Intermediate Financial Management*, 7th ed. New York: Thomson South-Western, 2002.

C.B.C. Enterprises v. United States, 978, F2d 669 (Fed. Cir. 1992).

Cerillo, William A., *Proving Business Damages.* Santa Ana: CA, James Publishing, 1989, 1-18–1.19.

Childres, Robert and Robert K. Burgess, "Sellers Remedies: The Primacy of UCC 2-708 (2) 48 *N.Y.U.L.*" Rev. 831 (1973).

Clayton v. Howard Johnson Franchise Systems, Inc. 954 F2d 645 652 (11th Cir. 1992) and *General Devices v. Bacon,* 888 S.W. 2d 497 (Tex. App. 1994).

Copeland, Thomas, Tim Koller, and Jack Murrin, *Valuation: Measuring and Managing the Value of Companies*, 3rd ed. New York: Wiley, 2000.

Dunn, Robert L., *Recovery of Damages for Lost Profits,* 5th ed., vol. II. Westport, CT: Lawpress, 1998.

Evans, Elizabeth, "Interaction Between Accountants and Economists," in *Litigation Services Handbook*, 3rd ed., Roman Weil, Michael Wagner, and Peter B. Frank, eds. Wiley, 2001.

Foster, Carroll B., and Robert R. Trout, "Computing Losses in Business Interruption Cases." *Journal of Forensic Economics* (December 1989).

Francis, Jack C. and Roger Ibbotson, *Investments: A Global Perspective,* Englewood Cliffs, NJ: Prentice-Hall, 2002.

Gaughan, Patrick A., *Mergers and Acquisitions.* New York: HarperCollins, 1991.

Gaughan, Patrick A., *Mergers, Acquisitions and Corporate Restructuring,* 3rd ed. New York: Wiley, 2002.

Gaughan, Patrick A., and Henry Fuentes, "The Minimization of Taxable Income and Lost Profits Litigation." *Journal of Forensic Economics* 4(1) (winter 1990): 55–64.

Gaughan, Patrick A., Henry Fuentes, and Laura Bonanomi, "Cash Flows versus Net Income: Issue in Commercial Damages Litigation." *Litigation Economics Digest* 1 (1) (fall 1995).

General Devices v. Bacon, 888 S.W. 2d 497 (Tex. App. 1994).

Graphics Directions, Inc. v. Bush, 862 P.2d. 1020 (Colo. Ct. App. 1993).

Heatransfer Corp., 553 F2d at 986.

Jarocz, John, "Considering Taxes in the Computation of Lost Business Profits." *Creighton Law Review* 25 (1991): 41–72.

Joseph Sandler and Law-A-Mat of Penn-Jersey, Inc. v. Lawn-A-Mat Chemical & Equipment Corp. et al., 141 N.J. Super. 437; 358 A.2d 805; 1976.

Juengel Construction Co., Inc. v. Mt. Etna, Inc., 622 S.W. 2d 510, 1981.

Kinich, Jeffrey H., "Cost Estimation," in *Litigation Services Handbook*, 2nd ed., Roman Weil, Michael Wagner, and Peter Frank, eds. Wiley, 1995.

Known, Arthur, John D. Miller, J. William Perry, and David F. Scott, *Financial Management: Principles and Applications*, 9th ed. Upper Saddle River, NJ: Prentice-Hall, 2002, 482–486.

Lee v. Durango Music, 355 P. 2d, 1083, 1088, (Colo. 1960.)

Martin, John D., J. William Petty, and David F. Scott, *Financial Management: Principles and Applications*, 9th ed. Upper Saddle River, NJ: Prentice-Hall, 2002.

Mathis, Stephen A., and Janet Koscianski, *Microeconomic Theory: An Integrated Approach.* Upper Saddle River, NJ: Prentice-Hall, 2002.

Mech-Con Corp., ASBCA No. 45105, 94-3 BCA ¶ 27,252, at 135,784.

Micro Motion, Inc. v. Exac Corp., 761 F. Supp. 1420 (N.D. Ca).

Moyer, Charles R., James R. McGuigan, and William J. Kretlow, *Contemporary Financial Management*, 9th ed. New York: Thomson South-Western, 2003.

Oliver B. Cannon & Son v. Dorr-Oliver, Inc., 394 A. 2d 1160 (Del 1978).

Perloff, Jeffrey M., *Microeconomics*, 2nd ed. New York: Addison Wesley, 2001.

Polaroid Corporation v. Eastman Kodak Company, 16 U.S.P.Q., 2d, 1481, 1990.

Rielly, Frank K., and Keith C. Brown, *Investment Analysis and Portfolio Management*, 6th ed. Fort Worth, TX: Dryden Press, 2000.

Ross, Archibald T., "Stock Market Reaction to the Depreciation Switch-Back." *Accounting Review* 47 (1) (January 1972).

Ross, Stephan A., Randolph W. Westerfield, and Bradford Jordan, *Essentials of Corporate Finance*, 4th ed. New York: Irwin, 2004.

Scullin Steel Co. v. PACCAR, Inc., 748 S.W. 2d 910 (Mo. App. 1988).

Sierra Wine & Liquor Co. v. Heublein, Inc., 626 F2d 129 (9th Cir. 1980).

Speidel, Richard E., and Kendall O. Clay, "Sellers Recovery of Overhead Under UCC Section 2-708 (2): Economic Costs Theory and Contractual Remedial Policy." 57 *Cornell Law Review* 681 (1972).

Stockney, Clyde P., and Paul Brown, *Financial Reporting and Statement Analysis.* Fort Worth, TX: Dryden Press, 1999.

Sunder, S., "The Relationship Between Accounting Changes and Stock Prices: Problems of Measurement and some Empirical Evidence." *Empirical Research in Accounting: Selected Studies* (1973).

Terrell v. Household Goods Carriers' Bureau, 494 F2d 16, 23.

Trout, Robert R., and Carrol B. Foster, "Economic Analysis of Business Interruption Losses," in *Litigation Economics*, Patrick A. Gaughan and Robert Thornton, eds. Greenwich, CT: JAI Press, 1993, 151–174.

Universal Power Systems, Inc. v. Godfather's Pizza, Inc., 818 F2d 667 (8th Cir. 1987).

Wagner, Michael, "How Do You Measure Damages: Lost Income or Lost Cash Flow." *Journal of Accountancy* (February 1990): 28–33.

Wecker, William, and Roman L. Weil, "Statistical Estimation of Incremental Cost Data from Accounting Data," in *Litigation Services Handbook*, 2nd ed., Roman L. Weil, Michael J. Wagner, and Peter Frank, eds. Wiley, 1995.

Willred Co. v. Westmoreland Metal Manufacturing Co., 200 F. Supp. 59 (E.D. Pa. 1961).

Willred Company and Professional Metal Manufacturing Company v. Westmoreland Metal Mfg. Co., 200 F. Supp. 59, 1961.

7

TIME VALUE OF MONEY CONSIDERATIONS

Given that the plaintiff may incur a loss prior to and after a judgment date, the computation of a potential award needs to take into account the opportunity costs of past losses and simultaneously assign a present value to losses expected to occur in the future.[1] Whether the expert puts forward past losses inclusive of such opportunity costs depends on the position of the court on this issue. The discounting of future losses is more straightforward.

If it were established that a plaintiff lost a certain historical sum as a result of a business interruption, an award to the plaintiff of the exact sum would be an undercompensation. Had those monies been available at the time of the loss, they could have been invested thus equaling a greater amount on the trial date. Therefore, a rate of return needs to be applied to convert the monies that are being awarded "late" to trial date terms. Similarly, the reasoning for discounting future losses is that if it is established that the plaintiff will lose certain sums in the future, then awarding the projected future amounts on the judgment date overcompensates the plaintiff. This overcompensation comes from the fact that the plaintiff is getting access to the sums earlier than it otherwise would in the normal course of business. The monies that are received early can then be invested and grow to an even greater amount in the future. To prevent overcompensation, a rate of return must be incorporated into the award computation process to determine the *present value* of the projected future losses.

The computation of the present value of a loss can be broken down into two parts: the selection of the appropriate discount (prejudgment) rate and the compu-

---

[1]John C. Kier and Robin C. Kier, "Opportunity Cost: A Measure of Prejudgment Interest," *Business Lawyer*, vol. 39 (November 1983): 129–152.

tation of the present value using the selected rate of return. Prior to discussing the application of a prejudgment return and the process of discounting, the reader is provided some background on interest rates and securities markets. Experts need to have a clear understanding of the sources of the various rates that can be chosen to compute the time value of money. Such an understanding should include knowledge of the risk characteristics of the securities that offer different rates.

DETERMINATION OF INTEREST RATES

Interest rates reflect the rate of return that an investor may earn by forgoing consumption until a future time period. The lender provides capital to investors who use it to attempt to generate a rate of return that is sufficient to compensate the lender for the foregone consumption. For a compounded rate of return, this relationship is summarized by the following formula:

$$Y = X\,(1 + r)^n \qquad\qquad (7.1)$$

where X = amount lent
         r = annual rate of return
         Y = amount that must be paid back
         n = investment period

When the capital is invested for more than one period, that is when n in Equation 7.1 is greater than 1, investors enjoy a compounded rate of return where interest is earned on interest. This contrasts with *simple interest,* where interest is computed only on the original principal and does not include any accrued interest (see Equation 7.2).

$$Y = Xrn \qquad\qquad (7.2)$$

TYPES OF INTEREST RATES

When interest rates are discussed in the media, one can get the impression that there is only one interest rate. In fact, there are many rates. Fortunately, they tend to move together, so when some rates rise most of the others move in the same direction. That is, there is a risk-return relationship between the perceived risk of various securities and their return. When there is a change in the rate of return of some instruments, such as an increase in the rate of return for some of the low-risk securities, those securities with a higher perceived risk must increase their return in order to be competitive. This adjustment process may take place through changing prices offered for the affected securities. The risk-return relationship is discussed in greater detail later in this chapter. Some of the more common interest rates that are cited and used in commercial damages analysis are discussed below.

FINANCIAL MARKETS: MONEY MARKET VERSUS CAPITAL MARKET

There are two broad categories of financial markets: the money market and the capital market. These are not physical markets in the sense that the New York Stock Exchange is a physical market. Rather, they are defined by the term and the risk level of the securities included in the various market categories.

MONEY MARKET SECURITIES AND INTEREST RATES

The money market consists of short-term, low-risk financial instruments.[2] The market is a subsector of the fixed income market and features low-risk, highly marketable, short-term debt securities.[3] These securities have a maturity of 270 days or less, except for one-year Treasuries which are also included in this market. They differ from their long-term counterparts in that they do not have to be registered pursuant to Federal securities laws. Indeed, securities with maturities in excess of 270 days have to be registered and incur the costs of that registration process. Table 7.1 describes some of the major money market securities.

Table 7.1 Major Money Market Securities

Treasury Bills	These are the short term obligations of the Federal Government. They vary in maturity which can be as long as one year. T-bills are sold at a discount from their face value with the difference, as a percent of the purchase price, being the interest return. These securities enjoy the greatest marketability of all money market securities. T-bills are regularly sold with 91-day and 182-day T-bills being sold weekly and one year T-bills being sold monthly.

---

[2]See Frank Fabozzi and Franco Modigliani, *Capital Markets: Institutions and Instruments*, 3rd ed. (Upper Saddle River, NJ: Prentice-Hall, 2003), 400–416.

[3]Ziv Bodie, Alex Kane, and Alan J. Marcus, *Investments* (New York: McGraw-Hill, 2002), 28–34.

Table 7.1   Major Money Market Securities *(continued)*

Federal Funds	Federal funds consist of the required reserve balances that a bank must maintain in an account with the Federal Reserve. Banks may borrow or lend excess reserves with other banks. The price of these funds is called the Federal Funds rate. The Federal Reserve Bank focuses on this rate when it is attempting to implement monetary policy. Changes in this federal funds rate are an important indicator of the tightness or looseness of monetary policy and thus affect rates on other securities.
Commercial Paper	These are short term promissory notes of well-known corporations. They are considered low-risk as the issuers are usually well established companies and the issues are typically backed by a line of credit. They have maturities that vary between five and 270 days but many have maturities of one to two months. They are issued in multiples of $100,000. While the maturities tend to be short, companies can extend the maturity by rolling over the issue. Investors try to gauge the risk of a given issue by examining its rating, which is issued by one of the major ratings agencies such as Standard & Poor's or Moody's.
Negotiable Certificates of Deposit	These are time deposits with a bank that are issued in denominations $100,000 or more and are usually negotiable. They are quite marketable, although the marketability may be lower for certificates with longer maturities. They have the advantage of being insured by the FDIC up to $100,000 which lowers their riskiness.
Repurchase Agreements	These are agreements for the trading of government securities on an overnight basis. A trader, such as a government securities dealer, may sell the security and agree to buy it back at a certain time (such as the next day) at a slightly higher price that becomes the interest return.
Banker's Acceptances	These are bank obligations used in international trade. For example, an importer may want a bank to accept its debt obligation and pay an exporter's bank. Banker's acceptances are like a post-dated check that is stamped or accepted by a bank; it then assumes the responsibility for the ultimate payment of the obligation. These acceptances may then trade in the market at a discount to the face value of the obligation just like other money market securities.

One can learn what the relevant money market rates are in several ways, but one of the most common sources is the credit markets section of most major newspapers. A sample of the type of interest rate data that are depicted in such media is provided in Table 7.2.

Major Money Market Rates

The different securities shown in Table 7.1 offer different interest rates. However, a few money market rates, such as those shown in Table 7.3 and Exhibit 7.1, are very often cited and serve as benchmarks for other rates in the marketplace.

Table 7.2   Example of Money Market Rates and Their Sources, as of July 21, 2003

Type of Money Market	Rate	Source
Prime Rate:	4.00%	The Federal Reserve
Discount Rate:	2.00%	The Federal Reserve
Federal Funds:	1.02%	The Federal Reserve
Commercial Paper (AA Financial 30 day):	1.01%	The Federal Reserve
Certificates of Deposit:	1.06%	The Federal Reserve
Bankers Acceptances:	1.05%	Prebon Yamane (USA), Inc.
London Interbank Offered Rates		Money Rates,
(LIBOR) (6-month):	1.11%	*Wall Street Journal*
Treasury Bills (short term, 6-month):	0.96%	The Federal Reserve
Overnight Repurchase Rate (Weighted Average):	1.01%	The Federal Reserve

CAPITAL MARKET

Securities with a maturity longer than 270 days are categorized within the capital market. Upon crossing this threshold, issuers of securities, with the exception of the U.S. Treasury, are required by the Securities Act of 1933 to register the securities with the Securities and Exchange Commission, a body formed as part of the Securities Exchange Act of 1934. Issuers of these securities use the proceeds from

Table 7.3   Often Cited Interest Rates

Prime Rate	This is the rate that banks charge their most credit worthy customers. Interest rates are often quoted as some increment above the prime rate such as "prime plus three."
Federal Funds Rate	This is the rate that banks charge each other in the trading of federal funds; it may take place through intermediaries. This rate is often used by the Federal Reserve Bank as a guide to the tightness of short term credit markets which, in turn, is used to guide monetary policy.
Treasury Bill Rate	T-bill rates are the rates on the lowest-risk money market investments offered by the U.S. Treasury. They are at the bottom of the yield curve. This curve usually slopes upwards; higher rates are associated with longer-term Treasuries.
LIBOR	This is the rate that large banks in London charge each other for interbank loans. The loans are short-term. LIBOR is typically about 1 percent above the short-term T-Bill rate.
Discount Rate	The discount rate is the rate charged on loans by the Federal Reserve Bank to member banks. The banks must present collateral, such as Treasury securities, and, in return, they receive an amount less than the face value of the securities. This difference as a percent of the loan amount is the discount rate. Changes in this rate are another way the Federal Reserve conducts monetary policy.

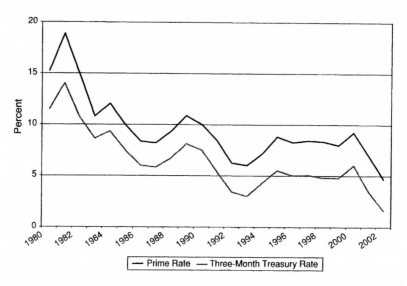

Exhibit 7.1   Prime rate and the three-month treasury rate: 1980–2002.

these offerings for long-term capital needs. With the additional length of term, purchasers of these securities must assume a greater risk and, therefore, expect a higher rate of return.

Table 7.4 describes the important categories of securities that trade in the capital market. Exhibit 7.2 shows the historical rates of return for some of these securities.

Table 7.4   Capital Market Security Categories

Treasury Bonds	Both Intermediate Term and Long Term Treasuries are considered capital market securities. Intermediate-term Treasuries have a maturity of one–ten years while long-term Treasuries have a maturity of ten years or more. With the longer term and the greater risk that this entails, they offer a higher rate of return. Unlike other capital market securities, this risk does not come from additional default risk, since the insurer is the U.S. Treasury. Given the creditworthiness of the U.S. Treasury, any additional default risk is considered negligible. The increased risk comes in the form of greater *reinvestment risk,* which is the risk that payments derived from these securities over the life of the investment. Such interest and principal payments are reinvested at a lower rate than the original investment.

Table 7.4 Capital Market Security Categories *(continued)*

Municipal Bonds	These are the debt obligations issued by state and local governments and various authorities. The interest payments on these bonds are exempt from federal taxation and from taxation in the locality in which they are issued.
Federal Agency Debt	These are the debt obligations of certain government agencies, such as the Federal National Mortgage Association (Fannie Mae) and the Government National Mortgage Association (Ginnie Mae). They issue these securities to finance their activities. Markets tend to assume that if there were a default, the federal government would step in to assist. Therefore, they are considered to be virtually free of default risk.
Corporate Bonds	These are the long-term debt obligations of corporations. They are a more risky investment than Treasury securities and, therefore, offer a higher rate of return.* The bonds may be secured by specific assets or unsecured, in which case they are called debentures. Companies may have several different issues outstanding, with certain issues being subordinate to others. Investors can assess the degree of risk of these bonds through a rating system offered by firms such as Standard & Poor's and Moody's. For example, Standard & Poor's rates the highest quality bonds as AAA while the lowest quality, those in default, are rated D. The lower the quality of a corporate bond, the higher the rate needed to compensate investors for assuming the increased risk.
Common Stock	These securities constitute the equity interest of the owners of corporations. They are the first securities to be issued by a corporation and the last to be retired. Stockholders are compensated through dividend payments and capital gains (losses). These securities bear a higher degree of risk than corporate bonds, as the latter category of securities enjoy a preference in the bankruptcy liquidation process. In this process monies derived from the sale of liquidated corporate assets cannot be paid to equity holders until the claims of bondholders are satisfied. Given that stockholders often get little or nothing in liquidation, and often do poorly in corporate reorganizations, stock are considered more risky than bonds. However, stockholders participate in the prosperity of a company that enjoys increased profitability while bondholders, who hold fixed income obligations, receive payments that are usually fixed. Therefore, the return for stockholders is expected to be higher than those for bondholders, this reflects the greater risk and return of these securities.

*This discussion implies that the higher the level of risk the greater the rate of return. Strictly speaking however, this is not accurate. It has been demonstrated that the market will not compensate investors for all types of risk but only for those risks that cannot easily be avoided through diversification This risk is called systematic risk and there is a good relationship between rates of return and the level of systematic risk.

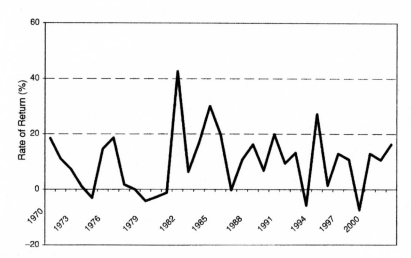

Exhibit 7.2a   Historical rates of return for long-term corporate bonds.

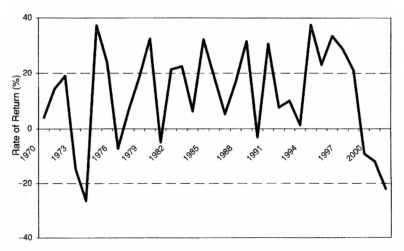

Exhibit 7.2b   Historical rates of return for large company stock.

REAL VERSUS NOMINAL INTEREST RATES

When lenders establish interest rates, they ensure that they are repaid by dollars that have at least the same buying power as the ones they lent. That is, they make sure that they earn a specific rate of return in excess of the rate of inflation. The inflation-adjusted return is known as the *real* rate of return. If, for example, a loan is made during a period of inflation, and the inflation was unanticipated, the dollars that are repaid may have less buying power than the dollars that were lent. Consider a loan that is made at a time when inflation was anticipated to be 3 percent. Based upon this belief, the lender loaned money at a 9 percent rate, seeking a 6 percent real rate of return. However, over the term of the loan, if inflation unexpectedly rose to 5 percent, it would erode the real rate of return to 4 percent from the anticipated 6 percent.

In inflationary periods where the inflation is unanticipated, borrowers gain because they pay back dollars that have a lower buying power than the dollars they lent. This gain comes at the expense of lenders who incorrectly anticipate the inflation. This loss and gain is known as the *redistribution effect* of inflation.[4] To avoid the adverse consequences of inflation, market participants must ensure that they correctly anticipate inflation. If inflation is stable, it is easier to anticipate inflation correctly. An unstable inflationary environment makes financial markets more difficult for participants and results in higher interest rates.

Fisher Equation

One of the first great American economists, Irving Fisher, clearly delineated the relationship between nominal and real interest rates.[5] This relationship has been termed the *Fisher Effect*.[6] This equation shows that the nominal rate of interest is equal to the real rate of return and the expected rate of inflation (see Equation 7.3).

$$(1 + r_n) = (1 + r_r) \times (1 + p) \qquad (7.3)$$

[4]Milton Friedman, *Dollars and Deficits* (Englewood Cliffs, NJ: Prentice-Hall, 1968).

[5]Irving Fisher, *Theory of Interest* (New York: A.M. Kelley Publishers, 1965). This book, however, was originally published in 1930.

[6]Stephen Ross, Randolph W. Westerfield, and Bradford Jordan, *Essentials of Corporate Finance,* 4th ed. (Homewood, IL: Irwin, 2004), 181–182.

where r_n = nominal rate of interest
        r_r = real rate of interest
        p = inflation rate

If we rearrange Equation 7.3, we get Equation 7.4:

$$(1 + r_n) = r_r + p + r_r \times p \qquad\qquad (7.4)$$

There are three components to the transformed Fisher equation. The first is the real return that an investor expects to receive on an investment. The second component of the nominal rate reflects inflationary expectations. The third component shows that the rate of return itself reflects the reduced buying power of the rate that is actually earned. This last component is usually small and is therefore often dropped to result in a short form. This simplified Fisher equation is shown in Equation 7.5:

$$r_n = r_r + p \qquad\qquad (7.5)$$

Example Using the Fisher Equation

Let us assume that the real rate of interest is 3 percent. Let us further assume that the inflation rate is 4 percent. The Fisher equation in 7.3 shows us that the nominal rate is as follows:

$$
\begin{aligned}
(1 + r_n) &= (1 + r_r) \times (1 + p) \\
&= (1.04)(1.03) \qquad\qquad (7.6) \\
&= 1.0712
\end{aligned}
$$

We can see that the simple Fisher equation indicates a nominal rate of 3 percent plus 4 percent or 7 percent.

Additional Comment of Nominal versus Real Rates in Business Interruption Analysis

It is important to know the distinction between nominal and real rates when one is applying and analyzing different interest rates. However, analysts and experts in litigation need to recognize that the rates with which they often deal—rates that are quoted in the marketplace—are quoted in nominal terms. Applying the Fisher equation allows one to gain a sense of how much of the quoted rate is due to price expectations. This, however, may not play a direct role in a particular case.

DETERMINANTS OF INTEREST RATES

In each market, interest rates are determined by the supply and demand of capital. The interaction of capital providers and those who want to borrow results in an equilibrium rate such as that shown in Exhibit 7.3.

If all other factors are constant, an increase in demand causes rates to rise, whereas a decline in demand causes rates to fall. This is demonstrated in Exhibit 7.4a. An increase in the supply of loanable funds causes rates to decline; a decrease in the supply of loanable funds will cause rates to rise (see Exhibit 7.4b).

Relationship between Risk and Return

The higher the level of risk of a security, the higher its rate of return. To understand this, consider two securities that are the same in all respects including their rates of return but which differ in their risk. Security Y has more risk than security X. Sellers seeking to sell both security X and Y will find that buyers are unwilling to buy Y—it offers only the same return as X but requires buyers to assume more risk than X. The only way that sellers will be able to sell Y is to offer a higher rate of return than X. How *much* higher depends on the risk that buyers perceive in Y. The result of this risk-return tradeoff process is a ranking of securities in the marketplace; securities with higher risk have to offer higher rates of return in order to compete for the available funds of investors.

Table 7.5 shows several average rates of return for securities that vary in their risk levels. Common stocks have higher risk than corporate bonds which, in turn,

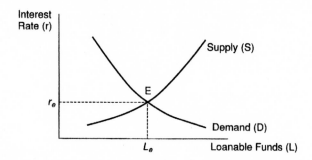

Exhibit 7.3   Demand and supply of loanable funds.

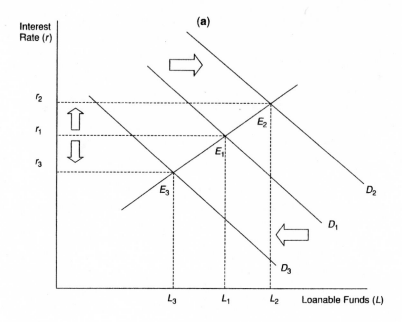

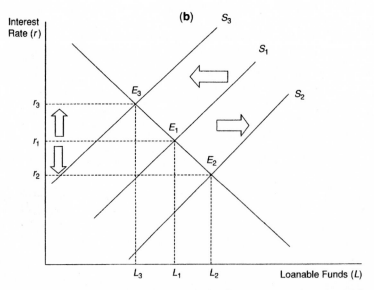

Exhibit 7.4   (a) Changes in demand for and, **(b)** changes in supply of loanable funds.

Table 7.5 Average Rates of Return

Average	Long-Term Treasury Bonds	Long-Term Corporate Bonds	Large Company Stocks
1980–2002	11.1%	11.0%	13.0%
1990–99	8.8%	8.4%	18.2%
1980–89	12.6%	13.0%	17.5%
1970–79	5.5%	6.2%	5.9%

Source: Calculated by Economatrix Research Associates, Inc. using data presented in *Stocks, Bonds, Bills and Inflation*® *2003 Yearbook,* © 2003 Ibbotson Associates, Inc. Based on copyrighted works by Ibbotson and Sinquefeld. All rights reserved. Used with permission.

have higher risk than Treasuries. Table 7.5 illustrates how these securities offer higher rates of return in accordance to the risk that the market perceives in these securities.

Sources of Rate of Return Data

The most frequently cited source of rate of return data is the annual volume *Stocks, Bills, Bonds and Inflation* published by Ibbotson Associates.[7] It is a book that every damages expert should own. The book is an outgrowth of a seminal study published by Roger Ibbotson and Rex Sinquefeld in 1976.[8] The study quantified the historical rates of return on various securities and became the start of the database that is published in the *Stocks, Bills, Bonds and Inflation* yearbook. The book provides a wide variety of rate of returns statistics as well as tables which allow the expert to look up the average rate of return for many broad categories of securities from 1926 through the last full year. The security categories covered by Ibbotson Associates are Treasury bills, intermediate-term Treasuries, long-term Treasuries, corporate bonds, large-capitalization common stocks, and small-capitalization common stocks. The book also includes many statistics on the variability of securities, helping to explain their risk and rate of return.

Calculating Rates of Return

Experts need to be aware of how the rates of return they use are computed as well as the difference between the rates quoted on a security and its rate of return. A one-period rate of return is defined as the income derived during the period divided by the purchase price. For a security such as a stock purchased at the start

---

[7]*Stocks, Bills, Bonds and Inflation*, annual, Ibbotson Associates, Chicago, Illinois.

[8]Roger Ibbotson and Rex Sinquefeld, "Stocks, Bills, Bonds and Inflation: Year-by-Year Historical Returns (1926–1974)," *Journal of Business* 49 (2) (January 1976): 11–47.

of the period, this could be the sum of any change in the price of the security plus any dividends received divided by the purchase price (see Equation 7.7).

$$\text{One-Period Rate of Return on a Stock} = \frac{(\text{Price change} + \text{Cash dividend})}{\text{Purchase Price}} \qquad (7.7)$$

For an interest-paying bond, the one-period rate of return is similarly computed as shown in Equation 7.8.

$$\text{One-Period Rate of Return on a Bond} = \frac{(\text{Price change} + \text{Interest Income})}{\text{Purchase Price}} \qquad (7.8)$$

Data sources such as Ibbotson Associates show various rates of return for large categories of securities of large-capitalization stocks. Such returns can be readily computed using the value of market indices such as the S&P 500. Periodic returns can be computed in a similar fashion as shown in Equation 7.9.

$$\text{One-Period Rate of Return for a Market Index} = \frac{(\text{Index value change} + \text{Cash flow income})}{\text{Index value at the beginning of the period}} \qquad (7.9)$$

Computing Average Rates of Return over Historical Periods

There are two ways that a historical average rate of return can be computed. These are the arithmetic and geometric mean. The arithmetic mean annual rate of return is the simple average of the annual rates of return over the historical period. This is expressed in Equation 7.10.

$$r_a = 1 / n \sum_{i=1}^{n} r_t \qquad (7.10)$$

where r_a = the arithmetic rate of return;
r_t = the rate of return generated over the period t and $t-1$
n = the number of periods used for computing the average

The geometric mean can be computed as follows:

$$r_g = [Y_n/Y_0]^{1/n} - 1 \qquad (7.11)$$

where r_g = the geometric mean
Y_n = the value at the end of period n
Y_0 = the value at time 0
n = the number of periods over which we are computing the geometric mean

The geometric mean generally is less than or equal to the arithmetic mean. However, the arithmetic mean better measures "a typical performance over single periods and serves as the correct rate for forecasting, discounting, and estimating the costs of capital."[9]

Term Structure of Interest Rates

Another important relationship involving rates that may be used to discount future losses or to being historical loss amounts to present value terms is what is known as the term structure of interest rates. This refers to the relationship between rates of securities at different maturities and of a similar credit quality.[10] The more common circumstance is for yields on longer term securities, such as long term Treasuries, to have a higher yield than their shorter term equivalents. There are various theories, which attempt to explain the common upward sloping nature of this relationship which is sometimes graphically depicted as a yield curve.[11] One of the more often cited theories is the expectation theory, which states that long term rates are a function of current short term rates and expected future short term rates. When future short term rates are expected to rise, then long term rates, being partially a function of future rates, have to be higher than short term rates. Sometimes, however, we can have a downward sloping yield curve. This is called an inverted yield curve. Some analysts believe that a flat or downward sloping yield curve is a predictor of recession. For experts in litigation, the yield curve enters the picture when they have to decide whether to use long term rates or short term rates to discount future losses to present value. While this will be discussed later in this chapter, at this point we will just state that many experts believe that one should roughly match the term of the securities being used as a guide to the discount rate, with the term or the loss stream being discounted.

PREJUDGMENT LOSSES

If the expert discounts future losses to present value, it would also be reasonable to bring historical losses to present value terms. In order to make the injured firm whole for past damages, one may need to apply a prejudgment rate of return to the projected past losses so as to convert them to current terms. The allowable

---

[9]*Stocks, Bills, Bonds and Inflation: 2003 Yearbook* (Chicago, IL: Ibbotson Associates), 100.

[10]Peter S. Rose, *Money and Capital Markets,* 8th ed. (New York: Irwin McGraw-Hill, 2003), 179–181.

[11]Jeff Madura, Financial Markets and Institutions, 6th ed. (New York: Thompson South-Western) 56–66.

rate of return may be established by a statute which defines the rate of prejudg-ment interest. If this rate is applied by the courts, the issue is elementary. In such instances, the court may want the expert to present losses without any adjustment for the historical time value of money. The court may want to independently do this computation and it may want to avoid the possibility of "double counting." However, if the court seeks testimony of the appropriate prejudgment rate, there are several alternatives that can be considered.

Selection of Appropriate Prejudgment Rate

There are differing views within economics and finance as to the appropriate rate of return to apply to historical damages to bring them to trial date terms. At a min-imum, past losses should be converted to present value terms using a risk-free rate such as the rate on U.S. Treasury bills.[12] Some believe that the defendant's debt rate should be used as the prejudgment rate of return based upon the theory that once the defendant engaged in its wrongful actions, it was, in effect, in debt to the plaintiff—as it "owed" the plaintiff its lost profits.[13] The use of the defen-dant's debt rate, which is higher than the risk-free rate, results in a higher present value of losses. This choice of prejudgment returns, however, is not generally accepted within this field. The use of the risk-free rate, or the defendant's debt rate, will not fully compensate the plaintiff for its opportunity costs. If the plain-tiff had received the lost profits at the time it would have earned them but for the actions of the defendant, it would have either reinvested them in the business and/or distributed a component to shareholders. The use of the lower rates de-scribed above may not compensate the plaintiff for the lost investment opportu-nities that it could have enjoyed. Another guide to use in the determination of the prejudgment rate is the plaintiff's cost of capital. This is the expected rate of return that the market requires in order to attract funds to a particular usage or investment.[14] This is the weighted average of each of the individual costs of cap-ital for each of the components in the company's capital structure. For example,

---

[12]R.F. Lanzillotti and A.K. Esquibel, "Measuring Damages in Commercial Litigation: Present Value of Lost Opportunities," *Journal of Accounting, Auditing and Finance* (1989): 125–142 and Franklin M. Fisher and R. Craig Romaine, "Janis Joplin's Yearbook and the Theory of Damages," *Journal of Accounting, Auditing and Finance* (1989): 145–157.

[13]James M. Patell, Roman L. Weil, and Mark A. Wolfson, "Accumulating Damages in Litigation: The Role of Uncertainty and Interest Rates," *Journal of Legal Studies* XI (2) (June 1982): 341–364.

[14]Shannon P. Pratt, *Cost of Capital: Estimation and Applications* (New York: Wiley, 1998), 3.

if the firm derived half its capital from borrowing and half from equity investments, each weight is 0.50. The rate of return on equity would be higher than the
debt rate due to the increased risk associated with equity investments. Let us
assume that the debt rate is 10 percent and the equity rate is 15 percent. The
weighted cost of capital would be as follows:

$$\text{Cost of capital} = w_d r_d + w_e r_e \qquad (7.12)$$

where w_d = percent of debt in the capital structure
        w_e = percent of equity in the capital structure
        r_d = rate paid on debt
        r_e = rate of return on equity

Based on the parameters of the above example, the cost of capital would be:

$$0.50 \ (10\%) + 0.50 \ (15\%) = 12.5\%$$

When the firm has a more varied capital structure, with different layers of debt
and other forms of capital, such as preferred stock, the cost of capital can be
expressed in the following weighted average form:

$$\text{Cost of capital} = \sum_{i=1}^{n} w_i r_i \qquad (7.13)$$

where w_i = percent of total capital the ith type of capital in the firm's total
            capital structure
        r_i = rate of return on the ith capital source

Equation 7.13 simply means that the cost of capital is the weighted average of the
costs of the components of the firm's capital mix.

For a profitable firm, the return provided by the cost of capital may be lower
than the actual rate of return the firm earns in a given year (depending on how you
define this rate of return). The cost of capital, however, is a rate of return which is
sufficient for a company to meet its interest obligations and repay its debt principal, while also allowing for an equity return that is consistent with this type of
business. It is important to note that the payment of a rate of return equal to the
cost of capital is not a "break even" return. It is a return which is equal to the return
contracted for by new nonequity capital providers; it enables new equity holders
to receive the return they expected at the time they made their investment.

In computing damages for a division of a diversified firm that operates in
many lines of business and has several divisions, it may be more appropriate to
use the divisional cost of capital. When that is not easily defined, the economist
can look at the costs of capital for companies that are similar to the division in
question. The individual components of the capital mix of a firm and their respective costs are discussed.

COMPONENTS OF THE COST OF CAPITAL

Cost of Debt. The rate on debt is more straightforward than the equity rate. The debt rate is stipulated when the firm enters into borrowing agreements. For example, if the firm always borrows at the prime rate, this may be a good estimate of the debt rate. The situation becomes only slightly more complicated when the firm has more than one source of debt.

If the company has borrowed from banks at varying rates, a weighted average can be taken for a historical period such as five years. The weights used are the amounts borrowed. When the company has borrowed in securities markets by issuing corporate bonds, however, the rate on these securities needs to be added to the debt rate calculation in the same weighted manner as before.

It is the norm in corporate finance to express the debt rate on an after-tax cost basis.[15] This reflects the tax benefits which are derived through the tax deductibility of interest payments. On an after-tax basis, the cost of debt can be expressed as:

$$r_d^t = r_d \, (1 - t) \tag{7.14}$$

where t = firm's tax rate
r_d = before-tax debt rate
r_d^t = after-tax debt rate

For public debt in the form of corporate bonds, these rates can be further adjusted to reflect the flotation costs.

Preferred Stock. Preferred stock typically pays a constant dividend and is more similar to debt than common stock. The cost of preferred stock can be expressed in the following way:

$$r_p = \frac{d_p}{P_{net}} \tag{7.15}$$

where d_p = preferred stock dividend
P_{net} = net proceeds of the preferred stock offering after deducting flotation costs

Rate on Equity. The determination of the appropriate rate of return on equity is less straightforward. This is the rate of return which is expected by the firm's

---

[15]Eugene F. Brigham and Philip R. Davies, *Intermediate Financial Management,* 8th ed. (New York: Thomson South-Western, 2004), and R. Charles Moyer, James R. McGuigan, and William J. Kretlow, *Contemporary Financial Management*, 9th ed. (New York: Thomson South-Western Company, 2003).

equity investors. For publicly held companies, the historical return on equity is a readily available statistic. It tends to be higher for firms that are riskier. For newer firms, however, the rate of return on equity provided by securities markets may not be as useful. In such instances, it is valuable to consider the equity rates of *proxy companies*. Because these companies are in the same industry, are of similar size, and have similar risk characteristics as the injured company, the rate of return on equity for such companies can be used as a proxy for the injured company's equity rate.

The rate of return on equity may be different depending on whether the equity is derived from internal sources, such as retained earnings, or external ones. The cost of internal equity capital is often represented by the Gordon model as follows:[16]

$$k_e = d_1 / P_0 + g \qquad (7.16)$$

where k_e = the cost of internal equity
          d_1 = next period's dividend
          P_0 = the stock price at time 0
          g = the growth rate of dividends

Using another approach, the appropriate risk-adjusted return relationship can be approximated using the *capital asset pricing model* or CAPM. This model generates *betas* to weight the difference between the market rate of return and the risk-free rate. Betas are derived from a regression analysis of the historical movements of the individual firm's stock return (r_i) and the excess market return ($r_m - r_f$). Betas reflect the variability of the stock's return which can be explained by market movements. This is referred to as *systematic risk*. Systematic risk is that component of total risk which cannot be reduced through diversification. Each firm has its own beta which is used to adjust the excess return ($r_m - r_f$) and reflect the firm's unique risk characteristics. Using this model, the following equity rate can be derived as shown in Equation 7.17:

$$k_e = r_f + \beta_i (r_m - r_f) \qquad (7.17)$$

where k_e = cost of equity
      r_f = risk-free rate
      r_m = market rate of return
      β_i = beta for company i.

---

[16]For a discussion of the cost of equity capital see J. Fred Weston, Scott Besley, and Eugene Brigham, *Essentials of Managerial Finance*, 11th ed. (Fort Worth, TX: Dryden Press, 1996), 576–579.

The capital asset pricing model, and betas in particular, have been the subject of criticism.[17] The strength of the hypothesized positive, linear relationship between betas and security returns was challenged when Fama and French showed that the inclusion of other variables, such as size, significantly reduces the explanatory power of betas. They have expanded the usual CAPM into a *three-factor model* which includes other explanatory variables, such as firm size. Their results follow some other challenges to the capital asset pricing model. However, the CAPM has certainly not been discarded and continues to be a valuable tool in corporate finance.

Betas for many companies can be found in a variety of places. Many investment publications, such as *Value Line Investment Survey*, include betas in the collection of financial statistics they publish on the companies covered in their publication.[18] Another source is the *Beta Book* published by Ibbotson Associates.[19] A sample of the betas for the Dow Jones Industrial Average 30 companies derived from *Value Line* is shown in Table 7.6.

For privately held companies, the rate of return on equity is more difficult to establish. These statistics are not as readily available as they are for publicly held firms. The problem is even greater for the smaller private companies, which, since they are not encumbered by the requirement to meet expected returns for stockholders, tend to have higher "costs" than they otherwise would. The rates of return on equity for these businesses, therefore, are not comparable to those provided by securities markets. The rates for similar public firms can be used after the addition of a risk premium in order to account for the increased risk and illiquidity associated with many private firms. The expert needs to determine the appropriateness of this approach on a case-by-case basis.

Sources of Cost of Capital Data

The cost of capital for a company can be measured directly by determining the components in the company's capital mix and the relevant rate that the company pays for each one of them. Using these data, weights for each component can be computed and applied to the relevant rates to arrive at a weighted average cost of capital. These data may be acquired directly from the company or from public filings that the company has generated.

---

[17]Eugene F. Fama and Kenneth French, "The Cross Section of Expected Stock Returns," *Journal of Finance* (June 1992): 427–465.

[18]*Value Line Investment Survey* (New York: Value Line Publishing).

[19]*Beta Book* (Chicago, IL: Ibbotson Associates).

Table 7.6 Betas for the Dow Jones Industrial Average Companies

Components of Dow Jones Industrial Average		
Symbol	Company	BETA
AA	Alcoa Inc.	1.15
GE	General Electric Co.	1.30
JNJ	Johnson & Johnson	0.75
MSFT	Microsoft	1.15
AXP	American Express	1.50
GM	General Motors	1.20
JPM	JP Morgan Chase	1.55
PG	Procter & Gamble	0.60
BA	Boeing Co	1.00
HD	Home Depot Inc	1.40
KO	Coca Cola Co	0.70
SBC	SBS Comms	0.95
C	CitiGroup	1.55
HON	Honeywell Intl	1.25
MCD	McDonald's	0.95
T	AT&T Corp	NMF*
CAT	Caterpillar Inc.	1.10
HPQ	Hewlett-Packard	1.30
MMM	3M Company	0.90
UTX	United Tech CP	1.15
DD	DuPont Co	1.00
IBM	Intl Business Mach.	1.05
MO	Altria Group	0.70
WMT	Wal-Mart Stores	1.05
DIS	Walt Disney Co	1.15
INTC	Intel Corp	1.25
MRK	Merck & Co	0.95
XOM	Exxon Mobil	0.80
EK	Eastman Kodak	1.00
IP	Intl Paper Co	1.00

*Not measurable figure.
Source: The Value Line Investment Survey

Another source of cost of capital data is the *Cost of Capital Quarterly* year-book.[20] This data source includes capital costs, such as the cost of equity, and is organized by SIC code. Capital costs are available for approximately 300 different SIC codes. The data is organized by industry category rather than by company.

Ibbotson Associates culls these data from the Compustat data files. This is a data source published by Standard & Poor's that has financial data, including financial statements, for a large number of public companies.

[20]*Cost of Capital Quarterly* (Chicago, IL: Ibbotson Associates).

Cost of Capital as an Element of Damages

In one District of Columbia case, a plaintiff appealed a district court's award of the costs of capital which was applied to damages resulting from a breach of contract.[21] The Court of Appeals indicated that such an award is appropriate in a breach of contract claim but not in a negligence claim. In its ruling, the court stated as follows:

> It remains unclear whether pre-judgement interest (interest from the time of the tort to the date of court judgement) is available in a negligence action. Nonetheless, . . . in addition to finding Williams negligent, the District court had found that Straight has breached its contract with Smoot. Further, because Williams agreed to indemnify Straight in full, the court did not error by including the costs of capital in the damage award assessed against Williams—whether or not the court allows a cost of capital award in a negligence action.

Cost of Capital in Public Utility Environment

Cost of capital is a fundamental concept in the public utility rate-making process. Many hearings in which economic experts testified on the costs of capital have been held before various rate-making commissions. The commissions typically meet to decide whether a given utility may receive an increase in its rates to reflect higher costs as well as a return on invested capital. Courts ruling on related issues have endorsed the use of a rate of return which is sufficient to allow a company to *maintain its credit and attract capital.*[22] This rate has been found to be one which affords a rate of return similar to other investments which have comparable risk levels.

A type of lawsuit that occurs in the construction industry but also elsewhere is a suit that is the result of a plaintiff's loss. Construction contractors are often requested by purchasers of their services, such as other companies or governmental entities, to post a bond. The bond guarantees their performance and protects the purchasers from a variety of failures on the part of the contractor. Such bonds may be purchased by a surety. In making their assessment of the contractor's *bonding capacity*, they tend to look at a limited number of financial variables. Paramount among them is the liquidity of the contractor as measured by

[21]*Williams Enterprises, Inc. v. The Sherman R. Smoot Company*, 938 F2d 230, 290 U.S. App. D.C. 411 (October 8, 1991.

[22]*FPC v. Hope Natural Gas Co.* 320 U.S. 591, 64 S. Ct. 281, 88, L. Fd. 333 (1944).

the size of its working capital. Working capital is the difference between current assets and current liabilities. This is explained in the excerpts included below from *S.C. Anderson v. Bank of America*:[23]

> Anderson claimed consequential damages, consisting of lost profits, based upon an alleged impairment of bonding capacity.
>
> A contractor must furnish a performance bond if it is to be awarded a public works construction project. A bid bond is a document issued by a bonding company which is attached by the contractor to its bid. The bond represents to the project owner that the contractor is bondable, and if the contractor is awarded the job, the surety company will issue a performance bond covering the work.
>
> A surety, such as Travelers, calculates a contractors bonding capacity by assessing, among other things, the contractor's working capital. Working capital consists of current assets less allowed current liabilities. By mid-1986, Anderson's financial statements disclosed that the CPII and TAII receivables had not been paid for several months. This impacted Anderson's working capital and, in August, 1986, resulted in a reduction in Anderson's bonding capacity from an aggregate exposure of $10 million to an aggregate exposure of $5 million.

There are several ways to measure the damages that a plaintiff may suffer as a result of a loss of bonding capacity. One way is to measure the reduced amount of business the plaintiff experienced due to the lower bonding capacity. The lower capacity may prevent him from taking on projects beyond a certain combined level. Defendants should explore whether the loss of the bonding capacity is truly due to their actions or is the result of other factors, such as mismanagement by the contractor. Defendants should also be mindful that a lower total business volume does not necessarily imply lower overall profitability. Some companies can generate more total profits on a smaller business volume. Their pursuit of growth, however, may cause them to take on more business and dilute their overall profitability. It can also happen that the plaintiff is prevented from bidding larger jobs due to a lower bonding capacity but is able to bid a larger number of smaller jobs—some of which may not have the same bonding requirement of larger jobs. The defendant should compute the profitability margin by job for the plaintiff in order to assess the relative profit contribution of large versus small jobs.

Another factor that should be explored by defendants in cases over loss of bonding capacity is the cost of securing alternative bonding capacity. If alterna-

---

[23]*S.C. Anderson v. Bank of America*, 24 Cal. App. 4th 529 (1994).

tive bonding capacity can be acquired at a higher price, then this difference in price may be one measure of damages instead of a lost profits analysis. If that is the case, then the issue simplifies into a higher costs of capital analysis as opposed to a lost profits exercise.

Computation of Prejudgment Interest in Patent Infringement Cases

The courts have not presented a unified position on how to compute the prejudgment return in patent infringement cases. Several rates have been found acceptable, ranging from money market rates to the prevailing prime rate during the infringement period.[24] However, there have been cases in which a plaintiff was able to demonstrate that rates in excess of the prime rate, which were the rates that it had to pay to obtain capital to stay solvent during the infringement period, were appropriate.[25]

In patent cases, prejudgment interest is applied to what are known as *base damages*. Base damages are the amount of damages that are awarded. These usually are a measure of lost profits or a reasonable royalty. Punitive multipliers may also be applied to these base damages.[26]

Risk Adjustment of Past Losses

Past losses are usually not known with certainty—they have to be estimated. Given this uncertainty, their estimation should reflect some risk adjustment process. The uncertainty associated with past losses, however, is markedly different than that of future losses. There are a number of important deterministic variables that influence the level of sales and profits that a firm can receive. These include factors such as the overall level of demand in the economy, the performance characteristics of particular types of products, consumer preferences, actions of competitors, etc. In making an *ex-post projection*, some of these factors are already known. Indeed, the methodological framework presented in this book attempts to explicitly take into account such factors in the loss estimation process.

---

[24]*Uniroyal, Inc. v. Rudkin-Wiley Co.*, F2d 1540 (Fed. Cir. 1991).

[25]*Lam, Inc. v. Johns Manville Corp.*, 718 F2d 1056, 219 U.S.P.Q. 670 (Fed. Cir. 1983).

[26]*Gyromat Corporation v. Champion Spark Plug Company*, 735 F2d 549 (Fed. Cir. 1984).

Given the more complete nature of the information set that applies to past losses compared to future losses, there is a very different level of uncertainty associated with them. For future losses, many of the deterministic variables are unknown; for past losses, they are known historical values. To the extent that the historical loss estimation process already took the variation in the relevant risk factors into account, the past losses may already be risk-adjusted through the use of the information set that is available as of the date of the analysis. If the expert explicitly attempted to do this in the estimation process, then no further risk adjustment of past estimated losses is necessary. If not, then some accommodation for such uncertainty needs to be made. The risk adjustment process for past losses presents a fertile area for cross-examination when the expert has ignored this issue in estimating losses.

DISCOUNTING PROJECTED FUTURE PROFITS

Future projected losses must be converted to present value. The reason is that if an award of damages is made as of a trial date, but the future losses would not be incurred for some period of time in the future, then the early receipt of such an award would overcompensate the plaintiff—such monies could be invested and would equal an even greater amount in the future. A lesser amount, the present value of future losses, needs to be computed.

In order to compute the present value of a future amount, a *discount rate* must be selected. This rate may include a premium to account for the riskiness of a projected income stream. Generally speaking, risk is the possibility that the rate of return may deviate from expectations. In investment analysis, risk is the variability of an asset's returns.[27] This risk is quantified using statistical measures such as the variance and standard deviation of returns. In corporate finance, the risk adjustment process is focused on variables such as cash flows and is measured using a variety of statistical techniques.[28] If one were to graph the variability of common stock returns relative to a lower-risk security, such as long-term Treasuries, one would see a greater degree of dispersion for stock returns compared to the returns on long-term Treasuries.[29] This comparative variability is

---

[27]See Edwin J. Elton and Martin J. Gruber, *Modern Portfolio Theory and Investment Analysis* (New York: Wiley, 1995), 128–180.

[28]Aswath Damodaran, *Corporate Finance* (New York: Wiley, 1997), 286–326.

[29]Jack C. Francis and Roger Ibbotson, *Investments: A Global Approach* (Upper Saddle River: NJ: Prentice-Hall, 2002), 24.

shown in Exhibit 7.5. It contrasts the standard deviation of returns for large company stocks with long-term Treasury bonds. The standard deviation for larger
company stocks is, with exceptions, higher than the standard deviation for long-
term Treasuries. This is why, on average, stocks pay a higher return—but the variability of this return is greater than for Treasuries. This variability is the risk
associated with these different securities. It is why these securities offer different
rates of return. Using similar reasoning, the return and risk of corporate bonds are
generally lower than for common stocks but are higher than for Treasuries.

The convention in personal injury economic loss analysis is to select a risk-
free rate, or at least a rate that is free of default risk.[30] In effect, this assumes that
the projected wage and benefit stream is virtually certain. In this type of analysis,
economists make a risk adjustment by adjusting the future stream itself. This is
done by applying an unemployment adjustment factor or by curtailing the length
of the stream, as with projections to the worklife expectancy only. Therefore, the
use of a risk-free rate can be deceptive. It implies that there was no risk adjustment; in fact, the expert may have explicitly taken this into account. Moreover,
even personal injury cases vary: the use of a risk-free rate may be more appro-

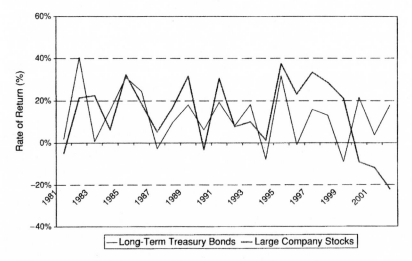

Exhibit 7.5.   Standard deviation of large company stock versus long-term
treasuries: 1981–2001.

---

[30]Michael Brookshire and Frank Slesnick, "A 1996 Study of Prevailing Practice in
Forensic Economics," *Journal of Forensic Economics* X (1) (winter 1997): 11.

priate in smaller awards if the income stream being replaced in the loss projection is essential for the survival of the plaintiffs. Some cases, however, that involve large awards that would reasonably be invested in a more balanced portfolio earning higher returns may require higher discount rates.

In lost profits analysis, the risk adjustment process is often incorporated into the discount rate.[31] This type of risk adjustment process is standard in corporate finance and is routinely done in capital budgeting analysis.[32] Capital budgeting is the area of corporate finance that deals with the analysis, evaluation, and selection of investment projects. In capital budgeting, projects are evaluated using techniques such as discounted cash flows and the internal rate of return. In discounted cash flow analysis, a risk-adjusted discount rate is used to convert projected future cash flows to present value terms. The discount rate is adjusted upward in accordance with the perceived variability of riskiness of the project's projected cash flows.[33]

One *possible* source of discount rates is the cost of capital of the corporation. Once again, the weighted average cost of capital can be employed but now as the discount rate to bring future projected losses to present value terms. If, however, the expert is measuring losses associated with a particular project, then it may be more appropriate to use the project's costs of capital if this cost is significantly different than the company's overall cost of capital.[34] Another alternative to using the weighted average cost of capital as the discount rate is to select a risk premium that can be added to the risk-free rate. Treasury securities provide several different risk-free rates (free of default risk) that vary according to the maturity of the security. The risk-free rate that is similar in length to the term of the loss projection should be selected. For example, in a ten-year future loss projection, the rate on ten-year Treasury Notes is applicable. To this risk-free rate is added a risk premium that as closely as possible reflects the anticipated variability in the projected stream of future losses. Once again, the securities market is used as a guide. For example, higher-risk securities, such as junk bonds (bonds with a Dun & Bradstreet rating of BB or lower), can be used to reflect the anticipated risk of the loss projection. If the perceived variability of the projected losses exceeds what is accounted for

---

[31]Jeffrey C. Bodington, "Discount Rates for Lost Profits," *Journal of Forensic Economics* V (3) (fall 1992): 209–219.

[32]Lawrence J. Gitman and Jeff Madura, *Introduction to Finance* (Boston: Addison Wesley, 2001), 343–345.

[33]James C. VanHorne and John M. Machowiz, *Fundamentals of Financial Management* (Englewood Cliffs, NJ: Prentice-Hall, 1995), 414–416.

[34]Richard A. Brealey, Stewart C. Myers, and Alan J. Marcus, *Fundamentals of Corporate Finance* (New York: McGraw-Hill, 1995), 262–263.

by junk bond returns, then other risk premia can be considered, such as the rates of return required for investments in closely held companies.[35]

This method of adding a risk premium to the risk-free rate, where the premium is derived from securities traded in the marketplace, is regularly used in the field of business valuations.[36] The method is referred to as the *build-up method*. The expert must judge whether the risk premia embodied in the rates of publicly traded securities are assumed to be comparable to the premia associated with the business activity whose income is being brought to present value terms. This method has the advantage of allowing the expert to tailor the discount rate to coincide with the specific risks that the expert perceives for the lost revenue and profits stream. For this reason, it *may* be preferable to the cost of capital method, although the two *may* end up being similar.

COMMON ERRORS MADE IN DISCOUNTING BY DAMAGES "EXPERTS"

Particularly when the expert lacks a good background in corporate finance, one of the most common errors is to use a discount rate that insufficiently accounts for the riskiness of the projected lost earnings stream. Naive experts often use a discount rate that is more closely associated with a low-risk or even riskless income stream. For example, it is not unusual in a lost profits analysis to see an "expert" use a Treasury security as the source of the discount rate. This selection implies that the expert considers the risk of the income stream that he has projected to have the same risk attributes, such as default risk, as a Treasury bond. Such an error results in an exaggerated loss estimate. The example shown in Table 7.7 depicts the magnitude of the exaggeration. It compares the differences in present value that results when an expert chooses a relatively low discount rate when a much higher discount rate would more fully account for the relevant risk factors, such as the various business risks. For example, over a five year period, a lost profits stream that is constant åt $10,000 and is discounted at 6% results in a cumulative present value of $52,123,638. However, when this same income

---

[35]This "build-up" discount rate is discussed in Robert R. Trout, "Introduction to Business Valuation," in *Litigation Economics*, Patrick A. Gaughan and Robert Thornton, eds. (Greenwich, CT: JAI Press, 1993), 107–150.

[36]Shannon Pratt, Robert F. Rielly, and Robert Schweihs, *Valuing a Business*, 3rd ed. (New York: Irwin Professional Publishing, 1996), 161–165, and Jay Fishman, Shannon Pratt, J. Clifford, and D. Keith Wilson, *Guide to Business Valuations* (Forth Worth, TX: Practitioners Publishing, 1995), 5-14–5-23.

Table 7.7   Present Value of a Lost Profit Stream Using 6% and 20% Discount Rates

Time (Years)	6% Discount Rate	20% Discount Rate
0	$ 10,000,000	$ 10,000,000
1	9,433,962	8,333,333
2	8,899,964	6,944,444
3	8,396,193	5,787,037
4	7,920,937	4,822,531
5	7,472,582	4,018,776
Cumulative Present Value	$ 52,123,638	$ 39,906,121

stream is discounted at a 20 percent rate, the cumulative present value is $39,906,121. The losses are exaggerated by $12,217,516, or by 30.6 percent!

The impact of the higher discount rate is greater the further into the future it is necessary to discount. In the first year, the difference in the discount factors is relatively small—94 cents on the dollar versus 83 cents. By the fifth year, this difference is considerably greater—75 cents on the dollar versus 40. Plaintiffs should make sure that their expert has not made such an error, for it is easily detected by a knowledgeable defense expert. Defendants must ensure that they retain an expert who can accurately determine the correct risk-adjusted discount rate so that losses are sufficiently discounted.

Discounting with Nominal versus Real Rates

There has been much debate in the forensic economics literature regarding whether discounting should be done using nominal or real interest rates.[37] Much of this debate has centered around personal injury litigation. However, many of the same principles apply to the measurement of commercial damages. Therefore, it is instructive to explore this debate and the court's position on it.

One of the simplest ways of projecting future earnings and then discounting them to the present is to simply assume that the rate of earnings growth is approximately equal to the interest rate used to discount the future earnings. The process of discounting then becomes quite simple: one simply needs to take the length of the loss period and multiply it by the annual loss in the first year of the loss. The result is an inflation-adjusted and discounted loss. This method is referred to as the *total offset method*. The courts have acknowledged the mathematical validity

---

[37]See W. Cris Lewis, "On the Relative Stability and Predictability of the Interest Rates and Earnings Growth Rate," *Journal of Forensic Economics* (winter 1991): 9–26, and Laura Nowak, "Empirical Evidence on the Relationship Between Earnings Growth and Interest Rates," *Journal of Forensic Economics* (spring/summer 1991): 187–202.

of using a net discount rate, one that deducts the inflation rate from the discount rate so that discounting is done using a real or inflation-adjusted rate. However, the courts have not accepted the simplistic total offset method.[38] Given that it can be shown that interest rates have been generally above the rate of inflation, it is difficult to justify using the total offset method.

The decision of whether to use a nominal versus real discount rate depends on how the inflation adjustment is done in the projection. If revenues and lost profits are projected using an annual inflation adjustment, then a nominal interest rate should be used to discount the projected amounts to present value terms. Only when the projection is not adjusted for the effects of inflation, would it make sense to use a real rate in the discounting process. Given that the methodology described in this book specifically incorporates inflation and growth into the projection process, nominal rates rather than real rates are used for discounting.

Court's Position on the Appropriate Risk Premium

The process of discounting to present value has been well received and accepted by the courts and there is abundant legal precedent to confirm this.[39] In fact, the Delaware Chancery Court has characterized the discount cash flow method of valuation, an application of discounting which will be discussed in Chapter Eight, as the preferred method of valuation.[40] Furthermore, Robert Dunn has observed that in the few instances in which the courts have refused to recognize that only discounted profits should be allowed, the defendant had failed to introduce proof as to what such discounted values would be.[41] This implies that at a minimum, a defendant should be mindful of the need to prove this issue to the court.

We have explored the reasoning behind all of the components that should be incorporated in the risk premium so as to arrive at a discount rate that fully reflects the risk of the projected future lost profits stream. Some courts, though, have been reluctant to accept a discount rate that incorporates all of this risk. For example, in *American List Corp. v. U.S. News & World Report*, the trial court accepted an 18 percent discount rate based upon the perceived risk associated with the plaintiff's

---

[38]*Jones and Laughlin v. Pfeifer*, 462 U.S. 523 (1983).

[39]For example, *Lee v. Joseph E. Seagram & Sons*, 552 F2d 447 (2d Cir. 1977).

[40]*Charles L. Gaines v. Vitalink Communications Corporation*, No. 12334, Del Ch. 1997 WL 538676 (August 28, 1997).

[41]Robert L. Dunn, *Recovery of Damages for Lost Profits*, 5th ed. (Westport, CT: Lawpress, 1998), 502–503.

ability to fulfill the contract in the future.[42] However, the New York Appeals Court rejected the 18 percent discount rate as too high and remanded for a recomputation of this discount rate. In stating its reasoning, the court asserted:

> Defendant argues that in discounting the total amount due under the contract to its present value, the court may factor in the risk that the nonrepudiating party will be unable to perform the contract in the future. Such a rule, however, does violence to the settled principles of the doctrine of anticipatory breach because it would require the nonrepudiating party to prove its ability to perform in the future, despite the fact the doctrine is intended to operate to relieve the nonrepudiating party from that very performance.

One court was reluctant to accept a higher risk premium. However, this should not preclude the expert from applying standard financial principles to construct a risk-adjusted discount rate that fully reflects the risk of the projected lost stream of lost profits.

Process of Capitalization and the Loss of an Indefinite Stream of Future Profitability

Assuming it is legally established that the plaintiff should be compensated for the loss of a stream of future profitability of indefinite length, it is possible for the expert to value such a stream using the process of *capitalization*. Applied to commercial damages analysis, this process values a continuous stream of projected future profits. This valuation is done by dividing the growth-adjusted capitalization rate into the next period's projected lost profits. The growth adjustment refers to the projected rate of growth of the profit stream. If, for example, the selected discount rate is 15 percent and the annual profit stream is projected to grow at a 5 percent rate, then the growth-adjusted capitalization rate equals 10 percent. Mathematically, dividing by 0.10 is the same as multiplying by 10. Similarly, using a growth-adjusted capitalization rate of 20 percent is equivalent to multiplying by five. For each rate that is used as a divisor, there is an equivalent multiplier that is implied by the divisor. The capitalization process is shown in Equation 7.18.

$$\text{Capitalized Value} = \text{Annual Earnings}/(k_i - g) \qquad (7.18)$$

where k_i = the capitalization rate for firm i prior to growth adjustment
          g = the growth rate of future annual earnings

---

[42]*American List Corp. v. U.S. News & World Report*, 75 N.Y. 2d 38, 550 N.Y.S. 2d 590 (1980).

Difference between a Capitalization Rate and a Discount Rate

When one forecasts specific future monetary amounts, such as cash flows, and then uses a discount rate to convert each of these amounts to present value terms, it is known as discounting. The rate used to convert the future amounts to present value terms is the discount rate. Continuous monetary streams that are growing at a certain positive rate or not growing at all are called *perpetuities*. Computing the present value of such a stream is called capitalization. The interest rate used for this present value conversion of a perpetuity is called a capitalization rate. Sometimes these terms are used interchangeably, but such usage is generally incorrect.

Using Capitalization in a Business Interruption Loss Analysis

This book discusses two ways of converting future loss amounts to present value terms. The first requires projecting specific lost profits into the future and then discounting them to present value terms using the relevant discount rate. The second is to stipulate a lost profit value for a forthcoming year and to assume that this earnings stream would continue indefinitely. If this occurs, the present value of such a stream can be computed by capitalizing it or, stated another way, by dividing it by the relevant capitalization rate. While the latter method is sometimes used to value businesses, especially closely held businesses, it is not generally used as the sole method of computing the present value of a lost profits stream. One of the reasons for this is the implied length of the earnings stream. In order to use capitalization, one has to assume that the lost profits stream would have continued indefinitely. A court has to accept the length of this earnings stream. If a court will only accept a more limited loss period, then one msut project specific annual losses for the relevant loss period and then discount them accordingly.

Sometimes the capitalization process may be used in conjunction with discounting. For example, assume that a business interruption has occurred two years prior to the trial date and the expert has projected losses for an additional three years into the future. The question may arise: *What about losses after that third year?* Would the plaintiff have been able to generate profits after the third year? Is it reasonable to conclude that the loss period would extend into the future indefinitely? If there is a case-specific reason why losses should be projected for three more years, such as that was the remaining length of a contract, then those losses may be projected separately. If, however, the plaintiff argues that it has lost an income stream of indefinite length, then this value can be shown by capitalizing the losses.

Unless there are case-specific reasons for extending losses for a period of indefinite length, the capitalization analysis may not be relevant. It is a calculation that may not necessarily be relevant depending on the facts of the case and the relevant law. Experts should make their retaining attorneys understand the nature of a capitalization calculation. This calculation assumes that the losses will go on for an infinite time period. This sounds like a calculation that results in an extremely high value solely due to its infinite length. In reality, however, the present value process that is implicit in the capitalization computation converts values far into the future into very low values. However, some of the pragmatic issues that have to be dealt with are the legal responsibility of the defendant for losses of such an infinite length in light of the plaintiff's obligation to mitigate its losses as time goes by. These issues may make the capitalization of losses calculation irrelevant to a case.

Statistical Stability of Capitalization Rates

One issue that affects the reliability of capitalization rates is the statistical stability of these rates. The issue of statistical stability is discussed in Chapter Five where the concept of stationarity was introduced. Nonstationary statistical series lack certain properties that affect the reliability of forecasts upon which they are based. This issue is relevant to capitalization rates if such rates are based on historical data, as is often the case. Bowles and Lewis investigated the time series properties of capitalization rates with an eye toward assessing the reliability of such rates as they are used in a litigation context.[43] They wanted to determine if the historical mean of a capitalization rate series was covariance stationary. If it was, they concluded that it would be appropriate for present value calculations. They did this research using aggregated macroeconomic data where g was the quarterly change in after tax profits in the economy and r was the rate of return of the S&P 500. They applied time series tests to these two series and a combined capitalization rate series based upon the difference between r and g. Their research allowed them to reject a null hypothesis of a unit root for all of these series, leading them to conclude that capitalization rates are stationary and therefore useful to present value calculations.

The Bowles and Lewis research is useful, but readers must bear in mind that it is based on broad-based macroeconomic data. The capitalization rate, however, that an expert uses in a particular case would presumably be based on a firm-specific g which might not have the same statistical properties.

---

[43]Tyler J. Bowles and W. Cris Lewis, "Time Series Properties of Capitalization Rates," *Litigation Economics Review,* 5 (2) (winter 2001): 27–31.

SUMMARY

The time value of money is a fundamental concept in economics and finance and also plays an important role in commercial damages analysis. It is based on the rates of return that are available in financial markets. The rates are offered by numerous securities which vary according to their maturities and their risk levels. As a rule, the longer the term to maturity, the higher the rate. The greater the level of risk, the higher the rate of return. Securities with greater risk levels have higher risk premia built into their rates of return; this compensates security holders for this higher level of risk.

One of the ways in which the time value of money enters into commercial damages analysis is through the use of a prejudgment rate of return. Such a return is designed to compensate a plaintiff for receiving its past damages on the trial date (as opposed to when these damages were actually incurred). Several alternative prejudgment rates are available for a court to apply. The selection process may be simplified if a statutory rate exists within the relevant jurisdiction applied to all historical losses. If the law is not clear on this issue, then there may be room for testimony on what rate would fully compensate the plaintiff for receiving these monies late. One option is to select relatively low money market rates to bring the historical losses to present value terms. Other options include the cost of capital, which may more accurately reflect the plaintiff's opportunity costs.

The other way in which the time value of money enters into commercial damage analysis is when projected future losses are converted to trial date terms. This process involves selecting a discount rate which fully reflects the risk or expected variability of the future loss stream that the expert has projected. The more the perceived risk, the higher the discount rate. The higher the discount rate, the lower the resulting present value. The further into the future the projected amount, the lower its present value. Experts look at the variability in returns of securities traded in public markets as their guide to selecting an appropriate rate to discount the future losses. Courts, however, have not been fully receptive in uniformly accepting these high risk-adjusted rates normally accepted in financial markets. This is probably attributable to the presentations made in these cases that dealt with this issue.

REFERENCES

American List Corp. v. U.S. News & World Report, 75 N.Y. 2d 38, 550 N.Y.S. 2d 590 (1980).

Beta Book. Chicago, IL: Ibbotson Associates.

Bodie, Ziv, Alex Kane, and Alan J. Marcus, *Investments*. New York: McGraw-Hill, 2002.

Bodington, Jeffrey C., "Discount Rates for Lost Profits." *Journal of Forensic Economics* V (3) (fall 1992).

Bowles, Tyler J., and W. Cris Lewis, "Time Series Properties of Capitalization Rates." *Litigation Economics Review* 5 (2) (winter 2001): 27–31.

Brealey, Richard A., Stewart C. Myers, and Alan J. Marcus, *Fundamentals of Corporate Finance.* New York: McGraw-Hill, 1995.

Brigham, Eugene, and Philip R. Davies, *Intermediate Financial Management,* 8th ed. New York: Thomson South-Western, 2004.

Brookshire, Michael, and Frank Slesnick, "A 1996 Study of Prevailing Practice in Forensic Economics." *Journal of Forensic Economics* X (1) (winter 1997).

Charles L. Gaines v. Vitalink Communications Corporation, No. 12334, Del Ch. 1997 WL 538676 (August 28, 1997).

Cost of Capital Quarterly Chicago, IL: Ibbotson Associates.

Damodaran, Aswath, *Corporate Finance.* New York: Wiley, 1997.

Dunn, Robert L., *Recovery of Damages for Lost Profits,* 5th ed. Westport, CT: Lawpress, 1998.

Elton, Edwin J., and Martin J. Gruber, *Modern Portfolio Theory and Investment Analysis.* New York: Wiley, 1995.

Fabozzi, Frank, and Framco Modigliani, *Capital Markets: Institutions and Instruments,* 3rd ed. Upper Saddle River, NJ: Prentice-Hall, 2003.

Fama, Eugene, and Kenneth French, "The Cross Section of Expected Stock Returns." *Journal of Finance* (June 1992).

Fisher, Franklin, M., and R. Craig Romaine, "Janis Joplin's Yearbook and the Theory of Damages." *Journal of Accounting, Auditing and Finance* (1989).

Fisher, Irving, *Theory of Interest.* New York: A.M. Kelley Publishers, 1965.

Fishman, Jay, Shannon Pratt, J. Clifford, and D. Keith Wilson, *Guide to Business Valuations.* Forth Worth, TX: Practitioners Publishing, 1995.

FPC v. Hope Natural Gas Co. 320 U.S. 591, 64 S. Ct. 281, 88, L. Ed. 333 (1944).

Francis, Jack C., and Roger Ibbotson, *Investments: A Global Approach.* Upper Saddle River: NJ: Prentice-Hall, 2002,

Friedman, Milton, *Dollars and Deficits.* Englewood Cliffs, NJ: Prentice-Hall, 1968.

Gitman, Lawrence J., and Jeff Madura, *Introduction to Finance.* Boston: Addison Wesley, 2001.

Gyromat Corporation v. Champion Spark Plug Company, 735 F2d 549 (Fed. Cir. 1984).

Ibbotson, Roger, and Rex Sinquefeld, "Stocks, Bills, Bonds and Inflation: Year-by-Year Historical Returns (1926–1974)." *Journal of Business* 49 (2) (January, 1976).

Jones and Laughlin v. Pfeifer, 462 U.S. 523 (1983).

Kier, John C., and Robin C. Kier, "Opportunity Cost: A Measure of Prejudgment Interest." *Business Lawyer,* vol. 39 (November 1983).

Lam, Inc. v. Johns Manville Corp., 718 F2d. 1056, 219 U.S.P.Q. 670 (Fed Cir. 1983).

Lanzillotti, R.F., and A. K. Esquibel, "Measuring Damages in Commercial Litigation: Present Value of Lost Opportunities." *Journal of Accounting, Auditing, and Finance* (1989).

Lee v. Joseph E. Seagram & Sons, 552 F2d 447 (2d Cir. 1977) .

Lewis, Cris W., "On the Relative Stability and Predictability of the Interest Rates and Earnings Growth Rate." *Journal of Forensic Economics* (winter 1991).

Madura, Jeff, *Financial Markets and Institutions,* 6th ed. New York: Thompson South-Western, 56–66.

Moyer, Charles R., James R. McGuigan, and William J. Kretlow, *Contemporary Financial Management,* 9th ed. New York: Thomson South-Western, 2002.

Nowak, Laura, "Empirical Evidence on the Relationship between Earnings Growth and Interest Rates." *Journal of Forensic Economics* (spring/summer 1991).

Patell, James, Roman L. Weil, and Mark A. Wolfson, "Accumulating Damages in Litigation: The Role of Uncertainty and Interest Rates." *Journal of Legal Studies* XI (2) (June 1982).

Pratt, Shannon P., *Cost of Capital: Estimation and Applications.* New York: Wiley, 1998.

Pratt, Shannon P., Robert F. Rielly, and Robert Scheihs, *Valuing a Business,* 3rd ed. New York: Irwin Professional Publishing, 1996.

Rose, Peter S., *Money and Capital Markets,* 8th ed. New York: Irwin McGraw-Hill, 2003, 179–181.

Ross, Stephen, Randolph W. Westerfield, and Bradford Jordan, *Essentials of Corporate Finance,* 4th ed. Homewood, IL: Irwin, 2004.

S.C. Anderson v. Bank of America, 24 Cal. App. 4th 529; 1994.

Stocks, Bills, Bonds and Inflation: 2003 Yearbook Chicago, IL: Ibbotson Associates.

Trout, Robert R., "Introduction to Business Valuation," in Patrick A. Gaughan and Robert Thornton, eds. *Litigation Economics.* Greenwich, CT: JAI Press, 1993.

Uniroyal, Inc. v. Rudkin-Wiley Co., F2d 1540 (Fed. Cir. 1991).

Value Line Investment Survey. New York: Value Line Publishing.

VanHorne, James, and John M. Machowiz, *Fundamentals of Financial Management.* Englewood Cliffs; NJ: Prentice-Hall, 1995.

Weston, Fred J, Scott Besley, and Eugene Brigham, *Essentials of Managerial Finance,* 11th ed. Fort Worth, TX: Dryden Press, 1996.

Williams Enterprises, Inc. v. The Sherman R. Smoot Company, 938 F2d 230, 290U.S. App. D.C. 411 (October 8, 1991).

8

BUSINESS VALUATIONS

In lawsuits where the business has been interrupted so significantly that it ceases to exist or where its value has changed significantly, the appropriate method to measure the loss may be to do a business valuation. The field of business valuations has grown dramatically over the past two decades. Numerous books have been written on the methodology of business valuation. In addition, many articles and periodic newsletters are available to keep experts aware of the latest developments in the field.[1] Therefore, this chapter provides only an overview of the methods involved; references in which readers can find a more expanded treatment of the topic are also included. The additional focus of this chapter is to show how business valuation methods can be applied in cases of business interruption.

LEGAL STANDARD FOR BUSINESS VALUATIONS IN BUSINESS INTERRUPTION CASES

A recent U.S. Supreme Court decision clarified the court's position on the relevance of business valuations to business interruption matters. The case, *Coastal Fuels of Puerto Rico, Inc. v. Caribbean Petroleum Corporation*,[2] is quite useful even though it is actually an antitrust case—not a straightforward business interruption. Coastal Fuels of Puerto Rico had won a price discrimination decision at a lower court level against Caribbean Petroleum Corporation (CAPECO) but had failed to win a Section One Sherman Act claim of monopolization. The Supreme Court had earlier vacated a jury verdict on damages: they thought that the total damages might have been too high as the antitrust verdict had included damages for monopolization. The price discrimination claim was retired and, ironically, the verdict on this second trial was three times higher than the original damages value.

---

[1]*Business Valuation Review.*
[2]*Coastal Fuels of Puerto Rico, Inc. v. Caribbean Petroleum Corporation.*

The total damages verdict in the second proceeding, $4.5 million before tre-
bling, included $2 million for "going concern damages." The issue of going con-
cern damages, the value of the business, became a main focus of the Court in its
review of the analysis that had been presented. In reaching its decision, the Court
relied upon *Farmington Dowel Products Co. v. Foster Manufacturing Co.*[3] In citing the *Farmington* court, the Court established that if lost value is to be a measure of damages for a company that went out of business due to the defendant's
actions, the value should be measured as of the date that the company went out
of business—not its value as of the trial date. In explaining why the value as of
the trial date is inappropriate, the *Farmington* court stated that a valuation:

> . . . would have required an estimate of profits for a period of some ten years dur-
> ing which the company neither existed nor made, plus an estimate of the going con-
> cern value . . . of a company which had ceased being a going concern over ten years
> before, which estimate would have involved a further estimate of profits for a more
> remote future period.

The Court in *Coastal Fuels* concluded that it faced the same situation. The
only meaningful difference was that the period of time between the trial date and
the date when the plaintiff went out of business was four years instead of ten. The
Court agreed with the *Farmington Dowel* court when it concluded that valuing a
company long after it had gone out of business relied "too heavily on speculation
and conjecture." The Court was very clear in its opinion:

> We conclude that the *Farmington Dowel* framework—that going concern value
> should be evaluated as of the time the plaintiff goes out of business and actual lost
> profits awarded only up to that date—is and should be the norm. It may be that in
> some situations the difference between the date the company went out of business
> and the date of trial is not great and the issue does not arise in any significant sense.
> But here, more than four years had passed. We do not adopt a per se rule that four
> years is inherently too great a gap, but we think it raises such risks of speculative
> evidence that the *Farmington Dowel* framework presumptively applies.

LOST PROFITS VERSUS LOST BUSINESS VALUE

The Court in *Coastal* went on to clarify the circumstances in which lost profits
are appropriate and in which the value of the business is the relevant measure. It

---

[3]*Farmington Dowel Products Co. v. Forster Manufacturing Co.*, 421 F2d 61 (1st Cir.
1970).

did so by once again adopting the court's reasoning from the *Farmington Dowel* case. In *Farmington Dowel,* that court allowed lost profits to be the appropriate measure until the date the plaintiff went out of business. The appropriate measure of damages was then the value of the business. The court in *Farmington* was clear that a plaintiff could not claim both post-trial future profits as well as the lost value of the business. It said:

> To do so would result in a clear duplication [the plaintiff] would get its present value as a going concern plus its future profits, but the latter figure would be a major element in determining the former figure.

BUSINESS VALUATION FRAMEWORK

Exhibit 8.1 provides a basic framework for the valuation process. It shows that this process can be conceptually broken down into stages. In the initial stages, shown at the top of the chart, the expert does his preliminary investigation into

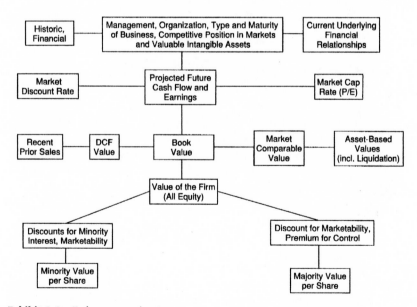

Exhibit 8.1   Pathway to valuation.
Source: Robert Trout, "Business Valuations" in *Measuring Commercial Damages* (New York: Wiley, 2000), 237. This material is used by permission of John Wiley & Sons, Inc.

the nature of the business and the purpose of the assignment. The expert then selects the appropriate techniques to be used to value the business. These are shown in the middle of the chart. By employing these methods, the expert is able to arrive at a value for the equity of the business. This equity value may then be subject to certain adjustments such as those shown at the bottom of Exhibit 8.1. The remaining part of this chapter takes the reader through the steps in the valuation process.

THEORETICAL VALUE OF A BUSINESS

The value of a business should be a function of the future benefits that will accrue to the owners of the business. For publicly held business, these benefits may come from future dividends and increases in the price of the stock. For closely held businesses these benefits can be derived in different ways than publicly held firms. Whichever the case, the valuation exercise involves defining the benefits and projecting them into the future. The higher the value of such benefits, the greater the value of the business. The identification and analysis of such benefits is the subject of the valuation process.

Methods of Business Valuation

In a business valuation, an analyst assigns a value to a financial asset for which there is often either no market, or only a limited one, available to value it. Businesses whose equity or debt securities are actively traded on securities exchanges are regularly valued on a daily basis. Such companies are known as publicly held companies based upon the "public" ownership of their equity. For larger companies, the ownership is usually held by a large number of stockholders. Issuing companies have to adhere to Securities and Exchange Commission (SEC) filing and disclosure requirements as well as other state regulations.

PUBLIC VERSUS PRIVATE COMPANIES

There are significant differences in the valuation process for public and private companies. The shares of public companies are traded in securities markets where they get regularly revalued. For large Fortune 500 companies which trade on the New York Stock Exchange, the values of their shares can greatly assist the analyst in determining the value of the company. For other public companies which trade infrequently on the over-the-counter market, the quoted value of the shares contains less information content on the value of the company. Private companies, however, do not have organized markets for their shares. The expert has to do other analysis, such as trying to find comparable companies that are public and using information about their stock prices to ascertain how the market would value the private company. This method, called comparable multiples, is discussed later in this chapter.

Another way in which public and private companies differ is in their financial statements. As part of the securities registration process required by national securities laws, public companies must have audited financial statements. Private companies, on the other hand, can have compiled or reviewed statements. Compilations are restatements of the financial data provided by the company without any meaningful verification. Review statements feature more verification than compiled statements. Under a review process, the accountants investigate certain aspects of the statements but employ significantly fewer verifications than they do in an audit.

The fact that these statements are not audited does not mean that they are unreliable or cannot serve as the basis for an accurate valuation. However, the evaluator must understand that audited and reviewed statements differ in the degree to which the data they contain have been verified for accuracy.

BUSINESS VALUATION PARAMETERS

At the start of a business valuation, two parameters need to be established. These are:

1. *Purpose of the Valuation.* It is assumed that the business is being valued as a result of an interruption in the operations of the plaintiff. This interruption has either caused the company to go out of business or resulted in a decline in its value. The expert's task is then to compute the value prior to the business interruption and compare it to the value at some other date.

2. *Valuation Date.* A business's value changes over time. Therefore, it is important to stipulate the date as of which the value is to be computed. This date is often selected based upon legal assumptions that would be provided to the expert. The *Coastal Fuels* court indicated that this date should not be beyond the date that the company went out of business.

Factors to Be Considered When Doing a Business Valuation

Several factors need to be analyzed when conducting a business valuation.These include firm-specific factors as well as external variables such as the state of the economy and the condition of the industry. These external factors define the environment within which the firm operates. Firm-specific factors reflect the unique aspects of the firm as it operates in this economic environment.

REVENUE RULING 59-60
AND FACTORS TO CONSIDER IN VALUATION

A number of revenue rulings clarify the factors that tax courts consider when evaluating valuation analyses. Perhaps the most frequently cited of these rulings is Revenue Ruling 59-60. It is particularly relevant in the valuation of closely held businesses. It lists some of the factors that evaluators of closely held businesses should consider as part of the valuation process. Although some experts may disagree as to how these are presented and what other factors should be considered in a valuation, it is helpful to consider these factors—particularly when certain courts place significant weight on them.

Revenue Ruling 59-60

- The nature of the business and the history of the enterprise from the inception
- The economic outlook in general and the condition and outlook of the industry in particular
- The book value of the stock and the financial condition of the business
- The earnings capacity of the company
- The dividend-paying capacity
- Whether or not the enterprise has goodwill or other intangible value
- Sales of the stock and the size of the block of stock to be valued
- The market price of stocks of corporations engaged in the same or a similar line of business whose stocks actively trade in a free and open market, either on an exchange or over-the-counter

---

Firm-Specific Factors

One of the first steps in the valuation process is to conduct research into the background of the company. This involves an investigation into its history. Often this includes a site visit. The expert identifies the senior management, their backgrounds, and compensation levels. In addition, the company's principal products and services are identified. Various lists are often prepared that delineate the company's main facilities and other details relevant to a valuation of the company. In doing such an investigation, the expert tries to identify those aspects of the company that contribute to the overall value of the company. For example, a company might have a well-established brand name for some of its products and this may create the expectations that it may have dependable cash flows in the future. Another company might find great value in its experienced work force which its competitors may lack. The identification of these value drivers can play an important role in the overall valuation process.

Having done a review of the company's history and products, the expert needs to review the company's finances. This includes its sources of capital and how it has financed its assets. A review of the company's current and historical capital structure then leads to a consideration of its expected future financing needs. Questions need to be answered, such as *Will the company have sufficient access to capital to be able to grow at the rates that are incorporated in the valuation process?*

Each valuation presents its own set of firm-specific factors that the expert must consider and analyze. It is not possible to give one all inclusive list which fits all valuation. Each valuation is different and after an initial review, the expert compiles a list of unique factors that have to be considered.

Economic Factors

An evaluator of a business needs to understand the overall economic environment within which the business operates. More precisely, this is the macroeconomic environment. Various economic aggregates, such as those discussed in Chapter Three, are useful when assessing the state of the macroeconomy. The interrelationship between the business, its sales and the performance of the economy needs to be assessed when valuing a business, just as it does when measuring lost profits from a business interruption.

Depending on the nature of the business, and the extent to which its derives its demand from a specific region of the country, a regional economic analysis may be needed. This type of analysis is also discussed in Chapter Three. That chapter explores the abundant sources of macroeconomic data that are available to the expert. In doing an analysis of these data, the expert can evaluate the extent to which the firm's net earnings and cash flows are influenced by business fluctuations.

Industry Factors

The state of the industry needs to be analyzed when doing an evaluation of a specific business within an industry. This component of the overall analysis is similar to what is covered in Chapter Four. It involves an analysis of the condition of the industry, including a consideration of the level of competition and the profitability of the industry over time. The evaluator should be able to determine whether profitability has been stable or was increasing or decreasing as of the evaluation date. All other things constant, businesses that operate in highly competitive environments are exposed to greater degrees of competitive pressure which may result in lower profit margins. If the level of competition has recently changed, or is expected to change, such as through a process of deregulation of the industry, the value of the business may change. If deregulation results in lower margins and profits, the value may fall correspondingly.

Financial Analysis

Following an analysis of the overall economy and the industry, the expert may want to conduct a financial analysis of the company. This often includes a financial ratio analysis.[4] These ratios consider five main characteristics of a company: liquidity, assets activity, financial leverage, performance, and profitability. A list of the standard financial ratios is presented in Table 8.1.

The liquidity ratios provide information on the ability of the company to meet its short-term obligations. Activity ratios indicate how quickly the company turns over or converts certain assets into sales, such as inventories or accounts receivable. Financial leverage ratios consider a company's capital structure and how much debt versus equity it utilizes to finance its assets. Profitability ratios measure

---

[4]For a good review of financial ratio analysis see Eugene F. Brigham and Philip R. Davies, *Intermediate Financial Management,* 7th ed. (New York: Thomson South-Western, 2002), 215–241.

Table 8.1 Financial Ratios

Ratio Analysis: Altria Group (in millions)

Ratio	Ratio Formula	Year 31-Dec-99	Ratio	Year 31-Dec-00	Ratio	Year 31-Dec-01	Ratio	Year 31-Dec-02	Ratio
Liquidity									
Current Ratio	Current Assets / Current Liabilities	20,895 / 18,017	1.16	17,238 / 25,949	0.66	17,275 / 20,141	0.86	17,441 / 19,082	0.91
Acid Test Ratio	Current Assets–Inventories / Current Liabilities	11,867 / 18,017	0.66	8,473 / 25,949	0.33	8,352 / 20,141	0.41	8,314 / 19,082	0.44
Asset Management									
Inventory Turnover (Days)	Average Inventories / Cost Goods Sold / 360	9,237 / 82	112	8,897 / 81	110	8,844 / 93	95	9,025 / 91	99
Inventory Turnover (Days) (Alternative Calculation)	Average Inventories / Sales / 360	9,237 / 218	42	8,897 / 223	40	8,844 / 250	35	9,025 / 223	40
Receivable Turnover (Days)	Average Receivables / Sales / 360	4,502 / 218	21	4,666 / 223	21	5,084 / 250	20	5,144 / 223	23
Fixed Assets Turnover	Sales / Net Fixed Assets	78,596 / 12,271	6.41	80,356 / 15,303	5.25	89,924 / 15,137	5.94	80,408 / 14,846	5.42
Total Assets Turnover	Sales / Total Assets	78,596 / 61,381	1.28	80,356 / 79,067	1.02	89,924 / 84,968	1.06	80,408 / 87,540	0.92
Debt Management									
Total Debt to Total Assets	Total Debt / Total Assets	46,076 / 61,381	0.75	64,062 / 79,067	0.81	65,348 / 84,968	0.77	68,062 / 87,540	0.78
Times Interest Earned	Earnings before Interest & Taxes / Interest Charges	13,616 / 795	17.13	14,806 / 719	20.59	15,702 / 1,418	11.07	16,601 / 1,134	14.64

Table 8.1 Financial Ratios (continued)

Ratio Analysis: Altria Group (in millions)

Ratio	Ratio Formula	Year 31-Dec-99	Ratio	Year 31-Dec-00	Ratio	Year 31-Dec-01	Ratio	Year 31-Dec-02	Ratio
Profitability									
Net Profit Margin	Net Income—Preferred Dividends / Sales	$\frac{7,675}{78,596}$	0.10	$\frac{8,510}{80,356}$	0.11	$\frac{8,560}{89,924}$	0.10	$\frac{11,102}{80,408}$	0.14
Basic Earning Power	Earnings before Interest & Taxes / Total Assets	$\frac{13,616}{61,381}$	0.22	$\frac{14,806}{79,067}$	0.19	$\frac{15,702}{84,968}$	0.18	$\frac{16,601}{87,540}$	0.19
Return on Total Assets (ROA)	Net Income—Preferred Dividends / Total Assets	$\frac{7,675}{61,381}$	0.13	$\frac{8,510}{79,067}$	0.11	$\frac{8,560}{84,968}$	0.10	$\frac{11,102}{87,540}$	0.13
Return on Equity (ROE)	Net Income—Preferred Dividends / Average Common Equity	$\frac{7,675}{15,751}$	0.49	$\frac{8,510}{15,155}$	0.56	$\frac{8,560}{17,313}$	0.49	$\frac{11,102}{19,549}$	0.57
Market Value									
Price/Earnings Ratio	Price per Share / Earnings per Share	$\frac{23.00}{3.19}$	7.21	$\frac{42.25}{3.75}$	11.27	$\frac{45.85}{3.87}$	11.85	$\frac{40.53}{5.21}$	7.78
Price to Cash Flow	Price per Share / Operational Cash Flow per Share	$\frac{23.00}{4.73}$	4.86	$\frac{42.25}{4.87}$	8.68	$\frac{45.85}{4.02}$	11.40	$\frac{40.53}{\ }$	
Market to Book	Market Price per Share / Book Value per Share	$\frac{23.00}{6.36}$	3.62	$\frac{42.25}{6.61}$	6.39	$\frac{45.85}{8.87}$	5.17	$\frac{40.53}{9.14}$	4.43
	Outstanding Shares	2,406		2,269		2,212		2,131	

Source: Henry Fuentes and Patrick Gaughan, Economatrix Research Associates, Inc.

the company's ability to generate profits, such as gross and net profits, from its sales. Market ratios reflect how the market values the company.

Financial ratios provide more information content when they are compared to industry norms,[5] referred to as cross-sectional comparisons. In addition, the expert also reviews the trends in the ratios over time to see if there is an improvement or a deterioration in a particular aspect of the company's condition.

VALUATION CONCEPTS

There are several different valuation concepts which are used in the field of business valuation. Some have more relevance than others. These are:

- Liquidation Value
- Book Value
- Enterprise Value
- Fair Market Value
- Fair Value

Liquidation Value

This is the value that would be realized if the assets of the firm were sold and the proceeds used to satisfy outstanding liabilities. This value is influenced by the manner in which the assets are sold. In many liquidations, assets are sold at "fire sale" prices that are well below the values that would be realized in a more orderly sale. Higher value can be realized with a more orderly liquidation, for the seller may be more selective in the prices that it accepts.

Liquidation value is sometimes used as a *floor value* for a company. That is, it is considered a value which is below or, at worst, equal to the value that the expert would put forward in the valuation.

Book Value

Book value, which is also called net asset value, is the difference between the value of the company's assets and its liabilities. The value of the assets is the value that those assets carry on the company books. This value may be less than the

---

[5]See *Annual Statement Studies,* Robert Morris Associates, Philadelphia, PA.

market value due to the cumulative impact of depreciation. In some valuations, the expert can adjust this value to reflect more accurate market values, but the relevant data may not be available to do such an adjustment.

For some asset-oriented businesses, such as ones in the financial services industry, net asset value may be higher—the asset may be kept on the books at more accurate values. For other businesses, the asset side of the balance sheet may include various intangibles that are difficult to value. Accounting rules have recently changed regarding the valuation of goodwill. Goodwill must now be regularly reexamined and written down if its value is reduced.[6]

It is usually assumed that the liabilities are carried at accurate values on the company's balance sheet. However, certain categories of liabilities may be too uncertain to be valued and thus are included on the balance sheet. Potential litigation liabilities are an example. It may be that the market is aware that such liabilities are significant, but because accountants cannot construct a reliable estimate of their value, they are not included. When this happens, the expert needs to try to explicitly address this issue prior to issuing a total value for the company.

Enterprise Value

Enterprise value is a term that is used differently in different contexts. It reflects the value of the entire business rather than the value of the equity. If earnings-oriented methods are used to value a business, the resulting value does not necessarily reflect how the business was capitalized. This reflects the relevant components of debt and equity in the company's capital mix. Once the value of the liabilities is deducted from the total value, the value of equity can be distinguished from the enterprise value.

Enterprise value reflects the market value of the invested capital. Some users, however, are so concerned about the ambiguity of the usage of this term that they recommend avoiding its use in the valuation process.[7]

Fair Market Value

The term fair market value is defined as the value that would be realized in a transaction between a buyer and seller, each being full informed of the relevant

---

[6]SFAS 142.

[7]Shannon Pratt, Robert F. Reilly, and Robert P. Schweihs, *Valuing a Business,* 4th ed. (New York: McGraw-Hill, 2000), 24.

facts, and neither under a compulsion to pursue the transaction. In most contexts, having a willing buyer and seller means that the transaction is an arm's-length transaction. This rules out values that are derived from situations where the buyer or seller is unduly influenced to complete the transaction. Sometimes the term fair market value is used interchangeably with cash value or market value.

Fair Value

In some cases, an alternative to fair market value must be used according to the laws of the relevant jurisdictions. This value may be different than the market value, as the latter could be subject to various discounts which are discussed later in this chapter.

Fair value is usually understood to mean a legal standard that applies to certain types of valuations. It is commonly used in valuations for oppressed minority shareholder lawsuits. In such suits, this usually means the value that would prevail but for the actions of the oppressor. Often, the term fair value is discussed in state statutes that relate to such suits.

MOST COMMONLY USED VALUATION METHODS

There are several techniques that are commonly used to value closely held businesses. Some of these methods are more appropriate than others depending on the particular circumstances surrounding the business being valued.

- *Discounted future cash flows.* This method requires a projection of future cash flows and the selection of a discount rate to bring the future projected amounts to present value.
- *Capitalization of earnings.* Capitalization of future earnings treats the income stream as a perpetuity and values it by dividing a representative earnings base by the appropriate capitalization rate.
- *Comparable multiples.* This is a very common approach to valuing businesses. It involves the selection of certain comparable multiples and applying them to the target business to derive a value.
- *Asset-oriented approaches.* There are several asset-oriented approaches. Some are relevant to the valuation of both public and private businesses; others are applied more frequently to privately held businesses. They simply focus on the value of the assets in relation to the firm's liabilities with explicitly taking into account the future earnings of the business.

Discounted Future Cash Flows
or Net Present Value Approach

The discounted future cash flows approach to valuing a business involves three main analytical steps:

1. Projecting future cash flows
2. Measuring the length of the projection period
3. Selecting the appropriate discount rate

The value of a business using discounted cash flows can be expressed as follows:

$$\text{Value} = \sum_{i=1}^{n} CF_i / (1 + r)^t \qquad (8.1)$$

where CF_i = the ith periods cash flows
n = the number of periods
r = the risk-adjusted discount rate

We have already discussed the discount process in Chapter Seven. One of the key decisions in using the discounted cash flow approach is to select the proper discount rate. This rate must be one that reflects the perceived level of risk in the target company.

One of the steps in the valuation process is determining the length of the projection period. The cash flows are scheduled to grow at a rate g. Often this rate is derived from a consideration of the historical growth of the company's cash flows. Most analysts project the cash flows for a five-year period and then capitalize the cash flows that are projected for the sixth year and thereafter. This is expressed in Equation 8.2.

$$\text{Value} = \sum_{i=1}^{5} \frac{CF_t}{(1 + r)^t} + \frac{V_5}{(1 + r)^5} \qquad (8.2)$$

While many valuations that use discounted cash flows employ a five-year period for the first part of Equation 8.2, this is not a hard and fast rule. Other lengths, such as seven years, are also acceptable. One of the factors that determine the length of the future projection period is the length of time that the expert feels confident that he can accurately forecast.

The value in year five, V_5, is the capitalized value of the cash flows that the business would derive after the fifth year. These cash flows are treated as a perpetuity and are capitalized by dividing the cash flow value for the sixth year by the growth adjusted discount rate $(r - g)$. That is, the sixth year's cash flows are computed by multiplying the fifth year's cash flows, FCF_5, by $(1 + g)$. This is then divided by the capitalization rate which is the difference between the discount rate, r, and the growth rate, g. The value V_5 is a year five value and it must be brought to year 0 terms by dividing it by $(1 + r)^5$. This discounted value of the cash flows after year five is sometimes referred to as the *residual*.

CASE STUDY: APPLYING THE DISCOUNTED CASH FLOW METHOD OF BUSINESS VALUATION

This case study applies the discounted cash flow method of business valuation to a company that had $2.5 billion in sales in 2002. Sales are expected to grow at declining rates of growth over the next five years from 10 percent in 2003 to a maturity growth rate of 6 percent, g, after the fifth year. Free cash flow (FCF) is defined as the difference between net after tax operating income (NOPAT) and new net capital expenditures.

$$NOPAT = EBIT(1 - \text{tax rate})$$

$$FCF = NOPAT - \text{new net capital expenditures}$$

The discount rate is taken to be the weighted average costs of capital (WACC) for the company which this case study assumes is 12 percent, r. The capitalization rate which is used to compute the terminal value of the company after year five is the difference between this rate and the long-term growth rate:

$$WACC = r = 12\% \quad \text{and} \quad k = \text{capitalization rate} = r - g = 12\% - 6\% = 6\%$$

The enterprise value of the company is the present value of its future projected cash flows. This value is computed as the sum of the present value of the individually projected cash flows for the first five years and the capitalized terminal value. This value is computed as follows:

$$\text{Terminal Value} = FCF_6 / (r - g)$$

It is important to remember that this terminal value is itself a year five value as it is the value of the company's cash flows that are projected to be received after year five. Therefore, it must be brought to present value by dividing it by the PVIF applicable to year five or $1/(1.12)^5$.

Valuation Equation: $$\frac{FCF_1}{(1 + k)^1} + \frac{FCF_2}{(1 + k)^2} + \cdots + \frac{FCF_5}{(1 + k)^5} + \frac{FCF_6}{(1 + k)^5}(r - g)$$

Assumptions: Sales Growth: Growth at 10% per year declining by 5 and 6% thereafter.
Shares Outstanding (mil): 40

	Years				
	1	2	3	4	5
Sales growth rate	10.0%	9.5%	9.0%	8.0%	7.0%
After-tax operating margin	6.0%	6.0%	6.0%	6.0%	6.0%
Net op. cap. exp. %/sales	5.0%	5.0%	5.0%	5.0%	5.0%
Weighted Average Cost Capital (WACC)	12.0%				
Long run growth rate	6.0%				
Sales Base Level–2002:	2,500				
Free Cash Flows (1–5)					
Sales (mil $)	2,750.0	3,011.3	3,282.3	3,544.8	3,793.0
NOPAT	165.0	180.7	196.9	212.7	227.6
Net operating capital expenditures	137.5	150.6	164.1	177.2	189.6
Free Cash Flows (FCFs)	27.5	30.1	32.8	35.4	37.9
Present Value of FCFs	24.6	24.0	23.4	22.5	21.5

Terminal Value Calculation

Free Cash Flow Year 6	40.2
Term. Value of Company in Year 5	670.1
Present Value of Terminal Value	380.2

Total Enterprise Value

Present Value of FCFs (years 1–5)	116.0
Present Value Company's Terminal Value	380.2
Total Enterprise Value	496.2
Deduct market value of debt & preferred	100.0
Total Value Common Equity	396.2
Shares Outstanding	40.0
Price of Share of Stock	9.9

Discount Rate and Risk

Our discussion would be conspicuously incomplete if we did not briefly discuss the selection of the discount rate and the risk-adjustment process that was covered in great detail in Chapter Seven. The greater the risk associated with the projected cash flow stream, the higher the discount rate that is used. If the projected cash flow stream is considered highly likely, then a lower discount rate is used. For high-risk cash flow streams, a risk premium is added which increases the discount rate. The use of a higher discount rate lowers the present value of each annual projected income amount.

The discount rate is often set as the sum of a risk-free rate plus an appropriate risk premium. Experts often look to the variability of securities that are traded in the marketplace and the risk premium that they include. This risk premium is then added to the risk-free rate to arrive at the risk-adjusted discount rate.

CAPITALIZATION OF EARNINGS

The capitalization process allows the expert to determine the present value of a business's future income by treating it as a perpetuity. A perpetuity has no specific ending period. The capitalization process requires the expert to select an earnings base. The capitalization rate is then divided into that base to determine the present value of the earnings stream.

Some naive critics disparage the capitalization of earnings technique because, in their view, the process assumes that the business will be in existence for an infinite time period. This is not a valid criticism, because monies that would be received an infinite number of years from now would be worth nothing given the time value of money. Moreover, the present value of income that is received further into the future is worth less and less. The more distant the income that is received, the less valuable it is to an acquirer.

Capitalization Rates versus Discount Rates

The terms *capitalization rate* and *discount rate* are sometimes used interchangeably. When a specific projection of income has been developed for a certain time period, then the term *discount rate* is used. When the task is to value a business that is capable of generating an income stream for an indefinite period of time, then the term *capitalization rate* is used. The relationship between the capitalization rate and the discount rate is depicted in Equation 8.3.

$$ke = r - g \qquad (8.3)$$

where ke = the capitalization rate
r = discount rate
g = growth rate of the income stream being valued

COMPARABLE MULTIPLES

Comparable multiples are used to value a comparable business by deriving multiples that have been used to value companies, such as in acquisitions, and applying them to the business in question. The first step in the process is to determine comparable companies. These are sometimes referred to as proxy firms or guideline companies. The process of selecting comparable companies is similar to what the expert does when using the yardstick method to value lost profits in a business interruption. In this process, the expert seeks to find companies which market a similar product or service as the business in question. This is often done by searching databases which have historical acquisition/transactions data by SIC code and then selecting a set of comparable transactions. Several such databases exist and they vary in their attention to companies of different sizes.[8] The expert can search these databases, get several transactions, and then research the target companies more carefully to determine if they are really comparable. Sometimes some of the companies are eliminated from consideration due to certain differences between them. Perhaps one of the potential comparable companies is much larger than the company is question. Another possible reason for a rejection is if the company is in more than one line of business and these other areas are significantly different from the business that is being valued. Still another reason could be that the comparable value for one of the deals was so different from the others that it is considered an outlier or an anomaly. In this step of the valuation process, the expert makes a judgment call to eliminate certain companies.

There are several possible multiples that can be used to value businesses. Two of the most frequently cited are earnings before interest, taxes, depreciation, and amortization (EBITDA) and P/E multiples. Data of such multiples are readily available. EBITDA multiples were very popular in valuing acquisition targets in the fifth merger wave of the 1990s. With the sharp decline in some of these companies in the early 2000s, some have criticized using such multiples. Examples include cable companies—they may have been valued using EBITDA multiples that carry with them the assumption that depreciation is a good proxy for capital expenditures and that future capital expenditures will be similar to historical expenditures. Some of these companies had to invest significant sums to upgrade their networks after acquisitions. Some considered the problem to be the multiples which did not account for such changes in expenditures.

Other multiples, such as revenues multiples, may be more relevant for certain types of businesses such as some closely held companies. Revenues, as opposed

---

[8]See for example Pratt Stats and Biz Comps.

to earnings-oriented, multiples are used when there are concerns about the quality of the earnings data.

Users of this method may have to make additional adjustments after a value is determined by applying the multiple. Since the comparable multiples method is an earnings-oriented approach to business valuation, the expert may possibly choose to add in the value of nonoperating assets as they were not necessary to the generation of the earnings base to which the multiple was applied. Whether adjustments such as these are done depends on the particular circumstances of the valuation.

CASE STUDY:
USE OF MULTIPLES TO DETERMINE ENTERPRISE VALUE

Enterprise value can be measured in a variety of ways. The value of an enterprise is a function of the ultimate return that a potential investor will receive on her investment. One of the measures that can be employed in ascertaining the value of an enterprise is its performance relative to the performance of similar enterprises or the price that an investor has paid for other investments. We can ascertain the value attributable to both debt or equity interests or to equity interests alone.

The yardstick used in the determination of the enterprise value is usually expressed as a multiplier (referred to as a multiple) of some base figure which is used to measure the relative performance of the enterprise. Some of the more common performance measurements are:

- EBITDA–Earning before interest, taxes, depreciation, and amortization
- EBIT–Earning before interest and taxes
- Net Income–Earnings after interest and taxes
- Free Cash Flow–Operational cash flow less capital expenditures

Regardless of the basis utilized in assessing performance, a multiple can be determined by examining the acquisition prices paid for other entities and comparing it to the appropriate base. Table 8.2 illustrates the calculation of a multiple utilizing the EBITDA performance measurement.

Table 8.2 shows that the multiple derived is based on the relationship between the total enterprise value ($14,500,000) and EBITDA ($3,100,000). The application of the multiple indicated to the EBITDA performance of a target company to be acquired will result in an estimate of total enterprise value. Equity value can then be determined by deducting interest-bearing debt from total enterprise value.

An application of the comparable multiples theory is illustrated in the following case. We are attempting to determine the appropriate value of Wilson Company,

Table 8.2   EBITDA Multiple

Net Income	$ 2,000,000
Taxes	700,000
Interest	250,000
Depreciation and amortization	150,000
EBITDA	$ 3,100,000
Equity acquisition price	$12,000,000
Interest bearing debt	2,500,000
Total enterprise value	$14,500,000
Multiple	4.68

which is being acquired by OCI, Inc. OCI has made a number of acquisitions over the past years (see Exhibit 8.2). Historically, OCI has paid between seven and ten times EBITDA, averaging 8.6 times on an unweighted basis or 8.24 times on a weighted basis, dependent on the size of the transaction.

We can apply this multiple to the financial result of the Wilson Company, the target acquisition, to determine an approximate value to assign the Wilson Acquisition (see Table 8.3). It should be pointed out that the results of Wilson's historical financial performance should be adjusted for nonrecurring or unusual items, which are not anticipated in the future.

Asset-Oriented Approaches

Asset-oriented methods consider the value of a company's assets in relation to its liabilities. The simplest application of this is the determination of net asset

	Court Company	Rotary Company	Bay Products	Western Manufacturing
Net Income	748,125	304,000	776,000	2,374,000
Taxes	785,625	110,000	400,000	1,411,000
Interest	48,750	45,000	182,000	1,407,000
Depreciation/Amortization	458,125	233,000	392,000	3,498,000
EBITDA	2,040,625	692,000	175,000	8,690,000
Equity Acquisition Price	14,052,000	4,600,000	14,600,000	54,300,000
Interest Bearing Debt	498,000	1,863,000	2,616,000	15,954,000
Total Enterprise Value	14,555,000	6,463,000	17,216,000	70,254,000
Multiple	7.13	9.34	9.84	8.08
Average EBITDA Multiple	8.60			
Weighted Average EBITDA Multiple	8.24			

Exhibit 8.2   OCI, Inc., summary of acquisitions.

Table 8.3 Valuation of Wilson Company

Net Income	$ 1,539,000
Taxes	928,000
Interest	374,000
Depreciation and amortization	1,194,000
EBITDA	$ 4,035,000
Average Multiple	8.24
Total Enterprise Value	$332,484,000
Interest bearing debt	8,990,000
Total equity value	$ 24,258,400

value—also called shareholder equity. This is the difference between assets and liabilities on the company's balance sheet. It does not explicitly consider the earning power of the assets except what is explained by their values.

It is important to note that the value of a company's assets on its balance sheet is purchase price less accumulated depreciation. This value may be very different from an asset's market value. If there is reason to believe that the market value of a company's assets are very different than its book values, then asset-oriented approaches may be less helpful (unless adjustments to the asset values can be made). Most damages experts are not in a position to make such adjustments, although they may bring in other experts to help with such adjustments.

Intangible assets may present particular challenges to the valuation expert seeking to do an asset-oriented valuation. While recent changes in accounting rules require a regular examination of goodwill, this may not be sufficient for the expert who is valuing the entire business.[9]

The discussion of asset-oriented approaches assumes that the liabilities carried on the company's books are accurate values. If a liability is knowable and capable of being measured, accounting rules require it to be noted. However, certain off-balance sheet liabilities may not be on the balance sheet as they are uncertain and not measurable. This does not mean, however, that they are not significant and potentially sizable. The huge litigation liabilities of tobacco and asbestos manufacturers are a case in point.

ADJUSTMENTS AND DISCOUNTS

The expert may need to make various adjustments to the values he derived from the application of some of the methods already discussed. Two of the more common adjustments are marketability and minority adjustments.

---

[9]SFAS 142.

Marketability Discounts

Stock investments in some companies are more liquid than others. One major difference is in the liquidity of stock in closely held and public companies. The stock of closely held companies is distinctly different from that of public firms in that a market already exists for public stocks; the stock of private companies, however, has only limited marketability. Depending on where a public stock is traded, this investment can be quite liquid. Liquidity refers to the speed with which an asset can be sold without incurring a significant loss of value. Under normal conditions, the stocks of major companies that are traded on the New York Stock Exchange are liquid investments. Stocks of companies infrequently traded on the over-the-counter market are not as liquid. However, even these stocks have a market maker who will endeavor to buy and sell the shares. This is not the case for shares of closely held companies. Therefore, if the stock values of comparable public companies are used to value closely held shares, these derived values need to be reduced to reflect the relatively lower marketability of closely held shares.

There has been abundant research on marketability discounts. One body of research examined the prices of *letter stock*. Letter stocks are shares of public companies that are identical to the company's shares that are actively traded, except that the stock is restricted and cannot be traded for a specific time period. Companies issue restricted shares for a variety of reasons, including the financing of mergers or for the compensation of management. Because the lettered stock may not be traded in public markets, it lacks the marketability of the unrestricted shares. The price difference between these two categories of stock can be used as a guide to the value of this one attribute—marketability. Whatever discount that is derived from this research, however, underestimates the true marketability discount. This is because letter shares are usually restricted for a period of one to two years, at which point they become registered with the SEC and can be publicly traded. Therefore, this research measures only the discount due to the temporary lack of marketability and the indefinite lack of marketability of closely held stock.

Marketability Discount Research

A number of studies have tried to measure the value of the discount that the market puts on a lack of marketability. In the context of business valuations, marketability refers to the ability of an investor in a business to sell his investment without significant loss of value. Various studies that attempt to measure the discount that the market itself applies to less marketable investments are categorized according to the methodology that has been employed.

Restricted Stock Studies

One of the early studies on restricted stock discounts was the Securities and Exchange Commission's Institutional Investors Study.[10] The SEC's researchers examined companies that were traded on the New York and American Stock Exchanges, as well as OTC companies, and found an average discount of 25.8 percent. Shortly after the SEC study, Milton German examined 89 restricted stock transactions and found that the restricted shares sold at discounts equal to 33 percent of the unrestricted stock.[11] Similar results were obtained by Robert Moroney, who found a mean discount of 35.6 percent for 146 restricted stock transactions.[12] Robert Trout used a multiple regression model to estimate the marketability discount for 60 restricted stock purchases. He found an average discount of 33.45 percent.[13] Still another study, done by J. Michael Maher, found a similar mean discount of 35.43 percent.[14]

In the 1980s, using data from 28 restricted stock private placements from 1978 to 1982, Standard Research Consultants found an average discount of 45 percent. Williamette Management Associates, using data on 33 restricted stock private placements from 1981 to 1984, found an average discount of 33 percent. The results of these studies are summarized in Table 8.4.

Research on Private Transactions
before Initial Public Offerings

An alternative methodology for deriving the marketability discount is to examine the difference between the prices of private securities transactions prior to initial public offerings (IPOs) and the IPO prices. Two such studies were conducted, one by John Emory of Baird & Company and another by Williamette Management Associates. Emory examined 97 offerings during the period 1980–1981 and 130

---

[10]"Institutional Investor Study Report of the Securities and Exchange Commission," Washington, D.C.: U.S. Government Printing Office, Document no. 93–64, March 10, 1971.

[11]Milton German, "An Economist-Financial Analysts Approach to Valuing Stock of a Closely Held Company," *Journal of Taxation* (June 1972).

[12]Robert E. Moroney, "Most Courts Overvalue Closely Held Stocks," *Taxes* (March 1973): 144–154.

[13]Robert R. Trout, "Estimation of the Discount Associated with the Transfer of Restricted Securities," *Taxes* (June 1977): 381–385.

[14]J. Michael Maher, "Discounts for Lack of Marketability for Closely Held Business Interests," *Taxes* (September 1976): 562–571.

Table 8.4   Summary of Restricted Stock Studies

Study	Years Covered	Sample Size	Average Discount (%)
SEC	1966–69	398	25.8
German	1968–70	89	33.0
Trout	1968–72	60	33.45
Moroney	NA	146	35.6
Standard Research Consultants	1978–82	28	45.0
Management Planning	1981–96		27.1
Silber	1981–88		33.8
FMV Opinions, Inc.	1979–92		23.0
Williamette Management	1981–84	33	31.2

Source: Adapted from Shannon Pratt, Robert Reilly, and Robert P. Schweihs, *Valuing a Business,* 4th ed. (New York: McGraw-Hill, 2000), 404.

offerings during the period 1985–86.[15] He found that pre-IPO stock transactions, the prices of which were reported in SEC filings for a period five months prior to the IPO, traded at a mean discount of 60 percent from the IPO price.

Williamette Management Associates did a similar study covering parts of the period from 1975 to 1985.[16] Examining 665 transactions companies, they found discounts ranging from 41.7 percent to as high as 80 percent.

Conclusion of Restricted Stock and Pre-IPO Research

The research in this field shows that when public prices are used as a guide for the value of the stock of private companies, a marketability discount of at least one third is appropriate. The studies in this area support such a discount, if not an even higher one, from the public price.

Minority Discounts

A second discount might also be needed, depending on the percentage of owner-ship the privately held stock position constitutes. This is because control is an additional valuable characteristic that a majority position possesses a minority holding does not. A minority shareholder is often at the mercy of majority share-

---

[15]John D. Emory, "The Value of Marketability as Illustrated in Initial Public Offerings of Common Stock," *Business Valuation News* (September 1985): 21–24, and John D. Emory, "The Value of Marketability as Illustrated in Initial Public Offerings of Common Stock," *Business Valuation Review* (December 1986).

[16]Shannon Pratt, *Valuing Business and Professional Practices,* 3rd ed. (Homewood, IL: Dow Jones-Irwin, 1986), 250–255.

holders. The holder of a minority position can only elect a minority of the directors, and possibly none of the directors, depending on whether the corporation is
incorporated in a state that allows cumulative voting. Majority and minority
shareholders each possess proportionate rights to dividend distributions, but a
majority shareholder possesses the right to control the actions of the corporations
in addition to these dividend decisions. This is an additional characteristic and
commands an additional premium that must be paid. Looking at it from the
minority shareholder's viewpoint, the minority position is valuable and will trade
at a discount to account for the lack of control.

A guide to the appropriate minority discount is the magnitude of the average
control premium. Table 8.5 shows that the average control premium between
1980 and 1998 was 40.7 percent. This premium can be used to compute the
appropriate minority discount using the following formula:

$$\text{Minority discount} = 1 - [1/(1 + (\text{Avg. Premium})] \qquad (8.4)$$

Using the average control premium of 40.7 percent we get an implied minority discount of 28.8 percent.

Table 8.5   Control Premiums and Implied Minority Discounts

Year	Control Premium Minority Offer (%)	Implied Discount (%)
1980	49.9	33.3
1981	48.0	32.4
1982	47.4	32.2
1983	37.7	27.4
1984	37.9	27.5
1985	37.1	27.1
1986	38.2	27.6
1987	38.3	27.7
1988	41.9	29.5
1989	41.0	29.1
1990	42.0	29.6
1991	35.1	26.0
1992	41.0	29.1
1993	38.7	38.3
1994	44.1	54.5
1995	37.1	61.7
1996	36.6	29.4
1997	35.9	22.4
1998	40.7	39.5
1999	43.5	33.0
2000	49.1	53.8
2001	58.0	35.2
2002	59.8	39.9
Average	**42.7**	**34.2**

Source: Mergerstat Review, 2003.

Applying Marketability and Minority Discounts

Let us assume that a value of $40 per share has been computed for a 20 percent ownership position in a closely held firm. Assuming 33 percent marketability and minority discounts, the value of this stock position equals:

Unadjusted value	$40 / share
Less 33% marketability discount	26.80
Less 33% minority discount	17.96

The $17.96 per share value is the value of a nonmarketable minority position in this closely held business.

REFERENCES

Annual Statement Studies, Robert Morris Associates, Philadelphia, PA.

Brigham, Eugene F., and Philip R. Davies, *Intermediate Financial Management,* 7th ed. New York: Thomson South-Western, 2002.

Business Valuation Review.

Costal Fuels of Puerto Rico, Inc. v. Caribbean Petroleum Corporation.

Emory, John D., "The Value of Marketability as Illustrated in Initial Public Offerings of Common Stock." *Business Valuation News* (September 1985).

Emory, John D., "The Value of Marketability as Illustrated in Initial Public Offerings of Common Stock." *Business Valuation Review* (December 1986).

Farmington Dowel Products Co. v. Forster Manufacturing Co., 421 F2d 61 (1st Cir. 1970).

German, Milton, "An Economist-Financial Analysts Approach to Valuing Stock of a Closely Held Company." *Journal of Taxation* (June 1972).

"Institutional Investor Study Report of the Securities and Exchange Commission," Washington, D.C.: U.S. Government Printing Office, Document no. 93–64, March 10, 1971.

Maher, J. Michael, "Discounts for Lack of Marketability for Closely Held Business Interests." *Taxes* (September 1976).

Moroney, Robert E., "Most Courts Overvalue Closely Held Stocks." *Taxes* (March 1973).

Pratt, Shannon P., *Valuing Small Businesses and Professional Practices.* Homewood, IL: Dow Jones-Irwin, 1986.

Pratt, Shannon P., *Valuing a Business,* 2nd ed. Homewood, IL: Dow Jones-Irwin, 1989.

Pratt, Shannon P., "Discounts and Premia," in *Valuation of Closely Held Companies and Inactively Traded Securities.* Charlottesville, VA: Institute of Chartered Financial Analysts, 1990.

Pratt, Shannon P., *Valuing a Business,* 3rd ed. Homewood, IL: Dow Jones-Irwin, 1996.

Pratt, Shannon P., Robert Reilly, and Robert P. Schweihs, *Valuing a Business,* 4th ed. New York: McGraw-Hill, 2000.

SFAS 142.

Trout, Robert R., "Estimation of the Discount Associated with the Transfer of Restricted Securities." *Taxes* (June 1977).

Trout, Robert R., "Business Valuations" in *Measuring Commercial Damages.* New York: Wiley, 2000.

Van Horne, James C., and John M. Wachowicz, *Financial Management and Policy.* Englewood Cliffs, NJ: Prentice-Hall, 1996.

9

INTELLECTUAL PROPERTY

The field of intellectual property litigation has grown significantly in recent years. This has led to increased demand for the computation of damages for violation of intellectual property claims. Intellectual property issues revolve around four main types of intellectual assets. They are:

1. Patents
2. Copyrights
3. Trademarks
4. Trade Secrets

PATENTS

A patent is a grant of a property right that is extended by the Patent and Trademarks Office of the U.S. Department of Commerce. The right bestows upon the owner of the patent the right to exclude others from using it without permission from the holder of the patent.

There are two main components to a patent: its specification and its claims. The specification features a description of the invention and includes supporting documentation such as drawings, a description of the way the invention is used, and indications of prior art. The claims set forth what the inventor asserts are the relevant uses for which protection is requested. These include what are referred to as independent and dependent claims. These claims are drafted so as to try to prevent variations in the patent that would constitute infringement.

The property right that one receives from a patent is an exclusionary right. That is, it is the right to exclude others from making or using the product. The patent holder has the right to sue in federal district court those who violate the patent. In such a suit, the patent holder may seek two general types of relief—an injunction and damages.

There are three types of patents: utility, plant, and design patents. Utility patents are the ones that are most likely to involve a damages expert.[1]

Patent Time Periods

The three types of patents are divided into two categories based on their longevity. They are: utility and plant patents, and design patents. Utility and plant patents extend for 17 years from the approval date, whereas design patents last for 14 years. The 17-year time period may be extended up to an additional 5 years for pharmaceutical and medical devices. This extension was made possible by the efforts of the pharmaceutical industry who was coping with the delays in the Food and Drug Administration approval process.[2] Once patents expire the public may freely use the patented product.

Changing Legal Framework

The first patent act in the United States was written by Thomas Jefferson and was passed by Congress in 1790. In this initial version of the law, patent time periods were set at 14 years. The time period was extended in 1861 to 17 years. While the patent laws have evolved over the years, the legal treatment of patents underwent fundamental change in 1981 when the Federal Court system created a special Court of Appeals of the Federal Circuit. This court exclusively handles appeals of intellectual property lawsuits. This court has issued numerous decisions that have further defined the law in this area.

When an infringer claims a patent is invalid, the court places the burden of proof on the infringer who must prove the lack of validity. The standard of proof is demanding but if the use is invalid the infringer may demand significant damages. This has been underscored by several large damage awards. The costs of engaging in unauthorized use of patents have risen.

---

[1] Mark Glick, Lara A. Reymann, and Richard Hoffman, *Intellectual Property Damages: Guidelines and Analysis* (New York: Wiley, 2003), 125.

[2] J. Wheaton, "Generic Competition and Pharmaceutical Innovation: The Drug Price Competition and Patent Term Restoration Act of 1984," *Catholic University Law Review* 35 (1986): 433–487.

The owner of the intellectual property may ask the court for an injunction. However, courts have been somewhat reluctant to grant injunctions. In patent cases courts require the owner of the patent to meet certain standards such as a convincing likelihood of success and proof of irreparable harm which outweighs any harm the injunction inflicts upon the defendant. The key requirement is likelihood of success, and if this is met the court may simply presume the existence of other criteria such as irreparable harm.[3] The presumption of irreparable harm is partially based on the fact that a patent is only bestowed for a limited duration and continued use of the patent during that time period will erode the value of the patent to its holder.

Direct versus Contributory Infringement

Direct infringement refers to the unauthorized use of a patented product. The owner of the patent then has the right to bring an action against the infringer seeking damages. Contributory infringement occurs when one party facilitates the infringement by others. The owner of the patent then has the right to bring an action against the party who made it possible for others to infringe on the patent.[4] This creates certain opportunities for the patent owner, who may be able to pursue one action against the facilitator rather than pursuing many separate actions against a multitude of infringers (a more costly process).

Defenses Claimed by Alleged Patent Infringers

The users of intellectual property typically claim that they either did not infringe or that the patent is invalid. The lack of validity may be asserted by claiming that the invention was anticipated by a prior art and therefore was not patentable. The defendant may also claim that the United States Patent and Trademark Office failed in its duty to disclose the best prior art or research data which would not have supported the patent.[5]

---

[3]*Smith Int'l, Inc. Hughes Tool Co.*, 718 F2d 1573, 1581 U.S.P.Q., 686 (Fed Cir. 1983) *cert denied*, 464 U.S. 966 (1983).

[4]Jeffrey Samuels and Linda B. Samuels, "Contributory Infringement: Relief for the Patent Owner," *The Corporation Law Review*: 332–345.

[5]R. Peyton Gibson, "Infringement of Patents and Related Technology," *Commercial Damages: A Guide to Remedies in Business Litigation*, Charles L. Knapp, ed. (New York: Matthew Bender, 1997), 49-6–49-7.

Remedies Available to the Patentee

The patentee has several principal remedies available to it.[6] The most timely of these is the issuance of an injunction which would bar the infringer from continued use of the patent. The second type of remedy is an award of monetary damages in the form of a royalty or lost profits. In addition, the patentee may also seek compensation for legal fees and court costs.

COMPUTATION OF DAMAGES
FOR PATENT INFRINGEMENT

There are two categories of damages for owners of intellectual property: lost profits and royalties. Of the two alternatives, courts prefer to award lost profits. Royalties are used when the plaintiff cannot prove its lost profits, however.[7] While much of the discussion about the computation of lost profits discussed elsewhere in this book also applies to lost profits computation for intellectual property violations, there are certain differences.

LEGAL REQUIREMENTS NECESSARY
TO PROVE LOST PROFITS

As in most commercial damages cases, patent holders must first prove causality followed by a computation of damages. In the context of patent litigation, these requirements are encompassed in four factors which are called *Panduit Factors* from the case *Panduit Corp v. Stahlin Brothers Fiber Works, Inc.*[8] The four Panduit factors are:

1. *Market Demand.* The sales of the infringer may be used as proof that there was sufficient demand in the market for the product.[9] This is a known factor and therefore is not subject to speculation.

---

[6] Stanley M. Besen and Leo J. Raskind, "An Introduction to the Law and Economics of Intellectual Property," *The Journal of Economics Perspectives* 5 (1) (winter 1991): 3–27.

[7] *Hartness International, Inc. v. Simplimatic Engineering Co.*, 819 F2d 1100 1112 (Fed. Cir. 1987).

[8] *Panduit Corp v. Stahlin Brothers Fiber Works, Inc.*, 575 F2d 1152, 1156 (6th Cir. 1978).

[9] *Gyromat Corporation v. Champion Spark Plug.*, 735 F2d 5489, 552 (Fed. Cir. 1984).

2. *Unavailability of Noninfringing Substitutes.* This involves an examination of the characteristics of the product and the claimed substitutes. Court decisions have rendered this requirement less relevant as they have often found that no alternatives were acceptable unless there is a very strong similarity between the infringed product and the substitutes.[10]

Products may be very similar and thus be close substitutes. In other instances, the products differ in some attributes so as to not make them perfect substitutes. While an examination of the specific attributes of the products is helpful, a consideration of consumers' behavior in their consumption of the respective products is also very useful. Not all courts, however, have focused on consumers and some have only considered a product's technical attributes.

3. *Ability to produce and market product.* For many products, a variety of resources and capabilities are needed to successfully produce and market a product. While this is important and its consideration makes good common sense, this factor also may not be that important as the court may give the benefit of the doubt to the plaintiff.[11]

4. *Computation of the lost profits.* Since this book is about the computation of damages, this factor is discussed at length.

The Panduit factors represent an application of an array of 15 factors that the court set forth in *Georgia Pacific Corp. v. U.S. Plywood Champion Papers, Inc.* when it was establishing factors for determining a proper royalty. In *Panduit,* the court considered those 15 factors and applied them to the determination of lost profits.

The *Georgia Pacific* factors are discussed later in this chapter.

Computation of Lost Profits

Patent owners can incur lost profits in a number of ways. The most basic lost profits computation is to measure *incremental profits.* Incremental profits are defined as follows:

$$\text{Incremental profits} = (\text{Units sold by infringer}) \times (\text{Patentee's incremental profit margin}) \quad (9.1)$$

---

[10]R. Peyton Gibson, "Infringement of Patents and Related Technology," *Commercial Damages: A Guide to Remedies in Business Litigation,* Charles L. Knapp, ed. (New York: Matthew Bender, 1997), 49-26.

[11]*Gyromat Corporation v. Champion Spark Plug.,* 735 F2d 549, 554 (Fed. Cir. 1984).

The incremental profit approach is well established in the patent case law as set forth in cases such as *Paper Converting Machine Co. v. Magna-Graphics Co.*

> The incremental income approach to the computation of lost profits is well established in the law relating to patent damages. See *Lam, Inc. v. Johns-Manville Corp.; Levin Bros v. Davis Manufacturing Co.,* 72 F2d 163 (8th Cir, 1934). The approach that it does not cost as much to produce unit $N + 1$ if the first N (or fewer) units produced already have paid fixed costs. Thus fixed costs—those costs which do not vary with increases in production, such as management salaries, property taxes, and insurance—are excluded when determining profits.[12]

Consistent with the general methodology used in other types of commercial damage cases, fixed costs that do not vary with output are usually not included in the profit computation. In an effort to minimize its damages, infringers may focus on the magnitude of its sales of the infringed product as well as the costs included in the patentee's incremental profit margin.

One major difference between lost profits computations in patent infringement cases and other commercial damages cases is that there are lower requirements for proving demand for the product. The norm is to simply assume that the infringer's sales would have been the patentee's. It is usually not necessary to develop a more complete analysis of the demand determinants which normally would be done in a business interruption analysis. This sidesteps the questions of whether the patentee would have been able to sell as many units as the infringer did (from a demand-side perspective) and whether the patentee would have received the same price.

Measurement of the Infringer's Profit's

Prior to 1946, a plaintiff could recover both his lost profits and the infringer's profits. The Patent Statute was amended in 1946, though, to prevent the possibility of a double recovery.[13] The Supreme Court later interpreted the 1946 amendment to provide for the computation of the plaintiff's pecuniary damages as a result of the infringement.[14]

---

[12]*Paper Converting Machinery Co. v. Magna-Graphics Co.,* 745 F2d 11, 22 (Fed Cir. 1984).

[13]Mark Glick, "The Law and Economics of Patent Infringement Damages," *Utah Business Journal* 10 (2) (March 1997).

[14]*Aro Manufacturing Co. v. Convertible Top Replacement,* 377 U.S. 476 (1946).

The infringer's profits *may* not be very relevant to the computation of the plaintiff's lost profits. The key is determining what profits the patentee would have realized from the sales that the infringer made. However, the infringer's profits play a role when it is difficult to measure the patentee's profits. In such cases, the court looks to the infringer's profits to determine a reasonable royalty.

Lost Profits and Analysis of Market Share

One way that profits are measured in cases where substitutes for the infringed product exist is what is called the market share approach. It is an approach that has been accepted by courts.[15] Using this approach, an expert tries to measure the appropriate market share for the plaintiff. This is often done by considering the sales of the plaintiff in relation to the sales of other companies selling in the same market. A historical market share is established and the expert considers this when trying to establish what the plaintiff's market share would be but for the infringement of the defendant. That is, the expert attempts to create a "but for" market share. The expert cannot do this blindly; she also must consider other relevant factors, such as changes in the market and the economy that prevailed during the infringement period. If significant changes have taken place in the market and the economy such that the plaintiff would have had a different market share even in the absence of the infringement, then these factors need to be considered.

Comment on Capacity Considerations

The *Panduit* factors indicate that the plaintiff must show that it had the capacity and capability to produce and market the products whose sales the expert projects. This involves a consideration of several factors. One would be the physical facilities of the plaintiff—its total capacity. The damages expert may have to involve other experts to assist in this task if such an analysis requires this type of expertise. Each case dictates its own requirements. However, the expert needs to be aware that capacity includes more than physical facilities. Each business has a production function whereby it utilizes various inputs to generate an output. The input may include labor, management, equipment, facilities, etc. The company must be able to realistically integrate all of these components at the projected output level. This is easier to do if it can be shown that the company successfully

---

[15]*State Industries v. Mor-Flo Industries*, 883 F2d 1573, 1577-80 (Fed. Cir. 1989).

produced and marketed at that level in the past. If it had capacity constraints that indicate a lower capability than the projected level, then the expert must be able to show that this additional capability could have been successfully acquired, such as through the use of subcontractors. Any changes in the level of profitability at the "above capacity" level also need to be considered.

LOST PROFITS DUE TO PRICE EFFECTS

In addition to being deprived of the profits on sales made by the infringer, the profits actually received by the patentee could also be adversely affected by the infringer's actions. Had the infringer not entered the market with its unauthorized products, the owner would hold a monopoly position. As a monopolist, it would have the ability to pick the price-quantity combination on the product's demand curve which maximized its profits. However, when the infringer enters the market, the price may be affected as the owner and the infringer become competitors. This can lead to another form of losses—reduced prices received by the owner for the products actually sold. This is shown in Exhibit 9.1 where the increased output due to the entrant of the infringer causes a movement down the product demand curve from q_1 to q_2. A lower price of p_2 also results instead of the price associated with output level q_1 (which would have been p_1). The lower prices erode the owner's profit margin, leading to lower profits on the sales actually made by the owner.

It may be difficult to precisely measure the price effect that results from the *duopolistic* market structure (two sellers) in which the owner and the infringer are competitors. However, the court in *Kaufman Co. v. Lantech, Inc.* eased the bur-

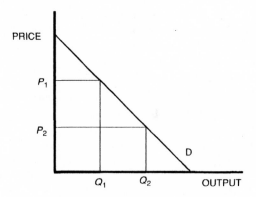

Exhibit 9.1 Lost profits due to price effects.

den of proof when measuring lost profits in a duopolistic market structure; it concluded that "when the patentee and the infringer are the only suppliers present in the market, it is reasonable to infer that infringement probably caused the loss of profits."[16] The improper competition changes the marketplace and economists have to estimate what the monopolist's price would have been in the absence of the competition. Economists have theoretically tried to trace the competitive effects of duopolists through game theory techniques which analyze the interactive effects of competitors.[17]

In *Polaroid Corporation v. Eastman Kodak Company*, the court explicitly recognized the need to consider the impact on the plaintiff's quantity sold due to the higher prices that the plaintiff claimed it would have received had it not been for the actions of the defendant.[18] In fact, the court rejected the view that Polaroid could have made more money if it had been able to raise prices:

> . . . I find that the higher prices that Polaroid says it would have charged would have depressed demand so substantially that the strategy the company historically pursued is actually the more profitable one.

Polaroid tried to prove its price erosion damages through an econometric model developed by one of its experts—Dr. Franklin Fisher. He concluded from his econometric analysis that from 1976–1990, Polaroid could have sold all of the cameras it had sold during this historical period plus all of the ones that Kodak sold while charging higher prices. The court summarized Fisher's model as follows:

> Professor Fisher constructed a model reflecting his judgements about what influences the demand for instant cameras and film. . . . Professor Fisher arrived at his model just as Professor Baumol did: by making assumptions about the influences on demand, entering the historical values of these influences and arriving at a mathematical relationship between the influences and the number of cameras that were purchased. Professor Fisher went one further step and used this framework of relationships to predict the future.

> In Professor Fisher's model, Polaroid charges more in the Kodak-free world and yet sells the same number of cameras from 1976–1990 that Polaroid and Kodak sold together from 1976–1985.

---

[16]*Kaufman Co. v. Lantech, Inc.*, 926 F2d 1136 (Fed. Cir. 1991).

[17]M. Shubik, "Information, Duopoly and Competitive Markets: A Sensitivity Analysis," *Kyklos* 26 (1973), and Charles R. Plott, "Industrial Organization Theory and Experimental Economics," *Journal of Economic Literature* 28 (December 1982).

[18]*Polaroid Corp. v. Eastman Kodak Company*, 16 U.S.P.Q. 2d 1481 (D. Mass) 1990.

I find that Polaroid would not have been able to raise its prices significantly without greatly reducing demand. Not surprisingly, Professor Fisher reaches a different conclusion. . . . Professor Christiansen, the econometrician who testified for Kodak, dissected the intricacies of Professor Fisher's model and exposed its unstated assumptions, biases and errors.

By not capturing the profound effect on the competition from conventional products, Professor Fisher overestimated the prices Polaroid could have charged for instant products.

The plaintiff's unsuccessful attempt to prove price erosion damages in *Polaroid v. Kodak* shows that any plaintiff must be able to reconcile claims of price erosion damages with the expected downward slope of a typical demand curve. If the plaintiff expects to prove a counter-intuitive result, it must be armed with a sound analysis that is going to withstand the challenges by equally qualified experts. Among the issues that have to be convincingly addressed is the price elasticity of demand over the relevant price range.[19] The need to address such issues through thorough economic analysis was clearly articulated by Judge Frank Easterbrook in *Mahurkar*. He criticized the lack of a meaningful economic analysis to support price erosion claims but also sought to substitute his own considerable knowledge of economics to try to determine what the relevant price elasticities were.[20]

Graphical Depiction of Lost Profits Inclusive of Price Erosion Damages

Losses from the sales of an infringer are shown in Exhibit 9.2. They are shown to include a component for price erosion damages, the difference between P_{NI} and P_I for all units that would have been sold without infringement, Q_{NI}, as well as the units that are sold with infringement, Q_I. The dotted area, $P_I GCD$, denotes the profits that the infringer realizes with the infringement. It can be seen that given the way the graph is drawn, these are well below the profits the patentee would have realized without the infringement—$P_{NI} AEJ$.

---

[19]Sumanth Addanki, "Economics and Patent Damages: A Practical Guide," Working Paper no. 21: National Economic Research Associates. (White Plains, NY, November 1993).

[20]*In re Mahurkar Double Lumen Hemodialysis Catheter Patent Litigation,* 831 F. Supp 1354 (N.D. 1993).

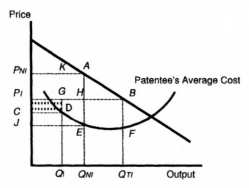

Exhibit 9.2 Patentee's lost profits.

LOST PROFITS DUE TO CHANGING COST CONDITIONS

Another less obvious way the owner can incur lost profits is by not realizing some of the economies of scale that it would have enjoyed had it been in a monopoly position (as opposed to the duopoly that would result from the owner being in competition with one infringer). Whether such losses exist depends on the cost function of the owner. Assume the owner's production process is characterized by economies of scale, such as that which is reflected in the average cost function depicted in Exhibit 9.3. Then, producing an output such as Q_1 where per-unit costs are AC_1 (as opposed to a higher output Q_2 where per unit costs are AC_2) results in higher costs equal to the $(AC_2 - AC_1)Q_1$.

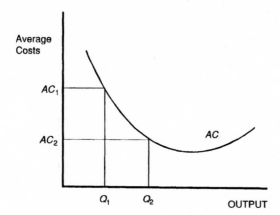

Exhibit 9.3 Changing cost conditions.

ROYALTY ARRANGEMENTS

The owner of the intellectual property may have chosen to license its use to users in exchange for a royalty. If the owner is already doing this, then the royalty that it charges authorized users *may* be used to compute the owner's losses. Royalty fees can also be used to construct the proper compensation for the owner even in cases where the owner is not authorizing users to use the product in exchange for a royalty. This method of compensation recognized that royalties are chosen by owners to obtain compensation from users. Therefore, in the absence of an explicit a priori arrangement, such a hypothetical royalty would be one way of compensating the owner. This method is helpful when similar products are traded in the marketplace using common royalty formulas. The existence of such formulas facilitates the damage computation.

Types of Royalties

There are two types of royalties: running royalties and lump sum royalties.[21] Running royalties are variable costs which are either computed as a percent of revenues or as a simple per-unit cost. An example of a running royalty is the 8 percent of infringing sales that was established in *H. K. Porter Co. v. Goodyear Tire and Rubber Co.* based upon expert testimony.[22] Lump sum royalties are a fixed sum that the user pays the owner. They give certain rights of use to the user in a manner that does not vary with the volume of use. An example of a lump sum royalty is the $2,600 annual fee per furnace that was established in *Trio Process Corp. v. L. Goldstein's Sons, Inc.* based upon a prior and existing license.[23]

Running royalties have certain efficiency effects on the market in that their variable nature is a factor that the user considers when determining its optimal profit-maximizing output. If this causes the user to put a lower output on the market than what it would in the absence of these additional variable costs, then economic theory indicates that a less-than-socially-optimal output reaches the market. In this sense, the lump sum royalty is more economically efficient; it transfers some of the profits that the user enjoys from selling its profit-maximizing output from the

---

[21]Elizabeth A. Evans, Martha S. Samuelson, and Robert A. Sherwin, "Economic Analysis of Intellectual Property Rights," *Litigation Support Handbook* (New York: Wiley, 2001).

[22]*H. K. Porter Co. v. Goodyear Tire & Rubber Co.*, 536 F2d 1115, 191 USPQ 486 (6th Cir. 1976).

[23]*Trio Process Corp. v. L. Goldstein's Sons, Inc.*, 612 F2d 1353, 204 USPQ 881 (3rd Cir. 1980) *cert denied*, 449 U.S. 827 (1980).

user to the owner without affecting the price-output combination. This is due to the fact that it is a *sunk cost* and thus should not affect decisions at the margin.[24]

Reasonable Royalties

The computation of royalties in patent infringement cases is different than the same computation in the normal operation of commerce. In patent cases, the standard is a *reasonable royalty*—not necessarily a commercially acceptable royalty. Courts have recognized that the computation of such an ex-post royalty is a legal fiction.[25]

In *Panduit Corp. v. Stahlin Brothers Fibre Works, Inc.*, the court stated:

> The setting of a reasonable royalty after infringement cannot be treated, as it was here, as the equivalent of ordinary royalty negotiations among truly "willing" patent owners and licensees. That view would constitute a pretense that the infringement never happened. It would also make an election to infringe a handy means for competitors to impose a "compulsory license" policy upon every patent owner.

A royalty may be computed even when the patent owner has not expressed any desire to license the product. The goal is to compute a royalty high enough to compensate the plaintiff who suffered due to the infringer's actions. However, in searching for a magnitude sufficient to compensate the plaintiff, courts have gone so far as to accept royalties that not only are greater than the standard royalties that prevail in commercial transactions but that have been as much as 50 percent of the product's price and more than 100 percent of the expected profits.[26] It seems that once the court concludes that the infringement has taken place, it moves to give the benefit of the doubt to the patentee.

Factors to Consider in Determining Royalties

The *Panduit* court referred to *Georgia Pacific Corporation v. U.S. Plywood-Champion Papers, Inc.*, a case in which that court delineated 15 factors that should be considered when determining a royalty rate. The court states that it

---

[24]Jack Hirshleifer and David Hirshleifer, *Price Theory and Its Applications,* 6th ed. (Upper Saddle River, NJ: Prentice-Hall, 1998), 174–175.

[25]*Georgia Pacific Corporation v. United States Plywood-Champion Papers, Inc.,* 446 F2d 295 (2d Cir. 1971).

[26]R. Peyton Gibson, "Infringement of Patents and Related Technology," *Commercial Damages: A Guide to Remedies in Business Litigation,* Charles L. Knapp, ed. (New York: Matthew Bender, 1997), 49-06.

derived these factors from several leading cases. In *Georgia Pacific*, the parties stipulated that a reasonable royalty was the proper measure of damages. The *Georgia Pacific* factors are:

1. The royalties received by the patentee for licensing of the patent in suit, proving or tending to prove an established royalty.
2. The rates paid by the licensee for the use of other patents comparable to the patent in suit.
3. The nature and scope of the license, as exclusive or nonexclusive; or as restricted or nonrestricted, in terms of territory or with respect to whom the manufactured product may be sold.
4. The licensor established a policy and marketing program to maintain his patent monopoly by not licensing others to use the invention or by granting licenses under special conditions designed to preserve that monopoly.
5. The commercial relationship between the licensor and the licensee, such as, whether they are competitors in the same territory in the same line of business; or whether they are inventor and promoter.
6. The effect of selling the patented speciality in promoting sales of other products of the licensee; the existing value of the invention to the licensor as a generator of sales of his nonpatented items; and the extent of such derivative or conveyed sales.
7. The duration of the patent and the term of the license.
8. The established profitability of the product made under the patent; its commercial success; and its current popularity.
9. The utility and advantages of the patent property over the old modes and devices, if any, that had been used for working out similar results.
10. The nature of the patented invention; the character of the commercial embodiment of it as owned and produced by the licensor; and the benefits to those that have used the invention.
11. The extent to which the infringer has made use of the invention; and any evidence probative of the value of that use.
12. The portion of the profit or of the selling price that may be customary in the particular business or in comparable businesses to allow for the use of the invention or analogous inventions.
13. The portion of the realizable profit that should be credited to the invention as distinguished to nonpatented elements, the manufacturing process, business risks, or significant features or improvements added by the infringer.

14. The opinion testimony of qualified experts.

15. The amount that a licensor (such as the patentee) and a licensee (such as the infringer) would have agreed upon (at the time the infringement began) if both had been reasonably and voluntarily trying to reach an agreement; that is, the amount which a prudent licensee—who desires, as a business proposition, to obtain a license to manufacture and sell a particular article embodying the patented invention—would have been willing to pay as a royalty and yet be able to make a reasonable profit and which amount would have been acceptable by a prudent patentee who was willing to grant a license.

Lost Profits versus Royalties

As noted above, courts view lost profits as the preferential measure of damages in patent infringement cases.[27] As stated in *Hansen v. Alpine Valley Ski Area, Inc.*, "If the record permits the determination of actual damages, namely, the profits the patentee lost from the infringement, that determination accurately measures the patentee's loss. If actual damages cannot be ascertained, then a reasonable royalty must be determined."

Plaintiffs may prefer lost profits if they exceed a reasonable royalty. Plaintiff's counsel may want to compute the losses both ways in advance of a trial as part of the selection of the best damages strategy to pursue. However, the court in *Hartness International, Inc. v. Simplimatic Engineering Company* endorsed using lost profits as the preferable method with a reasonable royalty being used "when actual lost profits cannot be proven."[28] Other courts have stated that the reasonable royalty should merely be used as the floor for damages.[29] Therefore, damages need to be computed using both approaches. In fact, there are cases where both lost profits and royalties have been awarded.[30]

Entire Market Theory

The entire market theory is the view that damages should be computed based on the market for an entire product which contained the infringed product. This

---

[27]*Hansen v. Alpine Valley Ski Area, Inc.*, 718 F2d 1075, 1078 (Fed. Cir. 1983).

[28]*Hartness International, Inc. v. Simplimatic Engineering Company*, 819 F2d 1100, 1112 (Fed. Cir. 1987).

[29]*Bandag, Inc. v. Gerrand Tire Co.*, 704 F2d 1578, 1583 (Fed. Cir. 1983).

[30]*Fonar Co. v. General Electric Co.*, 902 F. Supp. 330, 351 (E.D.N.Y. 1995).

means that if the infringed product is a component in an overall product, the patent damages should be computed based upon the market for the overall product. Courts may look to applying the entire market theory in cases where the infringed product plays a very large role in determining the value of the overall product.[31] This usually means that the products are physically part of the same machine.[32] Under the entire market value rule, damages are recoverable on the value of a patentee's entire apparatus containing several unpatented features where the patent-related feature is the basis for consumer demand."[33] In addition, the plaintiff may be able to claim damages resulting from lost sales of products that compete with the infringer's products.[34] Such an expanded base for damages can significantly increase the damages resulting from infringement. The U.S. Court of Appeals' articulation of the entire market theory is shown in an excerpt from *Rite-Hite Corporation v. Kelley Company.*

> Based upon the "entire market rule," the district court awarded lost profits on 1,692 dock levelers that it found Rite-Hite would have sold with the ADL-100 and MDL-55 restraints. Kelley argues that this award must be set aside because Rite-Hite failed to establish that the dock levelers were eligible to be included in the damage computation under the entire market rule. We agree.
>
> When a patentee seeks damages on unpatented components sold with the patented apparatus, courts have applied a formulation known as the "entire market rule" to determine whether such components should be included in the damage computation, whether for reasonable purposes, [cites omitted]. Early cases invoking the entire market rule required that for a patentee owning an "improvement patent" to recover damages calculated on sales of a larger machine incorporating that improvement, the patentee was required to show that the entire value of the whole machine, as a marketable article, was "properly and legally attributable" to the patented feature [cites omitted]. Subsequently, our predecessor court held that damages for component parts used with a patented apparatus were recoverable under the entire market rule if the patented apparatus "was of such paramount importance that it substantially created the value of the component parts" [cites

[31] *Julien v. Gomez & Andre Tractor Repairs, Inc,* 512 F. Supp. 955, 959 (M.D. La. 1981)

[32] Thomas L. Creel, "Patent Damages in the 90s," *Patent Litigation,* vol. II (New York: Practicing Law Institute, 1997).

[33] *Fonar Co. v. General Electric Co.,* 902 F. Supp. 330, 351 (E.D.N.Y. 1995) quoting *Rite Hite Corp. v. Kelley Co.,* 56 F3d 1538, 1544 (Fed. Cir. 1995).

[34] *Rite Hite Corp. v. Kelley Company, Inc.,* 56 F3d 1538, U.S.P.Q. 2d 1065, 1071 (Fed. Cir. 1995).

omitted]. We have held that the entire market rule permits recovery of damages based on the value of a patentee's entire apparatus containing several features when the patent-related feature is the "basis for consumer demand."[35]

The *Rite-Hite* decision broadened the measures of damages that may be claimed in patent lawsuits. The decision effectively allowed the recovery of damages for lost sales of goods not protected by the patent in suit.[36] Some have said that this decision could deprive the accused infringer of its day in court, while allowing the patentee to unlawfully extend the term and scope of protection of its patents.[37] Regardless of whether the decision will have such a far-reaching impact, it is clear that, under certain circumstances, *Rite-Hite* expanded the scope of damages that an expert may consider in such a calculation.[38] Collateral devices not covered by the patent but normally sold with the patented device now can be included in the damages analysis.

Computer Software

When the laws relating to intellectual property were first written, the computer industry was not near its current size. The computer software industry has since exploded. Given the valuable nature of proprietary computer software, companies want to protect and regulate its usage. In 1981, the U.S. Supreme Court removed legal barriers that had kept software from receiving some of the same protection of patent laws that other products enjoy. After that decision, computer software was protected by a patent. However, owners of the software may also choose to protect their assets through copyrights or as a trade secret.

---

[35]*Rite-Hite Corporation et al., v. Kelley Corporation,* 64 USL W 2032. 35 U.S.P.Q. 2d 1065.

[36]Brent Rabowsky, "Recovery of Lost Profits on Unprotected Products in Patent Infringement," *Southern California Law Review* (November 1996).

[37]Lisa Childs, *"Rite-Hite Corp. v. Kelley Co.:* The Federal Circuit Awards for Harm Done to a Patent Not in Suit," *Loyola University Chicago Law Journal* 27 (spring 1996): 665–713.

[38]Robert J. Cox, "Recent Development: But How Far? *Rite-Hite Corp. v. Kelley Co.'s* Expansion of the Scope of Patent Damages," *Journal of Intellectual Property Law* 3 (2) (spring 1996): 351–352.

COPYRIGHTS

A copyright protects the expression of an idea. However, it is the *expression* of the idea that is copyrighted rather than an idea itself. A copyright can be registered with the Copyright Office of the Library of Congress. It is typically accompanied by the symbol ©.

The Copyright Act of 1976, along with the Berne Convention Implementation Act of 1988, set forth the remedies for copyright infringement. These laws created the legal framework which had been governed by the Copyright Act of 1909.

Sections 102 and 103 provide copyright protection to the following types of work:

- Literary works
- Musical works as well as sound recordings
- Pictorial and other artistic works
- Pantomimes and choreographic works
- Motion pictures

Copyright Time Periods

Copyrights are protected for the life of an author plus 50 years. However, in the case of "works for hire," copyright protection lasts 75 years from the date of publication or 100 years from the date of creation. When the copyright expires it can be freely used by the public.

Remedies for Copyright Infringement

The Copyright Act provides various remedies for copyright violations including injunctions, impoundment, or destruction of the infringing items as well as damages. An injunction may be granted when the copyright owner can demonstrate a realistic likelihood of success in the action along with an expectation that the owner will incur irreparable injury. Irreparable injury normally means that damages cannot be adequately compensated for either due to their magnitude or the uncertainty in measurement. Courts, however, often simply presume the existence of irreparable damages leaving the defendant to prove otherwise.

Introduction to the Economics
of Copyright Law

An analytical framework for the economics of copyright law has been developed by William Landes and Richard Posner.[39] An overview of this framework is:

Let P = price of a copy

        $q(P)$ = market demand for copies of a work

          X = number of copies an author produces

          Y = number of copies copiers produce

          Z = the level of copyright protection

$Z \geq 0$ is a function of:

1. the degree of similarity between two works before infringement is determined
2. elements of the work that are protected
3. period of time work is protected

Assume   i. copiers supply copies up to point where $P = MC$ (marginal cost)

         ii. MC increases as the number of copies increases level of copyright protection increases

$$Y = Y(P, Z) \quad Y_p > 0 \; Y_z < 0 \qquad (9.1)$$

Author's profits are:

$$\Pi = (P - C)X - e(z) \qquad (9.2)$$

Substitutes for X:

$$\Pi = (P - C)[q(P) - Y(P, Z)] - e(z) \qquad (9.3)$$

where $e(z)$ = author's cost of expression

The greater the copyright protection is, the higher the author's cost of expression.

          R = author's gross profits

          N = number of works created

          $N = N(R, Z)$ where $N_r > 0$ and $N_z < 0$

---

[39]William E. Landes and Richard A. Posner, "An Economic Analysis of Copyright Law," *Journal of Legal Studies* XVIII (June 1989): 325–363.

The net effect in N of an increase in copyright protection depends on two effects:

1. As R increases, the number of works increases
2. As Z increases, the number of works decreases

At low Z, there is little incentive to produce works; free riders will dominate. Therefore, N increases as Z increases up to some level—Z^*. Beyond Z^* there are adverse effects on other potential authors. Some protection is good, but too much protection is bad. The solution is to find optimal Z^*.

Landes and Posner go on to show the welfare implications in deriving Z^*. Other conclusions of their framework is:

- At Z^*, the producer and consumer surplus per work exceeds the cost of producing the marginal work
- Optimal copyright protection should be set below the level that maximizes the number of works created
- The more valuable the work, the greater the optimal amount of copyright protection, as the cost of copying relative to the value received from copying will decline

Defenses in Copyright Suits

A defendant may assert various different defenses in copyright infringement lawsuits. One of the most fundamental is to assert that the copyright is invalid. This invalidity may be based on different theories, such as saying that the copyright was not sufficiently original. Another defense is the "fair use" defense in which the defendant is claiming that it is allowed the limited usage of the copyrighted material. Examples include newscasts, critics, research, and other normal usage. Whether such a defense is effective depends on the context within which the copyrighted material is used. Courts consider various factors such as the amount of the copyrighted material that was used. The more limited the use, the better the defendant's position is. Other factors are whether the material is essentially factual or fictional. The more it is a recitation of facts, the better the defense may be.

MEASUREMENT OF DAMAGES
FOR COPYRIGHT INFRINGEMENT

A copyright owner is entitled to its lost profits as well as those components of the defendant's profits not included in the copyright owner's lost profits computation. The award of the lost profits is designed to compensate the owner of the copyright while the award of the defendant's profits is designed to eliminate the incentive to infringe.

Copyright Owner's Lost Profits

The plaintiff's lost profits are usually measured by the plaintiff's lost sales less any cost savings from not producing these products. However, the plaintiff must measure these lost sales in a nonspeculative manner. The copyright owner cannot simply assume that the defendant's sales would have been its sales. Courts have held that various factors, such as the sales prices of both companies, need to be considered in the lost revenue projection process.[40] In cases in which the defendant sold the infringed product to the plaintiff's own former customers at similar prices, the assumption that the defendant's sales would have been the plaintiff's becomes easier for a court to accept.

In projecting lost sales due to copyright infringement, the forecasting methods discussed in Chapter Five are useful. Indeed courts have accepted significantly more basic projection techniques than those previously explained. For example, in *Taylor v. Meirick,* the court accepted a simple computation of the plaintiff's average sales for the two-year period prior to the infringement, without inflationary adjustment, as a nonspeculative forecast of what the plaintiff's sales would have been for the three-year infringement period.[41] Lost sales were then computed as the difference between these projected sales and the owner's actual sales. The simplistic nature of the damage estimation process is depicted in Exhibit 9.4.

Defendant's Profits

In order to prove the defendant's profits, the copyright owner only has to prove the infringer's gross revenues.[42] Once this is known, the defendant then has to establish what its costs are. Defendants may try to present a more full definition of its costs than what plaintiffs would prefer. At this point, the issue comes down to a

---

[40]*Stevens Linen Associates, Inc. v. Mastercraft Corporation,* 656 F2d. 11 (2d Cir. 1981)

[41]*Taylor v. Meirick,* 712 F2d 1112 (7th Cir. 1983).

[42]Ira Jay Levy and Paul S. Owen, "Infringement of Copyright and Literary Property," *Commercial Damages: A Guide to Remedies in Business Litigation* (New York: Matthew Bender, 1997).

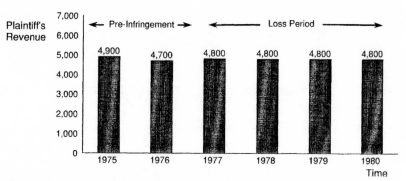

Exhibit 9.4 Simplistic revenue projection in *Taylor v. Meirick.*

cost analysis and the services of a good cost accountant can be invaluable. If, however, the defendant did not enjoy any profits from the infringement, then there are
no profits to award and the damages are simply the plaintiff's lost profits.

The analysis of the defendant's profits can be complicated when the costs
attributable to the infringed product and the defendant's other costs which are not
related to the infringed product cannot be easily separated. As with other types of
lost profits analysis, the goal is to measure the incremental costs associated with
the incremental revenues generated from the infringement. In *Deltrak, Inc. v.
Advanced Systems, Inc.,* the court recognized that fixed costs, such as rent or
depreciation, generally should not be included in this computation.[43] However,
other courts have found that overhead costs, which were measured by a simple
overhead costs/revenue ratio, should be applied to gross profits as an allowable
deduction.[44]

An excerpt from the court's opinion in *Deltrak v. Advanced Systems, Inc.,* a
case where the plaintiff sued for the improper use of architectural plans which
were used to build an apartment complex, is instructive in that it states what one
court found to be reasonable cost deductions:

> In consideration for the construction of the apartment complex and garage located
> at 1830-32 Knox Street, Empire paid Belmont $512,569 ($511,520 contract price
> plus $1,309 in reimbursed expenses). Belmont introduced evidence showing that it
> incurred $451,450.56 in direct deductible expenses, thus realizing a gross profit of
> $59,709.44 on the project. Belmont contends that it is entitled to deduct from the
> gross profit a portion of its administrative and general overhead expenses by a for-
> mula which would reduce its gross profit to a net profit of $12,878.94.

---

[43]*Deltrak v. Advanced Systems, Inc.,* 574 F. Supp. 400 (N.D. Ill. 1983).
[44]*Aiten v. Empire Construction Co.,* 542 F. Supp. 252 (D. Neb. 1982).

The rule is that overhead expenses which assist in the production of an infringing work are deductible from the gross profit of the infringer [cite omitted]. The burden is upon the defendant infringer to prove the actual expenditures for ordinary overhead and a fair method of allocating the overhead to the particular infringing activity in question [cite omitted]. The defendant need not, however, prove that each item of overhead was used in connection with the infringing activity [cite omitted].

The law requires no such minutiae, for it would make trial interminable. When appellant proved the actual expenditures for ordinary overhead, and a fair method of allocation, it carried its burden in the first instance. If, on cross examination or otherwise, it appears that ordinary overhead is not chargeable, in whole or in part, to the infringing business, then a proper charge only should be made. But all allowance should not be denied because stenographers, bookkeepers, janitors and presidents were not called to testify that they did perform specific tasks on this specific business. Courts and accountants resort to allocation to obviate this particular difficulty.

Statutory Damages

When the plaintiff's lost profits and the defendant's profits cannot be measured in a nonspeculative manner, the courts will look to an award of statutory damages. A plaintiff may elect to pursue statutory damages instead of its lost profits and the defendant's profits.[45]

Statutory damages are bounded within the monetary limits of greater than or equal to $750 but less than or equal to $30,000 for each infringement.[46] However, in cases where the courts find that the infringer was not aware of its infringement, it may reduce the statutory damage award.

TRADEMARKS

Companies may devote substantial resources to develop a trademark with which they hope that the market will associate the business and its products and services. In the traditional sense, trademarks are used to certify the authenticity of a product which, in turn, comes with the expectation on the part of a consumer of

---

[45]Ira Jay Levy and Paul S. Owen, "Infringement of Copyright and Literary Property," *Commercial Damages: A Guide to Remedies in Business Litigation* (New York: Matthew Bender, 1997), 50–52.

[46]Terry Lloyd, "Calculating Damages in Copyright Infringement Matters," *Litigation Services Handbook: The Role of the Financial Expert*, Roman L. Weil, Michael J. Wagner, and Peter Frank, eds. (New York: Wiley, 2001), 22-10.

the quality of the product or services. Trademarks for service providers are called *service marks*.

Trademarks provide protection for names associated with major brands. They also can provide protection for different products. They include fragrances, packaging, sounds, and designs, such as those embodied in clothing. The protection for trademarks is provided by the Lanham Act—it provides a variety of legal remedies including injunctive relief and monetary damages. This law deals with a broad array of business practices beyond just trademark infringement. Improper business practices, such as unfair competition, are made illegal by this law.

A candidate for a trademark applies at the Patent and Trademark Office to register the trademark. The applicant provides certain basic information such as the date of the first use of the trademark and indicates the products or services to which the trademark will apply. Once accepted, trademarks are published in the *Official Gazette*.

Trademark Time Periods

Trademarks have been defined by the Trademark Act of 1946. A trademark is valid for 20 years and may then be renewed for another 20 years, after which it may be renewed for another 20 years. The holder of the trademark, however, must attest to its continued use between the fifth and sixth year of its life lest the registration be canceled.

Economics of Trademarks

The main economic benefit of trademarks is that they reduce consumers search costs. Since the trademark is clearly identified with the marketer of the product, it is in the interest of the trademark owner to invest resources in maintaining the quality of the product or services. Landes and Posner express this in the form of a simple economic model as follows:[47]

$$\Pi = P + H(T; Y, W)$$

where Π = the full price of a good
   P = the money price
   H = search costs incurred by buyers
   T = trademark

---

[47]William M. Landes and Richard A. Posner, "Trademark Law: An Economic Perspective," *Journal of Law and Economics* XXX (2) (October 1987): 265–309.

$Y = $ a vector of factors other than T that affect search costs. These include advertising, value of consumers' time, number of competing products, etc.

$W = $ availability of words and symbols which can be used to construct a trademark (this is usually not relevant).

Landes and Posner show that firms with stronger trademarks (T) have lower search costs (H) and are able to command higher prices (P) due to the fact that the lower H is, the higher P can be without causing Π to change from its optimal level.

Trade Dress

An area related to trademark infringement is *trade dress*. Trade dress refers to the physical features of the product which have become known in the marketplace to be associated with a particular marketer of that product. These features signify what the source of the product is. One example is the pink color of Owens Fiberglass insulation.[48] When trade dress protection is afforded to a product, other companies are barred from duplicating these features. It is even possible for a company to qualify for trade dress protection on a product that was once patented but for which the patent has expired with the passage of time.

Damages for Trademark Infringement

Owners of trademarks can recover their damages (possibly in the form of a royalty) as well as the infringer's profits. In addition, they can recover other monetary relief such as treble damages, legal fees, and litigation costs. As with patent damages, lost profits must be proven in a nonspeculative way. Courts place the burden of proof on the plaintiff when it is trying to establish its damages. However, when the defendant's actions have made it difficult for the plaintiff to measure its damages, the defendant is generally not allowed to profit from this nor use this as a defense.

Recovery for damages from trademark infringement requires that the trademark owner demonstrate that it has been damaged, be able to measure these damages, and convincingly draw a causal link between the defendant's action and these damages.[49] A trademark owner is allowed to recover both its lost profits

---

[48]*In re Owens-Illinois Fiberglas Corp.*, 774 F2d 1116 (Fed. Cir. 1985).

[49]Ethan Horwitz, "Improper Use of Trademarks and Trade Names," *Commercial Damages: A Guide to Remedies in Business Litigation,* Charles L. Knapp, ed. (New York: Matthew Bender, 1997).

and the defendant's profits—but not when these come from some of the same sales.[50] If the plaintiff contends that the infringement caused confusion in the marketplace, resulting in it not being able to make certain sales, it must be able to demonstrate the ability to generate such sales in the marketplace in the absence of such confusion. If it cannot due to, for example, insufficient resources, then the court may not award the owner those damages.[51]

In establishing damages for trademark infringement, there is a high degree of proof required in establishing that damages actually occurred.[52] However, once this has been established, the courts are more lenient in the measurement of the actual damages; they may not require exactness. Courts have recognized that economic factors, such as the impact of the competition between the plaintiff and the defendant, may distort the market, making it more difficult to measure the plaintiff's lost sales.[53]

Plaintiff's Damages From Trademark Infringement

A trademark owner can be damaged in several ways when its trademark is violated. Sales can be diverted from the owner to the infringer. In addition, if the goods are produced in an inferior manner and the consumer believes that they are the products of the owner, the reputation of the owner may suffer resulting in diminished future sales. Other damages can occur from the owner using its marketing resources to build up a brand from which the defendant benefits without having to incur these costs. Ironically, the owner may then have to invest even more advertising and marketing monies to correct the consumer's perceptions. Such *corrective advertising* is another area in which the damage expert can be helpful.

Royalties as Measure of the Plaintiff's Damages
When royalties are the selected measure of the plaintiff's damages, their computation is straightforward when there is an existing agreement between the plaintiff and defendant that sets forth in an agreement between the plaintiff and

---

[50]*Polo Fashions, Inc. v. Extra Special Products, Inc.*, 208 U.S.P.Q. 421, 428 (S.D.N.Y. 1980).

[51]*Maltina Corporation v. Cawy Bottling Company*, 613 F2d 582 (5th Cir. 1980).

[52]Ethan Horwitz, "Improper Use of Trademarks and Trade Names," *Commercial Damages: A Guide to Remedies in Business Litigation,* Charles L. Knapp, ed. (New York: Matthew Bender, 1997), 51-27.

[53]*Donsco, Inc. v. Casper Corporation,* 205 U.S.P.Q. 246, 248 (E.D. Pa. 1980).

the defendant. When there was no agreement, then royalties may be measured by the standards in that industry. These standards may be established through expert testimony.[54]

Defendant's Profits

When the defendant's infringement is established, the plaintiff is awarded the defendant's profits so that the defendant cannot benefit from its illegal behavior. In computing these profits, the plaintiff must measure the value of the infringing revenues and then deduct the incremental costs associated with generating these revenues. This is the method used in a variety of business interruption cases.

As with patent infringement, all the plaintiff has to do is to prove the defendant's revenues. After that point the burden shifts to the defendant to prove its costs.[55] Courts have accepted simple measures of costs, such as using the ratio of infringing sales to the defendant's total sales and applying this ratio to the defendant's total costs.[56] However, courts have also accepted more sophisticated analysis of incremental costs which seek to identify only those costs incurred in the generation of the infringed sales. If the infringing sales are a more significant component of the defendant's total sales, then a portion of fixed costs may have to be included in total costs. If these sales are a small percent of total sales, then the court may disallow this deduction.[57]

TRADE SECRETS

Trade secrets come under the protection of the Uniform Trade Secrets Act. However, a firm and narrow definition of trade secrets is difficult as they can come in many forms and vary as business changes. It must, however, be information which allows the business to generate profits and enjoy some competitive advantage in the marketplace. The source of the profitability of the trade secrets may be from enhancing revenues, reducing costs, or both. The value of these

---

[54]*National Bank of Commerce v. Shaklee Corporation,* 503 F. Supp. 533, 207 U.S.P.Q. 1005 (W.D. Tex. 1980).

[55]*Playboy Entertainment, Inc. v. P.K. Sorren Export Company,* 546 F. Supp. 987, 997 (S.D. Fla. 1982).

[56]*Lawrence of London, Ltd. v. Count Romi, Ltd.,* 159 U.S.P.Q. 383 (N.Y. App. 1968).

[57]*S.C. Johnson & Son, Inc. v. Drop Dead Company,* 144 U.S.P.Q. 257, 260 (S.D.Cal. 1965).

secrets is underscored by efforts that the business exercises to keep the knowledge from leaking to competitors.

Some trade secrets are even patentable, but the business may decide not to apply for a patent so as to prevent competitors from using them after the life of the patent. Unfortunately, it may be difficult to maintain secrecy for such a time period. In addition, the law provides stronger protection for patents than it does for trade secrets.

Some of the forms of trade secrets are outlined below:

- *Compilations of Data.* These include various data which are used to generate profits. Such data are compiled in computer databases which may have helpful organizational features that the business has developed over time. A good example are databases of current and potential customers. However, in order for a company to prevent unauthorized use of customer lists, such as by former employees, the firm must maintain the list as a secret. Employees may be able to use remembered information on former customers.

- *Product of Experience.* This is the product of the company's experience which has led to perfecting certain procedures and processes. These also come in a variety of forms including machine settings, drawings, and manuals.

- *Formulas and Recipes.* Many manufacturers of food-related products closely guard the formulas for creating a product. The formula for Coca-Cola is a good example of this. Recipes can be jealously guarded by restaurants and chefs.

- *Research Findings and Test Results.* Companies involved in research and development closely guard the results of their research and preliminary tests. These secrets are often collected in research logs or preliminary reports which are considered proprietary.

In order for a trade secret to be legally protected, it must have economic value and the owner must have taken some measures to keep it secret. If one uses improper means to acquire a trade secret, such as engaging in industrial espionage, then a court may find that such users have to compensate the owner of the trade secret. However, if an individual or business acquires a trade secret through legitimate means, such as reverse engineering, then this is legal.

Damages for Misappropriation of Trade Secrets

There are two alternative measures of damages for trade secret misappropriation. One is the plaintiff's lost profits and the other is the defendant's gain. The plaintiff can recover one but not both. In order for the plaintiff to prove its losses, it may need to prove causality as well as the magnitude of damages.[58] Causality also involves showing that the sales diverted to a competitor would have been the plaintiff's sales but for the misappropriation of the trade secret.[59]

Trade secret damage analysis presents some interesting economic and accounting issues. For example, if the secret was the product of costly research, the defendant may be able to undercut the plaintiff's prices and take market share from the plaintiff. This could have an extended impact on the plaintiff if consumers are reluctant to pay the plaintiff's higher prices in the future.

In order to measure the defendant's profits derived from the use of the trade secret, an accounting of the defendant's profits attributable to the use of the secret needs to be compiled. Depending on the nature of the secret, it may or may not be easy to segregate these sales and profits from the other sales and profits of the defendant. Once the defendant's profits are measured, a court can consider remedies such as restitution. Another remedy is a royalty; however, it is not often used.[60] Royalties are used in trade secret cases when the plaintiff cannot prove its losses. In *Carter Products, Inc. v. Colgate Palmolive Company*, the court awarded royalties that were computed as a percent of the defendant's sales in addition to the defendant's profits.[61] Royalties may also be used when the defendant did not make a profit from use of the misappropriated secrets.[62]

Measuring the Plaintiff's Losses in Misappropriation of Customer Lists

The analysis of losses due to misappropriation of customer lists has to with the measurement of the plaintiff's losses and the defendant's gains from sales to customers on the misappropriated lists. In *Jet Spray Cooler, Inc. v. Crampton*, the court stated that the plaintiff may not recover both his own lost profits and those of the defendant.[63] This makes sense, because, but for the misappropriation, the

---

[58]Michael J. Herbert and William F. Johnson, "Improper Use of Trade Secrets and Customer Lists," *Commercial Damages: A Guide to Remedies in Business Litigation,* Charles L. Knapp, ed. (New York: Matthew Bender, 1997), 52-34.

[59]*Monsanto Chemical, Company v. Perfect Fit Product Manufacturing Company,* 349 F2d 389 (2d Cir. 1965) *cert denied,* 383 U.S. 942 (1966).

[60]Herbert and Johnson, op. cit., 52-40.

[61]*Carter Products, Inc. v. Colgate Palmolive Company,* 214 F. Supp. 383 (D. Md 1963).

[62]*University Computing Co. v. Lykes-Youngston Corp.,* 504 F2d 518, 535 (5th Cir. 1974).

[63]*Jet Spray Cooler, Inc. v. Crampton,* 385 N.E. 2d, 1356.

sale would not have been made twice (although a given customer could be sold to more than one time). The defendant may try to prove that the plaintiff would not have made the particular sales that the defendant made.[64] The burden of proof for this is on the defendant. In *Michel Cosmetics v. Tsirkas*, the court considered the trend in the plaintiff's sales and noted that its revenues and profits did not fall after the misappropriation. The court further noted that the sales were not even made in the plaintiff's territory.

One factor that needs to be considered in lost customer cases is the length of the projection. For long-term projections, the rate of customer attrition needs to be considered. The attrition rate and average customer duration is discussed in Chapter Five.

SUMMARY

Four different categories of intellectual property exist. They are patents, copyrights, trademarks, and trade secrets.

Patents are a grant of a property right by the Patent and Trademark Office of the U.S. government which give the patent holder the right to exclude others from using the patent for certain specific periods of time. Patents afford protection for 17 years in the case of utility or plant patents, while design patents last 14 years. A copyright protects the expression of an idea such as a literary or musical work. Copyright protection lasts for 75 years after the date of publication or 100 years after the date of creation. Trademarks are used to certify the authenticity of a product for consumers, who expect a certain level of quality for the product or services. A similar concept is trade dress, which refers to the physical features of the product that have become associated in the marketplace with a particular marketer of that product.

Two different types of infringement exist: direct and contributory infringement. Direct infringement refers to the unauthorized use of a patented item, whereas contributory infringement refers to facilitating others to engage in authorized use. Two types of damages can be awarded for patent infringement: lost profits and reasonable royalties. As with other types of commercial damages, lost profits must be measured within a reasonable degree of certainty. Certain factors, called *Panduit* factors, have been set forth by the courts as items that should

---

[64]*Michel Cosmetics v. Tsirkas*, 282 N.Y. 195, 26 N.E. 2d (1940).

be taken into account when attempting to measure lost profits. Reasonable royalties are used when lost profits cannot be measured within a reasonable certainty. A series of 15 factors has been presented by the courts as warranting consideration when determining a reasonable royalty.

Lost profits for copyright infringement must also be measured within a reasonable degree of economic certainty. If the copyright owner is not able to measure such losses, then it may be entitled to statutory damages. A copyright owner may be entitled to receive the infringer's profits. In making this computation, the plaintiff need only prove the infringer's revenues.Then the burden shifts to the defendant to prove the costs associated with these revenues.

Trademark owners may also be entitled to damages which are based upon a royalty or are focused on the infringer's profits. Other economic issues that the damages expert may have to focus on include possible damage to the reputation caused by the infringer and possible corrective advertising.

Trade secrets come in a variety of forms. They include data compilations, formulas, recipes, and research findings and test results. Damages arise from factors such as diverted sales and cost advantages.

Much of the methodology that has been developed in the overall damages framework presented in Chapters One through Five can be applied to measuring damages in intellectual property litigation. However, the area does provide some interesting variants, such as measuring the defendant's profits, in addition to simply focusing on the lost profits of the plaintiff. The expert should review some of the major cases, as the case law is different than the body of other commercial damages case law.

REFERENCES

Addanki, Sumanth, "Economics and Patent Damages: A Practical Guide." Working Page no. 21, White Plains, NY: National Economic Research Associates (November 1993).

Aiten v. Empire Construction Co., 542 F. Supp. 252 (D. Neb. 1982).

Aro Manufacturing Co. v. Convertible Top Replacement, 377 U.S. 476 (1946).

Bandag, Inc. v. Gerrand Tire Co., 704 F2d 1578, 1583 (Fed. Cir. 1983).

Besen, Stanley M. and Leo J. Raskind, "An Introduction to the Law and Economics of Intellectual Property." *The Journal of Economics Perspectives* 5 (1) (winter 1991): 3–27.

Carter Products, Inc. v. Colgate Palmolive Company, 214 F. Supp. 383 (D. Md 1963).

Childs, Lisa, "*Rite-Hite Corp. v. Kelley Co.:* The Federal Circuit Awards for Harm Done to a Patent not in Suit." *Loyola University Chicago Law Journal 27* (spring 1996): 665–713.

Cox, Robert J., "Recent Development: But How Far? *Rite-Hite Corp. v. Kelley Co.*'s Expansion of the Scope of Patent Damages." *Journal of Intellectual Property Law* 3 (2) (spring 1996): 351–352.

Creel, Thomas L., "Patent Damages in the 90s," *Patent Litigation*, vol. II. New York: Practicing Law Institute, 1997.

Deltak v. Advanced Systems, Inc., 574 F. Supp. 400 (N.D. Ill. 1983).

Donsco, Inc. v. Casper Corporation, 205 U.S.P.Q. 246, 248 (E.D. Pa. 1980).

Evans, Elizabeth A., Martha S. Samuelson, and Robert A. Sherwin, "Economic Analysis of Intellectual Property Rights." *Litigation Support Handbook: The Role of the Expert in Litigation*, 3rd ed. New York: Wiley, 2001.

Fonar Co. v. General Electric Co., 902 F. Supp. 330, 351 (E.D.N.Y. 1995).

Georgia Pacific Corporation v. United States Plywood-Champion Papers, Inc., 446 F2d 295 (2d Cir. 1971).

Gibson, R. Peyton, "Infringement of Patents and Related Technology." *Commercial Damages: A Guide to Remedies in Business Litigation,* Charles L. Knapp, ed. New York: Matthew Bender, 1997.

Glick, Mark, "The Law and Economics of Patent Infringement Damages." *Utah Business Journal* 10 (2) (March 1997).

Glick, Mark, Lara A. Reymann, and Richard Hoffman, *Intellectual Property Damages: Guidelines and Analysis.* New York: Wiley, 2003, 125.

Gyromat Corporation v. Champion Spark Plug, 735 F2d 5489, 552 (Fed. Cir. 1984).

Hansen v. Alpine Valley Ski Area, Inc., 718 F2d 1075, 1078 (Fed. Cir. 1983).

Hartness International, Inc. v. Simplimatic Engineering Company, 819 F2d 1100, 1112 (Fed. Cir. 1987).

Herbert, Michael J., and William F. Johnson, "Improper Use of Trade Secrets and Customer Lists" *Commercial Damages: A Guide to Remedies in Business Litigation,* Charles L. Knapp, ed., New York: Matthew Bender, 1997, 52-1–52-51.

Hirshleifer, Jack, and David Hirshleifer, *Price Theory and Its Applications,* 6th ed. Upper Saddle River, NJ: Prentice-Hall, 1998.

H.K. Porter Co. v. Goodyear Tire & Rubber Co., 536 F2d 1115, 191 USPQ 486 (6th Cir. 1976).

Horwitz, Ethan, "Improper Use of Trademarks and Trade Names." *Commercial Damages: A Guide to Remedies in Business Litigation,* Charles L. Knapp, ed. New York: Matthew Bender, 1997.

In re Mahurkar Double Lumen Hemodialysis Catheter Patent Litigation, 831 F. Supp 1354 (N.D. 1993),

In re Owens-Fiberglas Corp., 774 F2d 1116 (Fed. Cir. 1985).

Jet Spray Cooler, Inc. v. Crampton, 385 N.E. 2d, 1356.

Julien v. Gomez & Andre Tractor Repairs, Inc., 512 F. Supp. 955, 959 (M.D. La. 1981).

Kaufman Co. v. Lantech, Inc., F2d 1136 (Fed. Cir. 1991).

Landes, William M., and Richard A. Posner, "Trademark Law: An Economic Perspective." *Journal of Law and Economics* XXX (2) (October 1987).

Landes, William M., and Richard A. Posner, "An Economic Analysis of Copyright Law." *Journal of Legal Studies* XVIII (June 1989): 325–363.

Lawrence of London, Ltd. v. Count Romi, Ltd., 159 U.S.P.Q. 383 (N.Y. App. 1968).

Levy, Ira Jay, and Paul S. Owen, "Infringement of Copyright and Literary Property." *Commercial Damages: A Guide to Remedies in Business Litigation*, Charles L. Knapp, ed. New York: Matthew Bender, 1997.

Lloyd, Terry, "Calculating Damaging in Copyright Infringement Matters." *Litigation Services Handbook: The Role of the Financial Expert*, Roman L. Weil, Michael J. Wagner, and Peter Frank, eds. New York: Wiley, 2001, 22-10.

Maltina Corporation v. Cawy Bottling Company, 613 F2d 582 (5th Cir. 1980).

Michel Cosmetics v. Tsirkas, 282 N.Y. 195, 26 N.E. 2d (1940).

Monsanto Chemical Company v. Perfect Fit Product Manufacturing Company, 349 F2d 389 (2d Cir. 1965) *cert. denied*, 383 U.S. 942 (1966).

National Bank of Commerce v. Shaklee Corporation, 503 F. Supp. 533, 207 U.S.P.Q. 1005 (W.D. Tex. 1980).

Panduit Corp. v. Stahlin Brothers Fiber Works, Inc., 575 F2d 1152, 1156 (6th Cir. 1978).

Paper Converting Machinery Co. v. Magna-Graphics Co., 745 F2d 11, 22 (Fed Cir. 1984).

Playboy Entertainment, Inc. v. P.K. Sorren Export Company, 546 F. Supp. 987, 997 (S.D. Fla. 1982).

Plott, Charles R., "Industrial Organization Theory and Experimental Economics." *Journal of Economic Literature* 28 (December 1982).

Polaroid Corp. v. Eastman Kodak Company, 16 U.S.P.G. 2d 1481 (D. Mass) 1990.

Polo Fashions, Inc. v. Extra Special Products, Inc., 208 U.S.P.Q. 421, 428 (S.D.N.Y. 1980).

Rabowsky, Brent, "Recovery of Lost Profits on Unprotected Products in Patent Infringement." *Southern California Law Journal* (November 1996).

Rite Hite Corp. v. Kelley Company, Inc., 56 F3d 1538, U.S.P.Q. 2d 1065, 1071 (Fed. Cir. 1995).

Rite Hite Corp. v. Kelley Company, 64 USL W 2032. 35 U.S.P.Q. 2d 1065.

Samuels, Jeffrey, and Linda B. Samuels, "Contributory Infringement: Relief for the Patent Owner." *The Corporation Law Review*: 332–345.

S.C. Johnson & Son, Inc. v. Drop Dead Company, 144 U.S.P.Q. 257, 260 (S.D.Cal. 1965).

Shubik, M., "Information, Duopoly and Competitive Markets: A Sensitivity Analysis." *Kyklos* 26 (1973).

Smith Int'l, Inc. v. Highes Tool Co., 718 F2d 1573, 1581 U.S.P.Q., 686 (Fed Cir. 1983) *cert denied*, 464 U.S. 966 (1983).

State Industries v. Mor-Flo Industries, 883 F2d 1573, 1588-80 (Fed. Cir 1989).

Stevens Linen Associates, Inc. v. Mastercraft Corporation, 656 F2d 11 (2d Cir. 1981).

Taylor v. Meirick, 712 F2d 1112 (7th Cir. 1983).

Trio Process Corp. v. Goldstein's Sons, Inc., 612 F2d 1353, 204 USPQ 881 (3rd Cir. 1980) *cert denied*, 449 U.S. 827 (1980).

University Computing Co. v. Lykes-Youngston Corp., 504 F2d 518, 535 (5th Cir. 1974).

Wheaton, J., "Generic Competition and Pharmaceutical Innovation: The Drug Price Competition and Patent Term Restoration Act of 1984." *Catholic University Law Review* 35 (1986): 433–487.

10

SECURITIES-RELATED DAMAGES

In the wake of the booming stock market of the 1990s and its subsequent collapse, a large volume of lawsuits ensued. Some were motivated by large-scale scandals such as Enron, Worldcom, and Global Crossing. Others were caused by the large losses some investors incurred in their portfolios. In 2003, the industry was experiencing a "tidal wave of arbitration" cases.[1] Such a volume of securities lawsuits expands the need for finance experts to analyze allegations of damages.

KEY SECURITIES LAWS

The two main securities laws in the United States are the Securities Act of 1933 and the Securities Exchange Act of 1934. Conceived during the Great Depression and after the stock market crash of October, 1929, these laws were designed to regulate securities markets through mandated disclosure of more accurate, verified financial information and through the prevention of improper activities.

Securities Act of 1933

This law states registration and distribution requirements for public issuers of securities. Companies that issue securities to the public are required to disclose accurate information in their filings and other communications to shareholders. The dissemination of information known to be inaccurate can give rise to a cause of actions by investors who were adversely affected through their reliance on this information. In the wake of scandals such as Enron, this has become a major

---

[1]"A Tortuous Road for Investors," *Business Week* (May 5, 2003): 85.

issue.[2] Fiduciaries and professionals, such as accountants, may be held liable for the inaccurate information. However, defendants in such actions may try to assert defenses such as stating that investors were aware of the inaccurate information or that they (the defendants) did not know the information was false. Such suits require that experts analyze the damages arising from cases in which investors lost some or all of their investment as a result of inaccurate or false information.

Securities Exchange Act of 1934

This law regulates the trading of securities in the secondary market following their issuance in the primary market. This law requires companies to regularly file statements containing financial and other relevant information with the Securities and Exchange Commission—an entity created by this law. The Securities Exchange Act has been amended several times since 1934. Its current form makes illegal practices such as insider trading and market manipulation. Examples of market manipulations include what is known as "pump and dump" transactions: individuals or firms engage in deceptive trades and disseminate inaccurate information to try to push the price of a security up only to sell it to other investors who are not aware that the market interest and rising prices were contrived. Such manipulations have plagued the penny stock market—unscrupulous investment bankers can more easily manipulate the market for lesser-known publicly held companies.

Rule 10b-5 of this law prohibits a variety of fraudulent practices, such as disseminating untrue or misleading information or simply engaging in what this section of the law considers fraudulent securities activities. Violations of this part of the law are often referred to as 10b-5 violations.

Securities Litigation Reform Act of 1995

This act was the first major revision of the above mentioned securities, It was partially designed to curb abusive litigation practices by plaintiffs—especially those related to class actions under Rule 10b-5. New requirements were imposed on such class actions. Although this law imposed new regulations on class actions, some of the largest class actions occurred after the law's passage.

The typical class action follows a drop in an issuing company's stock price. Plaintiffs file suit alleging that the company made overly optimistic disclosures

---

[2]"The Fall of Enron," *Business Week* (December 17, 2001).

in light of the information that led to the fall in the stock price. An example of the extreme abuses that the Act sought to correct is the abrupt lawsuit against Philip Morris that followed the "Marlboro Friday" announcement on the morning of April 2, 1993: Philip Morris announced a $0.41 drop in the price of a pack of Marlboro cigarettes.[3] Just five hours later, a class action suit was filed, followed by four more suits later in the day and five more the following Monday.[4] The courts found the poor quality of the complaints laughable. Plaintiff's counsel apparently overwrote files from a prior case featuring a toy company, discussing Philip Morris' future success in the *toy* industry. Clearly, the speed with which the cases were filed prevented any meaningful research into the grounds for the fraud claims.

Among the regulations this law added is the requirement that settlements be disclosed to the class. Plaintiffs in class actions are required to demonstrate that they did not purchase the securities at the direction of plaintiff's counsel, that they reviewed and authorized the complaint, and that they disclosed all of their trades of the security in question as well as their activity in other securities lawsuits. In part, the law was designed to try to curb law firms which were pursuing such suits to receive "fee-mail" in settlements and employing professional plaintiffs who purchase the shares with the intention of suing. The law also governed the use of forward-looking statements. Such statements need to be clearly labeled as forward-looking and they must include appropriate cautionary language.

From a damages perspective, this law required the plaintiff to demonstrate that the actions of the defendant directly caused the plaintiff's damages. For example, in cases where a plaintiff alleges that the defendants disseminated financial statements featuring inflated profits, he must demonstrate that the stock moved in a manner which adversely affected him owing to this false information (rather than market movements). In addition, this law also set forth parameters within which damages may be computed in fraud-on-the-market claims.

Sarbanes–Oxley Act of 2002

Although the Securities Litigation Reform Act of 1995 placed needed curbs on abusive plaintiffs and their law firms and thereby aided potential defendants, it

---

[3]*In re Philip Morris Sec. Litig.*, 872 F. Supp. 97 (S.D.N.Y. 1995), aff'd in part and rev'd in part, 75 F3d 801 (2d Cir. 1996).

[4]Richard M. Philips and Gilbert C. Miller, "The Private Securities Litigation Reform Act of 1995: Rebalancing Litigation Risks and Rewards for Class Action Plaintiff, Defendants and Attorneys," *The Business Lawyer* 51 (4) (August 1996): 1019–1069.

imposed greater requirements on potential defendants. Financial statements that are filed with the Securities and Exchange Commissions must now be certified by the chief executive and chief financial officers of the issuer who must clearly state that the statements do not contain any information known to be false. The law applies to both quarterly and annual financial statements and the filings which contain them—10Qs and 10Ks, respectively. The officers who sign such certifications are responsible for establishing controls that ensure their accuracy. Officers who violate this law are subject to fines which can be as high as $5 million; they also can face imprisonment for up to 20 years. If the financial statements have to be restated due to inaccuracies, the officers may also have their compensation forfeited.

The law also imposed restrictions on accountants who certify such statements. It attempted to eliminate a conflict of interest on the part of accountants who were auditing companies and at the same time profiting from other consulting work for the issuer. The law sets forth a variety of services, including actuarial, valuation, broker/dealer, and investment banking, which auditors are expressly prohibited from providing to their audit clients. Accounting firms may perform nonaudit services, but they must be approved by the audit committee and be disclosed in the periodic reports that are filed.

DAMAGES IN SECURITIES LITIGATION

Damages can take on different forms in securities litigation. The most common are:

- Fraud-on-the-market
- Mergers-related damages
- Churning and broker portfolio mismanagement

FRAUD-ON-THE-MARKET

Fraud-on-the-market refers to the sale of securities pursuant to some material misrepresentation which investors may have relied upon. Some have pointed out that part of the fraud-on-the-market argument relies upon a blind trust in the integrity of the market—a potentially higher standard than nonfinancial markets.[5]

---

[5]Nicholas L. Georgakopoulos, "Frauds, Markets, and Fraud-on-the Market: The Tortured Transition of Justifiable Reliance from Deceit to Securities Fraud," *University of Miami Law Review* (spring–summer 1995): 671–730.

It is an example of a violation of Rule 10b-5. One of the most common ways that this occurs is when an issuer has released financial information which creates an overly optimistic picture of the company's financial condition. For example, a company may have inflated its profits by releasing inaccurate financial data. This could come from overstated revenues or understated costs. Other examples of a fraud-on-the-market can come from misleading or inaccurate statements about events which affects the stock price. An example is a denial of merger negotiations when such negotiations were actually taking place. This is actually what occurred in the *Basic, Inc. v. Levinson* case.

Basic, Inc. v. Levinson

One of the most famous cases in this area was *Basic, Inc. v. Levinson.* In this case, representatives of Basic, Inc. denied in public statements that merger negotiations were ongoing. However, starting in the fall of 1976, representatives of Basic, Inc. had active discussions with Combustion Engineering, Inc. regarding the possibility of a merger. In December, 1978, some investors were surprised to learn that Basic, Inc.'s board of directors approved a merger with Combustion Engineering.

It was argued that had this fact been disclosed, the stock would have traded at a higher price. This is due to the fact that in acquisitions, target shareholders receive a premium above the stock's price.[6] Shareholders who sold their shares, believing that a takeover premium was not forthcoming, may have incurred damages by selling their holdings at a lower sales price. The plaintiffs in this case were one-time shareholders in Basic, Inc., a manufacturing company whose shares traded on the New York Stock Exchange. They successfully argued that they sold their shares at artificially depressed prices due to the fact that the market was not aware of the impending tender offer from Combustion Engineering.

Basic, Inc. v. Levinson and Market Efficiency

In its ruling, the court in *Basic, Inc. v. Levinson* endorsed the *efficient markets hypothesis.*[7] This theory of financial markets considers the speed or efficiency with which financial markets internalize new information into the prices at which

---

[6]Patrick A. Gaughan, *Mergers, Acquisitions, and Corporate Restructuring,* 3rd ed. (Wiley, 2002).

[7]For a very readable discussion of the efficient markets hypothesis and the related literature see Burton Malkiel, *Random Walk Down Wall Street,* 4th ed. (New York: W.W. Norton, 1993).

securities trade.[8] There are three versions of the efficient markets hypothesis: strong form, semi-strong form, and weak form. In the strong form, all information (both public and private) is internalized in securities prices. The semi-strong version assumes that the market is efficient with respect to public information only. The weak form focuses on one type of public information—prior trends in security prices, and assumes that the securities prices internalize this particular type of information. In *Basic, Inc. v. Levinson,* the court endorsed the semi-strong version of the efficient markets hypothesis. In doing so, it assumed that if information on merger discussions had been given to investors, the market would have incorporated this into the prices of Basic's stock. The extent to which markets are considered efficient has been one of the most actively researched topics in finance.[9] Much of the research literature in this area relies on *event studies*; they look at the market's security price reaction to the dissemination of a particular type of information. For example, studies have looked at the market's reaction to annual or quarterly earnings reports, as well as a variety of other types of announcements, such as new products or exchange listings. While there are many studies that support market efficiency, there are many others that challenge some aspect of market efficiency. Several of these challenging studies show that market anomalies may exist in which investors may persistently enjoy extra-normal profits based upon the utilization of public information. One such example is the "turn-of-the-year effect" or "January anomaly"—it has been shown that trading motivated by tax loss can allow investors to realize above-normal profits.[10] Other oft-cited market anomalies are the *size effect* and *neglected firm effect* in which small firms or companies that are not as closely followed can be a source of above-normal gains.[11]

---

[8]Eugene F. Fama, *The Theory of Finance* (New York: Holt, Rinehart and Winston, 1972).

[9]Frank K. Rielly and Keith Brown, *Investment Analysis and Portfolio Management,* 6th ed. (Fort Worth, TX: Dryden Press, 2000), 213–253.

[10]Ben Branch, "A Tax Loss Trading Rule," *Journal of Business* 50 (2) (April 1977): 198–207, Donald B. Keim, "Size Related Anamolies and Stock Return Seasonality," *Journal of Financial Economics* 12 (1) (June 1983): 13–32.

[11]R.W. Banz, "The Relationship Between Return and Market Value of Common Stocks," *Journal of Financial Economics* 9 (1) (March 1981): 3–18, Marc R. Reinganum, "Misspecification of Capital Asset Pricing: Empirical Anomalies Based on Earnings Yield and Market Values," *Journal of Financial Economics* 9 (1) (March 1981): 19–46. S. Basu, "The Relationship Between Earnings Yield, Market Value and Return to NYSE Common Stocks," *Journal of Financial Economics* 12 (1) (June 1983): 129–156.

In a *"Basic*-type" argument, plaintiffs must prove that their shares traded in an efficient market.[12] The case law is not as developed in dealing with markets that are less efficient. In addition, issues such as the fact that the market may be more efficient at processing certain types of information than others has also not been as well developed in the case law. This may be less of an issue for major announcements pertaining to companies that trade on the New York Stock Exchange than it is for announcements relating to comparatively unknown companies that trade infrequently on the over-the-counter market.

Disgorgement

In Securities and Exchange Commission enforcement actions, the defendant, if found guilty, may be required to disgorge the ill-gotten gains. This precedent was established in the Texas Gulf Sulphur cases in which various employees of Texas Gulf Sulphur purchased stock and call options in the company prior to an announcement of a major mining discovery.[13] In these cases, the courts required the defendants to disgorge their profits. The amount to be disgorged can be either the actual profits that the defendant enjoyed or what is referred to as *paper profits*, defined as the difference between what the defendant paid for the shares and the value for them that the court assesses. This value is determined by relevant stock price data around the time of the event. In the case of positive information on which a defendant traded prior to the release of that information to the public, the paper profits are the difference between the price paid for the shares prior to the public announcement and the *full information price*. The full information price is determined by judgment based on the time that the market has finished reacting to the new information. Paper profits can thus be different from actual profits. If the illegal trader sells at the full information price, the two might be the same. However, if the trader holds on to the shares and other factors cause the stock price to move to another level, the actual profits will vary and will be determined at time of sale. Assume that the trader holds on to the shares and other factors cause the stock price to fall below the purchase price. If he sells the shares, he may be forced to disgorge positive paper profits when his overall trading in the stock actually resulted in losses.

---

[12]Jonathan R. Macey and Geoffrey P. Miller, "Good Finance, Bad Finance: An Analysis of the Fraud-on-the-Market Theory," *Stanford Law Review* 42 (April 1990): 1049–92.

[13]*SEC v. Texas Gulf Sulphur Co.,* 401 F2d 1301 (2nd Cir.), *cert denied,* 404 U.S. 1005 (1971).

Measuring Damages in Fraud-on-the-Market:
Out-of-Pocket Damages

The most common method of measuring damages for fraud-on-the-market is an out-of-pocket measure of damages.[14] This measure draws on the reasoning of Judge Sneed in *Green v. Occidental Petroleum Corp.*[15] Judge Sneed set forth an acceptable way of measuring such damages as the difference between what he called the *price line* and the *value line*. The price line reflects the "corporate defendant's wrongful conduct." In a case involving inflation of corporate profitability, this would be the stock price that was a function of the exaggerated income. The value line is the stock's price in the absence of exaggerated prices. This difference is depicted in Exhibit 10.1.

In Exhibit 10.1, the shaded area shows the magnitude of the damages that investors may have incurred. The two curves, called lines by the court, start off at the same point as t_i is assumed that this is the date when the misrepresentation occurs. At this time, it is assumed that an overly optimistic picture of the company's performance is portrayed, thus causing the market price (as reflected by the price line) to be above what its true value would be absent the misrepresentation.

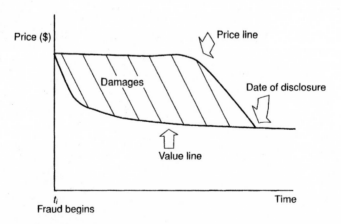

Exhibit 10.1   Price line versus value line.

---

[14]Bradford Cornell and R. Gregory Morgan, "Using Finance Theory to Measure Damages in Fraud on the Market Cases," *UCLA Law Review* 37: 883–924.

[15]*Green v. Occidental Petroleum Corp.*, 541 F2d 1335. C.A. Cal. 1976.

The measurement of damages can be divided into two parts:

1. *Establishment of the loss period.* The loss period usually begins with the date when the inaccurate information was released to the market. It usually ends with the date of disclosure.[16] If one assumes that markets are very efficient, then the time period narrowly focuses on these two dates. If, however, markets are not assumed to be very efficient, then the loss period becomes less clearly centered on these dates.

   The establishment of the loss period may not be very clear-cut. There is usually not just one improper announcement or material misrepresentation. Rather, there is often a series of such false statements. This requires the expert to make a judgment as to the correct start of the loss period. This judgment is made more difficult when there is a series of improper statements or misrepresentation; the expert must make a determination of when the inflating effects on the market began. The end of the loss period may also be unclear. It may be the case that the issuer makes a series of statements which address the initial misrepresentation. This could cause the market to correct in a series of steps. However, it could cause the market to overreact by thinking that the misrepresentation was greater than what it actually was.

2. *Measurement of damages.* In this model, the measure of damages is the difference between the price line and the value line multiplied by the number of securities in question. The number of shares are estimated using an analysis that attempts to determine how many shares were actually affected and eliminating shares in which gains offset losses.[17] The major challenge here is to calculate the *Value Line*. There are different ways to compute the *Value Line*. One is to arithmetically reconstruct what the stock price should have been during the loss period. This method examines the percent change of various other comparable companies and, in doing so, computes the relative change in the stock prices of these companies. This can be done using basic percentages or by employing regression analysis. More formally, the expert may employ what is known as *Comparable Index Approach*. It attempts to predict the security's return using explanatory variables such as the Market Return and the Industry Return.

---

[16]This is a very broad statement. Obviously, the fact of each case will determine what the true loss period is as well as the measure of damages.

[17]Janet Cooper Alexander, "The Value of Bad News in Securities Class Actions," *UCLA Law Review* 41 (August 1994).

Security and Market Returns

The percentage return of security is defined as the combined effects of the income that is received, such as the dividends from a share of stock, and the price changes of the securities (in the form of capital gains or losses). This percentage return has two components, one of which is the dividend yield. It is the component of the return that is attributable to the dividend income.[18] This can be expressed as follows:

$$\text{Dividend Yield} = D_{t+1}/P_t \qquad (10.1)$$

The other component of the total return is attributable to the security's price movements; it is called the capital gains return. This is expressed as follows:

$$\text{Capital Gains Yield} = (P_{t+1} - P_t)/P_t \qquad (10.2)$$

Both components of a security's return can be combined to form the percentage return of the security. This is shown in Equation 10.3.

$$R_t = \frac{\text{Dividends paid at end of the period} + \text{Change in the market value of the security}}{\text{Value of the security at the beginning of the period}} \qquad (10.3)$$

The return on the market can be computed in a similar manner using an accepted market proxy such as the Standard & Poor's 500 market index. This index uses the market value of the securities to measure the performance of the market.

COMPARABLE INDEX APPROACH

The comparable index method uses econometric methods to estimate the relationship between a security's return and the return of the market and the industry. The relationship is estimated and used to compute the security's "value." It is then compared to the security's actual price. In order to estimate the relationship, historical return data are gathered for the security, the industry, and the market. This period should be one that excludes the alleged fraud so the estimated relationship is not tainted by the events in question. The decision on the proper period to use

---

[18]For a discussion of the computation of returns see Stephen Ross, Randolph Westerfield, and Bradford D. Jordan, *Essentials of Corporate Finance,* 4th ed. (Homewood, IL: Irwin/McGraw-Hill, 2004), 290–294.

affects the value of the coefficients $\alpha_0 \ldots \alpha_2$ that are estimated. The estimated function is of the form shown in Equation 10.4.

$$R_{it} = \alpha_0 + \alpha_1 R_{mt} + \alpha_2 R_{It} \tag{10.4}$$

where R_{it} = the return on security i at time t

R_{Mt} = the return on the market at time t

R_{It} = the return on the industry at time t

The difference between the estimated security value and its actual price is sometimes referred to as the damage ribbon or, simply, inflation. This gap reflects the damages incurred by investors. The relationship between a hypothetical price and the value line is depicted graphically in Exhibit 10.1.

Example of the Comparable Index Approach

Assume that historical data have been used to estimate the following equation:

$$R_{it} = .005 + .70R_{mt} + .30R_{It} \tag{10.5}$$

The relationship is applied to the historical market and industry return data to compute the predicted return shown in Table 10.1. It is assumed that the security's value and its price are equal as of the full disclosure date. The value absent the fraud is then computed backwards from the full disclosure date using the predicted return as follows:

$$\text{Security Value}_{t-1} = \frac{\text{Security Value}_t}{\left(1 + \text{Predicted Return}_{t-1}\right)} \tag{10.6}$$

Once the security value has been computed, the difference between the "but for" value and the actual price can then be computed.

Now assume that the expert is trying to determine a security's value during a ten-day trading period prior to estimating the value line for a nine-day period through day ten. The expert has done some research which shows that the security's return can be explained by a combination of the market return and the industry return. Let us further assume that this research has resulted in the estimation of Equation 10.5.

Using this equation, we can derive the predicted return for each day. The predicted return is then used to retrospectively estimate the value line. For example, the 0.70 percent daily return is "backed out" of the $100 stock price to result in a $99.31 stock value. This value can then be compared to the actual stock price of $103 to result in a daily stock inflation of $103 − $99.31 or $3.69. The stock value

Table 10.1   Example of Computation of Security Price versus Security Value

			[Security Return = .005 + .07 (Market Return) + .30 (Industry Return)]		
Day	Market Return (%)	Industry Return (%)	Predicted Security Return (%)	Security Price	Security Value
1	3.10	2.75	2.07	130.00	85.80
2	−5.00	−2.50	0.85	135.00	87.57
3	2.50	1.50	1.86	140.00	88.32
4	1.30	5.00	2.28	125.00	89.96
5	−2.00	1.50	1.59	123.00	92.01
6	−1.50	−2.50	1.06	119.00	93.47
7	3.20	2.50	2.04	123.00	94.46
8	4.00	3.00	2.16	105.00	96.39
9	−1.50	1.00	1.55	103.00	98.47

for the days prior to day nine can be estimated in a similar manner. This is shown in Table 10.1.

Criticism of the Comparable Index Approach

As with any approach that relies on econometric analysis to estimate the best relationship among variables, there are often disagreements as to whether the expert-estimated relationship is the most accurate one. Some contend that the estimate is made more accurate if more explanatory variables, such as more than one index, are added to the model.[19]

Impact of the Private Securities Litigation Reform Act of 1995 on Damage Computations

The Private Securities Litigation Reform Act of 1995 addressed the way that damages are calculated in Rule 10b-5 cases. Section 21D (e) of the law states that a damage award shall not exceed the difference between the purchase price of the security and the mean trading price of that security over a 90-day period. This period begins with the day the full disclosure which corrected the misstatement was made to the market. An exception to this occurs when the security holder sells the shares or repurchases the security prior to the end of this 90-day period. In this case, the damages cannot exceed the difference between the pur-

---

[19]William Beaver and James K. Malernee, "Estimating Damages in Securities Fraud Cases," *Cornerstone Research* (1990).

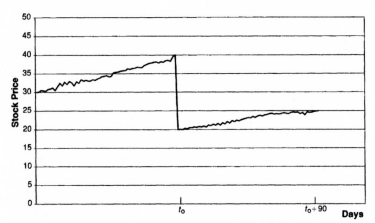

Exhibit 10.2   Graphical depiction of stock price cost.

chase price and the average of the security's price at the beginning of the full disclosure period and the price in the subsequent sales transaction.

In Exhibit 10.2, an investor purchases a stock at $30 and the stock price rises to $40. The plaintiffs allege that this rise was due to the false information disseminated by management. When the curative disclosure occurs at time t_0, the price falls to $20. Under the parameters of the new law, damages cannot be measured as the difference between the $40 price and the post-disclosure price—$20. Exhibit 10.3 shows that over the 90-day period, $t_0 + 90$, the stock price rebounded to $25. Given this rebounding price rise, the losses are the dif-

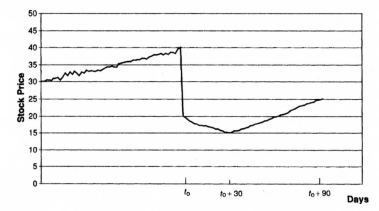

Exhibit 10.3   Graphical depiction of stock price damages: stock sold.

ference between the purchase price ($30) and this price, ($25) for a total per share damages of $5, not $20.

An exception occurs when the shares are sold during the 90-day period. In Exhibit 10.3, we assume that the investor bought the stock at the same price—$30. It rose to $40 and later fell to $20 on day t_0 after full disclosure. In this example, however, we assume that the stock price falls to $15 per share on $t_0 + 30$ when the investor sold the stock. The average price in the 30-day period before the investor sold the shares is $17.50. Damages are the difference between the purchase price ($30) and this average price, or $12.50. This example differs from that of Exhibit 10.2 in that not only was the stock sold prior to the 90 days, but the stock price continued to fall in the 30-day period—although not as sharply as it did on the announcement date. The further decline in the stock price expanded damages, although not by as much as the difference between the purchase price and the eventual sale price of $15. If the price rebounded steadily after t_0 as it did in Exhibit 10.1, damages would be less, although still higher than if the stock had been held for the full 90-day period.

EVENT STUDY APPROACH

The event study approach draws upon a methodology that has been extensively used in academia; it is used for conducting research on the impact of specific events on shareholder returns. The methodology is an application of econometric analysis to securities markets in a manner which allows the analyst to measure the impact of a particular event on the price and return of a security.[20] The methodology was developed by Eugene Fama, Franklin Fisher, Michael Jensen, and Richard Roll.[21] The model has come to be known as the FFJR model after its developers. Its application has led to the extensive analysis of a variety of events, such as earnings and new product announcements. Abundant research was conducted using this model in the 1970s and 1980s to test the efficiency of securities markets.

The event study methodology allows the user to filter out the influence of market forces. The user constructs a regression model which includes market returns as an explanatory variable. In doing so, a security's return is regressed against the

---

[20]A. Craig McKinlay, "Event Studies in Economics and Finance," *Journal of Economics Literature* XXXV (March 1997): 13–39.

[21]E. F. Fama, L. Fisher, M. Jensen, and R. Roll. "The Adjustment of Stock Prices to New Information," *International Economic Review* 10 (1) (February 1969): 1–21.

market returns. Equation 10.7 shows the mathematical expression of this relationship in what is known as the *market model*.

$$R_{it} = \alpha_i + \beta_i R_{mt} + \varepsilon_{it} \tag{10.7}$$

where α_i = the intercept term of the market model

β_i = the security's beta. Betas measure security's sensitivity to market returns.

ε_{it} = the model's deviations at time t

Exhibit 10.4 shows a graph of a hypothetical security's return against the market's return which is measured as the rate of return of some market index such as the Standard & Poor's 500.

Exhibit 10.4 shows that there is a linear relationship between the security's return and the market's return. The event study methodology uses this relationship to compute what the security's return would have been had it not been for the "event" that is the subject of the litigation. However, the event study model computes the relationship between the security's return and the market's return prior to the event; it uses the mathematical relationship to forecast the "but for" return of the security. This return can then be compared with the actual post-event return to measure the excess return of the security. This excess return, in the absence of other explanatory factors, can then be used to measure the magnitude of the loss.

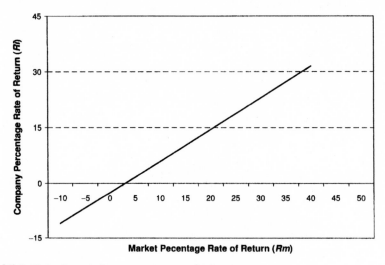

Exhibit 10.4   Security's return versus market's return.

Abnormal Returns of the Event Study Methodology

The market model allows for the separation of the total return of a security into systematic and unsystematic components. The systematic component is the part that can be explained by the market's return—$\alpha_i + \beta_i R_{mt}$. According to the market model, the part that cannot be explained by the market's influences is attributed to firm-specific effects and is statistically subsumed with the "remainder factor" in the market model's equation—ε_{it}. That is, ε_{it} captures the variety of firm-specific factors including those which are the subject of the litigation—the alleged fraudulently inflated profits of the previous example. The impact of ε_{it} can be more readily discerned by arranging Equation 10.7 as follows:

$$\varepsilon_{it} = R_{it} - (\alpha_i + \beta_i R_{mt}) \tag{10.8}$$

The historical data on R_{it} and R_{mt} for the period prior to the event in question, which is taken to be $t = 0$, are used to econometrically estimate α and β. The value of these two parameters are then used to compute a predicted return R_{it}, and its resulting deviation ε'_{it} which can then be compared to ε_{it}. This represents the deviation of the actual return, inclusive of the effects of the fraudulent behavior, from the predicted return as measured using the market model's estimated parameters α and β. This discussion is sometimes also expressed through the estimation of abnormal returns where abnormal returns are equal to:

$$AR_{it} = R_{it} - \alpha'_i + \beta' R_{mt} \tag{10.9}$$

where AR_{it} = abnormal returns
        α'_i = the estimated alpha
        β' = the estimate of beta

Example of a One-Period Abnormal Return

As an example of a one-period abnormal return assume that:

$$R_{it} = -9.5\%$$
$$\alpha'_i = -0.15\%$$
$$\beta' = 1.40$$
$$R_{mt} = -3.5\%$$

The one-period abnormal return is simply:

$$AR_{it} = -9.5\% - 0.15\% + (1.40 \times -3.5\%)$$
$$= -4.75\%$$

The abnormal returns computed above apply to just one period, i, which may be one day. When the event window is longer, then it is necessary to compute the cumulative abnormal returns (CAR). This is a running total of the one-period abnormal returns for the length of the study period. This is mathematically expressed as:

$$CAR_T = \sum_{t=1}^{T} (1 + AR_i) - 1 \qquad (10.10)$$

where T = the length of the study window.

When we compute CAR_T, we have a measure of the total impact of the event.

Examining the Variation in Abnormal Returns

Once the security's return has been computed, it may be useful to examine the variability in the return. In analyzing the variation in a security's return, it is useful to compute the standard deviation of the return. A security's return does not stay constant—it normally varies. One simplifying assumption that is made is that the variation fits a pattern that would be expected if the return were normally distributed. While not perfect, the assumption of normality is commonly made in event studies.[22] The standard deviation of a security's returns can be computed as follows:[23]

$$s = \frac{\sqrt{\sum (R_i - \bar{R})^2}}{N - 1} \qquad (10.11)$$

where R = the mean or average return over the sample period.

The standard deviation can be used to test the statistical significance of the variation in a return. Using the assumption of a normal distribution, we expect that 68 percent of the returns will lie within one standard deviation of the mean. 95 percent of the deviations will lie within two standard deviations while 99.7 percent will be within three standard deviations. We can take the standard deviations that we have computed to arrive at what is called a Z-statistic. It can be applied to a standard normal distribution table found in every statistics textbook. It is computed as follows:

$$\text{Z-statistic} = \frac{(\text{actual return value} - \text{mean return value})}{\text{standard deviation}} \qquad (10.12)$$

[22]Stephen J. Brown and Jerold B. Warner, "Using Daily Stock Returns: The Case of Event Studies, *Journal of Financial Economics* 14 (1) (March 1985): 3–32.

[23]Cheng F. Lee, *Statistics for Business and Financial Economics* (Lexington, MA: D.C. Heath, 1993), 98–127.

Therefore, for each return or abnormal return, we can use the mean and standard deviation to compute that return's Z-statistic. This statistic is then used to determine how likely it is that a given observed return is a certain number of standard deviations from its mean by sheer chance. Given that the average daily return is close to zero for larger capitalization stocks, the application of the Z-statistic is tantamount to computing the probability that a given return is different from zero.[24]

Decision Rules in Assessing the Significance of a Particular Return Value

The Z test statistics discussed above can be used to assess whether a particular return value is as high or low as it is due to chance or to some nonrandom event. In statistics, the null hypothesis is that the return value is different from some other value by sheer chance. Differences from this selected value—here, the average daily return of the security—that are so large that they are above a certain threshold value, are then determined not to be a function of normal random movements of the market. They must therefore be caused by some nonrandom process.

A common standard is to use a 5 percent decision rule which is based on the normal distribution. This rule states that if a certain value is 1.96 standard deviations from the mean (above or below—that is, in absolute value), there is only a 5 percent probability that such a difference is caused by chance. We can make the rule even more stringent by going to a 1 percent standard; this equates to 2.58 standard deviations, in absolute value, from the mean. However, one can relax the decision rule to a 10 percent level of significance; this corresponds to 1.65 standard deviations from the mean.

Example of Using an Event Study in an Insider Trading Case

Mark Mitchell and Jeffrey Netter, both academic financial economists who were in the employ of the Securities and Exchange Commission, reported the results of an interesting event study analysis. It involved an executive recruiter who was accused of using information he acquired in the search process to buy stock.[25] The recruiter used the knowledge that the candidate whom his firm had recommended for the position of chief executive officer in a small fiber optics telecom-

---

[24]Jonathan R. Macey and Geoffrey P. Miller, "Lessons from Financial Economics: Materiality, Reliance and the Extended Reach of Basic v. Levinson," *Virginia Law Review* 77 (1991): 1017, 1020.

[25]Mark Mitchell and Jeffrey Netter, "The Role of Financial Economics in Securities Fraud Cases: Applications at the Securities and Exchange Commission," *Business Lawyer* 2 (2) (February 1994): 545–590.

munications company, Artel Communications, would be given the job on a given day. On the day he received the insider information, February 9, 1987, the president of the executive search firm purchased 23,500 shares of Artel stock for approximately $72,000. This translates to an average price of $3.06 per share. The purchase was made one day before the announcement of the appointment. Two years after the illegal trades, in April 1989, the SEC charged the president of the management recruiting firm with insider trading.

Although managerial appointments tend not to cause as dramatic stock price movements as other important events, such as new product announcements or impressive earnings reports, some research shows relatively small positive stock price effects.[26] Mitchell and Netter's table, reproduced here as Table 10.2, shows

Table 10.2   Stock Price Performance for Artel Communications

| | | | | | Cumulative | |
Date	Artel Price	Artel Volume	Abnormal Return (%)	Z-Statistic	Abnormal Return (%)	Z-Statistic
Feb. 4	$2.250	10,100	−6.22	−1.12	−6.22	−1.12
Feb. 5	2.250	4,400	−0.41	−0.07	−6.61	−0.84
Feb. 6	2.250	1,600	0.56	0.10	−6.08	−0.63
Feb. 9	3.250	72,000	45.38	8.20	36.54	3.30
Feb. 10	3.875	68,100	20.53	3.70	64.56	5.22
Feb. 11	3.750	65,200	−3.73	−0.67	58.43	4.31
Feb. 12	3.625	16,300	−2.50	−0.45	54.47	3.72
Feb. 13	3.750	6,800	2.47	0.44	58.28	3.72
Feb. 17	3.750	25,600	−1.39	−0.25	56.09	3.38
Feb. 18	4.500	57,000	20.25	3.67	87.70	5.01
Feb. 19	4.500	23,500	0.17	0.03	88.02	4.79
Feb. 20	4.625	23,600	3.09	0.56	93.83	4.89
Feb. 23	4.250	7,300	−6.92	−1.25	80.42	4.03
Feb. 24	4.250	7,900	0.17	0.03	80.72	3.90
Feb. 25	3.625	24,700	−14.74	−2.67	54.08	2.52
Feb. 26	3.625	6,200	0.61	0.11	55.02	2.49
Feb. 27	3.500	6,200	−3.50	−0.63	49.59	2.17

Notes: Returns are expressed in percents. Stock price data is from Center for Research in Security Prices (CRSP) at the University of Chicago. Marked model estimation period is Feb. 4, 1986 through Feb. 3, 1987. Market proxy is CRSP value-weighted index of NYSE, AMEX, and NASDAQ stocks. Beta estimate for Artel Communications is 0.96.
Source: Mark L. Mitchell and Jeffery M. "The Role of Financial Economics in Securities Fraud Cases: Applications at the Securities and Exchange Commission," *The Business Lawyer* 49 (2) (February 1994): 545–590. Reprinted by permission.

---

[26]Eugene P.H. Furtado and Vijay Karan, "Causes, Consequences and Shareholder Wealth Effects of Management Turnover: A Review of the Empirical Evidence," *Financial Management* (summer 1990): 60–75.

that the stock price rose sharply the day before and the day of the announcement. They computed abnormal daily returns of 45.38 percent and 20.53 percent, respectively, on these days. The table also shows that trading volume in this relatively thinly-traded security was substantially higher during the three-day period starting one day before and ending one day after the announcement.

Mitchell and Netter established that the research studies in the field show that the announcement of an executive appointment can show positive returns. They then set about to show that the stock price movement and related change in stock return were abnormal given the stock price history of this particular company. They computed the standard deviation in the stock price return over the one-year period prior to the event and found it to be 5.57 percent. Movement of at least two standard deviations, approximately 11 percent, would allow the researcher to conclude within a 95 percent level of assurance that the movement was unusual and not the product of normal fluctuations in this relatively more volatile stock. They concluded that the abnormal returns during the announcement period were very statistically significant.

Table 10.2 shows that the stock price remained at the "announcement level" until news was related in a trade publication that the new CEO would also remain on the board of directors of his former employer, where he was chairman. The article cited certain synergies that might be expected through future dealing between the two companies in the same industry. The stock price remained at that level until a negative quarterly earnings report was released towards the end of February.

The court heard arguments on the magnitude of any disgorgement that would be required. This was ironic in light of the fact that the defendant had actually incurred losses equal to about $17,000 on this investment. This is because he held on to the shares for approximately two more years, at which time he sold them at approximately $2 per share. In order to compute the disgorgement amount one needs to compute the "full information price." This is the stock price as of the date that the complete effect of the relevant information (the hiring of the new CEO) was internalized into the stock price.

In court, both sides argued about which date should be taken as the one from which to draw the full information price. The defense argued that it was the day after the announcement. The government argued that it extended to February 18, the date that the story came out about the new CEO remaining as director of his previous employer. This argument was based upon the assumption that he may have had information about this as well. The court accepted this latter date, and its full information price of $4.50 per share—as opposed to $3.75 per share on February 11. The difference between the purchase price and the full information price, less adjustments for commissions and the bid-asked spread, resulted in a computed disgorgement of $24,663.

Using an Enhanced Market Model

In the comparable index model, *both* market and industry effects are included as explanatory factors in calculating a predicted return. This has an advantage over the basic market model in that there may be important industry factors that are unique to the industry and which cannot be captured by the market's variation. These factors can be econometrically filtered by the direct inclusion of an industry return as a separate explanatory variable. This is shown in Equation 10.13:

$$R_{it} = \alpha_i + \beta_i R_{mt} + \beta_j R_{It} + \varepsilon_{it} \qquad (10.13)$$

where β_j = the coefficient of the industry index
R_{It} = the industry index return

The more important industry factors are in explaining the variation in the firm's return, the more important it is to use the industry-enhanced market model. Failing to do so can lead to the erroneous conclusion that all of the variation between the predicted and actual return is explained by firm-specific factors including the alleged fraudulent behavior. Including the industry return allows us to filter out industry influences and better isolate the firm-specific factors.

Factors to be Considered in Applying the Event Study Methodology

In using the event study methodology, a number of factors have to be considered. These factors can affect the usefulness of this approach as a tool in measuring damage. One of the most fundamental of these is the availability of the necessary. Another is the presence of confounding events which may skew the results. Still another is the time period or event window.

Data Availability

The event study approach works best when there is an abundant history of return data. Having ample return data enhances the statistical reliability of the forecasted "but for" projected return line. When this history is limited, the statistical reliability of the forecasted line may be low. This is reflected by relatively high "standard errors" which are statistical measures of the confidence one can have that the line lies within a certain range of values above and below the line. The fewer the data points, the wider this range is and the lower the statistical reliability of the forecasted values. Moreover, the fewer the data points, the less confidence one can have in the values that are forecasted further into the future. The more data points, the further into the future one can confidently project the "but for" return line.

The data availability problem is one of the reasons why it is more difficult to use the event study approach in markets for thinly traded securities. Thinly traded securities are those which have limited trading volume and thus a more sparse data point history. More obscure equities or certain bonds may fall in this category. Securities traded in more active markets, such as equities which are traded on NASDAQ or the major exchanges (the American and New York Stock Exchanges) are often good candidates for an event study.

Sources of Return Data

As noted, abnormal returns are defined as the ex-post return of the company's securities minus a normal return. Return data are available from the University of Chicago Center for Research in Security Prices database. This database is called the CRSP database. Many universities and some firms subscribe to this database as it is often used in empirical research studies. When using the CRSP database, one may want to use as a measure of market performance a value-weighted CRSP index of all New York Stock Exchange, American Stock Exchange, and NASDAQ stocks for the market proxy.

Existence of Confounding Events

The event study methodology is easiest to apply when the event in question can be readily isolated and when there are not other events occurring at the same time. In particular, other confounding firm-specific events can make the isolation of the event in question problematic. For example, in the case of a release of fraudulently inflated earnings information, the task of isolating the impact of this information on the security's return is made more difficult when it occurs at approximately the same time as a firm-specific event. If the company announces the hiring of potentially important management personnel or issues a press release about new product developments, the expert's job becomes more difficult. He needs to determine whether the security's return increase was due solely to the fraudulent earnings or whether the other factors which also had an uplifting effect on the security's return caused all or part of the increase. Each case is unique and requires the expert to exercise judgement when considering all relevant information. In the presence of such confounding events, the expert may have to employ more advanced statistical techniques which may enable him to filter out the influence of these confounding factors.

Defining the Event Window

One of the first factors to consider when doing an event study is to select a time period long enough to include the duration of the event. Generally, one should select a time period that is somewhat longer than the event period so that the returns during the event period can be compared to a period during which the events are not influencing the returns. It is wise to include some time before and after the event. These should be periods that are unaffected by the event. For a merger, this should be a period prior to the announcement of the merger and one that is also prior to any improper trading that is the subject of the litigation. In insider trading cases, one needs to identify the dates when the information is used by the illegal trader and the dates when the information reaches the market. The expert must use his own judgment in selecting a proper window. The window that is selected is a source of some controversy and may be one variable that affects the value of the monies to be disgorged.

Measuring the Number of Damages Shares

The above discussion presents a model for measuring per-share damages. However, the number of damaged shares still must be explained. Depending on the legal framework of the claims, the number of damaged shares may only include those that traded during the class period. If the number of these shares is known, then the computation involves simply applying the per-share loss to the number of shares.[27] Unfortunately, it may not be easy to quantify the exact number of damaged shares. The expert may have to resort to a simplifying process in order to estimate the number of damaged shares. To arrive at such an estimate, certain assumptions about the trading behavior of investors need to be made.

Equal Trading Probability Model

Certain models based upon different assumptions about trading behavior exist.[28] These models differ in how they treat the trading behavior of investors. In one version, the *equal trading probability model,* sometimes called the *one-trader model,* it is assumed that shares are only traded one time during the class period. This assumption can lead to the total number of shares traded exceeding the number of shares outstanding. The assumption is made more realistic by taking into account the fact that shares can be retraded. Under the one-trader model, the

---

[27]This statement makes the simplifying assumption that the dollar loss is constant throughout the loss period which may not be the case.

[28]William H. Beaver, James K. Malernee, and Michael C. Keeley, "Stock Trading Behavior and Damage Estimation in Securities Cases," *Cornerstone Research* (1993).

expert assumes that all shares entering the class have an equal probability of being traded as shares that have not yet entered the class. This results in the number of shares entering the class being a function of trading volume and the number of remaining shares that are not yet in the class. One of the criticisms of the one-trader model is that it does not differentiate between the different types of investors that hold shares in a company. It treats active traders and those who utilize a buy-and-hold strategy the same. This assumption has a significant impact on the damages that result from the use of this model.

Dual Probability Trading Model

An alternative to the equal probability model is the *dual probability model.* Under the dual probability trading model, sometimes referred to as the *two-trader model,* traders are categorized into two different classes: active traders and traders who utilize a buy-and-hold strategy. The model requires the expert to assume a certain probability of trading for active traders and inactive traders. The expert may also assume the percent of total shares outstanding held by these two groups of traders. Under this model, shares are retraded among active traders resulting in a lower number of shares entering the class. With a lower number of shares in the class, the dual probability trading model results in a lower damage estimate.

The dual probability trading model is more realistic than the equal probability trading model. The latter results in higher losses and thus is more in favor of the plaintiff. However, the dual probability model is influenced by the different trading probabilities and share percentages assigned to the two groups of traders. The expert may want to draw on research to support these assumptions. One such source of data is depository records which, when combined with trading volume data, may help the expert select the relevant parameters needed to use the dual probability trading model.

Proportional Trading Model

Still another stock trading model is the proportional trading model.[29] In this trading model, the number of shares traded is differentiated from those that were

---

[29]Dean Furbush and Jeffrey Smith, "Estimating the Number of Shares in Securities Fraud Litigation: An Introduction to Stock Trading Models," *The Business Lawyer* 49 (2) (February 1994): 527–543.

retained. The model assumes that there is an equal probability that a given share came from a pool of those shares that had already been traded during the loss period and those that were being traded for the first time. This assumption is applied on a daily basis throughout the loss period. The number of shares are retraded, as opposed to those that enter the class due to being traded for the first time, being derived process using the equal probability assumption. This differs from the dual probability model in which probabilities that may not be equal are assigned to the two groups of traders.

MERGERS-RELATED DAMAGES

Another type of lawsuit involving damages claims related to securities are merger-related suits. These lawsuits became a common occurrence in the 1980s and have continued throughout the 1990s as the pace of mergers reached record highs.

HISTORY OF MERGERS IN THE UNITED STATES

The United States is in the midst of another period of merger and acquisition activity that intensified in 1993. This is the fifth such period, often referred to as a *merger wave,* in U.S. economic history.[30] The first wave started at the turn of the century; the second occurred in the 1920s. The third merger wave occurred at the end of the 1960s. Merger and acquisition activity was relatively quiet, with some notable exceptions, until the mid–1980s when corporate America took off in a merger frenzy. This lasted until the end of the 1980s when various events, including the overall economic slowdown and the collapse of the junk bond market, brought about its end. After a comparatively short hiatus, merger and acquisition activity picked up in 1994 and quickly reached unprecedented levels by 1999 and 2000. This is apparent in both the number of deals and the dollar value of deals (see Exhibits 10.5a and 10.5b).

Merger Laws

Acquisitions of publicly held companies are subject to certain laws that regulate share purchases and takeovers. The most prominent of these is the Williams Act.

---

[30]For a discussion of merger waves see Patrick A. Gaughan, *Mergers, Acquisitions, and Corporate Restructuring,* 3rd ed. (New York: Wiley, 2002).

(a)

Number of Mergers and Acquisitions

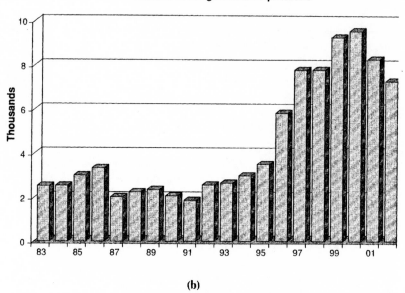

(b)

Dollar Value of Mergers and Acquisitions

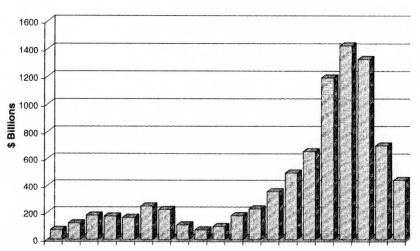

Exhibit 10.5   Mergers and acquisitions.
Source: Mergerstat Review 2003.

This law, enacted in 1968, is an amendment to the Securities and Exchange Act of 1934. In an effort to regulate hostile takeovers, the law sought to enhance the confidence of investors in securities markets by providing them with certain information and time to deliberate over such information.

Pursuant to Section 13(d), the Williams Act requires the filing of a Schedule 13D within 10 days of the acquisition of 5 percent of a public company's outstanding equity securities. The disclosure requires the acquirer of the stock to reveal certain information such as the identity of the purchaser, and the plans the purchaser has for the stock and the issuing company. Section 14(d) of the law requires the filing of a Schedule 14D-1 upon the initiation of a tender offer. Ironically, the Act did not define what a *tender offer* is. This was done by a subsequent court decision where a tender offer was defined by the presence of eight factors—called the *Eight Factor Test*.[31] Simply stated, however, a tender offer is an offer made directly to the shareholders of a public company.

The Schedule 14D-1 requires the disclosure of similar information as the Schedule 13D. In addition, the bidder has to reveal such relevant information as the terms of the offer as well as information on the bidder and its sources of financing. Due to the fact that target companies tend to receive a takeover premium (a monetary amount in excess of the stock price prior to the announcement) stock prices rise on the announcement of takeovers.[32] For this reason, bidders may try to conceal their plans when making share purchases. In this way, they try to avoid paying some component of the takeover premium when they accumulate the target's stock prior to the initiation of a formal bid. When such efforts lead to an evasion of the requirements of securities laws, the SEC or private parties may initiate a lawsuit.

Disgorgement in Merger Related Transactions

As noted above, acquirers of stock in targets or potential targets of takeovers may want to avoid the necessary filing such as the filing of a Schedule 13D. This allows the purchaser to buy the stock at a lower price than what he would have to pay if the market were aware of the information that it would have if disclosure pursuant to the Williams Act were provided to the market. There is support in the

---

[31]*Wellman v. Dickinson*, 475 F. Supp. (SD NY 1979), aff'd 632 F2d 355 (CA2 1982), *cert. denied* 460 U.S. 1069 (1983).

[32]Asquith Paul, "Merger Bids, Uncertainty, and Stockholder Returns," *Journal of Financial Economics* 11 (1–4) (April 1983): 51–83.

finance literature for a general positive stock price effect associated with Schedule 13D announcements (although the majority of such purchasers were not for the purposes of takeovers).[33] In the 1980s, certain individuals pursued various schemes including *stock parking*—the placing of purchased shares in names other than the true purchaser to avoid the requirements of Section 13D. There were various actions brought against them, including some high profile cases, in which the purchasers were found to be criminally liable.

A methodology similar to what is used in the event study approach can be applied to determine the purchaser's gains made through the evasion of the disclosure requirements of the Williams Act. The expert needs to compute the full information price—the price that the stock would have traded at had the market been aware of the purchaser's acquisition of the shares. The amount to be disgorged is the difference between the purchase price and the full information price times the number of shares involved.

Example of Using the Event Study Methodology to Measure the Disgorgement Amount in a Delinquent Schedule 13D Filing

Mark Mitchell and Jeffrey Netter report a case involving the failure to file a Schedule 13D within the time requirements of the Williams Act. On December 18, 1987, the president of Pizza Inn, Francis Spillman, purchased 50,000 shares of a chicken restaurant chain, Winners Corporation, which put his total stake in the company above the 5 percent threshold. This required him to file a Schedule 13D within ten calender days (by December 28). However, he did not file until January 6, 1988—eight days late. He also bought 45,000 more shares between December 28 and January 6. In December 1989, the SEC charged Spillman with violating Section 13(d). The price he paid for the shares he purchased between the required disclosure date and the actual disclosure date failed to reflect the information that would have been contained in the Schedule 13D.

Table 10.3 shows the stock price and return history of the Winners Corporation over a period before and after the trades in question. It shows that the stock price rose from $1.875 on December 28 to $3.00 on January 6—the day before the disclosure. Mitchell and Netter report that during this time period, Spillman's share purchase accounted for approximately 45.5 percent of the trading volume and that his purchases alone during this period often exceeded the historical average trading volume of this security.

---

[33]Wayne H. Mikkelson and Richard S. Ruback, "An Empirical Analysis of the Interfirm Equity Investment Process," *Journal of Financial Economics* 14 (4) (December 1985): 501–523.

Table 10.3 Stock Price Performance for Winners Corporation

Surrounding Spillman's Delinquent Schecule 13D Filing on January 6, 1988.
(Required filing on December 28, 1987)

Date	Winners Price	Abnormal Return	Z-Statistic	Cumulative Abnormal Return	Z-Statistic	Volume/Mean Volume	Spillman Volume/Mean Volume
Dec.11	1.500	8.71	1.62	8.71	1.62	0.25	
Dec.14	1.375	−10.92	−1.99	−3.16	−0.41	5.46	1.14
Dec.15	1.375	−0.06	−0.01	−3.22	−0.34	1.02	0.57
Dec.16	1.500	7.32	1.35	3.87	0.36	12.54	12.20
Dec.17	1.500	1.88	0.35	5.82	0.48	1.12	0.57
Dec.18	2.250	47.96	8.80	56.57	4.26	13.53	5.67
Dec.21	2.000	−11.22	−2.09	39.01	2.72	4.27	1.14
Dec.22	2.000	0.21	0.04	39.30	2.57	5.46	0.11
Dec.23	1.875	−7.29	−1.35	29.15	1.80	2.68	0.23
Dec.24	2.000	7.15	1.33	38.39	2.25	0.42	0.22
Dec.28	1.875	−3.58	−0.66	33.43	1.86	1.31	0.57
Dec.29	1.875	0.65	0.12	34.31	1.83	6.01	2.22
Dec.30	2.250	19.00	3.52	59.82	3.07	3.42	0.68
Dec.31	2.250	0.44	0.08	60.53	2.99	0.90	0.90
Jan.4	2.375	2.16	0.39	63.99	3.05	1.15	0.79
Jan.5	2.500	4.26	0.79	70.97	3.28	1.12	0.51
Jan.6	3.000	19.98	3.72	105.14	4.71	4.66	
Jan.7	3.000	−0.53	−0.10	104.06	4.53	3.95	1.25
Jan.8	2.875	2.23	0.38	108.6	4.58	0.78	0.34
Jan.11	2.875	−0.99	−0.18	106.56	4.38	0.70	0.57
Jan.12	2.750	−3.33	−0.62	99.67	4.00	5.23	3.97
Jan.13	2.500	−9.05	−1.68	81.60	3.20	1.21	0.57
Jan.14	2.625	5.20	0.97	91.05	3.50	1.98	0.57
Jan.15	2.625	−2.23	−0.41	86.78	3.26	0.84	
Jan.18	2.500	−4.58	−0.85	78.24	2.88	0.06	
Jan.19	2.500	1.01	0.19	80.04	2.89	0.77	
Jan.20	2.500	2.73	0.50	84.95	3.01	0.01	
Jan.21	2.625	5.06	0.94	94.30	3.28	6.13	4.62
Jan.22	2.750	3.72	0.69	101.53	3.48	0.11	

Notes: Returns are expressed in percents. Stock price and volume data is from Center for Research in Security Prices(CRSP) at the University of Chicago. Market model estimation period is December 11, 1986 to December 10, 1987. Marked proxy is CRSP value-weighted index of NYSE, AMEX, and NASDAQ stocks. Beta estimate for Winners 1.03.

Source: Mark L. Mitchell and Jeffery M. Netter "The Role of Financial Economics in Securities Fraud Cases: Applications at the Securities and Exchange Commission," *The Business Lawyer* 49 (2) (February 1994): 545–590. Reprinted by permission.

· One measure of the amount to be disgorged would be the difference between the full disclosure price, $3, and the various prices that Spillman paid for the shares. The SEC, however, took into account the fact that after the filing—which included Spillman's stated intention to initiate a tender offer filing—the stock price fell. They used the average price over a two-week period following the filing: $2.675.

CHURNING[34]

One aspect of the securities industry that seems to be ever present to varying degrees is churning litigation. Churning litigation is an outgrowth of broker-customer disputes. While both members and critics of the securities industry agree that the majority of brokers are honest professionals endeavoring to provide valued services to their clients, there is always a certain percentage of brokers who unscrupulously violate their obligations to their clients. Such violations comprise what is known as "churning" of customers' accounts. Churning is a fraudulent practice whereby brokers induce customers to excessively trade the securities in their accounts so as to generate greater commission income for the broker without regard to the financial interests of customers. This practice is a violation of a number of laws: the anti-fraud provisions of the Securities and Exchange Act of 1934 as well as specific rules put forward by the Securities and Exchange Commission, the National Association of Securities Dealers, and the New York Stock Exchange. Churning litigation presents another opportunity for the expert with a background in finance to provide useful quantitative analysis which can enable a court or arbitration panel to better analyze the claims of churning.

The execution of a churning claim by a customer generally takes place through the arbitration process. This was underscored by the June 1987 Supreme Court decision *Shearson American Express v. McMahon*. In this case, pre-dispute agreements requiring settlement of disputes through compulsory arbitration were held to be binding.[35] Following this decision, customers no longer had access to the courts and were bound by the arbitration process. Unfortunately, many brokerage customers with valid claims now find themselves in a less advantageous position

---

[34]This section is derived from Patrick A. Gaughan, "An Analytical Model of Securities Litigation," *Litigation Economics,* Patrick A. Gaughan and Robert Thornton, eds. (Greenwich, CT: JAI Press, 1993).

[35]*Shearson American Express v. McMahon*, 107 S.Ct. 2332 (1987). *Perry v. Thomas*, 107 S.Ct. 2520 (1987).

relative to their deep-pocket defendants. A customer who pursues a claim against a brokerage firm quickly realizes that the defendant usually has far more resources at its disposal than the claimant. In addition, the customer has entrusted most of his financial resources to an unscrupulous broker who then takes advantage of this trust to deplete the wealth of the customer. The financially weakened customer discovers that it is extremely difficult to effectively oppose a brokerage firm that possesses substantial financial resources and abundant in-house legal and expert talent. A customer first must retain legal counsel who is quite familiar with this area of the law in order to pursue the legal remedies available. However, legal counsel alone is generally not sufficient to successfully prosecute a churning claim. This is where the experts retained by the attorney comes into play.

Most attorneys seek to retain a former professional in the securities industry who can opine on the suitability of the types of securities that the broker purchased for the client. However, the industry expert's testimony is often more effective if he is armed with a presentation of a clear quantitative model which measures and summarizes the volume and nature of the trading that took place. This is where a financial economist plays an important role. Such an expert can analyze the volume and pattern of trades in the account(s) and present a concise and convincing analysis at the arbitration proceedings. The analysis must be cost-effective, particularly if the customer possesses only limited resources.

This chapter presents the framework of a model that can be used to analyze the trading of securities for a churning claim. The model is based on measures which were indicative of churning in various prior legal decisions. These measures are used to compare the volume of trading in the accounts in question with these accepted legal standards. The measures are used to determine if the trading reached a level which was, according to precedent, clearly excessive. While the focus of this chapter is on the use of this model in the liability part of a churning case, a brief discussion of the method for computing damages is also included.

Elements of a Churning Claim

There are four elements of a churning claim. They are:

1. Control
2. Suitability
3. Scienter
4. Excessive trading

Control refers to the extent of the customer's involvement in the trading decisions. Control is clear when the customer had no involvement with the trading decisions and when the broker did not have to consult the customer in order to make trades. Brokers or registered representatives often attempt to acquire such control through an explicit written agreement rather than through oral authority. The situation becomes less clear, however, when the customer provides such written authority but also orally instructs the broker to consider this authority limited to certain trades or types of securities. The fact that many customers fail to carefully read a written agreement and place greater weight on the oral representations of brokers makes some churning disputes problematic for arbitrators.

Suitability refers to the recommendation of certain investments that are suitable for the customer in light of his personal financial circumstances or investment objectives. Broker recommendations to purchase speculative securities for customers who lacked a background in finance or securities trading and who had limited financial resources have been found to be unsuitable. It may be the case that margin trading itself is indicative of unsuitability. In such cases, it may be necessary to present expert testimony on the degree of financial sophistication necessary to fully comprehend the risks of particular types of transactions. For example, such expertise is useful in demonstrating why buying uncovered call options is a speculative transaction. Expert testimony could be used to explain why a naive investor might have difficulty comprehending the risks and potential for gain in complex option trading strategies, such as the use of butterfly spreads or straddles.

In proving a churning claim, the plaintiff may need to demonstrate *scienter*. This refers to the assertion that the defendant acted either with the intent to defraud the customer or with careless disregard for the financial interests of the client. In 1976, scienter became necessary in order to establish a claim of churning under Section 10(b) of the Securities and Exchange Act of 1934. Used in the context of churning, scienter refers to a mental state embracing the intent to deceive, manipulate, or defraud. While scienter is an integral part of the churning claim, the financial expert may not play an active role in proving this allegation.

The final necessary aspect of a successful churning claim is the demonstration of *excessive trading* in light of the objectives of the account. Such a demonstration attempts to show that the volume of trading was so excessive that the goal of the trading activity was to generate profits for the broker rather than gains for the customer. It is here that certain quantitative measures of trading activity can be employed to relate the pattern of trading in the accounts to accepted legal standards of churning.

Quantitative Measures of Churning

There are three main quantitative measures of churning.

1. Turnover ratios
2. Average holding periods
3. Cost of investment services

A successful churning claim may require the combined use of all these measures. High turnover is often associated with a low holding period, which implies high trading costs. These high costs may mean that the trading strategy is required to yield a high rate of return simply to break even.

Turnover Ratios

The most common formulation of turnover ratios is the *Looper formula*. The Looper formula is defined as follows:

$$\text{Looper formula} = \frac{\text{total cost of purchases}}{\text{average equity}} \qquad (10.14)$$

Average equity is defined as follows:

$$\text{Average equity} = \frac{\text{beginning period equity} + \text{ending period equity}}{2} \qquad (10.15)$$

For example, an account that had an average equity of $100,000 and purchases of $850,000 in a given year has a turnover ratio of 8.5.

Two of the most commonly used periods are monthly and annual periods. Monthly periods can be particularly useful for higher volumes of trading. In the case of margin accounts, the debit balances must be deducted from the equity measure. In addition, it is generally better to include all accounts in the computation of average equity. For example, if the investor has both a cash and a securities account, both should be combined to arrive at total average equity. However, it may be useful to segregate the trading of certain accounts, such as options accounts. If this is the goal of the analyst, a separate turnover analysis can be computed which excludes the options account. Given the inherently short-term nature of options, it may be useful to present a separate analysis in which these trades are excluded. Another ratio, the contract index—which is the ratio of the number of option contracts bought or sold within a given period divided by the average equity—is sometimes used as an alternative to the traditional Looper turnover ratio.

Given the fact that both purchases and sales generate commissions for the broker, it might also be useful to include in the Looper formula both types of transactions in the numerator such as in Equation 10.16.

$$\text{Looper formula} = \frac{\text{total cost of purchases + total price of sales}}{\text{average equity}} \quad (10.16)$$

While the above formulation is more revealing about the total value of trading and the resulting commission income proportional to the trading volume, it may be counting the same trade twice. If a broker sells one security in order to buy another, this can be considered one transaction. The second security has replaced the first. However, as far as commission accounting is concerned, each is a separate transaction that generates a commission charge. The debate becomes moot, however, in light of the reasons for the computation of the turnover ratios. The value of the specific turnover ratio utilized is to derive a quantitative measure of trading activity which can be compared with other quantitative measures that have been indicative of churning in prior litigation. The standard that is therefore ordinarily relied on is the traditional Looper formula (Equation 10.14), which includes *only purchases* in the numerator. Although the analyst might find it enlightening to compute both measures, the standard Looper formula is more useful for comparison purchases.

Legal Guidelines for Turnover Ratios   The legal guidelines for turnover ratios as they relate to churning are grouped into four categories:

1. Turnover ratio less than two
2. Turnover ratio greater than two but less than four
3. Turnover ratio greater than four but less than six
4. Turnover ratio greater than six

Some writers in this area have simply categorized these ratios into those less than two and those greater than two. Goldberg, for example, states that the courts have been reluctant to find that trading which resulted in annualized turnover ratios of less than two was excessive. However, he points out that turnover ratios greater than two have been found to be indicative of active trading and have carried the inference of churning. In cases where the turnover ratio has exceeded four, the courts found that the volume of trading was such that a conclusion of excessive trading is reasonable. In instances where the turnover ratio is greater than six, the results may be even more conclusive.

It is important for both the expert and legal counsel to consider the turnover ratios in light of the investment objectives of the account. If the account was established as part of a long-term investment strategy that would provide predictable income with little risk of loss of principal for the customer, the higher turnover ratios cited above would seem to be indicative of churning. However, high turnover may be expected for an account that was established along more speculative lines. If the customer has approved an aggressive trading strategy that seeks to frequently trade securities in an attempt to sell at temporary highs while buying at temporary lows, high turnover may be a necessary component of this customer-approved trading strategy. In cases such as this, the courts have failed to find that the account was churned and have indicated higher turnover is expected in such trading accounts.

Holding Periods and In-and-Out Trading

Turnover ratios can be supplemented by other measures that help reveal the extent of the trading activity in the account. Therefore, it is most useful to combine the computation of the turnover ratios with a measurement of various average holding periods. Holding periods provide an indication of the average length of time that securities are held in a portfolio. This is useful if one is attempting to determine if there was a pattern of in-and-out trading. In-and-out trading is a pattern of trading in which the broker sells a security after a short holding period. This may even be followed by a series of sales and purchases of the same security. To compute the holding periods, the analyst must determine how long each security remained in the portfolio. The securities are then categorized into various holding periods. A common holding period categorization is as follows:

- Less than 30 days
- Less than 90 days
- Less than 180 days
- Less than 360 days

Holding periods can be measured in terms of the dollar value of securities or the total number of securities held. The dollar measure is more revealing than the number of securities since, in effect, the nonmonetary measure weights different dollar amounts equally. Nonmonetary measures treat a $70 share of stock as equal

Table 10.4   Summary Breakdown of Excessive Trading

Holding Periods	Excessive
Percent held for less than six months	75% or more
Percent held for less than three months	50% or more
Percent held for less than one month	25% or more

to a $5 share. Since commissions are based on the value of the transaction, a monetary measure is generally more appropriate.

Examples of some of the decisions which have used holding periods as benchmarks are shown in Appendix B. Based on an overview of numerous decisions, the summary breakdown in Table 10.4 is generally considered indicative of excessive trading.

Cost of Investment Services

Brokers charge a commission for each trade executed on behalf of the customer. Herein lies the potential conflict that sometimes induces brokers to churn their portfolios. Trading is the activity that generates commissions. This sometimes leads brokers to trade simply to increase their income rather than to advance the customer's wealth. This implies there is one level of commission costs that is associated with wealth-enhancing trading and another that is associated with churning. It is therefore useful to compute the costs of trading in comparison to both the profits generated and the average equity in the account. The economist's model may provide computations of the following:

- Total commissions and fees charged
- Total margin interest paid by the customer
- The sum of commissions, fees, and margin interest as a percentage of the total portfolio value on an annual basis, referred to as the cost/equity percentage
- The sum of commissions, fees, and margin interest compared to the income from trading on an annual basis

The cost/equity percentage is useful because it highlights the rate of return that would be necessary to simply break even. If this rate of return is unreasonably high, the broker's motives must be questioned. This is particularly the case if it can be shown that the broker has not generated such a rate of return in any of his or her other accounts.

Measuring Damages

The typical churning case involves a claimant who entrusted funds to a broker with the expectation of achieving rates of return that are consistent with the historical experience in the market. This may involve a diversified portfolio of stocks, bonds, and money market investments. If this is the case, the *expected value* of the portfolio can be measured using a historical weighted average rate of return based on readily available annual return statistics. However, the actual rate of return over the loss period is more relevant. This can be computed in the same manner using the actual rates that prevailed for each of the broad categories of stocks, corporate bonds, and Treasuries; these are combined in a manner that is similar to the composition of the portfolio. The end of the loss period is either the date of the litigation or the date that the claimant ended the relationship with the broker and withdrew the funds. The actual value of the portfolio at the end of this time period can then be deducted from the expected value to determine the damages.

The argument is sometimes made that broad market statistics are inherently different since they are based on a larger portfolio of securities. However, this argument is opposed by the abundant research in the field of finance which shows that as portfolios are diversified they approach the rate of return for the market. That is, as portfolios become increasingly diversified, the unique, unsystematic risk of the portfolio decreases and approaches that of the market. If the investment objective is simply to maintain an original portfolio, or if the broker uses his own judgment to purchase a specific portfolio which differs in performance compared to the market, a specific rate of return for the portfolio in question can be computed using the CRSP monthly return database discussed earlier in this chapter.

The loss computation can be complicated by the fact that there may be some withdrawals from or deposits into the account. Deposits can be handled individually using the same rate-of-return computation that is applied to the original portfolio but with a different starting date. Withdrawals are also handled using the same method, but they are given negative values to offset the larger portfolio-compounded values.

Punitive Damages in Securities Litigation

Federal securities laws do not include provisions for the award of punitive damages in civil litigation. Some state laws allow for an award of punitive damages in securities fraud cases. In March 1995, the U.S. Supreme Court upheld an arbitrator's power to award punitive damages in cases where a brokerage agreement contained a New York "choice of law" clause.[36] Prior to this decision, the *Mastrobuono* decision, the Second and Seventh Circuits had held that the *Garrity* rule which prohibited arbitrators from awarding punitive damages was the law.[37] Until *Mastrobuono,* this was in conflict with the position of the Court of Appeals of the First, Eight, Ninth, and Eleventh Circuits which supported the award of punitive damages.[38] Given that the *Mastrobuono* decision led brokerage firms to include a New York choice of law provision, this decision can have far-reaching effects depending on the position of the individual courts and how they interpret the brokerage agreements.

Conclusion of
Churning Analysis Model

The model and approach described in this chapter are methodologically straightforward, and the computations involve basic mathematics. However, the computations can be a time-consuming and arduous task. The analyst should therefore be able to rely on good spreadsheet or database software to generate the large volume of calculations that are often necessary in active brokerage accounts. While the calculations themselves are basic, their value in litigation can be substantial. Without definitive quantitative evidence, the claimant would have to rely simply on the impressions of the industry expert and the arbitration panel. However, with detailed quantitative analysis, the extent of the trading and its related costs can be precisely demonstrated. Such evidence can also enable the claimant to counter the internally generated analysis that is often presented by the defendants. In addition, a clear model such as the one presented in this chapter can also be invaluable to defendants in actions where churning has not occurred. The same analysis that a plaintiff might present in cases where there was excessive trading can also be used by defendants to show that the trading was not in excess of the legal standards.

---

[36]*Mastrobuono v. Shearson Lehman Hutton,* 115 S. Ct. 1212 (1995).

[37]*Garrity v. Lyle Stuart, Inc.* 40 N.Y.S. 2d 354, 353 N.E. 2d 793, 386 N.Y.S. 2d 831 (1976).

[38]Carroll E. Nesseman and Maren E. Nelson, "Securities Arbitration Damages," in *Securities Arbitration,* David E. Robbins, Chair (New York: Practicing Law Institute, 1996).

APPENDIX A: CASE STUDY:
IN RE COMPUTER ASSOCIATES,
INTERNATIONAL, INC.

This example is derived from a securities case that went to trial in the eastern District of New York involving allegation of insufficient or inaccurate disclosure by Computer Associates, Inc., a public company that trades on the New York Stock Exchange. The case centered around whether Computer Associates, Inc. had made sufficient and timely enough disclosure of performance that was less than expectations. The plaintiff retained an expert who measured a purported amount of the stock price inflation. The company made a disclosure on July 12, 1990 that indicated that performance would be less than what had been expected. The plaintiff contended that these expectations on the part of the market were caused by management's allegedly misleading statements. Below are various excerpts from the direct testimony of the plaintiff's expert.[39]

Q. Did you see any evidence of guidance of future performance as made at that meeting?

A. Yes, I did. The notes indicated that management in the May 22 meeting indicated that for the year, this is the fiscal year, there would be 20 to 25 percent revenue growth and that earnings would be higher than that.

    They also indicated that in the first quarter, earnings would be up over the corresponding quarter of a year ago, and that revenue would not be up as nearly as up for the year, it would be up, but it would be over the corresponding quarter of the year ago. . . .

Q. Do you view whether—what the company said seemed to be affecting the market price of the stock?

A. Yes, because what we saw here is a stock price that was trending upward, to the $16 level, consistent with an expectation of a substantial earnings improvement in fiscal 1991. The statements that were made on January 23, set the groundwork for that and on May 22, those statements were reiterated, and the period after May 22 the stock continued to trade at fairly high levels, relative to what happened, on July 12, which I think we'll get into later. . . .

---

[39]The excerpts that are shown and not complete passages and there are numerous sections left out. This is necessitated due to space limitations. However, it is believed that the included sections demonstrate some of the concepts that have been covered up to this point in this chapter.

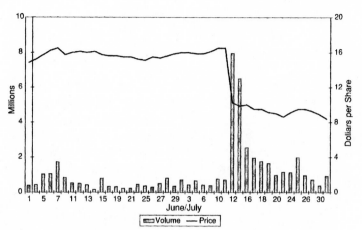

Exhibit 10A.1   Weekly trading volume and common stock price of Computer Associates, Inc.
Source: Computer Associates International, Inc.

Exhibit 10A.1 is a graph of the daily closing stock price of Computer Associates, Inc. over the first seven months of 1990. This period includes July 12, 1990, the day on which the company made an announcement of disappointing results. The depressing effect that such news had on the stock price can be more dramatically seen in Exhibit 10A.1; this shows the shorter two-month period of June 1990 through July 1990. In referring to similar graphs that were presented at trial, especially a graph that featured the first seven months, the expert at trial testified as follows:

> **A.** . . . It shows the stock price basically prior to July 12, sent three trending upwards slightly in the $12, $13 level, up to the $14, $15 level, back down a little bit and continuing up to the $16 level. Then it shows what occurred on July 12, when they announced that the earnings for the—that the sales were going to be off for the quarter and that earnings would be off for the quarter. The stock in one day went down from the $16 level to the $10 level. That was a one day drop. Very, very substantial drop. Approximately 40 percent. Then in one period after that drop, the stock drifted lower over a period of several months, getting as low as $5 and then by the end of the year it recovered to about $7, $8 level.

In addition to showing the stock price effects, the expert then went on to show the changes in trading volume that accompanied the July 12, 1990 announcement.

The variation in weekly trading volume for the two-month period of June 1990 through July 1990 is shown in Exhibit 10A.1.

A. . . . . I added the volume data. This time it's daily volume. You'd have to sum five days to get a week here, but this shows now on the daily volume, the scale is in millions of shares per day, from zero to ten million and you could see that the—in most days, prior to the announcement on July 12, the stock traded less than a million shares a day. A million shares would be good here.

There are a couple of dates when it traded up over a million, but at no point did it get over two million shares a prior to July 12. July 12, it traded up over seven and a half million shares in one day. July 12 was a Friday—excuse me, was a Thursday, July 13, which was Friday it again traded over six million on the 13 and then there was a weekend, and on Monday the 16 it traded over two and a half million shares. Those three days, you had just enormous trading volume.

Q. I don't know if you can tell us this. Do you know whether any other stock traded that many shares as did CA?

A. I believe CA was the largest number of shares to change hands that day.

Q. And, in the same way, did any stock move that much that day on the New York Stock Exchange?

A. They were down almost 40 percent, which is an unusually high drop and there was no other stocks that were down 40 percent in the New York Stock Exchange.

Q. Have you done any work to see how often a stock might change price 40 percent in one day?

A. Yes.

Q. Can you tell the jury what you have done?

A. We've done some research into just how often stocks change in price at various percentages, and a 40 percent drop in one day for a stock in the above $10 price level is extremely unusual. It almost never happens. Less than one in a hundred thousand chance of that happening.

A. What we've done here is we have constructed a graph to show how CA stock behaved relative to other computer software companies and what we've done here, we've taken the full year 1990, just like we started out with the price graph, and the red line is the price graph, that is CA. This is identical to the first chart that I showed you with the full year.

The red line on the first chart and the red line on this chart are identical. Now, we have added to that an index. I'll tell you what that is. H&Q stands for Hambrecht & Quist. They are a brokerage firm that specializes in technology stocks, and they have their own indices of groups of stocks and they have a software products index and what we've done here is we've slightly modified the index. CA was part of the index.

Well, we want to show what CA did relative to the other companies so we recalculated index with CA. I don't want to show you how CA did relative to itself, but how it did to the other companies. We recalculated the index taking out CA and what we did is we did something called indexing, which is that we made—we made the index equal to CA stock price to January 2, 1990.

A. . . . It's a little hard to visualize. When the lines are parallel, they are actually doing the same, it's when they are moving apart, when the gap is getting bigger is when the change is occurring. The gap got bigger between March and May and then it stayed about the same until April, then you have the plunge and the other stocks didn't plunge on that day, so this shows that CA going down 40 percent on July 12th has nothing to do with the other computer companies. They didn't go down 40 percent that day.

If they had the blue line would have gone down to here, it didn't. It went down slightly, but it did not go down 40 percent. Now, all of a sudden you see CA trading below the blue line. It's doing less well relative to starting on January 1. If you bought the average computer software company on January 2 and still held it as of July 12, you would be doing letter than CA, because CA is below the line.

And here you see that after the period of time, the stock drifts down, it's down to the $5 level, the index goes down as well, not quite as much, but then when CA comes back up, it comes up in line with the other software companies.

Essentially after the plunge, it then started at a lower level, lower level, $10 level, acting like the other software companies, so what this tells me is that there was an important event on July 12 that was only to do with CA that pushed that stock from $16 to $10. Otherwise, the stock behaved like other software companies.

A. There is a calculation where we're looking at the price decline on July 12. What I'm trying to do here, I'm trying to determine how much value came out of that press release on July 12. What was it worth, as a negative value, but still a value. One way of doing that is to look at the price of the decline on a one day basis. On July 11, the stock was 16 and a half, July 12, it was 10 and a quarter. That is a loss of $6.25.

The problem with one day declines, there is also a little bit of random movement in the stock prices and may not really tell you, you know, exactly what the loss of value is. One way of being a little more precise on the loss of value is to look at a few days beforehand and a few days afterwards and use average guess because sometimes stocks bounce around.

What I have done here, I have taken one trading week, five days before the decline and I have averaged them and that averaged price was $16 and 17 and a half cents. Then I looked at the average price after the decline and the average price after the decline as it continued down through the 18 is $9.82 and a half cents. So the stock price declined, based on a five-day average, before the bad news and a five-day average after the bad news would be $6.35. The difference between the two averages, $6.35.

Q. What is step one of your calculation, Mr. X?

A. Yes.

Q. Could you please explain step two of your calculation, Exhibit 1117?

A. Now, what I want to do is say, all right, maybe all software companies as measured by an average were going down. We don't want—we know the stock went down $6.35 average price one week before and one week after, but we don't—you can say that is damages, that is the value of the information, you have can say the 6.35 one day decline is the value of it.

But, to be a little more refined, you want to take out any drop that was due to a general decline in software companies. If all software companies were going down, I don't want to charge that as damages, I want to take that out of the damages. What I'm doing here, I'm looking at the value of the software index for those same five days. The 5 of July through the 11, and the 12 of July through the 18. And I see that the average was $16 and 17 and a half cents for the index the week before the decline, you have the index decline during that week. You can argue that the index declined because of the shock effect of CA that may have caused other stocks to go down.

That does happen and so you don't have to take this out of the damages, but let's assume that the others went down because it was a change in people's attitudes towards software industry that had nothing to do CA. The index did go down and it went down to $15.34 point two cents. I subtracted the two and said it was down 83.3 cents. That's what I have done here. Even though that index may have gone down because of the shock of what happened to CA.

Q, If you could tell the jury the third step?

A. Now, what I have done, I have combined the two, this step three shows the previous two charts, which is the CA calculation of the decline, the software products calculation, and its decline and I subtract from the $6.35 decline, the equivalent decline of the software, which is 83.3 cents and that's how I reached at the damage number, $5.51 point seven cents for approximately $5.52.

If you take out of the decline the entire—the entire decline of the other software companies, and just remove that and say that's not damages, that may be an economic condition, I come up with $5 and 51 point seven or 5.52.

The expert in this trial included certain graphical illustrations as part of his testimony. A graph similar to the one he presented is shown in Exhibit 10A.2. It is a price–value graph similar to the one shown in Exhibit 10A.1.

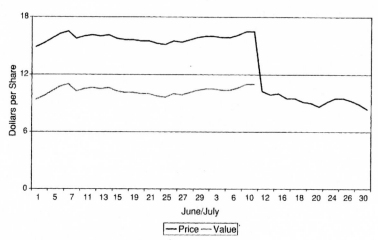

Exhibit 10A.2   Daily common stock price and value.
Source: Computer Associates International, Inc.

APPENDIX B:
CASES SETTING HOLDING PERIODS

Percentages	Case
	Holding Period Percentages within an Eight-Month Period
67%	*Matter of R. H. Johnson & Company,* 36 S.E.C. 467, 477 (1955), affirmed 231 F2d 523 (D.C. Cir. 1956).
77%	*Matter of R. H. Johnson & Company,* 33 S.E.C. 180. 182 (1952), affirmed 198 F2d 690 (2d Cir. 1952).
79%	*Matter of R. H. Johnson & Company,* 36 S.E.C. 467, 471 (1955), affirmed 231 F2d 523 (D.C. Cir. 1956).
86%	*Matter of Behel Johnson & Company,* 26 S.E.C. 163, 165–66, 167 (1947).
88%	*Matter of R. H. Johnson & Company,* 36 S.E.C. 467, 480 (1955), affirmed 231 F2d 523 (D.C. Cir. 1956).
	Holding Period Percentages within a Six-Month Period
21%	*Matter of Logan & Company,* 41 S.E.C. 88, 94 (1962), affirmed *Hersh v. S.E.C.* 325 F2d 147 (9 Cir. 1963).
56%	*Matter of Behel, Johnson & Company,* 26 S.E.C. 163, 167 (1947).
	Holding Period Percentages within a Thirty-Day Period
39%	*Stevens v. Abbot, Proctor & Paine,* 88 F. Supp. 836, 840 (E.D. Va. 1968. Merhige, J.).

REFERENCES

Alexander, Janet Cooper, "The Value of Bad News in Securities Class Actions." *UCLA Law Review* 41 (August 1994).

Asquith, Paul, "Merger Bids, Uncertainty, and Stockholder Returns." *Journal of Financial Economics* 11 (1–4) (April 1983).

Banz, R. W., "The Relationship Between Return and Market Value of Common Stocks." *Journal of Financial Economics* 9 (1) (March 1981): 3–18.

Basu, S., "The Relationship Between Earnings Yield, Market Value and Return to NYSE Common Stocks." *Journal of Financial Economics* 12 (1) (June 1983): 129–156.

Beaver, William H., and Michael C. Keeley, "Estimating Damages in Securities Fraud Cases." *Cornerstone Research* (1990).

Beaver, William H., James K. Malernee, and Michael C. Keeley, "Stock Trading Behavior and Damage Estimation in Securities Cases." *Cornerstone Research* (1993).

Branch, Ben, "A Tax Loss Trading Rule." *Journal of Business* 50 (2) (April 1977): 198–207.

Brown, Stephen J., and Jerold B. Warner, "Using Daily Stock Returns: The Case of Event Studies." *Journal of Financial Economics* 14 (1985): 3–32.

Business Week, "The Fall of Enron." (December 17, 2001).

Business Week, "A Tortuous Road for Investors," (May 5, 2003).

Cornell, Bradford, and Gregory R. Morgan, "Using Finance Theory to Measure Damages in Fraud on the Market Cases." *UCLA Law Review* 37: 883–924.

Fama, Eugene F., *The Theory of Finance*. New York: Holt, Rinehart and Winston, 1972.

Fama, E. F., L. Fisher, M. Jensen, and R. Roll, "The Adjustment of Stock Prices to New Information." *International Economic Review* 10 (1) (February 1969): 1–21.

Furbush, Dean, and Jeffrey Smith, "Estimating the Number of Shares in Securities Fraud Litigation: An Introduction to Stock Trading Modes." *The Business Lawyer* 49 (2) (February 1994): 527–543.

Furtado, Eugene P. H., and Vijay Karan, "Causes, Consequences and Shareholder Wealth Effects of Management Turnover: A Review of the Empirical Evidence." *Financial Management* (summer 1990): 60–75.

Garrity v. Lyle Stuart, Inc. 40 N.Y.S. 2d 354, 353 N.E. 2d 793, 386 N.Y.S. 2d 831 (1976).

Gaughan, Patrick A., "An Analytical Model of Securities Litigation," *Litigation Economics,* Patrick A. Gaughan and Robert Thornton, eds. Greenwich, CT: JAI Press, 1993.

Gaughan, Patrick A., *Mergers and Acquisitions.* New York: HarperCollins, 1994.

Gaughan, Patrick A., *Mergers, Acquisitions, and Corporate Restructuring,* 3rd ed. New York: Wiley: 2002.

Georgakopoulos, Nicholas L., "Frauds, Markets, and Fraud-on-the-Market: The Tortured Transition of Justifiable Reliance from Deceit to Securities Fraud." *University of Miami Law Review* 49 (spring–summer 1995): 671–730.

Green v. Occidental Petroleum Corp., 541 F2d 1335. C.A. Cal. 1976.

In re Philip Morris Sec. Litig., 872 F. Supp. 97 (S.D.N.Y. 1995), aff'd in part and rev'd in part, 75 F3d 801 (2d Cir. 1996).

Keim, Donald B., "Size Related Anomalies and Stock Return Seasonality." *Journal of Financial Economics* 12 (1) (June 1983): 13–32.

Lee, Cheng F., *Statistics for Business and Financial Economics.* Lexington, MA: D.C. Heath, 1993.

Macey, Jonathan R., and Geoffrey P. Miller, "Good Finance, Bad Finance: An Analysis of the Fraud-on-the-Market Theory." *Stanford Law Review* 42 (April 1990): 1049–92.

Macey, Jonathan R., and Geoffrey P. Miller, "Lessons from Financial Economics: Materiality, Reliance and the Extended Reach of *Basic v. Levinson.*" *Virginia Law Review* 77 (1991): 1017–1020.

Malkiel, Burton, *Random Walk Down Wall Street,* 4th ed. New York: W. W. Norton, 1993.

Mastrobuono v. Shearson Lehman Hutton, 115 S. Ct. 1212 (1995).

McKinlay, Craig A., "Event Studies in Economics and Finance." *Journal of Economic Literature* XXXV (March 1997): 13–39.

Mikkelson, Wayne H., and Richard S. Ruback, "An Empirical Analysis of the Interfirm Equity Investment Process." *Journal of Financial Economics* 14 (4) (December 1985), 501–523.

Mitchell, Mark, and Jeffrey Netter, "The Role of Financial Economics in Securities Fraud Cases: Applications at the Securities Commission." *Business Lawyer* 2 (2) (February 1994): 545–590.

Nesseman, Carrol E., and Maren E. Nelson, "Securities Arbitration Damages." *Securities Arbitration,* David E. Robbins, Chair, New York: Practicing Law Institute, 1996.

Perry v. Thomas, 107 S.Ct. 2520 (1987).

Philips, Richard M. and Gilbert C. Miller, "The Private Securities Litigation Reform Act of 1995: Rebalancing Litigation Risks and Rewards for Class

Action Plaintiff, Defendants and Attorneys." *The Business Lawyer* 51 (4) (August 1996): 1019–1069.

Posner, Norman, "Options Account Fraud: Securities Churning in a New Context." *Business Lawyer* 39 (2) (February 1984): 571–609.

Reinganum, Marc R., "Misspecification of Capital Asset Pricing: Empirical Anomalies Based on Earnings Yield and Market Values." *Journal of Financial Economics* 9 (1) (March 1981): 19–46.

Rielly, Frank and Keith Brown, *Investment Analysis and Portfolio Management*, 6th ed. Fort Worth, TX: Dryden Press, 2000.

Ritchken, Peter, *Options: Theory, Strategy and Applications*. Glenview, IL: Scott Foresman, 1987.

Robbins, David E., *Securities Arbitration: 1996*. New York: Practicing Law Institute, 1996.

Ross, Stephen, Randolph Westerfield, and Bradford D. Jordan, *Essentials of Corporate Finance*, 4th ed. Homewood, IL: Irwin/McGraw-Hill, 2004.

SEC v. Texas Gulf Sulphur Co., 401 F2d 1301 (2nd Cir.), *cert denied*, 404 U.S. 1005 (1971)

Shearson American Express v. McMahon, 107 S.Ct. 2332 (1987)

Stocks, Bills, Bonds and Inflation. Chicago, IL: Ibbotson Associates, 2002.

Van Horne, James C., *Financial Management and Policy*, 12th ed. Upper Saddle River, NJ: Prentice-Hall, 2002.

Wall Street Journal, "Suits Cloud AOL's Optimism." (May 11, 2003).

Wellman v. Dickinson, 475 F. Supp. (SD NY 1979), aff'd 632 F2d 355 (CA2 1982), *cert. denied* 460 U.S. 1069 (1983).

11

ANTITRUST

The world of antitrust enforcement has changed dramatically over the past century. It started at the end of the 1800s with the passage of the Sherman Antitrust Act and has moved along a winding path that featured periods of more and less antitrust enforcement. At present, there is relatively little antitrust enforcement compared to periods such as the 1950s and 1960s. Antitrust enforcement declined into the 1970s and became relatively dormant in the 1980s (see Exhibit 11.1).[1] In response to criticisms that antitrust was too inactive for the market's good, some defenders of the

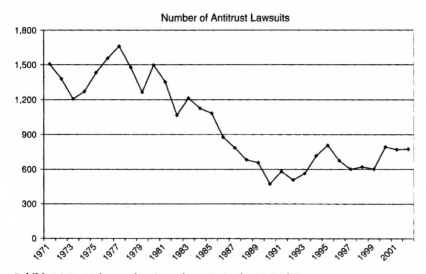

Exhibit 11.1   Volume of antitrust lawsuits in the United States.

[1]Carol Swanson, "Antitrust Excitement in the New Millennium: Microsoft, Mergers and More," *Oklahoma Law Review* (summer 2001): 285–338.

antitrust policies at that time asserted that the market was sufficiently competitive and did not need the assistance of the government as it did in the past. In the 1990s this changed somewhat. The antitrust enforcement authorities started to pursue antitrust enforcement with a somewhat greater vigor. This vigor reached a peak when the Antitrust Division of the Justice Department aggressively pursued Microsoft—one of the most successful companies in American history. Whether it is good for the economy or not, antitrust enforcement is alive and well in the 2000s.

Antitrust cases present opportunities for experts, typically economists, to express opinions on both the liability and the damages side of the case.[2] An antitrust case is typically a larger project than a commercial damages case. While economists are the most common type of expert working on antitrust cases, there are also opportunities for accountants to work on certain aspects of the analysis.

ANTITRUST LAWS

The main antitrust laws are as follows:

- Sherman Antitrust Act
- Federal Trade Commission Act
- Clayton Act
- Celler-Kefauver Act
- Hart-Scott-Rodino Act

Of these, the Sherman Act is the most important.

Sherman Act

The Sherman Act is the cornerstone of U.S. antitrust laws. Signed in 1890 by President Benjamin Harrison, it was named after Senator Sherman. The law was part of an effort to control the anticompetitive activities of large trusts that started to exercise growing influence over the corporate America of that time. The trusts were often under the control of major banks such as Morgan Bank. These trusts gained voting power over large amounts of equities of various companies and

---

[2]William F. Shugart, "Monopoly and the Problem of the Economists, *Managerial and Decision Economics* 17 (2) (March–April 1996): 221.

Table 11.1   Main Sections of the Sherman Act

Section One	This section outlawed all contracts and combinations which restrain trade.
Section Two	This section made the process of monopolization and attempts to monopolize illegal. It did not necessarily make monopolies illegal, but made actions a person or firm takes to monopolize a market illegal.

then used the voting rights associated with these shares to merge and combine various companies. The goal of these transactions was to try to create larger and more economically viable entities.

It is ironic that just after the passage of the country's first major piece of antitrust legislation, the first merger wave took place.[3] Between 1898 and 1904, a major wave of mergers and acquisitions occurred. This wave featured many horizontal combinations which resulted in markedly increased concentration in many industries. There are several reasons why the Sherman Act did little to influence the large number of horizontal combinations. Among them was the difficulty that the enforcers at the Justice Department had in interpreting a law which they wrongly believed was so broad that it could be applied to any commercial transaction. That, combined with the limited resources of the department, led them to put the Sherman Act to little use during the merger wave.

Sections of the Sherman Act
The two main sections of the Sherman Act are described in Table 11.1.

Given the uncertainty on the part of the courts and the Justice Department about how the Sherman Act should be used to foster competition, legislators passed two other laws in 1914 to facilitate antitrust enforcement. These were the Clayton Act and the Federal Trade Commission Act.

Clayton Act–1914

There are four main components of the Clayton Act; they are described in Table 11.2 along with the section of the Act to which they apply.

Federal Trade Commission Act

In 1914, the Federal Trade Commission Act was passed at the same time as the Clayton Act. Among its purposes was to establish an agency which would be

---

[3]Patrick A. Gaughan, *Mergers and Acquisitions* (New York: HarperCollins, 1991), 12.

Table 11.2   Main Components of the Clayton Act

Section Two	This section prevents price discrimination except that which can be justified by costs economies. This was further clarified and enhanced by the Robinson Patman Act of 1936.
Section Three	Tying contracts, which tie the purchase of one product to the purchase of another, as well as exclusive dealing, which results in the impairment of competition, are illegal under this section.
Section Seven	This section, under its original wording, made the purchase of stock of competing corporations, which result in reduced competition, illegal. This section was amended under the Celler-Kefauver Act of 1950 which closed the asset loophole and made the law apply to both stock and asset acquisitions. The Celler-Kefauver Act of 1950 also made vertical and conglomerate mergers and acquisitions illegal if they have an adverse effect on competition.
Section Eight	Interlocking directorates of competing corporations were made illegal by this section of the Clayton Act.

charged with the enforcement of anticompetitive practices and mergers. In 1938 the law was expanded to also focus on false or deceptive advertising. The Commission was given investigative powers and the ability to hold hearings and issue cease-and-desist orders.

Hart-Scott-Rodino Antitrust Enforcement Act of 1976

The Hart-Scott-Rodino Act was designed to prevent the completion of mergers and acquisitions which regulatory authorities might find objectionable and have to try to well after the deal had been completed. Under Hart-Scott-Rodino, a merger or acquisition cannot be completed until either the Justice Department or the Federal Trade Commission gives its approval. This approval process requires that the merging firms submit a 16-page form that includes various business data broken down by SIC codes. The Justice Department and the Federal Trade Commission decide between themselves which has jurisdiction.

Following the submission of the required forms, the regulatory authorities respond within certain stipulated time periods (which vary depending on whether the deal is a cash or securities offer). The authorities can extend the response period to an additional number of days; this is usually a sign that they have problems with the deal. Given the more relaxed pattern of antitrust enforcement in recent years, merging companies have been asking for an early termination of the Hart-Scott-Rodino waiting periods based upon a lack of antitrust concerns.[4]

---

[4]For a more detailed discussion of this law and its impact on mergers and acquisitions see Patrick A. Gaughan, *Mergers, Acquisitions, and Corporate Restructuring,* 3rd ed. (New York: Wiley, 2002), 83.

ANTITRUST ENFORCEMENT

Antitrust enforcement is the joint responsibility of both the Justice Department and the Federal Trade Commission. When the Justice Department wants to take action, it can bring a civil suit in federal court. Among the tools at its disposal are an injunction that it can wield to halt the objectionable activities. It can also pursue criminal proceedings against the targeted individuals or companies.

The Federal Trade Commission, however, can take action that is brought to an administrative law judge whose decision is then reviewed by the Federal Trade Commissioners. The Federal Trade Commission may get a cease-and-desist order to halt the illegal activities.

In addition to antitrust actions being pursued by the Justice Department and the Federal Trade Commission, individuals also have the right to file suits alleging antitrust violation. If successful, such suits can result in an award of treble damages.

ECONOMICS OF MONOPOLY

Antitrust laws are based on the principle that there are certain benefits of competition that are reduced when markets are monopolized. In order to understand these benefits, it is necessary to explore the microeconomics of market structures.

In microeconomics, there are several different broad forms of market structure. At one extreme is pure competition, which is a market structure characterized by many independent sellers each selling a small fraction of total market output. Being so small, their impact on the market is insignificant and they cannot do anything to influence market price. That is, the market price does not change when they vary their output. In addition, pure competition assumes that the products produced in the competitive market are homogeneous and undifferentiated. Based upon these assumptions, the firms in the industry are price takers, they cannot do anything to influence market price. The assumption of being a price taker means that the demand curve is a flat, horizontal line. This line also becomes the firm's marginal revenues curve. The marginal revenue function is the function that shows how much additional revenue a firm receives when it sells another unit of output.

The profit-maximizing output of the competitive firm is shown in Exhibit 11.2 as q_c. As with all types of firms, the profit-maximizing output is selected as the point where marginal revenue equals marginal costs. The difference in the case of pure competition is that the marginal revenue curve is flat and is the same as the demand curve.

In a monopoly, the only seller in the market is the monopolist. Therefore, the demand curve that the monopolist faces is the demand curve for the product itself.

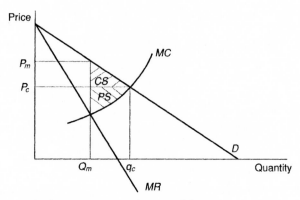

Exhibit 11.2   Perfectly competitive industry and firm.

Like all firms, even purely competitive ones, the monopolist selects its profit-maximizing output by where marginal revenue and marginal costs are equal. The difference between this market structure and pure competition is that with the demand curve having the usual downward-sloping structure given by the inverse relationship between quantity demanded and price, the marginal revenue is also downward-sloping and below the demand curve. The intersection of the upward-sloping marginal cost curve with the downward-sloping marginal revenue function gives us the profit-maximizing output Q_m shown in Exhibit 11.2.

It is possible for us to compare this monopolistic output with that of pure competition by trying to hypothesize what output this monopolist would produce if it acted as though it were operating under pure competition. Exhibit 11.2 shows that the purely competitive industry structure results in a larger market output which, in turn, causes market price to decline. These fewer units traded in monopoly result in a welfare loss—this is the loss of consumer and producer surplus. This is shown in the shaded region in Exhibit 11.2.

Fact versus the Amount of Damages in Antitrust Cases

Economic analysis in antitrust cases can be divided into two parts. It has much in common with other types of cases, such as employment and even personal injury analysis. First, it must be established that the plaintiff incurred measurable damages which were *caused* by the actions of the defendant. Some courts have referred to this process as establishing the fact and the amount of damages. The fact of damages itself has two parts: proving that the plaintiff was damaged and that these damages were caused by the defendant.[5] Establishing the fact of the damages is the key first hurdle that an antitrust plaintiff must traverse. Courts have used phrases such as *reasonable probability* (*Knutson v. Daily Review, Inc.*) and *reasonable certainty* (*Sunkist Growers v. Winkler & Smith Citrus Products Co.*) when describing the standard to be used in establishing the fact of damages and the causal relationship between the defendant's actions and the damages incurred by the plaintiff.

The strict requirements in establishing the fact of the damages present many opportunities for defendants to find other factors which could have caused the plaintiff's damages. These factors will vary from case to case, but often they may be found in the economic and industry analysis that was covered in Chapters Three and Four. The defendant may accomplish its goals even if it cannot conclusively prove that such other factors caused the plaintiff's damages. The defendant may be able to accomplish its goal by raising doubts about the causal link put forward by the plaintiff. For example, in the *United States Football League v. National Football League,* the defendant was able to establish that factors such as mismanagement were important explanatory variables.[6]

Once the fact of the damages has been established, courts tend to apply a more relaxed standard to measuring the amount of the plaintiff's damages.[7] This is partially due to the fact that once the world has been changed by the defendant's conduct, it is difficult to reconstruct the position of the plaintiff. While the burden of proof may be less for measuring damages, the analysis still must be nonspeculative. If the defendant can show that the plaintiff's damages analysis is speculative, then such damages may not be recoverable.

Interpretation of Antitrust Violations: Structure versus Conduct

There are two opposing schools of thought in antitrust enforcement. The *structure* school of antitrust sees that the mere possession of monopoly power is by itself an antitrust violation. Under this view, a firm is guilty of an antitrust violation

---

[5]*Bogosian v. Gulf Oil Corp.*, 561 F2d 434, 454 (3rd Cir. 1977), *cert denied*, 434 U.S. 1086 (1987).

[6]*United States Football League v. National Football League*, 842 F2d 1335 (2d Cir. 1988).

[7]*Van Dyk Research Corp. v. Xerox Corp.* 631 F2d 251, 255 (3rd Cir. 1980).

even if it did not engage in conduct that would otherwise be considered a violation of antitrust laws. Mere size alone would be enough to be found guilty of antitrust violations. This would be the case even if the firm did not do anything to limit the ability of other firms to enter the market and to limit the ability of the other companies in the industry to compete.

Under the *conduct* view, the mere possession of monopoly power is not a *per se* violation. The firm would have to engage in other unacceptable conduct in order for it to be guilty of antitrust violations. It is even possible that one firm that had a large market share but which did not engage in any anticompetitive behavior could be innocent of antitrust violations. At the same time, a firm with a smaller market share but which took actions to try to limit competition could be found guilty.

CHANGING PATTERN OF ANTITRUST ENFORCEMENT

In the early part of the century, the courts focused on a combination of structure and conduct. They sought companies that clearly had very large market shares but they also considered their anticompetitive conduct. These decisions quickly evolved into the *Rule of Reason* in which behavior became the main focus of the court.

Early Cases

In 1911, two major antitrust cases were brought against two companies that held dominant positions which they achieved through the use of various forms of anticompetitive behavior. The first of these is the *Standard Oil* case. The court focused on the many anticompetitive acts in which the company engaged to garner a 90 percent market share of the petroleum industry.[8] The court was suspect of the large market share. It was even more concerned, though, with the variety of anticompetitive behavior in which the company engaged to drive out competitors in order to achieve this market share. Such behavior included industrial espionage and local price wars. The court's solution was to require dissolution of the company; it was disassembled into 34 separate companies.

In the same year, the U.S. Supreme Court ruled against American Tobacco for similar reasons.[9] American Tobacco's market share was even greater than

---

[8]*Standard Oil Company of New Jersey v. U.S.* 221 U.S. 1 (1911).
[9]*U.S. v. American Tobacco Co.*, 221 U.S. 106 (1911).

Standard Oil's—American Tobacco dominated over 90 percent of the market. American Tobacco achieved this market share through a variety of questionable marketing and promotional tactics that were used to conduct large scale predatory campaigns designed to drive competitors out of existence. The company invested a large percent of revenues in advertising and marketing and used these resources in selective markets to eliminate competitors. This predatory behavior also included the establishment of "fighting brands" which were sold at predatory prices until the competitors acquiesced and sold out to American Tobacco and its CEO James Duke. Once again, the Court focused on the objectionable behavior, required dissolution of the company, and an oligopolistic market structure resulted.

Rule of Reason and the U.S. Steel Case

The evolution of the Rule of Reason took a major step with the U.S. Steel case.[10] Here U.S. Steel was shown to have a dominant position as evidenced by its market share—which was far larger than that of any of its competitors. The firm was formed through a consolidation of many different plants and competitors, leaving it with the majority of the market's production. This process was part of an overall consolidation that was occurring throughout the United States economy and constituted the first merger wave in American economic history. However, the court concluded that even though U.S. Steel did possess market power, it did not engage in any offensive conduct. The court found that even though the company accounted for approximately one-half of the market, its market share had actually fallen from as high as 66 percent.

In the U.S. Steel case, the court focused on the fact that the company did not make any attempt to price its products in a manner that would drive out competitors. In its decision, the court stated that size alone was not anticompetitive and U.S. Steel did not use its dominant position to limit competition.

Structure and the Alcoa Case

The position of the Court shifted in the 1945 when it moved away from the Rule of Reason and began to consider size by itself to be objectionable. In his decision,

---

[10]*U.S. v. U.S. Steel Corporation,* 251 U.S. 417 (1920).

Judge Learned Hand found that Alcoa had built up its bauxite reserves with the intention to monopolize the aluminum industry.[11] He was particularly impressed by the dominant position of Alcoa. Hand was concerned that even if the company had not used its market power to engage in anticompetitive conduct, the mere possession of such power, and the clear ability of a firm to dominate markets, was sufficient to constitute an antitrust violation. Judge Hand's solution was to force Alcoa to sell off parts of the company to competitors Reynolds Metals and Kaiser Aluminum and to not build any more plants for a period of time.

It is noteworthy to mention that the Alcoa decision was followed by another major antitrust decision in the following year. In 1946, the court continued a pattern of more intensive antitrust enforcement when it found the management of A&P guilty of anticompetitive behavior.[12] In later years, however, the "Alcoa doctrine" was discredited and the mere possession of a monopoly position was not construed to be a violation of antitrust laws.

1950s–1960s

Following the Alcoa and the A&P decisions, antitrust enforcement grew very intense. Antitrust laws were buttressed by the passage of the Celler–Kefauver Act in 1950. This law strengthened the Clayton Act. It bolstered the decisions of the 1940s to create an environment in which the Justice Department and the Federal Trade Commission wielded considerable power. There were not as many landmark decisions in this period but this was not indicative of the intensity of antitrust enforcement. Companies were often reluctant to pursue a case through trial and ended up settling by entering into agreements with the Justice Department.

When companies wanted to expand in the 1960s, they ran into extremely stringent antitrust enforcement. It limited their ability to expand within their own markets or even outside their usual industries. The intense antitrust enforcement of this period combined with the desire of companies to expand following the longest recovery in modern U.S. economic history caused the third merger wave. This wave, which took place in the late 1960s, featured conglomerate mergers— mergers outside of the company's industry.[13] Companies were reluctant to

---

[11]*U.S. v. Aluminum Company of America et al.*, 148 F2d 416, 424 (1945).

[12]*U.S. v. New York Great Atlantic and Pacific Tea Company et al.*, 67 F. Supp. 626 (1946), 173 F2d (1949).

[13]Patrick A. Gaughan, *Mergers, Acquisitions, and Corporate Restructuring*, 3rd ed. (New York: Wiley, 2002), 26–35.

expand within their own industries because they knew that such moves were often challenged. The antitrust enforcement became so intense that even conglomerate mergers were questioned.

On January 17, 1969, the last day of the Johnson administration, the government began its famous lawsuit against IBM.[14] The case dragged on for years but finally went to trial in 1975. The government alleged that IBM, which commanded approximately three-quarters of the mainframe computer market, engaged in various anticompetitive actions (such as predatory pricing), tying of various computer products (such as hardware and software), and other acts. The case was very costly and very time consuming; in the end, the government dismissed the case. Some have termed this case the Justice Department's Vietnam.

1970s–1980s

The 1970s and 1980s were periods of more relaxed antitrust enforcement. More pro-business administrations in Washington D.C. came to power and placed similarly-minded individuals in positions of power at the Justice Department. These individuals held the belief that even in oligopolistic market structures, there can be significant competition among the participants of the industry. Broader definitions of markets were applied, and consideration was given to factors such as global competitiveness.

One landmark antitrust development that took place in the 1980s was the dismantling of the Bell System. This event can be traced to a 1974 Department of Justice lawsuit that contended that AT&T was hindering competition of fledgling rivals such as MCI, and that AT&T obstructed telecommunications equipment companies from selling to the components of the Bell System which it controlled. The suit contended that AT&T used its monopoly of the local telecommunications market to dominate the long distance and equipment markets. AT&T argued that its control of the Bell System had resulted in the finest telecommunications system in the world. They stated that their dominant market position was actually good for the market. However, fearful that the ultimate legal result might be adverse, AT&T agreed to a consent degree which broke up the system. This break up separated the operating systems from the long distance entity while also releasing equipment component from the combined entity. The operating companies were grouped into seven large regional

---

[14]*United States v. Int. Bus. Mach. Corp.*, No. 69 Civ. 200 (S.D.N.Y., 1969).

holding companies, which were consolidated in later years through mergers and acquisitions. It is ironic that in the 1990s and 2000s these holding companies would compete with AT&T.

1990s

The 1990s marked a slight move away from the more relaxed posture of antitrust enforcement that was the norm during the 1980s. Mergers that may have not been questioned in the 1980s were given closer scrutiny by the Justice Department. Certain major firms that held dominant positions in markets, such as Microsoft, were watched carefully. They were challenged when they attempted acquisitions within their broadly defined industry category or when they tried to market products that could be construed as giving their products an unfair advantage over competitors. The Microsoft case was the highlight of the Justice Department's increased aggressiveness in the enforcement of antitrust laws. The Justice Department's suit alleged that Microsoft bundled its Web browser, Internet Explorer, with its dominant operating system in a manner that violated section one of the Sherman Act. The Justice Department argued that in doing so, Microsoft violated a 1994 order-and-consent decree when it bundled these products together in sales to original equipment manufacturers and consumers.

The Justice department experienced an initial victory that was greatly tempered by their subsequent setbacks. In *United States v. Microsoft Corp.*, the U.S. District Court found that Microsoft violated Sections 1 and 2 of the Sherman Act through what this court saw as Microsoft's efforts to use its Windows operating system to hold down competition in related areas such as Web browsers. The court based its decision in part on the *Jefferson Parish Hospital District No. 2 v. Hyde* and *Northern Pacific Railway Co. v. the United States* decisions.[15] However, the U.S. Appeals court for the D.C. Circuit affirmed the District Court's decision on monopoly maintenance but reversed its decision on attempted monopolization and tying as well as the District Court's suggested remedy.[16]

---

[15]Christopher Campbell, "Notes and Comments: Fit to Be Tied: How United States v. Microsoft Corp. Incorrectly Changed the Standard for Sherman Act Tying Violations Involving Software," *Loyola of Los Angeles Entertainment Law Review* 22 (2002): 583–612.

[16]John E. Lopatka and William Page, "Who Suffered Antitrust Injury in the Microsoft Case," *George Washington Law Review* 69 (October–December 2001).

ANTITRUST AND THE NEW ECONOMY

The Justice Department's pursuit of Microsoft drew attention to the application of traditional antitrust laws to "New Economy companies." Richard Posner defines new economy companies as firms operating in one of three areas:

1. Computer software manufacturers
2. Internet-based companies (such as AOL)
3. Communication services and equipment manufacturers designed to support the above two categories[17]

Posner points out that the economics of these industries differs markedly from the traditional capital-intensive industries that antitrust laws were designed to regulate. These traditional firms are so embedded in economics that they are used as the model for presentations on the determination of optimal output and price in many microeconomics textbooks. While such firms experience economies of scale in production, these scale economies are bounded by the limitations of the plant or plants they operate. This is not the case with many of the new economy businesses. They have falling average costs over large output ranges and, unlike their old economy predecessors, their businesses are not capital-intensive. The other obvious difference between these two types of industries is that the main output of the new economy companies is intellectual property. Such "goods" are characterized by very significant fixed, "upfront" costs but comparatively low marginal costs. The "production" component of these costs may be close to zero; however, there may be other nonzero marginal costs, such as selling costs.

MONOPOLIZATION AND ATTEMPTS AT MONOPOLIZATION

As noted earlier, Section 2 of the Sherman Act prohibits a company from monopolizing an industry or taking actions which are designed to achieve this goal. It is important to note, however, that it is not a violation of antitrust laws to develop a monopoly position by lawful methods. Monopolists can choose to compete as aggressively as competitive firms to achieve optimal profits.

---

[17]Richard A. Posner, "Antitrust in the New Economy," paper presented at the American Bar Association Antitrust Conference, New York City, September 14, 2000.

The situation is different when the monopoly position is attained or maintained by unlawful means. In this case, whether the firm truly has a monopoly position becomes more important. As part of the process of making a judgment on whether a firm has a monopoly position, various quantitative microeconomic measures can be employed. One of the first steps in this process is to define the relevant market.

Market Definition

The definition of a market determines the products and services that are competing with the product in question as well as the geographical area within which such competition occurs. Therefore, a market can be defined in two broad ways—geographic markets and product markets. Each way has its own quantitative measures that are employed.

Geographic Market Definitions

Geographic definitions of markets have varied considerably over time as the intensity of antitrust enforcement has varied. As markets have become broader and more internationalized, the definition of the relevant markets in some instances has widened. The degree to which increased internationalization is relevant to a case depends on the industry and the facts of the case.

Economists usually define the geographic boundaries of a market by judging whether an increase in the price in one market affects the price in the another market.[18] Other factors related to this market's definition are variables such as transportation costs that are incurred to move products from one market to the other. The more significant the transportation costs in the total costs of the product, the more likely that such costs might serve to segregate the market into separate markets. However, the expert needs to consider factors that could offset these costs, such as the existence of storage or distribution facilities.

Regulatory factors may play a role in the definition of a geographic market. For example, governmental regulations which prohibit selling the product or service outside certain boundaries may help define the geographical boundaries.

---

[18]Dennis Carlton and Jeffrey M. Perloff, *Modern Industrial Organization*, 3rd ed. (New York: HarperCollins Publishers, 1994), 807.

Such factors have played an important role in the banking industry, although their importance has declined significantly as the industry has undergone deregulation.

If marketing and advertising play a major role in generating demand for the product or service, then the geographic limitations of the often-used advertising media may help define the geographic market. However, as the marketing and advertising industry have themselves undergone major changes, the role of this factor may vary considerably.

Product Market Definitions

The broader the market, the less likely it is that a given firm is found to have monopolized it. Competitive products are those which are substitutes for one another. Products X and Y are *demand substitutes* for each other if an increase in the product X causes an increase in the quantity demanded of product Y. Products A and B are *supply substitutes* if an increase in the price of product A causes companies that are producing B to alter their production mix and increase their production of A.

Price and Substitutability

The degree of substitutability between two products is not constant; it varies as the price changes. At a low price, two products (X and Y) may not be substitutable, but at higher prices they may become substitutes. There tends to be a price at which consumers look for substitutes. The fact that at a higher price of good X its seller faces competition from substitutes does not mean that the company selling X lacks market power. Its market power may lie in the fact that it has the ability to sell the products at as high a price as possible before it faces significant competition.

Determining the Existence of Substitutes

A simple method of determining the degree to which products are considered substitutes is to survey the marketing and sales professionals in the industry. Salespeople without any knowledge of economics may know very well who their competition is as they try to sell their products. Marketing professionals who develop marketing campaigns usually also have intimate knowledge of who their major competitors are.

Using Correlation Analysis

If two products are substitutes, then presumably their prices move together as they engage in price competition. The degree to which these prices move together may be measured using correlation analysis. Correlation analysis is discussed in Chapter Two in the context of causality in commercial litigation. If the correlation coefficients are high, this usually indicates that the products are substitutes. Low correlations do not support the assertion that products are substitutes. However, this is not to imply that correlation analysis alone is conclusive.

Another method of determining whether or not a particular product, Y, may be a substitute for another one, X, is to find yet another product, Z, which is accepted as a substitute for X. Correlations of the movements in the prices of X and Z can be computed to measure their degree of association. This value is then used as a benchmark.[19] This correlation is then compared to the correlation between the prices of X and Y. Very different correlation coefficients fail to support the assertion that X and Y are in the same market. However, this is a general statement and each case has other factors that may offset this difference in the correlation coefficients.

Cross-Price Elasticity of Demand

A quantitative measure which may be useful in assessing the extent to which two products are substitutes is the cross-price elasticity of demand. It measures the percentage change in the quantity demanded of good X in response to a given percentage change in the price of good Y. This measure is expressed as follows:

$$\varepsilon_{xy} = \%\Delta Q_x / \%\Delta P_y = \Delta Q_x / Q_x / \Delta P_y / P_y = P_y / Q_x \Delta Q_x / \Delta P_y \qquad (11.1)$$

Two goods can have three different values for the cross-price elasticity of demand: positive, negative or zero. Such values reflect the extent to which they are substitutes, complements, or have no interrelation in consumption. Substitutes are goods which can be used in place of the good in question. This is because they have some similar characteristics in the eyes of consumers. Complements are goods that must be used together. Many consider tea and lemon complements; Coca Cola and Pepsi Cola are considered substitutes.

When the price of good Y increases and the quantity demanded of X increases, X and Y are said to be substitutes in consumption. When the price of Y rises and the quantity demanded of X decreases, the two goods are said to be complements.

---

[19]Dennis Carlton and Jeffrey M. Perloff, *Modern Industrial Organization*, 3rd ed. (New York: HarperCollins Publishers, 1994), 806.

If there is no change in the quantity demanded of X when the price of Y changes, the consumption of the two goods may not be interrelated. This relationship is summarized as follows:

$$\varepsilon_{xy} > 0 \quad X \text{ and } Y \text{ are substitutes}$$
$$\varepsilon_{xy} < 0 \quad X \text{ and } Y \text{ are complements}$$
$$\varepsilon_{xy} = 0 \quad X \text{ and } Y \text{ have no relationship in consumption}$$

Own-Price Elasticity of Demand versus Cross-Price Elasticity of Demand

The own-price elasticity of demand is the percentage change in the quantity of X that occurs as a result of the percentage change in the price of X. This is different than the cross-price elasticity of demand, which is the percentage change in the quantity of X in response to a percentage change in the price of Y. Both elasticity measures are relevant to antitrust analysis and a firm's market power. The own-price elasticity of demand is relevant to understanding the ability of the firm to raise price above marginal costs and enjoy above-normal profits; the cross-price elasticity of demand is also relevant in assessing competitive effects.

MARKET POWER

In microeconomics, market power is measured by the ability of the seller to charge a price above marginal costs. Marginal costs are taken to be the price that would prevail in a purely competitive market when sellers set price equal to marginal cost. However, few industries correspond to the exact characteristics of a purely competitive market. These characteristics are as follows:

- Many independent sellers
- Perfect information
- Homogeneous, undifferentiated products
- No barriers to entry

Most firms have some element of market power, whereas others possess significant market power. To the extent that a given firm has some market power, its price exceeds marginal costs. One of the problems of applying a concept such as marginal cost is that it is difficult to measure. If, however, a reasonable approximation can be made, then market power is measured using the *Lerner*

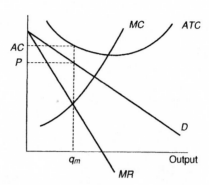

Exhibit 11.4 Average costs exceed price.

Index. This index, named after the economist Abba Lerner, may be expressed as follows:

$$\frac{(P - MC)}{P} = \frac{1}{\varepsilon} \tag{11.2}$$

The left hand side of this equation is called the *price-cost margin.* This margin is a function of the price elasticity of demand—ε. Specifically, the magnitude of the margin is inversely related to the price elasticity of demand. That is, when the price elasticity of demand is low, price is significantly greater than marginal costs. However, when the price elasticity of demand is high, marginal costs are very close to price.

The Lerner Index is useful in that it shows how a monopolist's market power is related to its ability to set price above marginal costs. The more inelastic demand is, the greater the monopolist's ability to widen the gap between price and marginal costs.

It is important to note, however, that merely having monopoly power, as measured by the ability to set price above *marginal* costs, does not mean that a firm makes a profit. It could be that the firm has fixed costs that make a positive profit at its optimal output—the output where marginal revenue equals marginal costs—impossible. This is shown in Exhibit 11.4. In this example, average costs (*AC*) are always above the demand curve which means that price (*P*) is always less than average costs even at the optimal output q_m.

MEASURES OF MARKET CONCENTRATION

In economics, there are two opposite types of market structure—pure competition and monopoly. In pure competition, the firms lack market power; in a monopoly, however, the monopolist has some degree of market power. In reality, most industries are neither monopolists nor purely competitive. However, depending on how close they are to either end of the industry spectrum, some of the characteristics of either form of industry structure may apply. Towards this end, it is useful to measure the degree of concentration in an industry. This can be done in different ways, the most basic of which is to use concentration ratios.

Concentration Ratios

Concentration ratios measure the amount of total market output that is accounted for by the top 4, top 8, or even top 12 companies in the industry. The greater the market share accounted for by a smaller grouping of firms, the closer an industry is to monopoly. Industries where the top four or eight companies account for most of the industry output usually are considered oligopolies. An example of the wide range of concentration ratios in different industries can be found in the Census Bureau's reports.[20] It is important to keep in mind that one cannot judge the degree of competition in an industry by looking at concentration ratios alone. An industry can have a significant degree of competition even when there are relatively few competitors.

Herfindahl–Hirshman Index

Concentration ratios are not very sensitive to changes in industry concentration caused by mergers among firms in the same size category. For example, if the top firms constitute 98 percent of total industry output and there is a merger between the sixth- and seventh-ranked companies in the industry, the top eight concentration ratio will shed little light on the competitive effects of this change in control. To remedy such problems, regulatory authorities rely on the Herfindahl–Hirshman Index (HHI). It is expressed as follows:

$$HHI = \sum_{i=1}^{n} s_i^2 \qquad (11.3)$$

where s_i = the market share of the ith firm.

---

[20]U.S. Bureau of the Census, 1982 Census of Manufacturers, "Concentration Ratios in Manufacturing," Washington, D.C. (April 1986).

Given that the market shares of the firms are squared, the index places disproportionately greater weight on larger firms. In the example above, the merger between the sixth- and seventh-largest firms has little impact on the top eight concentration ratio other than to promote the relatively small, previously ninth-ranked firm to the number eight spot. However, the HHI may rise significantly when the sixth- and seventh-ranked firms merge. In an effort to prohibit types of mergers and acquisitions that are unacceptable, the Justice Department has created merger guidelines in terms of the Herfindahl–Hirshman Index.

COMMON TYPES OF ANTITRUST CASES

With the dramatic increase in mergers and acquisitions that occurred in the 1980s and 1990s, lawsuits involving alleged increases in market power resulting from such transactions may require antitrust analysis. These cases draw on the type of analysis that was discussed earlier. However, in addition to allegations of basic monopolization of markets, there are certain other types of antitrust violations that arise. These are predatory pricing and tying contracts. Predatory pricing is a violation of Section Two of the Sherman Act; tying contracts violate Section Three of the Clayton Act. There is an abundant literature on each of these types of violations that is well beyond the scope of this chapter. However, an introduction is provided to some of the issues and tools that may be employed in a litigation environment.

Mergers and Acquisitions Antitrust Analysis

The 1980s featured a dramatic increase in both the number and size of mergers and acquisitions. This period was the fourth merger wave that occurred in U.S. economic history. It ended in the late 1980s with the collapse of the junk bond market. This helped fuel the high number of hostile deals that occurred as well as the overall slowdown in the economy. However, after a relatively short hiatus, the pace of mergers and acquisitions increased in 1993 and the resulting merger frenzy surpassed even the lofty levels reached in the 1980s. This period was the fifth merger wave.[21]

---

[21]Patrick A. Gaughan, *Mergers, Acquisitions, and Corporate Restructurings,* 3rd ed. (New York: Wiley 2002), 51–54.

Regulatory Framework

Mergers and acquisitions are highly regulated. Purchases of stock beyond the 5 percent threshold require the filing of a Schedule 13D disclosure statement pursuant to the Williams Act or Section 13(d) of the Securities and Exchange Act; tender offers require the filing of a Schedule 14D-1 pursuant to Section 14(d) of the same law. However, in addition to these securities laws, a special disclosure-related law exists for the antitrust ramifications of mergers and acquisitions. This law, the Hart-Scott-Rodino Antitrust Improvement Act, requires the filing of a form which includes data on sales by SIC code for merger partners above a certain size. This form is filed with both the Justice Department and the Federal Trade Commission who determine who between them has jurisdiction. If the transaction is objectionable, they may ask for more information (which is usually a sign of a potential problem) or they will indicate that they oppose the deal. The purpose of the law is to give merger partners an advance ruling. This prevents the government from having to file a lawsuit after the fact and having to try to disassemble the combined entities.

Horizontal Mergers and Acquisitions

Section 7 of the Clayton Act, which was amended in 1950 by the Celler-Kefauver Act to include asset transactions, makes illegal those deals in "any area of commerce" or in "any section of the country" that lessen competition or tend to create a monopoly. The wording of these excerpts from the law is revealing. The term "any area of commerce" implies that the industry definition is flexible. In addition, regional concentration becomes an issue under the wording "any section of the country." The phrase "tend to create a monopoly" makes the law applicable even if the deal did not result in a clear monopoly. Given its broad wording, this section of the Clayton Act and the Sherman Act are potent weapons in the hands of regulators who are predisposed to oppose such deals.

One of the most common antitrust complaints in mergers and acquisitions has to do with increases in market power caused by horizontal transactions, such as a merger between rivals. This claim was asserted more often in the mid-1990s as the industry consolidations of the fifth merger started to have an effect on the degree of concentration in some industries. The led to the Justice Department playing a more active role in examining, not merely "rubber stamping," the mergers that took place.

Predatory Pricing

Predatory pricing refers to the use of price competition to drive rivals out of business and to prevent competitors from entering into the firm's market. Obviously, one of the key tasks in a predatory pricing analysis is to determine whether the price competition was the product of ordinary competitive actions or was part of a predatory process. This is one of the problems of predatory pricing economic analysis—distinguishing predatory pricing from ordinary competition.[22] Courts have recognized that cutting prices is one of the main forms of competition.[23] In order to determine this, one must compare price to some measure of the alleged predator's costs. This usually involves showing that the predator incurred losses, usually short-run losses, in order to generate long-term gains.

Predation is more likely in markets where the predator has certain advantages over current or potential rivals. These advantages may come in the form of larger size or lower costs. Certain game-theory issues arise when the competitors do not know the other firm's cost structure; they merely formulate guesses based on a variety of observable variables, such as the rival's prices and responses to the prices of competitors.

Areeda and Turner's Marginal Cost Rule
of Predatory Pricing

One of the leading treatises in the area of predatory pricing was the 1975 article by Philip Areeda and Donald Turner.[24] Under the Areeda and Turner standard, pricing is predatory if it falls below the alleged predator's short-run marginal cost. This implies that costs above short-run marginal costs are lawful. However, given the difficulty in measuring marginal costs, Areeda and Turner suggest that average *variable* costs be used as a proxy for marginal costs. Alternatives to the Areeda and Turner average variable costs rule have been put forward. These include using long-run marginal costs as well as average total costs. Given that average variable costs are generally below average total costs, it may not be nec-

---

[22]Frank Easterbrook, "Predatory Strategies and Counterstrategies," *University of Chicago Law Review* 48 (2) (spring 1981): 263–337.

[23]*Eastman Kodak Co. v. Image Tech. Services,* 112 S. Ct. 2072, 2088 (1992).

[24]Philip E. Areeda and Donald F. Turner, "Predatory Pricing and Related Practices Under Section Two of the Sherman Act," *Harvard Law Review* 86: 697–733.

essary to look at both, because prices that are below average variable costs should be below average total costs.[25]

The courts have not put forward one accepted measure of costs. For example, this issue was sidestepped in both *Cargill, Inc. v. Monfort of Colorado* and *Matsushita Electrical Industrial Corp. v. Zenith Radio Corp. et al.* Even in *Brooke Group Ltd. v. Brown & Williamson Tobacco Corp.,* the court did not have to deal with this issue as both parties to the suit agreed that the appropriate cost measure was average variable cost. Another unresolved cost issue is how to treat fixed versus variable cost. This issue includes how to deal with costs that are fixed over one time period but vary as the time period expands.

Recouping of Losses

One important result that one can derive from *Brooke Group v. Brown & Williamson Tobacco* is that the plaintiff must demonstrate that the defendant has a reasonable probability of recouping the losses it incurred by allegedly pricing below costs. This process involves showing that over some reasonable time period the defendant would be able increase price above the competitive level.[26] The present value of these future profits must offset the present value of the costs incurred through the losses caused by the below-cost prices.

Criticisms of the Economics of Predatory Pricing Claims

There has been much criticism of the appropriateness of predatory pricing claims. Much of this revolves around whether predatory pricing can be an effective means of acquiring monopoly power.[27] Some question the sense of a competitor who prices at a level where it incurs losses simply to impose losses on other firms.[28] John McGee, a famous critic of rationality of predatory pricing claims,

---

[25]Paul L. Joskow and Alvin K. Klevorick, "A Framework for Analyzing Predatory Pricing Policy," *The Yale Law Journal* 89 (2) (December 1979): 213–270.

[26]Michael Denger and John A. Herfort, "Predatory Pricing Claims After Brooke Group," *Antitrust Law Journal* 62 (3) (Spring 1994): 541–558.

[27]B.S. Yamey, "Predatory Price Cutting: Notes and Comments," *Journal of Law and Economics* 15 (1972): 129.

[28]Richard Posner, *Antitrust Law: An Economic Perspective* (University of Chicago Press), 187.

has emphasized that there are much less costly ways to obtain the same advantages that predators are seeking, such as mergers.[29] In addition, he points out that once competitors perceive that the predator's actions are temporary, they may wait out the loss period with the predator. If the actions force them to leave the industry, McGee states that they may reenter. Others have questioned McGee's criticisms, saying that they seem accurate in theory but do not hold up when confronted with the realities of certain market situations.[30] When the predator is far larger than the rivals, they may not be able to wait out the losses as easily as a well-financed predator. In addition, rivals who were once forced out by losses incurred at the hands of a predator may think twice before devoting capital to an industry which has dealt them such unpleasant experiences. Other more attractive opportunities may exist.

Credibility and Alleged Predation over Time

In *Matsushita Electrical Co. Ltd. v. Zenith Radio Corporation et al.*, the Supreme Court questioned the soundness of claims of predatory pricing that extended over two decades. The Court concluded that it is not reasonable that any competitor would incur losses over such a long time period in the hope of recouping these gains at some indeterminate time in the future. Such a plan implies that the alleged predator is using a rather unreasonable discount rate in its competitive strategy. Ruling out such a strategy, the Court concluded that the prices must be the product of normal competition. One lesson that arises from this case is that the time period over which the alleged predatory pricing occurred must be of a reasonable length. It cannot be so long as to make the claims lack credibility.

Predatory "Costing"

An interesting variant of predatory behavior is where a firm seeks to drive out rivals not by lowering their revenues through predatory pricing but by taking

---

[29]John S. McGee, "Predatory Price Cutting: The Standard Oil Case," *Journal of Law and Economics* (October 1958): 137–169, and John S. McGee, "Predatory Pricing Revisited," *Journal of Law and Economics* (October 1980): 289–330.

[30]Douglas Greer, *Industrial Organization and Public Policy*, 3rd ed. (New York: Macmillian Publishing Company, 1992), 453–455.

actions which increase their costs. Competitors who have their costs increased may reduce output, potentially allowing the predator to increase its market share.[31]

Price Fixing

Price fixing is a violation of Section One of the Sherman Act. The law makes collusive behavior among competitors who seek to establish certain market prices illegal. This type of price fixing is called *horizontal price fixing*. Price fixing can also be vertical: a firm at one stage of the production-distribution chain seeks to change prices at another stage. An example is the manufacturer who wants to require distributors or retailers to maintain prices above certain levels.

Damages in Horizontal Price Fixing

In cases of horizontal price fixing, plaintiffs may pay higher prices than what they would have paid in the absence of price fixing. This difference in prices may be a measure of the plaintiff's per-unit damages. The price difference can then be applied to a quantity measure to arrive at a cumulative damages value. One of the difficult tasks facing the economist is to determine what prices would have been without the collusive behavior. One method that is used to determine such prices is the *before and after method*. This method looks to find a period of time during which there was no price fixing. Depending on the facts of the case, this time period could either be before or after the price fixing. The difference in prices between the "no price-fixing" time and the price-fixed period are then computed to measure the per-unit damages. One important analytical element of the before and after method is the economic comparability of the two time periods to rule out any other economic factors that may have been responsible for the price difference. This is an area that defendants may want to explore. One issue that is often not considered by courts is the quantity variation that might have occurred in response to the varying prices.

If there are no time periods without the presence of price fixing then an alternative to the before and after method is to find some proxy firms that are very

---

[31]Steven C. Salop and David T. Scheffman, "Recent Advances in the Theory of Industrial Structure," *Recent Advances in the Theory of Industrial Structure* 73 (2) (May 1983): 267–271.

similar but who are not involved in the price fixing. As was discussed in Chapter Two of this book, this method is referred to as the *yardstick method*.[32]

Measuring Damages in Vertical Price-Fixing Cases

The measurement of damages in a vertical price-fixing case involves establishing the per-unit damages as measured by the difference between the fixed price and an unaffected prices. The expert may be able to find examples of both prices when there are marketers who sell under the fixed as well as the unfixed price policy. An example is the manufacturer of a product who requires its distributors to sell at certain minimum prices. If the distributors try to sell at lower prices and the manufacturer responds by taking certain actions (like cutting off the distributors supplies), there may be readily available evidence of both sets of prices in the market.

One important component of the analysis is to show that there actually are damages. It could be the case that the manufacturer is trying to extract economic rent by imposing its fixed prices. If the defendant can establish that the plaintiff would have sold at the disputed prices even without the actions of the defendant, then no damages will be found.

Tying Contracts

Another common type of antitrust case is one in which there is an allegation of a *tying contract*. Tying contracts are agreements in which a seller requires a buyer to purchase products from it at certain prices which the buyer would otherwise not purchase. Such contracts are illegal pursuant to Section Three of the Clayton Act. Tying contracts are sometimes seen when the defendant is trying to extend the power it possesses in one market to another market where its lacks such power. This could occur, for example, if the defendant has a monopoly in one market but faces competition from several sellers in the other market. If the plaintiff needs both products for its production process, it can be forced to acquiesce to the seller's requirements. A famous tying contract case was *International Business Machines v. U.S.*[33] The Supreme Court concluded that IBM's require-

---

[32]*Fishman v. Estate of Wirtz*, 807 F2d 520, 551 (7th Cir. 1986).

[33]*International Business Machines v. United States*, 298 U.S. (1936).

ment that buyers of its machines also purchase its computer cards was an example of IBM using its market power—derived from its preeminent position in the computer industry—to engage in price discrimination. The more intensive users of the machines would purchase more cards and would, therefore, pay more in total than those who used the machines less intensively. Tying contracts were the means through which IBM became what is referred to as a *price-discriminating monopolist.*

Determining if Products are Truly Separate

One of the tasks of the economic expert in a tying contracts case is to determine if the products are truly separate or if they are naturally bundled together. If the latter is the case, it may be a costly task to unbundle them—this process may work to raise the ultimate price to the consumer. For example, in *Jefferson Parish Hospital District No. 2 v. Hyde,* the court determined that the services of anesthesiologists were separate from the services that a hospital offers.[34] The court concluded that the issue of there being two products centers not on their functional interrelationship but on the nature of the demand for the two products. That is, if the nature of the demand is such that there is a separate demand for each of the two products, then there are two products, not just one, that ties the two together.

A classic example of goods that are often tied together but do not necessarily have to be offered together are products that require service. The manufacturer may want to require buyers to purchase its service. One argument made by defendants in these types of actions is that substandard service may damage the product and affect the warranty.[35] This argument is weakened if the plaintiff service organization can demonstrate that they are capable of offering services of similar quality. Such cases have arisen when former service employees of a defendant leave its employ after having provided service to the defendant's consumers. After having been trained by the defendant, they enter into competition with the defendant in the services business. In such circumstances, the defendant needs to show why, in spite of these circumstances, there is a quality control issue.

One of the ways that manufacturers try to make it difficult for third-party service organizations to enter the services market is to refuse to sell parts to such

---

[34]*Jefferson Parish Hospital No. 2 v. Hyde,* 466 U.S. 2 (1984).
[35]*Jerrold Electronics Corp. v. United States,* 187 F. Supp. 545 (1961).

organizations. Faced with such a shortage of parts essential to provide timely service, these companies often resort to purchasing used equipment and dismantling it for parts. Even in this case, the manufacturer has an advantage in that it may be able to claim that it has only new parts. Competing services companies offer used parts that may not perform as well. Probably the most well-known case in this area is *Eastman Kodak Co. v. Image Technical Services*.[36] The definition of market was crucial in this case. The independent services organizations (ISOs) conceded that Kodak, which had less than a 25 percent market share, did not have power in the market for the copiers that they sold and which were being serviced by the ISOs. However, the ISOs asserted that Kodak had a monopoly in the market for the parts used in Kodak's own products. A divided Supreme Court concluded, however, that the absence of market power at the initial product level did not necessarily preclude the exercise of anticompetitive market power in the aftermarket.[37] Kodak had argued that assertions that it would raise prices in the aftermarket above competitive levels did not make sense. This is because the new prices would raise the total cost of the product, hurting Kodak's competitive position in the equipment market. This view is espoused by some economists who assert that the market power for these interrelated products and systems is very interdependent.[38] While some see this as a rejection of pure economic theory, the Court did conclude that markets may not work perfectly. These imperfections may make the simplistic theory of equipment market competition fail to prevent aftermarket anticompetitive activities.[39] Others do not see this as a rejection of pure economic theory, or what some refer to as Chicago economic theory. They see the courts moving to a more modern, or post-Chicago, stance in which a variety of economic factors that include more recent developments in the field of industrial organization are taken into account in reaching modern antitrust decisions.[40] Other economists do not think that the Court went far enough and assert that the competition in the equipment market may have little effect on a manu-

---

[36]*Eastman Kodak Co. v. Image Technical Services*, 112 S. Ct. 2072 (1992).

[37]*Image Technical Services, Inc. v. Eastman Kodak Co.*, 903 F2d, 612, 617 (9th Cir. 1990).

[38]Carl Shapiro and David Teece, "Systems Competition and Aftermarkets: An Economic Analysis of *Kodak*," Antitrust Bulletin 39 (1) (spring 1994): 135–162.

[39]Benjamin Klein, "Market Power in Antitrust: Economic Analysis After *Kodak*," *Supreme Court Economic Review* 3 (1993): 43–92.

[40]Steven C. Salop, "Kodak as Post-Chicago Law and Economics," Charles River Associates, April 1993.

facturer's attempt to monopolize its aftermarket.[41] At the time of writing, this issue remains hotly debated in the economics profession.

It is useful to consider how the alleged tying affects the market and consumers. In *Microsoft*, the court noted that not all ties are bad.[42] Prior cases such as *Jefferson Parish* only focused on the tying—it did not go further to determine if the tying was necessarily bad. However, the "Supreme Court has already held that tying arrangements as a category are a type of business relationship that experience has shown always hurts competition."[43]

Measuring Damages from Tying

Damages analysis for tied products is similar to the analytical process used for horizontal price fixing. The expert may measure the difference between the price that would have been paid had there not been tying and the price that was actually paid.[44] This price difference can be applied to a measure of quantity to arrive at the amount of damages.

Part of the damages investigation process may be to try to determine if, but for the tying, there were other substitute products that were available at lower prices. If this cannot be done, then there may not be a basis for a damages claim. The expert's research needs to establish that the products were comparable in their features and characteristics.

Distributor Termination and Antitrust

Termination of distributors is a common type of case in which there are antitrust allegations along with possible other claims such as breach of contract. In order

---

[41]Severin Borenstein, Jeffery MacKie-Mason, and Janet S. Netz, "The Economics of Customer Lock-In and Market Power in Services," *The Service Productivity and Quality Challenge,* Patrick T. Harker, ed. *International Studies in The Service Economy* 5 (Dordrecht; Boston and London: Kluwer Academic, 1995): 225–250.

[42]*U.S. v. Microsoft Corp.*, 253 F3d at 87.

[43]Samuel Noah Weinstein, "Antitrust: Sherman Act Violations: 1. Monopolization a) Tying: United States v. Microsoft Corp.," *Berkeley Technology Law Journal* 17 (2002): 273–294.

[44]*Northern v. McGraw-Edison Co.*, 542 F2d 1336, 1347 (8th Cir. 1976), *cert. denied,* 429 U.S. 1097 (1977).

to seek relief under antitrust laws, the plaintiff ex-distributor needs to show a conspiracy on the part of the defendant to terminate the distributor as part of a process to reduce competition or monopolize a given market.

The methods used to measure damages from a termination of a distributor's agreement are similar to what has been discussed in this book. They often involve a measurement of reduced sales and an application of a relevant profit margin which will be applied to the amount of lost sales. One analysis that the expert may do in an antitrust case and not in another type of business interruption claim is an additional economic analysis. It is done to establish the economic effects of the anticompetitive behavior. This may be done to establish liability while the traditional damage measurement methods may be used to quantify the damages.

In cases where the terminated distributor has gone out of business it may be necessary to do a business valuation. This is done for the entire business in cases where it has closed, or it is done for a component of the business which may have ceased operating. If the plaintiff can establish that this segment of its overall operation could have been sold separately in a market for such entities, then the valuation may be easier to perform. The valuation may either show a diminished value or a loss of the entire value in cases where the entity no longer exists. The process of business valuation is discussed at length in Chapter Eight.

Just as in other types of damages analysis, the terminated distributor needs to take steps to mitigate its damages. This may involve locating alternative supply sources. If the plaintiff fails to take such reasonable steps, the court may find that the defendant is not liable for the plaintiff's damages, for they could have been avoided.[45]

However, changing suppliers may impose additional and unique costs on the plaintiff which may add to its damage claim. For example, there may be a variety of additional costs that the plaintiff incurred, ranging from a changeover of marketing materials, sales support items, etc. These costs may be added to the total damages.

SUMMARY

The field of antitrust litigation has grown in recent years after it declined for a period of time. Antitrust litigation presents many opportunities for experts to present economics damages testimony. Such work calls for experts to potentially

---

[45]*Golf City, Inc. v. Wilson Sporting Goods Co.*, 555 F2d 426, 436 (5th Cir. 1977).

present testimony on both the liability and the damages side of the case. While economists are the more common type of expert doing such work, accountants are also needed for certain aspects of the analysis that may be necessary.

Experts working in this area need to possess a strong background in microeconomics—particularly the subspecialty of industrial organization. However, both economists and accountants may provide valuable testimony on the damage-related issues of an antitrust action.

Several key laws provide the regulatory framework for antitrust enforcement. Primary among these is the Sherman Antitrust Act. This law is the cornerstone of U.S. antitrust laws. Other important laws include the Clayton Act, Federal Trade Commission Act, Celler-Kefauver Act, and the Hart-Scott-Rodino Antitrust Improvements Act. These laws have been interpreted, sometimes in conflicting ways, by many court decisions.

Antitrust laws are designed to prevent the formation of a monopoly, a market structure in which there is only one seller. In such a market structure, less output is sold in the market and the price is higher than what would occur in a more competitive market structure. As a market moves toward a more competitive structure, societal welfare may be increased.

Various quantitative methods can be employed to analyze the degree of competition in a given market. These methods may be used to assess the extent of any monopoly power that a firm may possess. Using tools that are mainstays in the world of industrial organization, the expert may be able to provide valuable assistance to the court in an antitrust proceeding.

REFERENCES

Areeda, Phillip E., and Donald F. Turner, "Predatory Pricing and Related Practices Under Section Two of the Sherman Act." *Harvard Law Review* 86.

Bogosian v. Gulf Oil Corp., 561 F2d 434, 454 (3rd Cir. 1977), *cert denied*, 434 U.S. 1086 (1987).

Borenstein, Severin, Jeffrey K. MacKie-Mason, and Janet S. Netz, "The Economics of Customer Lock-In and Market Power in Services." in *The Service Productivity and Quality Challenge*, Patrick T. Harker, ed. *International Studies in the Service Economy* 5. Dordrecht, Boston and London: Kluwer Academic, 1995.

Campbell, Christopher, "Notes and Comments: Fit to Be Tied: How *United States v. Microsoft Corp.* Incorrectly Changed the Standard for Sherman Act Tying Violations Involving Software." *Loyola of Los Angeles Entertainment Law Review* 22 (2002): 583–612.

Carlton, Dennis, and Jeffrey M. Perloff, *Modern Industrial Organization*, 3rd ed. New York: HarperCollins Publishers, 1994.

Denger, Michael L., and John A. Herfort, "Predatory Pricing Claims After Brooke Group." *Antitrust Law Journal* 62 (3) (spring 1994).

Easterbrook, Frank, " Predatory Strategies and Counterstrategies." *University of Chicago Law Review* 48 (2) (spring 1981).

Eastman Kodak Co. v. Image Tech. Services, 112 S. Ct. 2072, 2088 (1992).

Fishman v. Estate of Wirtz, 807 F2d 520, 551 (7th Cir. 1986).

Gaughan, Patrick A., *Mergers and Acquisitions.* New York: HarperCollins, 1991.

Gaughan, Patrick A., *Mergers, Acquisitions, and Corporate Restructuring*, 2nd ed. New York: Wiley, 1996.

Gaughan, Patrick A., *Mergers, Acquisitions, and Corporate Restructuring*, 3rd ed. New York:Wiley, 2002.

Golf City, Inc. v. Wilson Sporting Goods Co., 555 F2d 426, 436 (5th Cir. 1977).

Greer, Douglas, *Industrial Organization and Public Policy.* New York: Macmillan Publishing Company, 1992.

Image Technical Services, Inc. v. Eastman Kodak Co., 903 F2d, 612, 617 (9th Cir. 1990).

International Business Machines v. United States, 298 U.S. (1936).

Jefferson Parish Hospital No. 2 v. Hyde, 466 U.S. 2 (1984).

Jerrold Electronics Corp. v. United States, 187 F. Supp. 545 (1961).

Joskow, Paul L., and Alvin K. Klevorick, "A Framework for Analyzing Predatory Pricing Policy." *The Yale Law Journal* 89 (2) (December 1979).

Klein, Benjamin, "Market Power in Antitrust: Economic Analysis After Kodak." *Supreme Court Economic Review* 3 (1993).

Lopatka, John E. and William Page, "Who Suffered Antitrust Injury in the Microsoft Case." *George Washington Law Review* 69 (October–December, 2001).

McGee, John S., "Predatory Price Cutting: The Standard Oil Case." *Journal of Law and Economics* (October 1958).

McGee, John S., "Predatory Pricing Revisited." *Journal of Law and Economics* (October 1980).

Northern v. McGraw-Edison Co., 542 F2d 1336, 1347 (8th Cir. 1976), *cert. denied*, 429 U.S. 1097 (1977).

Posner, Richard A., *Antitrust Law: An Economic Perspective.* University of Chicago Press, 1987.

Posner, Richard A., "Antitrust in the New Economy," paper presented at the American Bar Association Antitrust Conference, New York City, September 14, 2000.

Salop, Steven C., "Kodak as Post-Chicago Law and Economics." Charles River Associates (April 1993).

Salop, Steven C., and David T. Scheffman, "Recent Advances in the Theory of Industrial Structure." *Recent Advances in the Theory of Industrial Structure* 73 (2) (May 1983).

Shapiro, Carl, and David J. Teece, "Systems Competition and Aftermarkets: An Economic Analysis of Kodak." *Antitrust Bulletin* 39 (1) (spring 1994).

Shugart, William F., "Monopoly and the Problem of the Economists." *Managerial and Decision Economics* 17 (2) (March–April, 1996): 221.

Standard Oil Company of New Jersey v. U.S. 221 U.S. 1 (1911).

Swanson, Carol, "Antitrust Excitement in the New Millennium: Microsoft, Mergers and More." *Oklahoma Law Review* (summer 2001): 285–338.

U.S. Bureau of the Census, 1982 Census of Manufactures, "Concentration Ratios in Manufacturing." Washington, D.C. (April 1986).

United States Football League v. National Football League, 842 F2d 1335 (2d Cir. 1988).

U.S. v. Aluminum Company of America et al., 148 F2d 416, 424 (1945).

U.S. v. American Tobacco Co., 221 U.S. 106 (1911).

United States v. Int. Bus. Mach. Corp., No. 69 Civ. 200 (S.D.N.Y., 1969).

U.S. v. Microsoft Corp., 253 F3d at 87.

U.S. v. New York Great Atlantic and Pacific Tea Company et al., 67 F. Supp. 626 (1946), 173 F2d (1949).

U.S. v. U.S. Steel Corporation, 251 U.S. 417 (1920).

Van Dyk Research Corp. v. Xerox Corp. 631 F2d 251, 255 (3rd Cir. 1980).

Weinstein, Samuel Noah, "Antitrust: Sherman Act Violations: 1. Monopolization a) Tying: United States v. Microsoft Corp." *Berkeley Technology Law Journal*, 17 (2002): 273–294.

Yamey, B. S., "Predatory Price Cutting: Notes and Comments." *Journal of Law and Economics* 15 (1972): 129.

12

THE ECONOMICS
OF PUNITIVE DAMAGES

The topic of punitive damages has evoked great debate both in the field of law and within the economics profession. Various groups, especially those representing potential defendants, have claimed that such damages are often inappropriate and "out of control." Such groups claim that the imposition of punitive damages often constitutes a violation of their right to due process. This chapter addresses the economics of punitive damages as they relate to corporations. The extent to which punitive damages serve the goals set forth in the law is explored. The chapter points out the various areas in which such damages may not serve the purposes of punitive damages as presented in the law. In addition, it reviews some of the approaches used by plaintiffs when making presentations to juries on punitives. Given that there are problems with some of these types of presentations, this chapter focuses on these problems and explores what can be done to address them.

EVOLVING POSITION OF THE U.S. SUPREME COURT
ON PUNITIVE DAMAGES

Punitive damages has a long history in the law. The doctrine of punitive damages can be traced with certainty back to English common law, although others have claimed that its roots begin even further back in history.[1] Punitive damages is a penalty that is applied in addition to compensatory damages when the defendant's conduct is judged to be particularly reprehensible.[2] While it has a long history, courts have struggled to reach a consistent position on punitive damages; they

---

[1]David Owen, "Punitive Damages in Products Liability Litigation," *Villanova Law Review* (June 1976): 1262.

[2]Second Restatement of Torts.

have yet to arrive at one. However, recent Supreme Court decisions have taken major strides in that direction.

Punitive damages are designed to further the twin goals of punishment and deterrence. In 1991, the U.S. Supreme Court, in *Pacific Mutual Life Insurance Co. v. Haslip,* articulated these goals when it stated that "punitive damages are imposed for purposes of retribution and deterrence."[3] In later decisions, the Court consistently reaffirmed these purposes. For example, in *Cooper Industries, Inc. v. Leatherman Tools Group, Inc.,* the Court stated:

> Punitive damages may properly be imposed to further a State's legitimate interests in punishing unlawful conduct and deterring its repetition.[4]

In 1993, in *TXO Production Corp. v. Alliance Resources Corp.,* the Court complicated matters by upholding a punitive damages award of ten million dollars with a compensatory damages amount of $19,000.[5] In this case, punitive damages were 526 times what the compensatory damages were. Some had concluded that the argument over the use of such a high ratio of punitive to compensatory damages as a violation of due process was a dead issue.[6] However, the issue of the magnitude of the punitive/compensatory multiplier is complex, because in this case, the Court also considered potential—not just actual—compensatory damages. Thus, the *TXO* decision was not an endorsement by the Supreme Court of such a high multiplier: it considered a denominator that was significantly higher.

In 1996, in *BMW of North America v. Gore,* the U.S. Supreme Court found that an award of $145 million in punitive damages and one million dollars in compensatory damages violated the due process clause of the Fourteenth Amendment of the United States Constitution.[7] In reaching its decision, the Gore court named three factors or guideposts that courts should consider when reaching a decision on punitive damages:

1. the degree of reprehensibility of the defendant's conduct
2. the disparity between the actual and potential harm
3. the disparity between a jury's award of punitive damages and civil penalties imposed in other cases

---

[3]*Pacific Mutual Life Insurance Co. v. Haslip,* 499 U.S. 1, 19 (1991).

[4]*Cooper Industries, Inc. v. Leatherman Tool Group, Inc.,* 532 U.S. 424, 433. (2001).

[5]*TXO Production Corp. v. Alliance Resources Corp.,* 509 U.S. 443, 475 (1993).

[6]Colbern C. Stuart, "Mean Stupid Defendants Jarring Our Constitutional Sensibilities," *California Western Law Review* 30 (1994).

[7]*BMW of North America v. Gore,* 517 U.S. 599. (1996)

In 2001, in *Cooper Industries, Inc. v. Leatherman Tool Group, Inc.*, the Supreme Court stated that the due process clause prohibited the imposition of "grossly excessive or arbitrary punishments."[8] In this decision, the Court stated that a trial court's application of the *Gore* guideposts was subject to *de novo* review.

On April 7, 2003, the Court more explicitly addressed the punitive multiplier as well as other factors taken into account when determining a punitive damages award. In *State Farm Mutual Automobile Insurance Co. v. Campbell et al.*, the Court applied the *Gore* factors to a Utah case involving an insurer's claims against their automobile insurance company.[9] In going through the factors, the Court clarified how they apply to different lawsuits. The *Campbell* decision did not prescribe a specific multiplier, but it did state that "few awards exceeding a single digit ratio between punitive and compensatory damages will satisfy due process." Indeed, the Court, in citing *Haslip,* did say "an award of more than four times the amount of compensatory damages might be close to the line of constitutional propriety." The Court found this ratio to be "instructive." This decision set a precedent in that it was only the second time that the Supreme Court reduced a punitive damages award that was handed down by a jury. Even though *BMW of North America v. Gore* seemed to lend some stability to the process of arriving at and evaluating punitive awards, various state courts have awarded punitive damages without bound or a reasonable basis. In *Engle v. R.J. Reynolds Tobacco Co.*, a class-action suit alleging smoking-related injuries in the State of Florida, a jury in 2002 awarded an unprecedented $144.8 billion in punitive damages.[10] The fact that this award far exceeds the defendants' ability to pay it (and will bankrupt them if the plaintiffs do not prevail on appeal) seemed to be lost in the verdict determination process. What is even more troubling are the specious analytical grounds upon which the verdict was based. The decision was later reversed by Florida's Third District Court of Appeal. This case shows that the problem of punitive damages remains one that is not fully understood by the court, particularly in the field of mass torts.[11] While it is the most extreme example, it is not an isolated case. In a more recent decision on March 21, 2003, in *Miles v. Philip Morris,* a class action, an Illinois court

[8]*Cooper Industries, Inc. v. Leatherman Tool Group, Inc.*, 532 U.S. 424, 433 (2001).

[9]*State Farm Mutual Automobile Insurance Co. v. Campbell et al.* No. 01–1289.

[10]*Engle v. RJ Reynolds Tobacco Co.* No. 94–08273 (Fla. 11th Cir. CT. Nov. 6, 2000–final judgment).

[11]Brian H. Barr, "*Engle v. R.J. Reynolds:* The Improper Assessment of Punitive Damages for an Entire Class of Injured Smokers," *Florida State Law Review* 28 (spring 2001): 787.

entered a judgment against Philip Morris for $10.1 billion in total damages of which $3.1 were punitive.[12]

Some have theorized that part of the purpose of the Court's decision in *BMW of North America v. Gore* was to send a message to lower courts to "tighten its grip on punitive awards." If this is so, then it is clear that many state courts have yet to receive the message.[13]

The *State Farm v. Campbell et al.* decision addressed other areas that are quite relevant to the economic of punitive damages. Specifically, these include the inclusion of out-of-state factors as well as the potential bias in the intro-duction of net worth measures. These will be addressed separately later in this chapter.

FREQUENCY OF PUNITIVE DAMAGES

Punitive damages are awarded relatively infrequently. It is well known that the majority of cases do not go to trial; however, of those that ultimately do, only a minority feature punitive damages. For example, Landes and Posner found that only 2 percent of product liability cases result in punitive damages.[14] Another study showed an even smaller percentage. In looking at certain localities, the Rand study found punitive damages occurred in only 1/10 of 1 percent in Cook County and even less in San Francisco.[15] Rustad and Koenig could only locate 344 cases with punitive damages in a quarter of a century of cases.[16] Other stud-ies show a somewhat higher incidence of punitive damages. For example, the American Bar Foundation study found punitive damages in 4.9 percent of all ver-

---

[12]*Miles v. Philip Morris,* 2003

[13]Brian McKee, "The Implication of *BMW v. Gore* for Future Punitive Litigation: Observation from a Participant," *Alabama Law Review* 175 (1996), and Meghan A. Crowley, "From Punishment to Annihilation: *Engle v. R.J. Reynold Tobacco Co.*—No More Butts: Punitive Damages Have Gone Too Far," *Loyola Los Angeles Law Review* (June 2001): 1513–1532.

[14]William M. Landes and Richard A. Posner, "New Light on Punitive Damages," *Regulation* (September–October 1986): 33.

[15]Mark Peterson et al., "Punitive Damages: Empirical Findings," Rand Institute for Civil Justice (1987): R–3311–ICJ.

[16]Michael Rustad, "In Defense of Punitive Damages in Product Liability: Testing Tort Anecdotes with Empirical Data," *Iowa Law Review* 78 (1992).

Table 12.1 Punitive Awards Across Selected Industry Categories

Type of Case	# Awards	Punitive Awards as % of # Verdicts	Mean Punitive Awards (1992 $)
Insurance	134	13	7,933,676
Employment	125	17	2,689,033
Securities	6	21	30,269,389
Real Property	113	12	2,100,000
Other Contracts	258	15	6,283,804
Other Commercial	11	36	1,654,966

Source: Adapted from CitiGroup Smith Barney, April 7, 2003, Industry Note, "Damages Ruling May Limit Corporate Exposure."

dicts in their research sample.[17] A study conducted by the Justice Department found a somewhat higher rate—6 percent.[18]

Variation in Punitive Damages Across Industries

Some industries seem to be more of a target for punitive damages than others. A study by the Rand Institute showed that for their sample, the average punitive award in the securities industry was almost four times greater than awards in the insurance industry (see Table 12.1). Compared to other industry categories, such as real property, the awards were more than 14 times greater in the securities industry.[19] The variability across industry categories has given rise to concerns about uniformity and fairness.

FREQUENCY OF PUNITIVE DAMAGES AND THE SHADOW EFFECT OF PUNITIVE DAMAGES

A look at the relative frequency of punitive damages in verdicts might initially lead one to incorrectly conclude that because they are so infrequently awarded they need not be a major source of concern. However, the threat of punitive dam-

---

[17]Steve Daniels and Joanne Martin, "Myth and Reality in Punitive Damages," *Minnesota Law Review* 1 (1990).

[18]Carol DeFrances et al., "Civil Jury Cases and Verdicts in Large Counties," U.S. Department of Civil Justice, 1995.

[19]CitiGroup Smith Barney, April 7, 2003, Industry Note, "Damages Ruling May Limit Corporate Exposure."

ages permeates the negotiations of many more lawsuits than the aforementioned studies indicate. Intimidated by the threat of punitive damages, defendants who fear a runaway punitive verdict often settle for a probability-adjusted amount that includes their assessment of the likelihood of a punitive damages award. This is what is known as the *shadow effect of punitive damages.*

Defendants had long contended that the shadow effect was very significant. Few, however, were able to specifically quantify it. One attempt to do so was conducted by Koenig, who gathered insurance adjustor data and sought to determine what component of total settlements they allocated to punitive damages. He found that claims adjusters allocated a specific amount of total settlement values, 11 percent, to avoid claims of punitive damages.[20] Eleven percent may seem relatively small, but when this amount is combined with the fact the percent of cases that award punitive damages is also relatively small, the amount becomes quite significant.

Taxes, Insurance, and the Incidence of Punitive Damages

Even in settlement data, punitive damages are difficult to identify. This is due to the fact that when arriving at a settlement agreement, both the plaintiff and the defendant, but especially the plaintiff, have incentives to not identify settlement amounts as punitive damages. Settlement amounts designated as compensatory damages may not be taxed.[21] The Federal tax laws were amended by the Omnibus Budget Reconciliation Act of 1989 to expressly exclude punitive damages.[22] Having an award designated as taxable significantly lowers the net after-tax benefits to the plaintiff.

Some courts have demonstrated a reluctance to enforce insurance agreements for punitive damages. This, combined with the fact that insurance against such damages is difficult to acquire, may give defendants an incentive to not identify a settlement amount as punitive damages.[23] The economic incentives are such that designating parts of a settlement as punitive damages lowers the benefit to

---

[20]Thomas Koenig, "The Shadow Effect of Punitive Damages," *Wisconsin Law Review* (1998): 169–209.

[21]Section 104 of the Internal Revenue Code.

[22]Joseph M. Dodge, "Taxes and Torts," *Cornell Law Review* (January 1992).

[23]George L. Priest, "Insurability and Punitive Damages," *Alabama Law Review* 40 (3) (spring 1989): 1009–1012.

the plaintiff and may possibly raise the cost to the defendant. This is why even in settlement data, it is difficult to parse out the punitive component. However, it is reasonable to assume that it is there even if it is not designated as such.

PURPOSES OF PUNITIVE DAMAGES

As discussed earlier, it is well accepted that the twin purposes of punitive damages are punishment and deterrence.[24] The Supreme Court, in its recent decisions relating to punitive damages, *Cooper Industries v. Leatherman* and *State Farm Mutual v. Campbell,* has confirmed this. Punitive damages are "not compensation for injury. Instead, they are private fines levied by civil juries to punish reprehensible conduct and to deter its future occurrence."[25] They are awarded for acts that are so extreme that the trier of the facts seeks additional penalties beyond compensatory damages. Punishment in the form of monetary penalties is not designed to compensate victims but is instead directed at the wrongdoer. These penalties seek to punish the defendant for its wrongful acts.

Deterrence can take two forms: specific and general deterrence.[26] Specific deterrence is designed to prevent the defendant from engaging in similar acts in the future. General deterrence is designed to prevent parties other than the defendant from pursuing similar acts. Of the two goals of punitive damages, there is some support in the literature for deterrence as the more important of the two goals.[27]

Although one might think that it is desirable to take whatever measures are necessary to avoid all wrongful acts, economists believe that it is most efficient to pursue optimal deterrence and to avoid underdeterrence or overdeterrence. Overdeterrence occurs if resources devoted to deterrence are in excess of the value of the harm that was avoided. Underdeterrence occurs when insufficient resources are devoted to avoidance when comparing the value of the harm to the resources expended. Economists generally agree that there is an efficient level of deterrence and that either overdeterrence or underdeterrence is not desirable from a societal perspective. For companies producing socially desirable products, such

---

[24]Second Restatement of Torts (second), 908 (1) 1979.

[25]*Gertz v. Robert Welch, Inc.,* 418 U.S. 323, 350 (1974).

[26]Dorsey D. Ellis, "Fairness and Efficiency in the Law of Punitive Damages," 56 S. *California Law Review* 1 (1982): 8–9.

[27]David G. Owen, "Symposium: Punitive Awards in Product Liability Litigation: Strong Medicine or Poison Pill?: A Punitive Damages Overview: Function, Problems and Reform," *Villanova Law Review* 39 (1994).

as pharmaceutical companies, overdeterrence could mean that some products never get produced and marketed if a company believes that the potential litigation costs are too high. This could have serious adverse effects for consumers who would benefit from such products. Ironically, this overdeterrence can spill over to companies in other industries as they worry about being the target of suits that have affected other companies.

PUNISHMENT OF CORPORATIONS AND CORPORATE GOVERNANCE

There are very significant differences between the punishment of individuals and the punishment of corporations. When a trier of the facts concludes that an individual defendant needs to be punished, it is easy to focus on that defendant and to know that he or she will bear any penalty that is imposed. The situation is much less clear in the case of corporate defendants.[28] This is due to the nature of corporate organizations.

The ultimate owners of corporations are shareholders who elect directors to serve as their fiduciaries and to oversee the management so as to maximize the value of their investment. These directors select managers who run the corporations on a day-to-day basis. Some managers also serve as directors; they are referred to as inside board members. As a result of recent scandals involving companies like Enron, Worldcom, and Tyco, there has been pressure on outside board members to exercise closer scrutiny on their corporations.

Corporations group together various stakeholders toward some common economic activity. These stakeholders typically include equity and nonequity stakeholders. Equity stakeholders hold an ownership interest in the company. Nonequity stakeholders include employees, management, suppliers, communities, recipients of tax receipts, and possibly others, depending on the circumstances.

SPILLOVER EFFECTS AND PUNISHMENT OF CORPORATIONS

One of the problems with punishing a corporation is that the pain inflicted may be felt by those other than the wrongdoers. This is made possible by the doctrine

---

[28]John Coffee, "No Soul to Damm, No Body to Kick," *Michigan Law Review* (January 1981).

of *vicarious liability* whereby an employer can be found liable for acts of its employees. This is also known as the *respondent superior rule*. The concept of spillover effects is well known in microeconomics—especially in the field of public finance. Spillovers are what are referred to in microeconomics as externalities. These effects are defined as "A cost or benefit resulting from some activity or transaction that is imposed or bestowed on parties outside the activity or transaction. Sometimes called spillovers or neighborhood effects."[29]

It is difficult to isolate and punish the individual wrongdoers in a company. If one chooses to use the blunt tool of punitive damages, it is likely that innocent parties will bear the adverse effects of such an imprecise instrument. The guilty individuals, however, may have "long departed the scene." The latter becomes particularly likely when the lawsuit reaches trial many years after the alleged acts. The tobacco and asbestos lawsuits present some examples of such scenarios.

It is useful to focus on who the various stakeholders in a corporation are and see how they could be affected by a punitive award.

Equity Stakeholders

Shareholders are the true owners of the corporations. Stock is the first security to be issued when a corporation is formed and the last to be retired. Equityholders are entitled to a share of the profits from the corporation's business activities after other claims holders, such as creditors, have been paid. Since they profit from the company's activities through dividends and possible capital gains, it would initially seem appropriate that they should bear the impact of a punitive penalty. However, there are problems with such reasoning. One has to do with the nature of stock ownership of many corporations. For many closely held corporations, there may be little distinction between the owners of the company and the company's management and decision makers. Such companies may be run like sole proprietorships who are seeking the protection of the limited liability features of the corporate business form. Here, the corporate decisions which resulted in the imposition of the penalty may have been made by the same parties who are entitled to receive the residual profits. In such cases, the wrongdoer and the ones who bear the penalty may be one and the same. This may even be true for smaller publicly held companies in which share ownership is concentrated in the hands of few shareholders who may also take an active role managing the company. However,

---

[29]Karl Case and Ray Fair, *Principles of Economics*, 6th ed. (Upper Saddle River, NJ: Prentice-Hall, 2002): 318.

as one's focus moves to larger publicly held corporations, the gap between owner-ship and control becomes wider. In such larger publicly held companies, share-holders typically have little control. Shares tend to be widely distributed and few shareholders amass a significant percentage of the corporation's total shares outstanding.

Nature of Stock Ownership in the United States

The ownership of the stock of U.S. corporations has become increasingly con-centrated in the hands of institutions.[30] The three largest types of institutions are mutual funds, pension funds, and insurance companies. Each of these three types of organizations holds shares on behalf of many individuals who typically have little control or even contact with the corporations. While institutions have be-come somewhat more activist, they are still relatively passive and cannot be involved in the micromanagement of corporations. Each company may com-prise a relatively small part of its overall portfolio. In addition, through the risk-reduction benefits of portfolio formation, an institution's exposure to the troubles of a single corporation—what is refered to in corporate finance as unsystematic risk—tends to be limited.[31]

Nonequity Stakeholders

There are two groups of nonequity stakeholders: internal and external. Internal stakeholders include management and nonmanagement employees. Both groups have a vested interest in the success and growth of the corporations; they gener-ally derive their livelihood from the business. Managers attempt to direct the company's activities while nonmanagement employees generally carry out these decisions. Even within the management group, however, managers may make very different types of decisions. In the case of punitive damages, the wrongful acts could be committed by mid-level managers without the knowledge of either upper management or other employees. The problem of isolating the wrongdoers

---

[30]Carolyn Brancato and Patrick Gaughan, "The Growth of Institutional Investors in U.S. Capital Markets," Columbia University School of Law, *Center for Law and Economic Studies Monograph* (fall 1988).

[31]Stephen Ross, Randolph Westerfield, and Bradford Jordan, *Essentials of Corporate Finance*, 4th ed. (Boston: Irwin, 2004), 333.

becomes even more complicated when one considers employee turnover. This issue is discussed later in this chapter in the context of punishing the wrongdoers.

In addition to management, other stakeholders are nonmanagement employees. At most corporations, the ranks of nonmanagement employees are larger than those of management. However, in addition to employees, other stakeholders include suppliers who may depend on a defendant's corporation for an important component of its business. When a customer's business increases, its suppliers are positively impacted. The reverse is often true. Increased costs, such as litigation-related costs, may cause a company to cut back on the scale of its operations, and this may have an adverse effect on nonequity stakeholders.

Shareholder Wealth Effects

Litigation-related payments, like any other cost, lowers profitability and reduces the pool of monies available for dividends, thereby impeding capital gains. For this reason, large litigation payments can lower stock values. Research studies have shown the impact that litigation has on stock prices.[32] This impact can be very significant. A good example of this was the 42 percent decline in the stock price of the Halliburton Company in response to a $30 million verdict in favor of five plaintiffs (see Exhibit 12.1).[33] This was one of many asbestos cases brought against the company.[34] Over the previous quarter of a century, the company had settled almost 200,000 asbestos claims, but these claims were usually settled for modest amounts. The market reacted to that recent verdict as it marked a possible change in the asbestos litigation environment.

Securities firms have attempted to measure the magnitude of the large tobacco liabilities on Philip Morris Companies, Inc. By the end of 2002, Philip Morris USA, the tobacco subsidiary of Altria, had been the object of 1,500 tobacco law-

---

[32]John M. Bizjak and Jeffrey L. Coles, "The Effect of Private Antitrust Litigation on the Stock Market Valuation of the Firm," *The American Economic Review* 85 (3) (June 1995): 436–461.

[33]Neela Banerjee, "Halliburton Battered as Asbestos Verdict Stirs Deep Anxieties," *New York Times* (December 8, 2001): C1.

[34]It should be noted that Halliburton stock's price had been declining since May 2001, when the stock price was as high as $49.25, due to not only asbestos liabilities but also to a general market decline as well as due to fallout from the Enron debacle. However, the sharp decline on December 7, 2001 can be more directly attributed to the recent asbestos verdict.

Exhibit 12.1   Stock performance of Halliburton, Co.

suits.[35] Some of these suits were class actions and multiple-plaintiff suits. For example, in West Virginia, the company was the object of a class action involving 1,250 plaintiffs. Analysts at Goldman Sachs issued a report in February 2001 in which they did a "sum of the parts" analysis. They computed the enterprise value of the company by applying multiples that would be relevant to the four industry segments that at that time composed the overall parent entity—Philip Morris Companies, Inc.[36] This study showed that the "litigation overhang" was equal to $91.5 billion.[37] That is, without the impending litigation liabilities, which are inherently difficult to measure with precision, the value of the equity of Philip Morris Companies, Inc. should have been equal to $200 billion. However, the value that the market placed on the equity was $108.7 billion. The analysts at Goldman Sachs attributed this very significant difference to the market's allowance for the uncertain tobacco liabilities.

The Goldman Sachs analysis is but one of many examples of how stocks can be negatively affected by litigation liabilities. The relevance of these effects to puni-

---

[35]Altira Annual Report: 2002.

[36]Since the issuance of that report Philip Morris Companies, now Altria, has merged its Miller Brewing subsidiary into the South African Brewing Company to form SABMiller plc.

[37]Goldman Sachs Analyst Report, February 13, 2001.

tive damages is that the imposition of a significant punitive award may cause stock prices to decline. As a result, shareholders may lose part or all of the value of their investments. Markets tend to anticipate relevant changes in economic conditions and are generally efficient with respect to the processing of relevant information.[38]

While shareholders bear some of the costs of a punitive award, they are generally removed from the decision-making process. As such, they are not in a good position to take actions to prevent such losses. Some assert that shareholders can use the corporate election process to try to bring about changes in management's behavior. However, this is a very expensive and difficult process that is usually unsuccessful—even for shareholders holding sizeable stock positions.[39] Prior to reaching a decision on punitive damages, juries should be aware of the potential impact an award may have on shareholders. They should also know who these shareholders are and what responsibility, if any, they bore for the wrongful conduct. It is often the case that most of the shares are owned by large institutions managing share holdings on behalf of many individuals, such as those who have entrusted their wealth to a pension fund management firm. For this reason, juries might feel differently about making an award that would hurt such shareholders.

Another group of securities holders who may be adversely affected by litigation-related liabilities are bondholders and other creditors. If the bond market perceives that a lawsuit will threaten the ability of a defendant corporation to meet the stipulated bond interest and principal payments, the demand for bonds may fall, causing the price to decline. Rating agencies, such as Standard & Poor's and Moody's, monitor such events and may respond to a significant change in a company's bond ratings. This may cause adverse wealth effects for bondholders who are clearly not responsible for the actions that are at issue in a lawsuit. An example of such recent ratings declines came in May 2003 when Fitch Ratings slashed its overall rating of some of the bonds of RJ Reynolds Tobacco Holdings as a result of the $10.1 billion judgment against Altria's Philip Morris USA unit.[40] The ratings on these bonds were reported to have fallen below investment grade status to junk bond levels.

---

[38]There is an abundant literature in corporate finance on market efficiency which refers to the speed with which markets process and respond to relevant information. There is still a wide debate in finance as just how efficient markets are and to what extent there exist market anomalies or exceptions to market efficiency.

[39]See John Pound, "Shareholder Activism and Share Values," *Journal of Law and Economics* (October 1989): 357–379, and Patrick A. Gaughan, *Mergers Acquisitions, and Corporate Restructurings,* 3rd ed. (New York: Wiley, 2003), 265–281.

[40]Vanessa O'Connell, "Cigarette Industry Debt Ratings Cut by Fitch," *Wall Street Journal,* May 7, 2003, p. B6.

Regional Economic Effects

Various economic entities can be adversely affected by a litigation-induced cut-back in the level of a defendant's business operations. Among the entities which may experience such adverse effects are suppliers whose volume of business is tied to the defendant's purchases. Such suppliers may, in turn, respond to a lower volume of business by enacting their own cutbacks. In addition to suppliers, other stakeholders sometimes includes communities in which the defendant corporations do substantial business. Communities may depend on corporations for direct charitable contributions and for the positive economic effects that such entities have on the regional economy. This is why when plants are forced to close, communities often suffer significant adverse effects such as rising unemployment and other financial burdens. Companies which are encumbered by large litigation liabilities may be forced to engage in mass layoffs. This was the case, for example, when ABB announced that it was eliminating 12,000 jobs, over 7 percent of its workforce, as a result of the combined pressure of litigation expenses, a weak economy, and its own debt burden.[41] Displaced workers may be forced to replace their high-paying manufacturing jobs with positions that pay much less.[42] Such effects are immediately apparent in communities where specific corporations comprise a high percentage of a community's total employment. An example includes the negative economic effects that the Pennsylvania communities of Allentown and Bethlehem experienced when the steel industry contracted and companies were forced to lay off workers and close plants.[43]

Other spillover effects on stakeholders can occur if the costs of the litigation cause a defendant corporation to downsize or limit expenditures it would have devoted to other stakeholders such as communities (in the form of charitable contributions, for example). Macroeconomic theory shows that such cutbacks in expenditures have total adverse effects that are a multiple of the original reduction.[44] Insofar as the affected corporations are regionally concentrated, these adverse effects are also more concentrated within a region. Regional expenditure

---

[41]"ABB to Make Deeper Cuts," October 24, 2002, CNN.com.

[42]Elizabeth Patch, *Plant Closings and Employment Loss in Manufacturing* (New York: Garland Publishing, 1995), 7–9.

[43]John Strohmeyer, *Crisis in Bethlehem: Big Steel's Struggle to Survive* (Pittsburgh, PA: University of Pittsburgh Press, 1994).

[44]Such expenditures are explained in a major principles of economics textbooks in the contest of Keynesian expenditure multipliers. See for example Paul Samuelson and William Nordhaus, *Economics,* 16th ed. (New York: McGraw-Hill, 1998), 446–462.

multipliers that attempt to measure the aggregate impact of expenditures may be used to quantitatively measure the total adverse impact that a cutback in corporate expenditures has. These multipliers try to measure how many dollars are ultimately spent when a given dollar is spent. Economic models exist that attempt to measure the magnitude of such multipliers.[45] Such multipliers can be employed when trying to measure the adverse impact that a reduction in expenditures, caused by cutbacks in the wake of a significant punitive award, may have.

For economically diverse regions that are not dependent on a single company or industry for a large percentage of their employment, litigation-induced downsizing by a defendant may have less painful effects. For regions that are less economically diverse, however, the alternative employment opportunities are often more limited.[46] In addition, an accurate evaluation of the impact of litigation-related downsizing must also consider the total compensation of the lost jobs and the replacement positions. For example, if unionized manufacturing jobs are lost, and are replaced by low-paying service positions, then there would be significant adverse employment effects.[47]

Government and Public Sector Effects

Still another community effect derives from the fact that a punitive damages award is a taxable expense. Whether such damage awards should be tax-deductible has been a contentious issue. Some assert that allowing defendants the expense of punitive damages frustrates public policy which seeks to have corporations avoid behavior which a jury might determine to be reprehensible.[48] Although this issue has come up for debate, Congress has not changed the

[45]Dan S. Rickman and R. Keith Schwer, "A Comparison of the Multipliers of Implan, REMI and RIMS II: Benchmarking ready made models for comparison," *The Annals of Regional Science* 29 (1995): 363–374. The inclusion of this reference should not be construed as a verification or validation of this particular model but is merely included to show that models which attempt to measure regional multipliers do exist.

[46]Elizabeth P. Patch, *Plant Closings and Employment Loss in Manufacturing* (New York: Garland Publishing, 1995).

[47]Ronald Ehrenberg and Robert Smith, *Modern Labor Economics,* 7th ed. (New York: Addison Wesley and Longham, 2000), 508.

[48]Kimberly Pace, "The Tax Deductibility of Punitive Damage Payments: Who Should Ultimately Bear the Burden for Corporate Misconduct," *Alabama Law Review* 47 (spring 1996).

deductibility of this expense. This implies that recipients of tax revenues and tax-payers will bear some of the burden of the award. Given the tax effects which give plaintiffs an incentive to request that defendants do not designate the monies paid as punitive damages, this is less of an issue than it would be without such a plaintiff-based preference.

As part of the economic impact analysis of a punitive damages award, the tax payments made by a defendant may be another facet of the overall economic picture. Communities that depend on the receipts of taxes paid by a defendant may be adversely affected when a defendant downsizes as a result of a significant punitive award (or a series of such awards). However, if competitors expand to absorb the market share lost by a defendant, the net effects would be the relevant ones. A complete analysis of these effects can be complicated. If the competitors are in a different region, then federal taxes paid may offset each other. However, the regional tax effects would constitute a gain to the competitor's communities and their tax base and a loss to the defendant's community. Juries may be more sensitive to economic effects closer to their own community than those farther from their borders.

Consumers

One other major affected group of stakeholders are consumers of the defendant's products. This group may also feel the effects of a punitive damages award through a price adjustment. Prominent examples include the tobacco and pharmaceutical industries. One example is the increase in cigarette prices in response to the Master Settlement Agreement and its billion dollar payments.[49] In the pharmaceutical industry, research has also shown how drug prices are higher in a more active litigation environment.[50] Price increases brought on by litigation-related costs are similar to per-unit or excise taxes; microeconomic theory has shown this to be a form of regressive taxation. "Taxes on tobacco and alcohol are examples of regressive taxes, since poor individuals spend a larger fraction of their income on these goods."[51] If punitive or other damage awards cause corpo-

---

[49]Master Settlement Agreement Between the States and the U.S. Tobacco Producers, 1998.

[50]Richard Manning, "Products Liability and Prescription Drug Prices in Canada and the U.S." *Journal of Law & Economics* (April 1997): 203–243.

[51]Joseph E. Stiglitz, *Economics,* 2nd ed. (New York: Norton, 1997), 526.

rations to react by increasing prices, poorer consumers may bear a disproportionate burden relative to their income levels.

The extent to which prices increase in response to cost increases by producers is determined by the price elasticity of demand for the products. With an inelastic demand, prices may increase with a comparatively smaller quantity decrease (see Exhibit 12.2a). With an elastic demand, the quantity demanded responds comparatively more (see Exhibit 12.2b). Various factors determine a product's price elasticity including availability of substitutes, tastes and preferences, and the percent of an individual's total budget the product constitutes.[52] The price elasticity of demand tends to be higher in the long run than in the short run.[53] In the case of cigarettes, various estimates of elasticities exist. One such estimate is that the short-run price elasticity of demand is 0.4 and the long-run is 0.70—both of which are in the inelastic range.[54] However, these estimates are drawn from a different time period in which prices were lower and quantity demanded was less elastic than it now appears to be.

Although the initial responsiveness was relatively sluggish, the cigarette industry does provide an informative showcase for how litigation-related cost

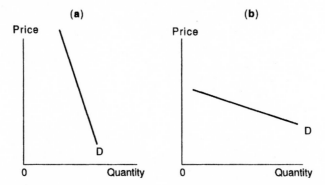

Exhibit 12.2   (a) Inelastic demand curve. (b) Elastic demand curve.

---

[52]John Taylor, *Economics,* 2nd ed. (New York: Houghton Mifflin, 1998), 98–100.

[53]Michael Parkin, *Economics,* 5th ed. (New York: Addison-Wesley Longham, 2000), 94.

[54]Michael Grossman, "The Economics of Substance Use and Abuse: The Role of Price," Economic analysis of substance use and abuse: The experience of developed countries (*Academia Studies in Asian Economies,* Cheltenham, U.K. and Northampton, MA: Elgar; distributed by American International Distribution Corporation, Williston, VT), 2001.

increases affect the quantity consumed and the market share of defendants in mass tort cases. Initially, presumably due to the inelastic nature of the demand for the product, while sales of cigarettes declined, though some of the manufacturers were able to maintain profitability for a period of time through the price increases. However, many consumers of this industry's products, who, on average, have somewhat lower incomes, did respond by switching to cheaper cigarettes from smaller manufacturers.[55] At the time the Master Settlement Agreement was signed, the major cigarette manufacturers commanded close to 100 percent of the market share. By 2002, the lesser known manufacturers accounted for 10 percent of the total U.S. cigarette market.

It is difficult for a jury to make a determination of the price effects and impact on consumers. Data on historical elasticities are not very helpful if prices change significantly and there is a new, more responsive or elastic part of the demand curve, assuming the curve does not shift due to other factors (see Exhibit 12.3). However, a jury may not be able to ignore the fact that when a company's costs change, prices may increase in response. Punitive damages are a cost, and corporations have to address these changing costs and the potential impact this may have on prices. These price effects can bring about a change in quantity demanded (the extent of which will depend on the relevant price elasticity of demand), a factor that a jury may want to consider after hearing economic expert testimony.

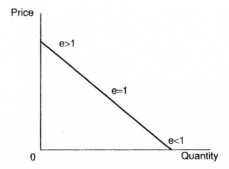

Exhibit 12.3   Elasticity of demand curve.

[55]Gordon Fairclough, "Four Biggest Cigarette Makers Can't Raise Prices as They Did," *Wall Street Journal* (October 25, 2002): 1.

Punishment of Corporations
and Focusing on the Wrongdoers

Having discussed the nature of corporations, which are broad entities composed of different groups of stakeholders, it is not hard to understand that the use of punitive damages may fail to inflict punishment on the wrongdoers. This is not a novel concept; it has been debated in law journals for decades.[56] As noted earlier, the parties responsible for the wrongful acts could be mid-level managers. They may have left the employ of the corporation prior to trial. It may even be the case that the upper management of the company was not aware of the actions of these employees.

The problem of isolating the wrongdoers is complicated by employee turnover. It has increased greatly over the past few decades. This is even true for upper managers and directors. Brickley showed that the average tenure of a chief executive is eight years.[57] A recent Booz Allen study provides some evidence that the rate of CEO turnover may be accelerating.[58] Hameralin and Weisbach showed that the average tenure of a corporate directors is nine years.[59] Given the length of time between a wrongful act that results in a lawsuit and the date of trial, it is conceivable that many, if not all of the wrongdoers, are not even with the company at the time of trial. Plaintiffs who seek punitive damages may not even care if the individual wrongdoers are pursued as they may only seek an outcome that yields the greatest financial payout. In such instances, however, punitive penalties are paid by those other than the wrongdoers.

The imposition of punitive damages may not hurt the wrongdoers but may cause various stakeholders to pay a financial penalty for actions in which they had no part. This problem is particularly true in cases where there is a long lag between the alleged wrongdoing and the trial. A jury should be made aware of the expected effects so it can make an enlightened judgment.

---

[56]John Coffee, "Corporate Crime and Punishment: A Non-Chicago View of the Economics of Criminal Sanctions," *American Criminal Law Review* 17 (1980): 419–476.

[57]James Brickley, "What Happens to CEOs After They Retire? New Evidence on Career Concerns, Horizon Problems and CEO Incentives," *Journal of Financial Economics* 52 (1999): 341–377.

[58]CEO Turnover Study, Booz Allen Hamilton, 2003.

[59]Benjamin E. Hameralin and Michael S. Weisbach, "The Determinants of Board Composition," *Rand Journal of Economics* 29 (4) (winter 1988): 589–606.

DETERRENCE THEORY
AND THE CHANGING LITIGATION ENVIRONMENT

The role of the probability of detection and deterrence theory were analyzed at length by Polinsky and Shavell.[60] Their approach to computing a punitive penalty is not new and can actually be traced to Jeremy Bentham and the Utilitarians.[61] However, Polinsky and Shavell provide a clear framework for how, theoretically, the probability of detection could be incorporated into the process of determining a punitive award. Because from a societal perspective it is not optimal to have either too many or too few precautions, they reasoned that total damages should equal the harm caused. If the probability of being found liable, however, is less than one, then there could be a need for punitive damages to make up for the shortfall between the value of the harm caused (H) and the expected damages (p)H, where p is the probability of being found liable. Using these calculations, they expressed a total damages multiplier and a punitive damages multiplier as follows:

$$\text{Damages Multiplier:} = (1/p) \qquad (12.1)$$

where H = harm caused, p = probability of being found liable, and D = total damages

$$D = H/p = H \,(1/p) \qquad (12.2)$$

while the Punitive Damages Multiplier = $[(1 - p)/p]$

The probabilities of being detected and found liable may be different at the time the wrongful act was committed and at the trial. This lag can be many years. If a jury is attempting to assess the deterrence effects and utilize a Polinsky–Shavell type of probability analysis, it is useful to differentiate between *ex ante* and *ex post* probabilities. The *ex ante* probability is the probability of being found liable as of the time the act is committed. While a plaintiff may want to assert that this is the relevant probability (assuming that such plaintiffs choose to put forward such reasoning at trial), the *ex post* probability—the one that exists at the time a jury makes a decision—is the more relevant. This is due to the fact that deterrence is forward-looking. Punishment is backward-looking.[62] To the extent that the litigation envi-

---

[60]A. Mitchell Polinsky and Steven Shavell, "Punitive Damages and Economic Analysis," *Harvard Law Review* III (1998): 870-962.

[61]Jeremy Bentham, *Theory of Legislation* (1881).

[62]Dorsey Ellis, "Fairness and Efficiency in the Law of Punitive Damages," 56 *S. Calif. Law Review* 1 (1982): 8–9.

ronment has changed during the period between the wrongful act and the trial date in a manner that increases this probability, the punitive damages multiplier declines. The advances made by the plaintiff's bar, as evidenced by the spate of new asbestos cases and recent high-profile pharmaceutical industry lawsuits, give weight to such a conclusion in certain litigation markets. An aggressive, organized, and well-financed plaintiff's bar stands ready to attack potentially liable deep-pocketed defendants.[63] The latter may have had advantages in the past, such as being able to outspend plaintiffs; however, these advantages have declined and, in some cases, may not be relevant. This changing environment is underscored by the following section from an article about the increasing volume of lawsuits against pharmaceutical companies.

> These days the battle between the drug companies is no longer one between corporate goliaths and individual advocates on a shoestring budget.
>
> "We've got plenty of a war chest," said J. Michael Papantonio, a lawyer in Pensacola, Fla., who is a leader in drug litigation. It's a different day out there. Its not like they going to look across the table from us and say, 'We're going to dry you up.'"
>
> Plaintiffs' lawyers can now finance enormously complicated suits that require years of pre-trial work and substantial scientific expertise, in the hope of a multi-billion-dollar payoff. Scores of firms collaborate on a case, with some responsible for finding claimants, others for managing the millions of documents that companies turn over, others for the written legal arguments, and still others for presenting the case to a jury. Some 60 firms have banded together, for example in the Baycol litigation.[64]

The probability analysis makes for an interesting economics discussion, although some research implies it may be less relevant from a practical viewpoint. Using a sample of 500 jury-eligible citizens, Professor W. Kip Viscuisi has shown that sample juries failed to properly apply probability-based negligence rules.[65] This is not surprising as most juries do not have any exposure to probability theory.

Deterrence: Comparing Gains and Losses

In mass torts a company may make payments in each of thousands of lawsuits it faced. Some have even paid billions of dollars in settlement payments. For exam-

---

[63]Mike France, "The Litigation Machine," *Business Week* (January 29, 2001): 115–123.

[64]Alex Berenson, "Trial Lawyers Are Now Focusing on Lawsuits Against Drug Makers," *New York Times* (May 18, 2003): 29.

[65]W. Kip Viscuisi, "Jurors, Judges and the Mistreatment of Risk in the Courtroom," *Journal of Legal Studies* XXX (1) (January 2001): 89–142.

ple, as of 2003, Wyeth had paid in excess of $14 billion in connection with its diet drug litigation. As part of the evaluation of the deterrence effects, a jury may want to consider the costs of the litigation, including settlement payments and legal fees, compared to the gains that the defendant made from the product. These gains are normally the profits that the company derived from the product. It may be the case in some mass torts that the gains are small compared to the costs that the company incurred. In addition, the costs may involve more than merely the direct litigation expenses. Other costs, such as adverse publicity and tarnished reputation can be quite significant.[66] These costs are discussed separately later in this chapter.

It may be the case that a simple comparison shows that the costs far outweighed the gains. Corporations try to avoid projects that pay a rate of return less than threshold levels such as the cost of capital.[67] Generating losses is an obvious problem. This serves both specific and general deterrence in that other companies which see the defendant make costly investments obviously do not want to replicate such errors.

DETERRENCE AND REGULATORY PROCESSES

Earlier discussions have shown that using punitive damages to try to achieve deterrence means using a very imprecise tool. Doing so may have significant adverse effects with little assurance that the guilty parties will feel the effects of the punishment. However, a jury may want assurance that deterrence will be accomplished so that similar acts do not occur in the future. Juries need to look at the regulatory processes that are in effect in the industry and determine if these processes address the need for deterrence. Some industries have strong deterrence measures in place. For example, as a result of the Master Settlement Agreement, the marketing activities of the tobacco industry are overseen by the National Association of Attorneys General (NAAG). This body meets regularly, has a specific tobacco committee, and is empowered to take aggressive legal actions. Juries wanting to deter one of the major tobacco companies from engaging in improper marketing activities, should consider that NAAG is better able to prevent such actions. A jury may hope that an additional monetary penalty for an act

---

[66]Jonathan M. Karpoff and John R. Lott, "On the Determinants and Importance of Punitive Damage Awards," *Journal of Law and Economics* (April 1999): 527–573.

[67]Arthur Keown, John D. Martin, J. William Petty, and David F. Scott, Financial *Management: Principles and Applications,* 9th ed. (Upper Saddle River, NJ: Prentice-Hall, 2002), 281–286.

that occurred many years before, on top of the billions of dollars in payments that this industry has made and will continue to make through the MSA, would better accomplish this. However, NAAG is but one of several regulatory bodies that exert regulatory pressures on the tobacco industry.

Some industries are closely regulated—others are not. The insurance industry in the United States, which has been the target of many lawsuits, is an example of a closely regulated industry. Insurance companies must be authorized to do business in each state in which they market insurance. State insurance regulators are empowered to restrict the ability of an insurance company to do business if it fails to adhere to that state's insurance requirements.[68] Regulatory processes work much better than attempted deterrence through the court system. An example is the high number of vanishing premium lawsuits that have been brought against life insurance companies.[69] These suits allege that life insurance companies did not properly inform purchasers of insurance that premiums for certain types of insurance policies could possibly not vanish if investment gains in the value of the policy were insufficient. By the time many of these lawsuits went to trial, the problem (to the extent that the problem ever did exist, an issue which is disputed by defendants) was already dealt with by the regulators of the industry. The National Association of Insurance Commissioners issues model regulations that are subsequently adopted by the various state insurance regulators. In this case, a specific model regulation was put forward to regulate the representations that insurance company salespeople could make. This is an example of how regulators can very directly identify the problem and construct a specific regulatory solution to eliminate it. When such regulatory structures are in place, jurors can have confidence that a process is in place which can better deal with the problem than they can. When there is a long time lag between the alleged wrongful acts and the trial, a jury may be able to look back and see that deterrence has already been achieved.

Each industry is different. In light of the fact that regulators may be able to effectively accomplish deterrence, juries should be made aware of what regulatory processes exist and how effective they can be in achieving deterrence. Once the regulatory–deterrence context has been established, a jury can try to determine if punitive damages will accomplish *additional* deterrence.

---

[68]Daniel R. Fischel and Robert S. Stillman, "The Law and Economics of Vanishing Premium Life Insurance," *The Delaware Jurnal of Corporate Law* 22 (1) (1997): 1–36.

[69]Kenneth Black, Jr. and Harold D. Skipper, *Life and Health Insurance,* 13th ed. (Upper Saddle River, NJ: Prentice Hall, 2000), 949–964.

Deterrence and Punishment and Mergers and Acquisitions

A record volume of mergers and acquisitions occurred in the fifth merger wave, which began in 1993–94 and ended approximately in 2001.[70] With the acquisitions of the assets of these various companies came the assumption of their liabilities including some difficult to predict and even foresee, off balance sheet liabilities such as litigation obligations. These contingent liabilities can be so difficult to predict that they may not be carried on the balance sheet as a known liability. It may only be years after an acquisition that the liability becomes more fully known and quantifiable. The serious potential that such liabilities can have was discovered in the 1990s and 2000s when various corporations that made acquisitions of companies became a target of a whole new wave of asbestos lawsuits and were pulled into bankruptcy as a result of these deals. As an example, Halliburton Corporation was forced to file for bankruptcy due to asbestos liabilities incurred by its Dresser Industries units, which it acquired in 1998 for $7.7 billion. With this acquisition, however, came 200,000 asbestos claims.[71] Other companies that inherited asbestos liabilities as a result of acquisitions include McDermott, International, Inc., which incurred them as a result of its acquisition of its Babcok & Wilcox unit. Still another company which inherited large litigation-related liabilites is ABB, a Zurich-based international conglomerate, which inherited its asbestos liabilities as a result of its $1.6 billion acquisition of Combustion Engineering in 1990.[72] It is ironic that ABB sold Combustion's operations in 2000 but was still forced to bear the liabilities for Combustion's asbestos exposure.

While punitive damages may often be inappropriate for companies not involved in acquisitions, they may be even more difficult to justify in the case of acquired entities. The management of the acquiring entity does not necessarily have any knowledge of the actions that may result in these lawsuits in the future. When a company completes the acquisition, however, it may be assuming such obligations. An acquirer may exercise due diligence, but the unpredictable nature of some types of obligations make it difficult to foresee these possible claims. It was believed that asbestos lawsuits were under control when a whole new wave of asbestos claims emerged in the 1990s using new legal theories. Many of these

---

[70]Daniel Fischel and Robert Stillman, "The Law and Economics of Vanishing Premium Life Insurance," *The Delaware Journal of Corporate Law,* 22 (1) (1997): 1–36.

[71]Andrew Clark and Lorraine Woellert, "Halliburton: Halfway Home?," *Business Week* (December 23, 2002): 54–55.

[72]ABB Completes Acquisition, *Wall Street Journal* (December 18, 1989).

defendants did not believe that the companies they were acquiring would have such a high volume of potential claims that would subsequently force them into bankruptcy. For companies in such a situation, what role would punitive damages serve? An acquirer may have no involvement with the target over the time period when the target engaged in the alleged wrongful acts. If this is the case, the acquirer who becomes the defendant in the lawsuit may not need to be deterred as it did not engage in any wrongful acts. Nonetheless, it and its stakeholders may bear the punishment for any punitive penalties that are imposed.

Punitive damages for acquirers often makes little sense. It makes even less sense to substitute the financial resources of the acquirer as indicia or gauges for the magnitude of punitive damages. If this is allowed, the magnitude of punitive damages could be far greater if a company whose employees may have engaged in wrongful acts is acquired by a large "deep-pocketed" corporation. How can it be reasonable to have one level of punitive damages if the company remains independent and another, far greater, level of punitive damages if this corporation is acquired? Clearly, the acts of the wrongdoers are the same and the magnitude of the harm, for which compensatory damages has presumably fully compensated the plaintiffs, is invariant. The only factor that differs is the respective wealth of the two corporations.

TYPICAL FINANCIAL MEASURES USED
IN THE DETERMINATION OF PUNITIVE DAMAGES

Many states allow juries to consider the wealth of the defendant when determining the magnitude of a punitive award. For example, the punitive damages statute of the State of Texas decrees that a jury can consider the net worth of the defendant. According to these researchers, states vary in their use of net worth as a guide to determining punitive damages.[73] While many punitive damages statutes discuss net worth, the simplistic application of net worth can often be of little value to a jury, and at times, can actually be very misleading.

Many states explicitly allow a consideration of net worth in the determination of punitive damages. Some states, such as Nevada and Missouri, only allow net worth to be considered in a second punitive phase. In this way, the magnitude of the defendant's wealth does not provide the jury with an opportunity to engage in

---

[73]Peter Frank, Christopher S. Kelkar, and Erica Sulkowski, "Punitive Damages," *Litigation Services Handbook,* Roman Weil, Michael Wagner, and Peter Frank, eds. (New York: Wiley, 2001), 12.1–12.49.

income redistribution to aid an injured plaintiff, even if the deep-pocketed defendant is not culpable. What is clear, however, is that if net worth is introduced, defendants need to make sure that the jury is also given additional financial information so as to better understand what this measure actually represents.

In *State Farm Mutual Automobile Insurance Co. v. Campbell et al.,* the U.S. Supreme Court addressed the inclusion of the net worth of State Farm in the determination of punitive damages. The Court had already expressed concerns in *BMW v. Gore* when it stated that the wealth of the defendant "provides an open-ended basis for inflating awards when the defendant is wealthy (Justice Breyer concurring)." The *Campbell* court also expressed reservations about the use of evidence on a defendant's wealth when it stated that "reference to its assets (which, of course, are what other insured parties in Utah and other States must rely upon for payment of claims) had little to do with the actual harm sustained by the Campbells. The wealth of the defendant cannot justify an otherwise unconstitutional punitive damages award." In addressing the plaintiff's attempts to introduce the wealth of the defendant, the Supreme Court expressed clear concerns that the wealth of a large defendant could bias the jury and possibly result in an award that bore little relationship to the actual harm caused. That is, if the wealth of a defendant is allowed to be a factor for the jury to consider, then the punitive/compensatory multiple could be far higher for a rich defendant than for a poorer one. The Supreme Court in *Campbell* was concerned about multiples greater than single digits. The only role for net worth, then, is in the determination of whether the defendant can pay a specific punitive award which the jury has already decided upon, rather than as a factor which the jury would consider as part of the punitive award calculus. The problem with including net worth, even in this more limited role, is that it may not necessarily provide useful information on what a defendant can actually pay.

NET WORTH

Net worth is the difference between the value of a company's assets and liabilities on its balance sheet.[74] One of the problems with using net worth is that the balance sheet is not designed for serving as a guide for juries to assess punitive damages. The assets on a balance sheet include both tangible and intangible assets. Among the intangible assets on a company's balance sheet is goodwill. Goodwill is created

---

[74]R. Charles Moyer, James R. McGuigan, and William J. Kretlow, *Contemporary Financial Management* (Mason, OH: Thomson South-Western, 2003), 66.

in acquisitions and is an accountant's way of dealing with the difference in the value of a previously acquired company's assets and the total purchase price of the company. Goodwill and other intangible assets cannot be used to pay a fine. Yet, since various courts allow net worth to be considered, these assets are part of what courts have said juries can look to when determining the magnitude of a punitive award.

One solution to the problem of intangibles embodied in the net worth of some companies is to substitute *tangible net worth*. This measure removes intangible assets from total assets prior to deducting total liabilities. It still is not without its own drawbacks, but for the purposes of considering the wealth of a defendant that could possibly be used to pay a punitive award, it is more appropriate than total net worth. The difference between total net worth and tangible net worth can be significant. For example, Table 12.2 shows that in 2002, Bristol Myers Squibb had a total, unadjusted net worth of $8.967 billion, while its tangible net worth was negative $2.199 billion—a very different value![75] The difference between total net worth and tangible net worth was the $4.864 billion of goodwill that the company reported as goodwill as well as $1.904 billion that it reported as intangibles.

It is generally assumed that the goal of using punitive damages is not to put the defendant out of business. Indeed, the Fifth Circuit in *Jackson v. Johns Manville Sales Corp.* expressed concerns that punitive damages could result in the destruction of the corporate defendant.[76] Including the full value of a company's assets fails to consider the uses of those assets and their role in the maintenance of the company's viability. A company needs to maintain a certain level of liquid assets to maintain its solvency. Other assets, such as illiquid equipment and real estate may be necessary to maintain the operations and continuity of the business. For example, Bristol Meyers Squibb's property, plant, and equipment equal approximately $5.321 billion—almost half of unadjusted total shareholder equity.

The Supreme Court, in *State Farm v. Campbell el al.*, expressed clear reservations about the use of net worth when is stated: ". . . the presentation of evidence of a defendant's net worth creates the potential that juries will use their verdicts to express biases against big businesses, particularly those without strong local presences." More fundamentally, net worth is simply not designed to be a gauge by which a jury determines punitive damages. However, as flawed as it is, other measures sometimes used by plaintiffs are even worse. One such measure is market capitalization.

---

[75]Bristol Myers Squibb Annual Report: 2002.
[76]*Jackson v. Johns Manville Sales Corp.*, 727 F2d 506, 526.

Table 12.2 Bristol-Myers Squibb, Inc. Consolidated Balance Sheet

Dollars in Millions	2002
ASSETS	
Current Assets:	
Cash and cash equivalents	$ 3,978
Time deposits and marketable securities	11
Receivables, net of allowances of $129 and $122	2,968
Inventories, including consignment inventory	1,573
Prepaid expenses	1,445
Total Current Assets	9,975
Property, Plant and Equipment, net	5,321
Goodwill	4,864
Intangible Assets, net	1,904
Other Assets	2,810
Total Assets	**$24,874**
LIABILITIES	
Current Liabilities:	
Short-term borrowings	$ 1,379
Deferred revenue on consigned inventory	470
Accounts payable	1,553
Dividends payable	542
Accrued litigation settlements	600
Accrued expenses	2,374
Accrued rebates and returns	819
U.S. and foreign income taxes payable	483
Total Current Liabilities	8,220
Other Liabilities	1,426
Long-Term Liabilities	6,261
Total Liabilities	**$15,907**
STOCKHOLDERS' EQUITY	
Preferred stock, $2 convertible series: Authorized 10 million shares; issued and outstanding 8,308 in 2002 and 8,914 in 2001, liquidation value of $50 per share	—
Common stock, par value of $.10 per share: Authorized 4.5 billion shares: 2,200,823,544 issued in 2002 and 2,200,010,476 issued in 2001	220
Capital in excess of par value of stock	2,491
Other accumulated comprehensive loss	(1,102)
Retained Earnings	18,860
	20,469
Less cost of treasury stock—263,994,580 common shares in 2002 and 264,389,570 in 2001	(11,502)
Total Stockholders' Equity	8,967
Total Liabilities and Stockholders' Equity	**$24,874**

MARKET CAPITALIZATION

Market capitalization is the product of a company's stock price and its total shares outstanding. Sometimes this value is used by plaintiffs as an alternative to net worth. One of the appealing features it has for plaintiffs over net worth is that it may be significantly higher. As an example, Table 12.3 shows the value of the net worth of the companies that are included in the Dow Jones Industrial Average. At the time the data were assembled for Table 12.3, market capitalization was 279.93 percent higher than net worth as of December 2002. The reason for this difference is that assets are not recorded on a company's balance sheet at market values. Unfortunately, as far as the determination of punitive damages is concerned, this measure is even more flawed than net worth.

The most fundamental flaw of using market capitalization as a gauge in determining punitive damages is that it is not an asset of the corporation and it does not represent an asset that a company can use to pay an award. Market capitalization represents the value of the total outstanding equity of a public company at a moment in time. It represents a claim that equity holders have against the future gains of the company. Shareholders may not have any responsibility for, or any knowledge of, the acts that are the subject of the litigation. Using market capitalization as part of the punitive damages decision-making process raises serious questions of fairness. Moreover, since the company is not in a position to use these assets to pay a punitive award, the market capitalization becomes totally inappropriate.

Another flaw of market capitalization as a measure is that it is not stable. While total shares outstanding are often relatively stable, market capitalization varies with the movement in share prices. The significant variability of share prices is well known. The relevance of this to punitive damages is that if a punitive award is based on an unstable measure of wealth, there could be widely varying amounts of punitive damages depending on what the market capitalization is at the time the measure is presented to the jury. As an example, assume that the Schering-Plough Corporation was determined by a jury to be liable for punitive damages, and that a jury based the amount of the award on the market capitalization of the company which as of April, 2003 would be very different from the value that prevailed for the prior year. This is shown in Exhibit 12.4 which reveals that stock prices for Schering-Plough had fallen from $34.98 on March 1, 2002 to $3 in 2003 just a year later—a decline of greater than 50 percent.[77] The figure

---

[77] The stock price trends of Schering-Plough are used as an example to show the variation in a company's equity values. No separate investigation has been done on the source of this equity variation.

Table 12.3 Current Components for Dow Jones Industrial Averages—as of 12/02

No.	Company	Ticker	Share Price as of 5/15/03	Traded Volume as of 5/15/03	Mkt Cap ($ Bn) as of 12/02	Net Worth ($Bn) as of 9/02	Difference (%)
1	Alcoa Inc.	AA	22.86	3,053,909	18.96	9.93	79%
2	American Express Co.	AXP	40.99	4,696,400	46.02	13.86	245%
3	Boeing Co.	BA	30.16	4,674,300	26.08	7.70	138%
4	Citigroup Inc.	C	39.45	11,349,800	178.94	86.72	127%
5	Caterpillar Inc.	CAT	53.40	1,738,000	15.51	5.47	163%
6	E.I. DuPont de Nemours & Co.	DD	42.60	3,589,200	41.40	9.063	276%
7	Walt Disney Co.	DIS	18.46	6,800,900	33.30	23.29	54%
8	Eastman Kodak Co.	EK	30.02	1,632,700	9.96	2.78	261%
9	General Electric Co.	GE	28.48	16,075,100	239.87	63.71	318%
10	General Motors Corp.	GM	34.85	8,952,300	20.07	6.814	8%
11	Home Depot Inc.	HD	29.37	12,929,500	55.94	20.12	210%
12	Honeywell International Inc.	HON	25.15	4,225,500	20.34	8.93	105%
13	Hewlett-Packard Co.	HPQ	17.63	10,262,100	52.56	36.26	53%
14	International Business Machines Corp.	IBM	89.90	7,102,900	132.98	22.78	523%
15	Intel Corp.	INTC	20.00	71,834,200	102.03	35.47	241%
16	International Paper Co.	IP	37.42	1,894,300	16.83	7.37	70%
17	Johnson & Johnson	JNJ	55.44	5,033,400	158.86	22.09	656%
18	J.P. Morgan Chase & Co.	JPM	30.49	10,648,700	46.62	42.31	11%
19	Coca-Cola Co.	KO	44.64	4,454,400	107.68	11.80	921%
20	McDonald's Corp.	MCD	18.60	8,349,000	20.38	10.28	105%
21	3M Co.	MMM	125.85	2,665,700	47.86	5.99	663%
22	Philip Morris Cos. Inc.	MO	33.74	7,012,900	81.18	19.48	311%
23	Merck & Co. Inc.	MRK	59.53	4,519,900	126.21	18.20	681%
24	Microsoft Corp.	MSFT	25.79	45,450,200	276.20	55.80	446%
25	Procter & Gamble Co.	PG	89.90	3,646,400	110.75	14.84	698%
26	SBC Communications Inc.	SBC	24.76	6,781,900	87.79	33.20	167%
27	AT&T Corp.	T	17.44	4,912,700	20.44	12.31	−50%
28	United Technologies Corp.	UTX	67.77	2,738,300	28.85	8.36	200%
29	Wal-Mart Stores Inc.	WMT	53.76	11,579,800	221.59	39.34	503%
30	Exxon Mobil Corp.	XOM	35.29	8,949,800	230.88	74.60	215%
	Average		**222.49**		**24.30**		**279.93%**

Note: Difference (%) shows how much higher the Market Cap over Net Worth
Net Worth (= Stockholders' Equity) is taken from the company's balance sheet (3rd Quarter)

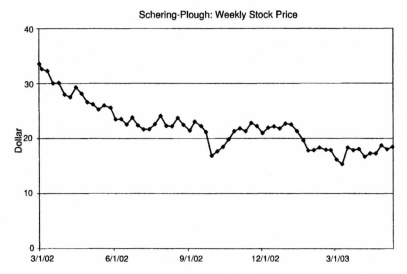

Exhibit 12.4   Stock prices of Schering-Plough.

shows that some of this decline can be attributed to a decline in the market and in the drug sector and another part is attributable to company-specific issues. This decline in the value of the stock implies that if the trial were held in the first quarter of 2002, the jury would be using a substantially higher gauge to determine punitive damages than what would prevail if the trial were delayed a year. This also implies that punitive damages could be substantially higher on one date (when the market was up) than on another date (when the market was down). Clearly, market capitalization fails in possessing one very desirable quality—stability. As such, it is simply not an appropriate measure in determining punitive damages.

Still another flaw of market capitalization is that the market reacts to news and tries to anticipate the outcome of relevant events. Assume that an award was made that was somehow based on market capitalization as a measure of the defendant's wealth. Between the time when the punitive verdict was announced and the time that the company had to make a payment, the market would react to the news of the verdict (if it had not already anticipated it). The stock price would fall in relation to the magnitude of the verdict. An example of this is the recent decline in the price of Altria's stock in response to the aforementioned Miles verdict.[78]

---

[78]*Susan Miles et al. v. Philip Morris Companies, Inc.,* Illinois Circuit Court, 2003.

The decline in the stock price around that announcement date is shown in Exhibit 12.5.

Once the news of an adverse punitive verdict reaches the market, the declining stock price means that the value of the company's market capitalization would be significantly lower on the date that the company has to make the payment than what it was when the jury reached its verdict. The market would try to adjust the value of the stock to reflect the losses associated with the payments. Insofar as market capitalizations were to somehow reflect an ability to make the punitive payment (which they do not), this ability would be reduced by the market's reaction to the impending payment.

Still another problem with market capitalization occurs when the defendant is a subsidiary. A subsidiary of a public company may not have a separate stock price. Such a company pays dividends "upstream" to a parent company. It may not have outstanding shares traded in the marketplace, however, and thus does not have a market capitalization. Citing the market capitalization of the parent company may be irrelevant. In cases such as this, market capitalization is not a viable measure to consider, assuming that it is otherwise appropriate (which it is not).

Lastly, given that the U.S. Supreme Court in *State Farm v. Campbell et al.* expressed its concern about the bias-related effects that net worth could have in the award determination process, it would seem that market capitalization, a measure which is often a multiple of net worth, would be even more problematic in the Court's view.

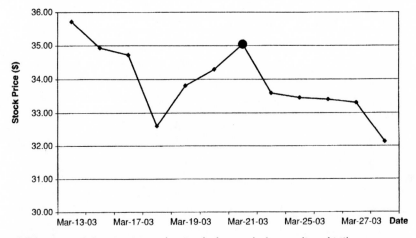

Exhibit 12.5   Philip Morris' stock price before and after verdict of Miles case.
Source: Historical Prices of Yahoo Finance (http://finance.yahoo.com)

Comparisons to the Finances of Individuals

Another approach espoused by some experts who testify for the plaintiffs is to compare a proposed punitive penalty to the impact of a fixed fine on an average household.[79] The median household income and wealth are often derived from surveys that are conducted by governmental entities such as the Federal Reserve Survey of Consumer Finances.[80] The approach that is often used is to compare a certain penalty imposed on a household, such as $100 or $1,000, and show what this amount is as a percentage of household income or wealth. This percentage is then applied to the income or net worth of the defendant corporation. Some assert that it is analogous to "common size statement" analysis that is done in corporate finance. The appeal of this for plaintiffs who are suing larger corporate defendants is that amounts of money that a typical juror considers large, appear relatively small when compared to a defendant's net worth or annual income. Plaintiffs' attorneys then tell the jury that they need to arrive at a larger amount in order to cause the corporation to "feel the same pain" that a household would if it were fined a certain percentage of its net worth. The problem with this exercise is that while the computation and application of the percentages are easy to perform, and may have great appeal for plaintiffs, the comparison of the finances of a corporation to those of a household is irrelevant and misleading. Corporations are far more complex structures than a family. The workings of major corporations involve different stakeholders who may be far removed from the decision-making process. Corporations compete for market share and maintain resources so as to retain and enhance their competitive position. Corporations engage in many other activities, such as acquiring other companies, that highlight the stark differences between corporate structures and families.

Even the data for family finances that are used in comparisons with corporations are misapplied. The data from the Survey of Consumer Finances lacks the reliability of data on corporate financial statements that has undergone an audit process. The Federal Reserve has grappled for years with the reliability of its data. Theses data are derived from voluntary surveys of respondents who are sometimes asked to provide instant recall to complex questions about their finances. Some do not know the answers to the questions and others may simply not want to respond accurately. The comparison of the two inherently different

[79]Everett Dillman, "Punitive and Exemplary Damages," *Litigation Economics,* Patrick A. Gaughan and Robert Thornton, eds. (Greenwich, CT: JAI Press, 1993), 91–108.

[80]Federal Reserve Bank, *Survey of Consumer Finances,* 2001.

data sets makes for a very misleading result. The data from the Survey of Consumer Finances were designed for other research purposes, such as informing the central bank about trends in the banking and savings behavior of households. It may serve this purpose well, but fails when it is put to a use for which it was never intended.

Reputation Costs

Corporations devote significant expenditures to public relations (PR). A recent Harris/Impulse Research survey of corporations that had average annual revenues of three billion dollars showed that such companies spent an average of $2.7 million on public relations.[81] These amounts of PR expenditures do not include the internal salaries of staff devoted to public relations. This is part of an effort to develop a positive image. Most companies believe that having a good image in the market and being considered a "good citizen" is good business. Generally, having a negative image creates a more difficult sales environment. Being the target of punitive damages claims, whether legitimate or not, carries with it costs beyond the direct monetary penalties the defendant faces. These costs have been documented in various research studies. Karpoff and Lott have shown that such costs can be substantial. They measured them by examining the stock market declines around the announcements of suits involving punitive claims.[82] They found that the market declined by more than what could be explained by the compensatory and punitive damages awarded. Karpoff and Lott also conducted earlier studies which showed how reputational penalties are reflected in stock market declines.[83] Other economists have found that media coverage of punitive verdicts was skewed. Steven Garber found that media coverage of punitive verdicts was higher the greater the size of the award; defense verdicts, however, garnered virtually no newspaper coverage.[84]

---

[81]2002 Public Relations Client Survey, Thomas Harris/Impulse Research Survey, September 23, 2002.

[82]Jonathan M. Karpoff and John R. Lott, "On the Determinants and Importance of Punitive Damage Awards," *The Journal of Law & Economics* (April 1999): 527–573.

[83]Jonathan M. Karpoff and John R. Lott, "The Reputational Penalty Firm Bear from Committing Criminal Fraud," *The Journal of Law & Economic* (October 1993): 757–801.

[84]Steven Garber, "Punitive Damages, Business Decisions and Economic Outcomes," *Wisconsin Law Review* (1998).

The same was true when large awards were reduced—the reductions received minimal media coverage. Given the orientation of the media in their treatment of punitive damages, companies have great incentives to try to avoid being the target of such suits.

THE UNCERTAIN LITIGATION ENVIRONMENT

Another interesting aspect of the litigation market is that companies are often not good at predicting what the volume and outcome of future lawsuits will be. Companies that are the targets of multiple lawsuits or serial tort suits often take charges and acknowledge liabilities based on their best estimates of the magnitude of the litigation-related exposure. Such liabilities are referred to as contingent liabilities, and accounting rules require that they be accrued when they are highly probable and estimable.[85] Some firms have indeed attempted to apply sophisticated statistical analysis to calculate litigation reserves.[86] While one assumes that these statements represent companies' best estimates, the number and outcome of current and future cases are often quite uncertain. This became particularly true in the 1990s and early 2000s when the volume of certain types of cases grew dramatically. A remarkable example is the asbestos lawsuits.[87] The now defendants in these suits, companies who at some point in time had an affiliation with asbestos manufacturers, thought that they had these suits behind them. A settlement was entered into on January 15, 1993 that was supposed to include a future claim against the entity founded by the asbestos defendants—the Center for Claims Resolution.[88] In 1997, however, the U.S. Supreme Court decided that the settlement did not meet the requirements for class certification under the Federal Rule of Civil Procedure 23. Many previously healthy companies were forced to file for Chapter 11 bankruptcy due to the sheer volume of these cases. Table 12.4 shows a few of the major companies that filed Chapter 11, some of whom are leading names in American industry.

---

[85]Jamie Pratt, Financial Accounting in an Economic Context, 5th ed. (New York: Wiley, 2003): 432–433.

[86]Marc A. Allen and Sam Savage, "Calculated Risk: Monte Carlo Modeling Reduces the Gamble When It Comes Time for CFOs to Set Loss Reserves for a Company's Pending Litigation," *The Daily Deal* (January 29, 2003): 7.

[87]Walter K. Olson, *The Rule of Lawyers* (New York: St. Martin's Press, 2003), 181–208.

[88]*Georgine v. Amchem,* Eastern District of Pennsylvania.

Table 12.4   Selected Asbestos Chapter 11 Filers

Company	Date Filed
Armstrong World Industries	December 2000
W.R. Grace	April 2001
Owens Corning	October 2000
GAF Corporation	January 2001
Pittsburgh Corning	April 2000
Babcox & Wilcox	February 2000

The asbestos defendants thought that they had the litigation problem contained through the *Georgine* settlement—they did not. The uncertainty of litigation is underscored by the dramatic reversals that this litigation took, ultimately forcing otherwise viable companies into bankruptcy. For companies facing mass tort lawsuits, the outstanding volume of litigation and the potential impact this may have on the health of the company should be considered in the determination of punitive damage amounts.

An example of the difficulties involved in predicting the impact of potential litigation exposure on the financial well-being of a corporation is found in *Owens Corning Fiberglas Corporation v. Roy Malone et al.* In this case, the Supreme Court of Texas agreed with the trial court and the court of appeals in concluding that a punitive award would not have an adverse effect on the financial health of Owens Corning. The court stated:

> The trial court considered OCF's "enough is enough" evidence from the post-trial hearing and determined that OCF's financial position is not so precarious that further punitive damages awards against it should be disallowed. We agree. The evidence is that OCF is a solvent, healthy company. In 1993, shortly before this case was tried, OCF reported to its shareholders that "at the end of 1991, our company was valued by the market at $932 million; 12 months later, the market value of the company was in excess of $1.5 billion, an increase of 60%!" Moreover, in March, 1993 OCF reported to the SEC that "the additional uninsured and unreserved costs which may arise out of pending personal injury and property damages asbestos claims and additional similar claims filed in the future will not have a materially adverse effect on the Company's financial position." We cannot say that the prior paid punitive damage awards against OCF, combined with the punitive damage awards here, have exceeded the goals of punishment and deterrence.[89]

---

[89]*Owens Corning Fiberglas Corporation v. Roy Malone et al.,* 972 S.W. 2d 35; 1998 Tex. Lexis 97; 41 Tex Sup. J. 877.

The court examined what the company said about its own assessment of its ability to survive the volume of litigation and concluded that the company had to be in a better position than the court in assessing the impact on the company. If the company states it can survive, how is the court able to conclude otherwise? However, in retrospect, both were wrong. Armed with hindsight that the Texas Appeals Court did not have at the time, we know that such reasoning was flawed. The lesson one can take from this is that in spite of optimistic statements that a company makes in its filings and submissions to shareholders, the company may not be able to accurately assess the potential exposure from future lawsuits—particularly when there are many of them outstanding. It has become very difficult to predict what the future litigation volume will be. However, at a minimum, one can conclude that the jury should at least consider the volume of other cases. Believing that the company would not be in jeopardy from such cases, the court in *Malone* did not allow the jury to consider other lawsuits and their potential effects.

Apportionment and Punitive Damages

It may be misleading to present to a jury in a particular venue the total value of whatever financial measures are to be presented. For example, assume that the defendant is a corporation that does business throughout the United States but not abroad, and is subject to lawsuits for mass torts throughout the United States. Considering the full value of the various financial measures, such as total corporate net worth, may in the aggregate lead to a consideration of financial values well in excess of the company's total financial resources. One way to deal with this problem is to apportion the financial values to fit the volume of business in the venue where the litigation is centered. This may mean that the defendant in a statewide class action presents a percentage of the total measures (for example, net worth—assuming for the purposes of this example that unadjusted net worth is an appropriate measure). This would represent that share of the defendant's total national business that the state comprises. The U.S. Court of Appeals for the Ninth Circuit agreed that apportionment was appropriate in *White and White v. Ford Motor Company*. It concluded that "extraterritorial conduct" should not be considered by a jury to impose a punitive penalty which would, in effect, punish a defendant for harm outside of the relevant jurisdiction. This court concluded that the jury should only consider the business in the State of Nevada rather than the national sales of the product in question.[90] This percentage may vary over

---

[90]*White and White v. Ford Motor Company et al.,* 2002, U.S. App. Lexis 24364.

time and experts may need to evaluate more than one year of data when putting forward a percentage.

The Supreme *Court in State Farm v. Campbell et al* also echoed a similar theme when it stated that out of state conduct should not be considered when determining awards within a given state. The court stated "Due Process does not permit courts to adjudicate the merits of other parties' hypothetical claims under the guise of a reprehensibility analysis. Punishment on these bases creates the possibility of multiple punitive awards for the same conduct, for nonparties are not normally bound by another plaintiff's judgment." This decision implies that not only should conduct be restricted to the state in question, but also other measures, assuming they are appropriate, such as net worth, should also be restricted or apportioned to apply to the state, as opposed to presenting numbers reflecting the company's national business. In a product liability case one guide to doing this analysis would be to take the percentage of the defendant's total national sales that have been made over a relevant time period in the state in which a state action has been brought. The apportionment process becomes more complicated when the venue is not a state, such as in a statewide class action, but a more narrowly defined case involving an individual or group of plaintiffs. In this instance, there may be a basis for more narrowly defined apportionment, such as to the county level or another relevant subsector.

SUMMARY

The issue of punitive damages continues to be hotly debated. This is the case even though punitive damages are awarded in only a small minority of lawsuits. Some assert that this relative infrequency implies that punitive damages should not be a cause for concern. Others point out that such damages are unpredictable and are often explicitly incorporated into settlement values. This process is sometimes referred to as the shadow effect of punitive damages.

The courts have been clear that the twin purposes of punitive damages are punishment and deterrence. However, punitive damages applied to corporations differs from those applied to individuals. The reason is that corporations are very different than individuals. A corporation is a group of various stakeholders who are affected, in different ways, by a punitive verdict. Examples of stakeholders are shareholders, employees, consumers, suppliers, and communities. A punitive award is a cost like any other cost that a company faces. Increased costs can have ripple effects on the stakeholders. This is an economic effect that a jury may want to know more about prior to rendering a verdict.

Plaintiffs often present certain financial measures for a jury's consideration in determining punitive damages. They may include measures such as a corporation's net worth. The use of these measures can be quite misleading, however, as they may suggest to a jury that a company's ability to pay a judgment is greater than it actually is. If such measures are deemed to be appropriate, they should be adjusted for components such as goodwill and other intangibles.

Punitive damages may involve more costs than the monetary award itself. In addition to defense costs, companies that are the targets of punitive suits may incur significant reputational costs. They may incur these costs when suits are filed or following punitive awards, but may not necessarily see them go away even if awards are reversed on appeal.

REFERENCES

"ABB Completes Acquisition." *Wall Street Journal* (December 18, 1989).

"ABB to Make Deeper Cuts." October 24, 2002, CNN.com.

Allen, Marc A. and Sam Savage, "Calculated Risk: Monte Carlo Modeling Reduces the Gamble When It Comes Time for CFOs to Set Loss Reserves for a Company's Pending Litigation." *The Daily Deal,* January, 29, 2003, 7.

Altria Annual Report: 2002.

Banerjee, Neela, "Halliburton Battered as Asbestos Verdict Stirs Deep Anxieties." *New York Times* (December 8, 2001): C1.

Barr, Brian H., "*Engle v. R.J. Reynolds:* The Improper Assessment of Punitive Damages for an Entire Class of Injured Smokers." *Florida State Law Review* 28 (spring 2001): 787.

Bentham, Jeremy, *Theory of Legislation,* 1881.

Berenson, Alex, "Trial Lawyers Are Now Focusing on Lawsuits Against Drug Makers," *New York Times* (May 18, 2003): 29.

Bizjak, John M. and Jeffrey L. Coles, "The Effect of Private Antitrust Litigation on the Stock Market Valuation of the Firm." *The American Economic Review,* 85 (3) (June 1995): 436–461.

Black, Kenneth Jr. and Harold D. Skipper, *Life and Health Insurance,* 13th ed. Upper Saddle River, NJ: Prentice-Hall, 2000.

BMW of North America v. Gore, 116 S.Ct. 1589 (1996).

Booz Allen Hamilton, CEO Turnover Study, 2003.

Brancato, Carolyn and Patrick Gaughan, "The Growth of Institutional Investors in U.S. Capital Markets." Columbia University School of Law, *Center for Law and Economic Studies Monograph* (fall 1988).

Brickley, James, "What Happens to CEOs After They Retire? New Evidence on Career Concerns, Horizon Problems and CEO Incentives." *Journal of Financial Economics* 52 (1999): 341–377.

Bristol Myers Squibb Annual Report: 2002.

Bullock v. Philip Morris Inc. Superior Court of California.

Case, Karl and Ray Fair, *Principles of Economics,* 6th ed. Upper Saddle River, NJ: Prentice-Hall, 2002.

CitiGroup Smith Barney, April 7, 2003, Industry Note, "Damages Ruling May Limit Corporate Exposure."

Coffee, John, "Corporate Crime and Punishment: A Non-Chicago View of the Economics of Criminal Sanctions." *American Criminal Law Review* 17 (1980): 419–476.

Coffee, John, "No Soul to Damm, No Body to Kick." *Michigan Law Review* (January 1981).

Cooper Industries, Inc. v. Leatherman Tool Group, Inc., 532 U.S. 424, 433. (2001).

Daniels, Steve and Joanne Martin, "Myth and Reality in Punitive Damages." *Minnesota Law Review* 1 (1990).

DeFrances, Carol, *et al.,* "Civil Jury Cases and Verdicts in Large Counties." U.S. Department of Civil Justice (1995).

Dillman, Everett, "Punitive and Exemplary Damages." *Litigation Economics,* Greenwich, CT: JAI Press, 1993).

Dodge, Joseph M., "Taxes and Torts." *Cornell Law Review* (January 1992).

Ehrenberg, Ronald and Robert Smith, *Modern Labor Economics,* 7th ed. New York: Addison Wesley and Longham, 2000.

Ellis, Dorsey D., "Fairness and Efficiency in the Law of Punitive Damages." 56 S. *California Law Review* (1982): 1, 8–9.

Engle v. RJ Reynolds Tobacco Co. No. 94–08273 (Fla. 11th Cir. CT. Nov. 6, 2000.—final judgment).

Fairclough, Gordon, "Four Biggest Cigarette Makers Can't Raise Prices as They Did," *Wall Street Journal* (October 25, 2002).

Federal Reserve Bank, *Survey of Consumer Finances,* 2001.

Fischel, Daniel and Robert Stillman, "The Law and Economics of Vanishing Premium Life Insurance," *The Delaware Journal of Corporate Law,* 22 (1) (1997): 1–36.

France, Mike, "The Litigation Machine." *Business Week* (January 29, 2001): 115–123.

Frank, Peter, Christopher S. Kelkar, and Erica Sulkowski, "Punitive Damages." *Litigation Services Handbook,* 3rd ed., Roman Weil, Michael Wagner, and Peter Frank, eds. New York: Wiley, 2001.

Garber, Steven, "Punitive Damages, Business Decisions and Economic Outcomes." *Wisconsin Law Review* (1998).

Gaughan, Patrick A., *Mergers, Acquisitions, and Corporate Restructurings,* 3rd
ed., New York: Wiley, 2002.

Georgine v. Amchem, Eastern District of Pennsylvania.

Gertz v. Robert Welch, Inc., 418 U.S. 323, 350 (1974).

Goldman Sachs Analyst Report, February 13, 2001.

Grossman, Michael, "The Economics of Substance Use and Abuse: The Role of
Price," Economic analysis of substance use and abuse: The experience of
developed countries and lessons for developing countries (*Academia Studies
in Asian Economies,* Cheltenham, U.K. and Northampton, MA: Elgar; distributed by American International Distribution Corporation Williston, VT),
2001.

Hameralin, Benjamin E. and Michael S. Weisbach, "The Determinants of Board
Composition." *Rand Journal of Economics* 29 (4) (winter 1988):589–606.

Jackson v. Johns Manville Sales Corp., 727 F2d 506, 526.

Karpoff, Jonathan M. and John R. Lott, "On the Determinants and Importance of
Punitive Damage Awards." *Journal of Law and Economics* (April 1999):
527–573.

Karpoff, Jonathan M. and John R. Lott, "The Reputational Penalty Firm Bear
from Committing Criminal Fraud." *The Journal of Law & Economics*
(October 1993): 757–801.

Keown, Arthur, John D. Martin, J. William Petty, and David F. Scott, *Financial
Management: Principles and Applications,* 9th ed. Upper Saddle River, NJ:
Prentice-Hall, 2002, 281–286.

Koenig, Thomas, "The Shadow Effect of Punitive Damages." *Wisconsin Law
Review* (1998): 169–209.

Kranhold, Kathryn, "Megadamages Against Industry May Be History." *Wall
Street Journal* (April 9, 2003): B1.

Landes, William M. and Richard A. Posner, "New Light on Punitive Damages."
Regulation (September–October 1986): 33.

Manning, Richard, "Products Liability & Prescription Drug Prices in Canada &
the U.S." *Journal of Law & Economics* (April 1997): 203–243.

Master Settlement Agreement Between the States and the U.S. Tobacco Producers,
1998.

McKee, Brian, "The Implication of *BMW v. Gore* for Future Punitive Litigation:
Observation from a Participant." *Alabama Law Review* 175 (1996), Meghan
A. Crowley, "From Punishment to Annihilation: *Engle v. R.J. Reynolds
Tobacco Co.*—No More Butts: Punitive Damages Have Gone Too Far."
Loyola Los Angeles Law Review (June 2001): 1513–1532.

452   THE ECONOMICS OF PUNITIVE DAMAGES

Miles v. Philip Morris, 2003.

Moyer, R. Charles, James R. McGuigan, and William J. Kretlow, *Contemporary Financial Management.* Mason, OH: Thomson South-Western, 2003.

O'Connell, Vanessa, "Cigarette Industry Debt Ratings Cut by Fitch," *Wall Street Journal* (May 7, 2003): B6.

Olson, Walter K., *The Rule of Lawyers*, (New York: St. Martin's Press), 2003.

Owen, David G., "Punitive Damages in Products Liability Litigation." *Villanova Law Review* (June 1976).

Owen, David G., "Symposium: Punitive Awards in Product Liability Litigation: Strong Medicine or Poison Pill?: A Punitive Damages Overview: Function, Problems and Reform." *Villanova Law Review* 39 (1994).

Owens-Corning Fiberglas Corporation v. Roy Malone et al., 972 S.W. 2d 35; 1998 Tex. Lexis 97; 41 Tex Sup. J. 877.

Pace, Kimberly, "The Tax Deductibility of Punitive Damage Payments: Who Should Ultimately Bear the Burden for Corporate Misconduct." *Alabama Law Review* 47 (Spring 1996).

Pacific Mutual Life Insurance Co. v. Haslip, 499 U.S. 1, 19 (1991).

Parkin, Michael, *Economics,* 5th ed. New York: Addison-Wesley Longham, Inc., 2000.

Patch, Elizabeth, *Plant Closings and Employment Loss in Manufacturing.* New York: Garland Publishing, 1995.

Peterson, Mark, *et al.*, "Punitive Damages: Empirical Findings," (Rand Institute for Civil Justice, 1987), R–3311–ICJ.

Polinsky, A. Mitchell, and Steven Shavell, "Punitive Damages an Economic Analysis." *Harvard Law Review* III (1998): 870–962.

Pound, John, "Shareholder Activism and Share Values." *Journal of Law and Economics* (October 1989): 357–379.

Pratt, Jamie, *Financial Accounting in an Economic Context,* 5th ed., New York: Wiley, 2003.

Priest, George L., "Insurability and Punitive Damages" *Alabama Law Review* 40 (3) (spring 1989): 1009–1012.

Rickman, Dan S. and R. Keith Schwer, "A Comparison of the Multipliers of Implan, REMI and RIMS II: Benchmarking ready made models for comparison." *The Annals of Regional Science* 29 (1995): 363–374.

Ross, Stephen, Randolph Westerfield, and Bradford Jordan, *Essentials of Corporate Finance,* 4th ed. Boston: Irwin, 2004.

Rustad, Michael, "In Defense of Punitive Damages in Product Liability: Testing Tort Anecdotes with Empirical Data." *Iowa Law Review* 78 (1992).

Samuelson, Paul and William Nordhaus, *Economics,* 16th ed. New York: McGraw-Hill, 1998.

Second Restatement of Torts (second), 908 (1), 1979.

Section 104 of the Internal Revenue Code.

State Farm Mutual Automobile Insurance Co. v. Campbell et al. No. 01–1289.

Stiglitz, Joseph E., *Economics,* 2nd ed. New York: Norton & Company 1997.

Strohmeyer, John, *Crisis in Bethlehem: Big Steel's Struggle to Survive.* Pittsburgh, PA: University of Pittsburgh Press, 1994.

Stuart, Colbern C., "Mean Stupid Defendants Jarring Our Constitutional Sensibilities." *California Western Law Review* (1994).

Susan Miles et al. v. Philip Morris Companies, Inc., Illinois Circuit Court, 2003.

Taylor, John, *Economics,* 2nd ed. New York: Houghton Mifflin Company, 1998.

2002 Public Relations Client Survey, Thomas Harris/Impulse Research Survey, September 23, 2003.

TXO Prod. Corp. v. Alliance Resources Corp., 509 U.S. 443, 475 (1993).

Viscuisi, W. Kip, "Jurors, Judges and the Mistreatment of Risk in the Courtroom." *Journal of Legal Studies* XXX (1) (January 2001): 89–142.

White and White v. Ford Motor Company et al., 2002, U.S. App. Lexis 24364.

INDEX

Printed in the United States
49342LVS00002B/312

9 780471 266563